FANTASTIC WORLDS

Fantastic Worlds

Myths, Tales, and Stories

Edited and with Commentaries by

Eric S. Rabkin

New York   Oxford
OXFORD UNIVERSITY PRESS
1979

Copyright © 1979 by Oxford University Press, Inc.

Printed in the United States of America

Library of Congress Cataloging in Publication Data
Main entry under title:

Fantastic worlds.

  Bibliography: p.
  1. Fantastic literature. I. Rabkin, Eric S.
PN6071.F25F34   808.83'876   78-11482
ISBN 0-19-502542-3
ISBN 0-19-502541-5 pbk.

ACKNOWLEDGMENTS

CHINUA ACHEBE: "Why Tortoise's Shell Is Not Smooth" from *Things Fall Apart.* Reprinted by permission of William Heinemann Ltd., London.

ALEKSANDR AFANAS'EV, ED.: "The Magic Swan Geese" from *Russian Fairy Tales,* trans. Norbert Guterman. Copyright 1945 by Pantheon Books, Inc.; renewed 1973 by Random House, Inc. Reprinted by permission of Pantheon Books, a Division of Random House, Inc., and Sheldon Press, London.

HANS CHRISTIAN ANDERSEN: "The Tinderbox" from *The Complete Fairy Tales and Stories,* trans. Erik Christian Haugaard, foreword by Virginia Haviland. Copyright © 1974 by Erik Christian Haugaard. Reprinted by permission of Doubleday & Co., Inc., and Victor Gollancz Ltd., London.

DONALD BARTHELME: "The Piano Player" from *Come Back, Dr. Caligari.* Copyright © 1963 by Donald Barthelme; originally appeared in *The New Yorker.* Reprinted by permission of Little, Brown & Co. and International Creative Management.

PETER BICHSEL: "There Is No Such Place as America" from *There Is No Such Place as America,* trans. Michael Hamburger. Copyright © 1969 by Hermann Luchterhand Verlag GmbH, Neuwied und Berlin; translation copyright © 1970 by Michael Hamburger; originally published in German under the title *Kindergeschichten* by Luchterhand/ Edition Otto F. Walter; first published in England by Calder and Boyars Ltd., London. Reprinted by permission of Delacorte Press/Seymour Lawrence & Marion Boyars Publishers Ltd.

JORGE LUIS BORGES: "Pierre Menard, Author of the *Quixote*" from *Labyrinths,* trans. James E. Irby. Copyright © 1962 by New Directions Publishing Corp. Reprinted by permission of New Directions, New York, and Laurence Pollinger Ltd., London.

RICHARD BRAUTIGAN: "Homage to the San Francisco YMCA" from *Revenge of the Lawn.* Copyright © 1963, 1964, 1965, 1966, 1967, 1969, 1970, 1971 by Richard Brautigan. Reprinted by permission of Simon & Schuster, a Division of Gulf & Western Corp., and Jonathan Cape Ltd., London.

ITALO CALVINO: "All At One Point" from *Cosmicomics.* Copyright © 1965 by Giulio Einaudi editore s.p.a., Torino; English translation © 1968 by Harcourt Brace Jovanovich, Inc., and Jonathan Cape Ltd.; originally appeared in *Playboy*. Reprinted by permission of Harcourt Brace Jovanovich, Inc., and Roslyn Targ Agency.

A. W. CARDINALL, ED.: "The Eye of the Giant" from *Tales Told in Togoland*. Reprinted by permission of the International African Institute and Mrs. Ada Cardinall.

ARTHUR C. CLARKE: "The Star" from *The Other Side of the Sky*. Copyright 1955 by Royal Publications. Reprinted by permission of Harcourt Brace Jovanovich, Inc., the author, and the author's agents, Scott Meredith Literary Agency, Inc., 845 Third Avenue, New York, N.Y.

ROBERT COOVER: "The Marker" from *Pricksongs & Descants*. Copyright © 1969 by Robert Coover. Reprinted by permission of E. P. Dutton, and Jonathan Cape Ltd., London.

JULIO CORTAZAR: "Axolotl" from *End of the Game and Other Stories*, trans. Paul Blackburn. Copyright © 1967, 1963 by Random House, Inc. Reprinted by permission of Pantheon Books, a Division of Random House, Inc., and Joan Blackburn.

JACK FINNEY: "The Third Level" from *Short Science Fiction Tales*. Copyright © 1950, renewed 1977 by Jack Finney. Reprinted by permission of Harold Matson Co., Inc.

E. T. A. HOFFMAN: "Ritter Gluck" and "The Sandman" from *Tales of E. T. A. Hoffman*, trans. Leonard J. Kent and Elizabeth C. Knight. Copyright © 1969 by the University of Chicago. Reprinted by permission of the University of Chicago Press and Leonard J. Kent.

SPENCER HOLST: "The Zebra Storyteller" from *The Language of Cats and Other Stories*. Copyright © 1971 by Spencer Holst. Reprinted by permission of the publishers, E. P. Dutton.

NORTON JUSTER: "The Royal Banquet" from *The Phantom Tollbooth*. Copyright © 1961 by Norton Juster. Reprinted by permission of Random House, Inc., and Collins Publishers, London.

FRANZ KAFKA: "The Judgment" from *The Penal Colony*. Copyright © 1948, renewed © 1975 by Schocken Books, Inc. "A Common Confusion" from *The Great Wall of China*. Copyright 1946, renewed 1974 by Schocken Books Inc. Reprinted by permission of Schocken Books, Inc., and Martin Secker & Warburg Ltd., London.

TOMMASO LANDOLFI: "Pastoral" from *Gogol's Wife and Other Stories*, trans. John Longrigg. Copyright © 1963 by New Directions Publishing Corp. Reprinted by permission of New Directions, New York.

H. P. LOVECRAFT: "The Picture in the House." Reprinted by permission of Arkham House Publishers, Inc., Sauk City, Wisconsin.

OVID: "The Myth of Actaeon," "The Myth of Narcissus," and "The Myth of Philomela" from *Metamorphoses*, trans. Mary M. Innes. Copyright © 1955 by Mary M. Innes. Reprinted by permission of Penguin Books Ltd.

BRUNO SCHULZ: "Cockroaches" from *The Street of Crocodiles,* trans. Celina Wieniewska. Copyright © 1963 by C. J. Schulz. Reprinted by permission of Walker & Co., Inc.

ESTHER SHEPHARD: "On the Columbia" from *Paul Bunyan.* Copyright 1924, 1952 by Esther Shephard. Reprinted by permission of Harcourt Brace Jovanovich, Inc.

JAMES THURBER: "The Secret Life of Walter Mitty" from *My World— and Welcome To It.* Published by Harcourt Brace Jovanovich; originally printed in *The New Yorker.* Copyright © 1942 by James Thurber, © 1970 by Helen Thurber. Reprinted by permission of Helen Thurber, and Hamish Hamilton Ltd.

J. R. R. TOLKIEN: "Leaf by Niggle" from *Tree and Leaf.* Copyright © 1964 by George Allen & Unwin Ltd. Reprinted by permission of Houghton Mifflin Co., and George Allen & Unwin Ltd., London.

AMOS TUTUOLA: "How I Brought Death into the World" from *The Palm-Wine Drinkard.* Copyright © 1953 by George Braziller. Reprinted by permission of Grove Press, Inc., and Faber and Faber Ltd., London.

KURT VONNEGUT, JR.: "EPICAC" from *Welcome to the Monkey House.* Copyright © 1950 by Kurt Vonnegut, Jr.; originally published in *Collier's.* Reprinted by permission of Delacorte Press/Seymour Lawrence, Jonathan Cape Ltd., London, and Donald C. Farber as attorney for Kurt Vonnegut, Jr.

SYLVIA TOWNSEND WARNER: "The Five Black Swans" from *The Kingdoms of Elfin.* Copyright © 1973 by Sylvia Townsend Warner. Originally appeared in *The New Yorker.* All Rights Reserved. Reprinted by permission of Viking Penguin Inc., Chatto & Windus Ltd., London, and the author's literary Estate.

H. G. WELLS: "The Star" from 28 *Science Fiction Stories.* Reprinted by permission of the Estate of the late H. G. Wells.

For David

PREFACE

This anthology is intended to serve the rapidly growing interest in the literature of the fantastic in three ways: by offering together a full range of materials that make possible an enriched understanding of the fantastic, by outlining a theoretical understanding of the fantastic that both puts these narratives into significant relation to each other and places fantastic literature in the wider field of literature, and by exemplifying a number of analytic methods of general utility that are particularly useful for and clarified by a study of the fantastic. In addition, some new theoretical positions are urged as a consequence of this study. The presentation of a large body of primary materials is intended to make this collection not only enjoyable but representative. As such, it can be used both to build traditional ideas about criticism and fantastic literature and also to test the ideas new to this book. In short, the arrangement of materials and the editor's essays are intended to offer alternatives to the usual points of view, just as the stories themselves rejuvenate the familiar by transplanting it to the wonderful soil of fantastic worlds.

E. S. R.

Ann Arbor, Mich.
November 2, 1978

TABLE OF CONTENTS

FANTASTIC WORLDS

Introduction

FANTASTIC WORLDS

The problem with the real world, frankly, is that it is the only one we have. To be sure, the real world is not an intolerably restricted world, at least not for most of us in the industrialized nations with our jet travel and air conditioning and long-distance telephone communication, but once you have been frisked at airport security a few times or have paid those ever-rising electric bills or have been called out of the bath by enough wrong numbers, you might well prefer a flying carpet or changeless Cockaigne or telepathy. Where do you find them? In fantastic worlds.

Fantastic worlds, when first we enter them, whether with the sigh of relief or the gasp of terror, come alive for us as alternatives to the real world. The real world is a messy place where dust accumulates and people die for no good reason and crime often pays and true love doesn't conquer much. In one sense all art is fantastic simply because it offers us worlds in which some order, whatever that may be, prevails. In our real lives, street noises occur randomly; they are indifferent to the shape we try to sense in our lives. But in a novel, street noises may keep the hero awake just before some crucial task in order to heighten the fear in the reader that the hero may be unready to meet his test or in order to justify his failure at that crucial task; the street noises may keep him awake before a day of the same old routine so that we can understand that the whole world is an annoyance to our hero or so that he can suddenly realize that the next day promises only the same old routine—and that he wants out. In art worlds, the street noises are never indifferent. The fact that traffic and crying neighbor babies and howling sirens should coordinate themselves in order to add shape to the life of our hero is fantastic, a true alternative to the real world.

If, in addition to hero-responsive street noises, a story had a dragon marauding in the countryside or a time machine or a cure for death, that story would be more fantastic still. This anthology collects a great diversity of these more fantastic worlds. Such worlds are not merely *different* from our own, but *alternative* to our own. Fantastic worlds—perhaps paradoxically—are defined for us and are of interest to us by virtue of their relationship to the real world we imagine to have been thought normal when the story was composed. Even though today we can often restart a stopped heart with a defibrillator, we still understand Frankenstein's awakening of his demon to be fantastic in the real world to which Mary Shelley's novel offers an alternative. Read as responses to the real world, fantastic worlds take on great significance. The marauding dragon, destroying farms, may symbolize natural infertility; when the handsome prince kills the dragon he simultaneously wins—and weds—the princess and thus restores fertility to the kingdom. The dragon is a fantastic dramatization of a real-world problem; the simple solution of the story poses a satisfying alternative to the complexities of the real world. In the same way, a time machine may serve to move the story's viewpoint to a time when something in our own world is grossly exaggerated, just as the dragon may exaggerate diminished crop production. In Jack Finney's "The Third Level," the alternative time is a wished-for past. The time machine that shuttles between our time and another makes clear the connectedness of the real world with fantastic worlds. The cure for death, in a similar way, is of dramatic interest for us only because we do perceive death as a significant problem in the real world; one never reads a story motivated by a cure for hangnails. To be allowed a world in which we can contemplate the solution of the problem of mortality may be satisfying, exciting, or—depending upon the treatment—terrifying. Regardless of what makes a particular story fantastic, that story will be important in the measure that it engages in its fantastic ways concerns of the real world.

ORGANIZATION OF THE BOOK

Certain questions seem universally to have occupied people's minds since prehistoric times. Where did the world come from? How can one explain the feelings of awakened sexuality? Why must there be death? Is there an afterlife? Fantastic worlds dramatize answers to these real questions for the ease of the questioners. In their oldest forms, these answers are the myths that cultures live by; in somewhat more modern forms, these answers become the folktales by which cultures entertain themselves; and in yet more modern forms, these answers become the fairy tales through which cultures amuse—and thereby educate—their young.

The first part of this anthology presents all three types of fantastic world from diverse cultures in order to provide a sample of the universal sources of the fantastic. Once a modern literary tradition becomes established, writers can capitalize on the conventional knowledge of readers. We all know that "Once upon a time" leads into stories about golden-haired princesses and evil stepmothers and handsome princes. When one of those characters enters the scene, we recognize that entrance as fitting. Similarly, we know that stories that begin around fireplaces on Christmas Eve always have ghosts in them. And what are ghosts, after all, for those of us who have not actually met one, but ectoplasmic embodiments of literary tradition? A writer is expected to know that his audience knows that vampires cannot see themselves in mirrors and that fake medieval syntax doth proclaim for those who will attend thereunto the deeds of the nobles of yore. Whether the conventional signals, then, are standard phrases or elements of setting or linguistic habits or anything else, the literary tradition can and does use convention to build fanastic worlds economically. "If I had not myself experienced what I am about to relate, I would not believe . . ." already tells us that the story to follow will be chilling, perhaps supernatural, and certainly set in an isolated environment. Would any among us be surprised to discover that the story concerned a murder in a crumbling castle, that the owner was a recluse, a cousin of the narrator, and that his mother had died in giving him life? Of course we would not be surprised. In fact, once conventions become established a creative author needs to supersede them lest they define too narrowly the stories he can tell.

The second part of this anthology presents stories within the English-language literary tradition in order to show how conventions can lead economically to the creation of fantastic worlds and how the repeated creation of those worlds leads in turn to the development and change of the conventions. Hoffmann's work is included here, although he wrote in German, because it had such a profound influence on such authors as Poe who initially established the conventions for the diverse branches of fantastic literature. Only some branches of this luxuriant and magical tree are represented. However, the stories collected here include work by nearly all of the great authors whose names are most commonly associated with fantasy.

Every fully developed literary tradition has its own heritage of fantastic literature, a heritage that reaches back to the oldest sacred texts and extends through the advent of a wide reading public knowledgeable in the literary conventions themselves. Fantastic worlds, like ghosts, begin to take on an independent life, and newer fantastic worlds can be constructed as alternatives to the older fantastic worlds (and through them as alternatives to the real world). In our modern world of hyper-accelerated change one would expect fantastic worlds that twist and reverse other fantastic worlds; in our modern world in which traditional answers are ever more frequently discarded as outmoded, one would expect literary experimentation and the search for further alternatives. Both of these forces combine to generate internationally a modern form of fantastic literature that is openly conscious of its fantastic nature and means to flaunt it. Some of the most exciting writing of this century has gone into the development of this new sort of fantastic world; the third part of this anthology presents an international sample of some of the best.

This book, then, proceeds in a developmental, approximately chronological way. The first part offers a selection of stories from oral and early literacy periods of many cultures in order to reveal some of the pervasive human questions that find treatment through the fantastic. In the second part, the enormous growth of fantastic codes in a single culture illustrates how refined can be the artistic response to our continuing need to face such fundamental issues. The third part, by virtue of its internationalism, implies that the work of fantasists, even after the development of literary traditions, bears a common stamp and fulfills a common need. Each of the widely different pieces in this anthology, and in the wider universe of fantastic worlds, reveals on close examination some of those elements found always and everywhere in the art people produce in expressing their common need for alternatives to our one real world.

ANALYZING THE FANTASTIC

J. R. R. Tolkien, author of *The Hobbit* (1937) and the Lord of the Rings trilogy (*The Fellowship of the Ring,* 1954; *The Two Towers,* 1955; *The Return of the King,* 1956) is universally acknowledged as one of the most important fantasists of this century. His somewhat Norse/somewhat Old English/somewhat original world of balrogs and hobbits is too extensive to be properly felt in an excerpt that would fit appropriately in this volume. However, we can turn to other work of this master for an example of distilled prose that captures much of what is crucial in fantastic literature. Here are two apparently simple sentences from Tolkien's eighty-page social satire called "Farmer Giles of Ham" (1949):

> "So knights are mythical!" said the younger and less experienced dragons. "We always thought so."

To see just how these sentences—and the fantastic—have their effect on a reader, let us examine these few words one by one.

So: This word, especially coupled with the emphatic "are" ("'So knights *are* mythical!'"), indicates that the speakers (younger dragons) feel a sense of satisfaction at having had a prejudgment confirmed. This is a feeling we can all share when, after "Once upon a time," we read of the expected "golden-haired princess." Temporally, the "so" connects us automatically to the earlier state of the dragons' knowledge, in which the belief was held but its confirmation was in suspense. The structure of confirmation of suspended belief is typical of much art, particularly so-called "romance" (including Gothic romance, love stories, and so forth), tales in which the reader's ideals are confirmed. When these ideals clearly flout reality, as, for example, when the ideal is that hidden guilt will be uncovered—although in real life most crimes go unsolved—the particular romance is obviously fantastic in more than the minimal sense common to aesthetically ordered art. Tales of Great Detectives, then, like those about Sherlock Holmes or Nero Wolfe, are fairly fantastic; they are fairy tales for adults in which the unworldly ideal is first suspended ("*Will* the guilty part be discovered?") and then confirmed ("Ah *so!*").

Knights: This word automatically activates a literary tradition that includes feats of derring-do, ornate armor, virgins with unicorns, and noble service to King and God. In other words, although there are historical knights, the term "knight" in a modern literary context refers not to parasitic landlords but to heroes who are foreknown to be larger than life, that is, alternative to the real world. Knights habitually participate in such super- natural events as pulling enchanted swords from enchanted rocks, falling prey to love potions, and, most important in this context, killing dragons. Thus, if against all the odds stacked up by reading the beginning of Tolkien's story, one were to read "knights" and think of both the fantastic and the historical con- texts, the word "dragons" would quickly settle us into our choice for the fantastic. In addition to this activation of literary codes and a sense of adventure, the word "knights" brings us back to an earlier time in our own English-speaking culture. The desire for a throwback way of life, for atavism, is common even to those fantastic worlds ostensibly set in the future, as we will dis- cuss in another section. Atavism is a reasonable fantasy when one considers that we all know that Western Civilization has, after all, made it through the Middle Ages intact; we are not nearly so sure we will make it through the Nuclear Ages at all. By contrast, the old times offer a wonderful alternative to the real world, an alternative that must be fantastic since the very fact of history demonstrates that Western Civilization could not fix itself at the year 1400.

Mythical: One of the commonest meanings of "mythical" is "untrue." All fantastic worlds, of course, are mythical, and the worlds of myths, even if they are symbolically true, are obviously not historically true. No one believes that someone named Pro- metheus stole fire from the gods, brought it to Earth, and, as punishment, was chained to Mount Caucasus. Nonetheless, myths are stories which the cultures that support them find significant. Western Civilization has consistently felt fear of the power conferred on it by increasing knowledge, and this fear has been given dramatic life in the story of Prometheus. Prometheus suffered daily for us; the fault in our having fire was his, not ours; the sense of fear we have need not turn into guilt for fires gone out of control. The myth, obviously, plays a crucial role in offering a fanastic world, an alternative to the real world in which the fire-making human may be the destroyer of home and family willy-nilly. In this sense of "untrue," "mythical" may be a magical word used to banish fears: "Oh, the Mafia is only mythical." Myths, like so many fantastic stories, handle fears for us. In Tolkien's lines, the dragons' fear that the word "mythical" tries to banish is a fear of knights, people we readers know existed in the real world. One ignores a real-world problem at one's peril, as the chief dragon discovers later in the story. Myth and history make an impractical combination. Mythical time is time out of time, a time unconnected with historical, real-world time. If this is 1980, then we know that World War II started 41 years ago; that the Declaration of Independence was signed 204 years ago; that Julius Caesar was killed 2024 years ago. How long ago did King Arthur ride? All events in the real world are connected by the clock called history; the events of myth are not. Hence, mythical elements—like "knights" here—are an alternative to the real world of the speaker. Part of the joke for the reader, of course, is that the real world for the speaking dragon is mythical for us reading humans. This sense of continuous reversal is the heart of fantasy. The repeated application of fantastic reversal to traditional materials is one of the chief mechanisms by which the fantastic myths of old become the fantasies of our own era.

Younger: This word puts the reader in mind of children. In our era, and since at latest the beginning of the nineteenth century, literature that was recognized as fantastic was usually thought somehow to be most fit for children. This agism, however, did not always exist. Myths, especially sacred tales, have been and are taken to be serious adult material in those cultures for which the myths seem an adequate explanation of some facet of reality. Devout "Fundamentalists" who believe in the historical accuracy of the Bible find that the account of Creation in Genesis is worth extended contemplation as adults. Most people, however, in our post-Enlightment and relentlessly "scientific" age, believe at most that the biblical account of Creation has only literary (that is, artistic; that is, at least minimally fantastic) value, and they find Genesis a fit object for study by children in Sunday school but not worth much concern to an adult.

Adults, mature adults, have learned to distinguish the real world from their own fantasies. Good adults know which side their bread is buttered on, never volunteer, keep a stiff upper lip, and learn to accept "the way things are." Children, on the other hand, do not yet know irrevocably how things are and so have the delightful habit of accepting them as they are not. Just because a place is called "Never-Never Land" does not mean it "never-never" was. Oh, to be sure, children do know that Barrie's fantastic world is fantastic; but children are not yet so willing to accept reality that they are unable to accept the unreality as well. Adults, most of whom began as children, are similarly ambivalent. A good adult would have no interest in Peter Pan, but the child who refused to grow up inside the adult can be captivated by Peter Pan so long as this captivation passes the adult's ingrown social censor. The best way to quiet this curmudgeon, as everyone knows, is to make believe that Peter Pan's story is a story for children. And it is that, of course, a tale in which children can indulge in fantasies of power and flight and adventure and freedom from parental restraint; but the play ends with the children quite happy to return to the home run by their parents, and the final image of outgrown Peter is really quite sad. Finally, this children's fantasy is much more for adults; it is a fantasy that panders to the childhood fantasies still in us and then confirms the adult fantasy that the stable world we have bought was worth the price of our youth. That price, mortality, is a terrible one. Fantastic worlds may indulge our atavism not only in presenting an earlier time of our culture, but an earlier time of our selves. For a brief moment of reading time in Tolkien's story, we share the adventure of new-found knowledge—and confirmation of belief—with those who are "younger."

Less experienced: This phrase underscores an attribute one necessarily finds among the young: ignorance. You cannot make a grown-up believe in Santa Claus or convince a two-year-old that he is unimportant. Experience is an opposite of innocence, especially in our culture, which often sees innocence as goodness and experience as corruption. Experience means experience of the real world. Although it is objectively clear that the real world offers us examples of love, say, and happiness, experience as the opposite of innocence has usually been taken to mean the experience of a real world of lust and filth and hunger and violence, a world on which some have focused so exclusively that these extremities characterize a romantic style of writing called "Naturalism."

In using the word "experienced," Tolkien reveals the fundamental connection of his fantastic world with the real world to which it offers an alternative. In having his speakers be "less experienced," he hints that they will eventually learn better and have to reverse their attitudes. Since they have just concluded that knights are mythical, a conclusion we already know to be false, we can confidently expect that this implication of the phrase "less experienced" will be borne out by the story. At one reading moment the word "younger" allows us an atavistic identification with the joys of youth and at the next its apparent synonym, "less experienced," allows us the smug adult satisfaction of knowing better. This is the same covert movement we noted in *Peter Pan*. "Less experienced," then, connects the fantastic world with the real world, promises alternatives (reversals) of the speakers' attitudes, and creates a world alternative to that of the childhood fantasy of two words earlier. This continuous use of reversal is at the heart of fantastic literature.

Dragons: This is a conventional word that calls to mind fire-breathing beasts, princesses in distress, and mortal combat. Fertility is very much at issue when there is a dragon on the scene. Dragons are also called serpents and worms, phallic symbols, perhaps; certainly symbols identifiable with the tempter of Eve in the Garden. The association with agricultural fertility has already been mentioned. For prepubescent boys, tales in which the fearful sleeping power of sexuality is put to rest by an older, wiser Saint George offer psychic consolation. Tolkien here offers a fantastic reversal of the traditional fantastic materials, for his innocent ("less experienced") dragons are relieved to discover that the danger (sexual potency) symbolized for them by knights need not be feared. Nonetheless, "dragon" does call to mind for most human readers an atavistic, mythic time of easy right-versus-wrong conflicts, sex, danger, adventure. At the same time that "dragon" by itself vivifies these conventional associations, "dragon" in its particular usage in this sentence has in part the effect of reversing those associations.

Every sentence carries more information than the mere words of which it is composed. For example, "The boy goes shopping" presupposes, among other sentences, a sentence that says "There exists a boy." The speaker who says "The boy goes shopping" may or may not be lying about what the boy does, but we take him to be seriously asserting in his implicit way that there exists such a thing as a boy, that there exists such an activity as shopping. Had Tolkien's sentence read, " 'So knights are mythical!' the *lunatic* exclaimed," we readers would have taken all of the markers of the fantastic to apply to the private world of the insane speaker. The narrator would have been asserting merely that "There exists a lunatic." In the actual Tolkien sentence, however, the prior sentence that we suddenly must recognize asserts that "There exists such a thing as a dragon," thus not only making a joke but offering a reversal of the very narrative ground rules by which, for example, we have been able to follow the orderly development from "younger" to "less experienced."

While the dragons, whom we know to be nonexistent, are ignorant enough to assert that knights are mythical, our narrator—with whom we must necessarily share a point of view—is ignorant enough to assert that dragons exist. This has the effect of our asserting, by reading the narrator's sentence, that dragons exist. In other words, we make the same mistake as the dragon-speakers: wrongly assigning an element to the real or fantastic world. We suddenly share something with the dragons and thus the fantastic world is forced on us by this fundamentally fantastic technique of reversal.

We: This word, which should apply to the dragons alone, seems in part to apply to us now because we have been made to share not only the viewpoint of the narrator (who is presumably human) but the viewpoint of the dragons (who are mythical— are they not?). Thus the plural pronoun implies in a minor way that we are dragons (but we are not mythical—or are we?). We have been implicated in this vertiginous process of reversal and re-reversal. Yet the appeal of the mythic time, the time out of time, is dependent in large part on its stability. Although the real Middle Ages obviously did not last, that is no reason not to hope against hope that a fantastic world that returned us to the Middle Ages might prove stable. Why are we reading fantastic literature, after all, if not to find an alternative to the real world, that ever-shifting and never-understood real world? How can Tolkien's fantastic world be itself so shifting? This continuous reversal makes Tolkien's world even more fantastic than the relatively stable fantastic worlds of, say, the Grimms' fairy tales. "We" never enter those worlds directly; they exist, as they are supposed to, changelessly, always.

Always: When the dragons use this word, its very stability highlights the instability of the situation we are in. Further, as a stable concept, it stands fantastically as an alternative to the real world of fluctuations and growth. And finally, the way "always" offers a temporal extension backward into the hazy, changeless past promises that what we are involved with is a fundamental value that had been suspended but now is to be confirmed. That is, our fantastic world of linguistic reversal is simultaneously a world of psychological wish fulfillment. This surely functions as an alternative to the real world which is usually indifferent to our thoughts.

Thought: What is crucial for the dragons, and for us, is not what was *known* to be so, that is, previously experienced, but what was *thought* to be so, that is, previously desired. What is known is known, and there is no use worrying about it. One can accept it, reject it, work to change it, or try to ignore it, but what is, is. The true field of freedom is in consideration of what is not, what might be, what we think. What we think and how we think (are the dragons in the story any more mythical than the knights?) are inevitably crypto-subjects of fantasy, even when the overt subjects may be quite different. To have "always thought" something is, of course, impossible, so long as one recognizes that one was born at any time later than Creation. To identify "always" with one's own recollections of one's own thoughts is a kind of egocentric projection of the self onto the world that we normally associate with the very young, but clearly, as Tolkien's story for adults makes obvious, the young still live somewhere inside even the oldest of us. Or in our thoughts.

So: As we noticed in beginning this close analysis, the word "so" expresses the satisfaction of the confirmation of a belief that had been held in suspense. Now we can see that the belief, the desired freedom from fear (especially sexual fear), has been held since "always." Certainly it has been held since the beginning of the two lines we have been examining. In poetry, rhyme creates in the reader a sense of satisfaction, a sense often made most obvious when it is missed: "Roses are red / Violets are blue / Sugar is sweet / And so is ice cream." The failure of this quatrain to end with "you," or at least some rhyme of "blue," feels wrong because the structure of the quatrain has set us up to expect the rhyme. In the same way, despite all the reversals of meaning and convention and hidden beliefs, hopes and fears, a fantastic narrative—because it is art—ends by reasserting order. In these lines from Tolkien, the word "so" ends the passage with what amounts to a rhyme by repeating the word "so" with which the passage began. This significant repetition of word (which is paralleled in fantastic narratives by repetitions of setting, plot element, and much more) bounds the passage, contains it, and tames the narrative word to show us that, even with dragons in it, Tolkien's world is a safe one. As such, it offers another kind of alternative to the turmoil of the real world. That we are mostly unconscious of the wealth of association and the nuances of change that the words ring only reveals how it is that we can give ourselves up so uncaringly to the fantastic world. The sense of artistic safety that Tolkien creates is a fantasy that old and young can all share because it is built upon a subtle and inspired manipulation of each reader's response.

THE FANTASTIC AND FANTASY

A reader's response to a given text depends on many things, among them, of course, the words of the text. But in addition to these words themselves, as the preceding section has argued, words, and words in certain contexts, call up many associations that may well be important in creating within a reader the experience of the fantastic. For any given reader, these associations might seem to be either impersonal and somehow outside him or personal and inside him. Every reader knows, for example, that his association of knights with a romanticized Middle Ages that never existed is knowledge in his own head, yet he understands nonetheless that this Arthurian mythology is part of the common heritage of readers, even those who have not encountered the particular text at hand, and hence that this mythology is part of an outside reality. Similarly, when the reader laughs at a joke in the text, he knows that every reader is supposed to laugh, but the laughter itself is his, part of his inside reality. Let us examine in more detail the outside and inside realities against which fantastic worlds are defined.

Outside reality comes most obviously from the worldly experiences of readers. These experiences, perhaps surprisingly, vary from era to era and from individual to individual. Aristotle wrote, and we often still say, that nature abhors a vacuum, which means that matter naturally disperses itself so that it fills up, however tenuously, the full volume available to it. Today, of course, we recognize that atoms, with their electrons probabilistically whirring around their relatively minute nuclei, are mostly nothing, just as our solar system, with the vast majority of its matter compacted into a few planets and moons and the sun, is also mostly nothing. So nature clearly prefers a vacuum.

When this fact first became clear, due to the experiments of Torricelli in 1643, the shock among those who understood the work was fantastic, quite literally. We live in a world that sees humanity as *Homo sapiens,* part of an evolutionary chain that will, we suppose, supersede us one day. The famous Scopes trial came about because to many people Darwin's ideas were literally fantastic. To people in some eras, the Earth was flat; now, for most of us, it is "obviously" round. The inventory of outside reality is not, then, fixed entirely by outside reality but reflects to a large extent the state of the cultures that view themselves as inhabiting that outside reality.

As readers of constructed worlds of art we are expected to engage our knowledge of the outside realities that have existed at different times. When the language of the art world conveys to us the impression that the text comes from the eighteenth century or later, then we know that dragons are to be taken as fantastic, alternatives to the real world in which, of course, dragons do not exist. But when the language of the King James Version of the Bible presents us with the dragon's prototype, the talking serpent, we do not take that as fantastic because we believe (rightly or wrongly) that for people living "back then" (King James died in 1625), dragons were thought possible even by those who had never seen one—just as we today believe in pandas. On the other hand, the text of Genesis makes it quite clear that Paradise itself is a world alternative to the outside reality inhabited by King James's subjects and hence we rightly read the account of Creation, with its shifts from no world to world and pure world to fallen world, as fantastic. An unsympathetic reading that does not respond to the clear intention of that text to provide alternatives for those readers misses the moral lesson which the alternative fantastic world is postulating for the reader's edification in this world.

Outside reality varies not only from era to era but from individual to individual. In a trivial sense, this merely reflects accidents of education. A French text can hardly be moving for a person who reads only German. But, in a significant sense, personal education reflects the stage one has arrived at in life. There are important and predictable differences between little children, for whom the world is egocentric, and somewhat older children; differences between these older children, who recognize the existence of physical danger, and children older yet, who recognize sexual dangers; differences between those who have felt the pressures of sexuality and those who have learned to live with them; differences between those who have merely begun their sex lives and those who have been changed by that fact into parents; differences between parents who are still children and parents who have lived through their own parents' deaths. We can, of course, project ourselves back into the persons we once were, retaining a certain double vision because we are no longer that person, but we cannot fully project ourselves into the persons we will become. For children, Ovid's tales of metamorphosis are fantastic not merely because the changing of a person into a stag or bird is an alternative to everyone's outside reality but because the underlying sexual forces are also alternative to children's reality. For Ovid's tale of metamorphosis into a flower, the underlying force is egocentrism, narcissism, and in reading this tale a child can take the change as less literal—and therefore less fantastic—and more metaphorical, just as an adult can take the changes to stag and bird as metaphoric. Hence, the degree to which an art world seems fantastic depends upon a reader's projection of an outside reality as it must conform to his assumptions about the culture of the text, the culture of the reader, and the life experience of the reader.

The fact of variable response to art worlds may imply to some that we are on shaky ground when we assert that something should or should not be taken as fantastic. And sometimes, of course, that is so. Jules Verne is generally thought today to have "predicted," among other things, the submarine. This thought follows from our own ignorance of history, an ignorance not shared by Verne's contemporaries who knew that a submarine had engaged in a naval battle in the American Civil War five years before the composition of *Twenty Thousand Leagues*

Under the Sea. However, such cases of mass mistake are comparatively rare because the outside reality that one believes to be implied by the text is continually checked by the inside reality that one experiences from the text.

The following passage comes from Lewis Carroll's "The Garden of Live Flowers":

> "Oh, Tiger-lily!" said Alice, addressing herself to one that was waving gracefully about in the wind, "I *wish* you could talk!"
>
> "We *can* talk," said the Tiger-lily, "when there's anybody worth talking to."
>
> Alice was so astonished that she couldn't speak for a minute: it quite seemed to take her breath away.

Although a given reader may believe that outside reality provides talking flowers, Alice's "wish" implies that at that moment in the world of this text Alice understands that flowers cannot talk. To read this passage properly, one must accept that ground rule as operating. Once accepted, the passage can then reverse the ground rule not only by creating a talking flower but by having the surprise of that fact make the child—usually quite talkative—mute. Just as the Tolkien passage made a small but stable narrative unit from "so" to "so," here we have a small but stable narrative unit that goes from our projection of floral silence to our projection of child silence. That such a reversal is indeed fantastic is signaled not only by the reversal in roles but by Alice's astonishment. The text trains us, word by word, to perceive reality—and shifting reality—in certain ways; it makes us pick from all possible outside realities the particular outside realities that make narrative sense of the text itself. Thus is created an inside reality, the moment-by-moment changing reality experienced by the reader.

It is important that we recognize that the fantastic comes not from mere violation of "the real world," but from offering an alternative to the real world; not from an alternative to some real world of immutable and universal law, but to a real world which our life and education have trained us to project as expectable as the context for a given text; and not to the projected real world

in the fullness of its infinite and often conflicting elements, but
to the particular real world which conforms to the needs of the
world inside the text itself. Because we believe that wizards "obviously" do not exist, we might naïvely suppose that their occurrence in a story would make that story fantastic. But if that story
cries out to be read as the life of a saint who performed miracles,
then for believing readers the text is clearly not fantastic. Similarly, perfectly ordinary things from our world can make a
moderately fantastic narrative world even more fantastic. For
example, if a story began with "Once upon a time," we would
not be surprised to find a dragon or a witch or a golden-haired
princess later. These would not elicit from us Alice's reaction of
shocked surprise. But consider a story that begins this way:
"Once upon a time there was a beautiful golden-haired princess
and she fell desperately in love with a plumber named Sid."
There is nothing in our world that is fantastic about there being
a plumber named Sid, but in the world promised by "Once upon
a time" Sid's presence violates the ground rules, and our added
astonishment should make this second beginning more fantastic
than the beginning of an ordinary fairy tale. The fantastic is
fantastic, then, not by virtue of simply violating some rules we
have picked up in the real world, but by virtue of reversing the
ground rules we are following at any given moment of reading.

To be sure, other things being equal, we allow our personal
and cultural sense of the real world to supply ground rules, but
other things are never completely equal. We may usually presume that the dead do not rise again (so that ghosts must be
fantastic), but, as we have seen, we presume in certain contexts
that dragons or wizards may be more or less expectable. Since
context is continuously created by the process of reading itself,
once we know that we are in a ghost story the later occurrence
of a ghost will not be particularly fantastic.

The key to the fantastic, then, is not to be found in simple
comparison with the real world but in examination of the reading process. We find the reader reaction that characterizes the
fantastic, a parallel of Alice's astonishment, when the operative

ground rules are reversed. Whether those rules come from our projection of the outside reality or are established by the inside reality of the text, the fantastic is an affect generated as we read by the direct reversal of the ground rules of the narrative world.

Many texts, such as standard fairy tales, make a host of reversals all at one moment. "Once upon a time" opens the world of Faërie which is, indeed, an alternative to our own world. But once in that world, fundamental reversal almost never occurs. Fairy-tale worlds—despite their ogres and spells—are stable literary worlds with foreknown rules. Neither the characters in fairy tales nor the readers of fairy tales are surprised when animals speak or magic spells work. But one could be surprised in a fairy tale either by the intrusion of the differently fantastic (backward time travel, for example, is not part of the conventional inventory of Faërie) or by the intrusion of the disconcertingly ordinary (Sid the plumber). In the very first chapter of *Alice in Wonderland,* for example, Alice takes a slow-motion fall to the bottom of a well, drinks a bottle of liquid that causes her to "shut up like a telescope," and so "she had begun to think that very few things indeed were really impossible." In such a context the shock of the fantastic might seem difficult to generate. Alice eats a small cake with the words "Eat Me" written on it in currants:

> She ate a little bit, and said anxiously to herself "Which way? Which way?" holding her hand on the top of her head to feel which way it was growing; and she was quite surprised to find that she remained the same size. To be sure, this is what generally happens when one eats cake; but Alice had got so much into the way of expecting nothing but out-of-the-way things to happen, that it seemed quite dull and stupid for life to go on in the common way.
>
> So she set to work, and very soon finished off the cake.

Carroll, by providing Alice with an ordinary experience, makes his narrative even more fantastic, for this ordinary experience functions as a reversal of the ground rules then operating, and it surprises both Alice and the reader. While fairy tales and other narratives that require one—but only one—set of reversals to be understood are fantastic, *Alice in Wonderland* is a true Fantasy.

The fantastic is the affect generated as we read by the direct reversal of the ground rules of the narrative world. Fantasy is that class of works which uses the fantastic exhaustively. One could not use the fantastic exclusively, since then there would be only reversal and no ground rules; so Fantasies must give some minimal sense of continuity, of reality. This conclusion accords well with our earlier observation that even the most realistic narratives must be fantastic to some minimal extent. Obviously literature presents us with a host of works that can be thought of as more or less fantastic (or realistic). The passage we have just noted from *Alice in Wonderland* comes from one of those rare, true Fantasies. Alice, in staying the same size, takes a non-action which, in context, is a fantastic bit of plot; in asking "Which way? Which way?" she reminds us of the theme of change and development, but that theme is suddenly reversed; although Alice seems ready for changes in herself, when the narrative world does not enforce such changes she immediately reverts to the basic function of eating, a backward movement in character; and when the narrator opposes "into the way" with "out-of-the-way" we get linguistic reversal. Moderately fantastic worlds, like traditional fairy tales and most ghost stories, can be recognized by the inventory of elements within them, such as fairy godmothers and family curses. But the vast literature of even more fantastic narratives, and those especially fantastic narratives for which we might rightly reserve the term Fantasy, are recognized by our sensitivity to the reversals within them. These reversals can most easily be thought of as occurring in the four levels we have just observed in Lewis Carroll: plot, thematic development, character development, and style. Narratives that keep reversing their ground rules at all four of these levels, like the works collected in the third part of this anthology, are as fantastic as any tales humankind has been able to construct since the prehistoric day when we first began using the fantastic to cope with fundamental questions about life and death and the real world.

EXPLORING THESE WORLDS

How might one use this book? The most obvious answer, of course, is that one should read these selections for entertainment. We have not, so far, talked about the fun of the fantastic and this has been intentional. The most common charge made against fantastic literature is that it is "merely entertainment" or that it offers "escape." There is nothing, however, wrong with escape. If one is imprisoned, the desire to escape is sane and valuable. If the real world oppresses a reader by the fact of mortality or the ambiguities of sex, a fantastic world that handles his fears for him or, at least for the time of reading, clarifies his confusion, is a world that offers not escape but liberation.

When people say that a work is "merely entertaining," they avoid a fundamental question: How is it that some works entertain us while others do not? There are, of course, effectively told and ineffectively told stories; matters of technique are not to be ignored. But more important than technique itself is the underlying story in the service of which that technique is used. *Hamlet* is a dour and grisly story and yet it is entertaining; the story of Genesis is in some sense terrifying and yet it too is entertaining. We are thrilled when Hamlet is first visited by the ghost of his dead father; we project ourselves into the scenes of Hamlet's vacillation; we are horrified and purged by Hamlet's death. In a similar way, we are awed when the Holy Ghost forms the world out of Chaos; we project ourselves into the world of the Garden; we are horrified and purged by the enormity of the Fall. Entertainment is not "mere"; it is the effective engagement of a text with issues of fundamental importance to the audience. We have argued that, in their special ways, depending on the reversals of ground rules, fantastic worlds give us precisely this sort of experience. So, read this book for its entertainment.

The human sources of fantastic entertainment are few but

important. The selections here are arranged in part so that comparisons will suggest themselves. The first two pieces are alternative Creation myths; the next two each concern the advent of death; the next three depend upon metamorphosis and two of those stand together as being sexually motivated changes. The introductions to the three parts will make these connections more explicit. At this point one should recognize that our treatment of the fantastic has been general and hence implies comparisons that would not be confined to the separate sections. Metamorphosis, for example, is a fantastic device used for making dramatic a quality which had previously been only a part of a character's psychology. This is true in the three early selections from Ovid and in the change of a living human into a ghost and in the exchange of personalities in the story by Cortázar. The fact of all art being to some extent fantastic has encouraged fantasists to explore repeatedly the relation between art and life, an exploration implicit in the narrative situations of the African folktales and explicit in the stories of pictures written by Poe and Lovecraft and thematically central in the modern pieces by Brautigan and Holst. The question of whether or not there is a life beyond human life figures significantly in the religious myths, in Tolkien's allegory, in the stories of curses and ghosts, and in Kafka's allusion to "The Judgment." These are all thematic concerns.

Thematic concerns include all of the psychological categories that we have seen dealt with in fantastic literature and such matters as the nature of art, of human perception, and of escape. In addition to thematic comparisons, one could profitably look for comparisons at the three other levels of narrative. For example, certain character developments recur: the hero learns that his early attitudes were wrong or that his early attitudes were right, that he must submerge himself in the community or that he must strike out on his own. At what stages does a culture pick one of these alternatives or another? In stories aimed at what age audience does one character development predominate over another? Plot comparisons are equally significant. We find the recurrence of the hero violating an injunction or falling into delusion or being forced to defend the status quo. In which types of stories is one plot element or another crucial? Style too invites comparisons. Some works, like fairy tales and heroic fantasies, are told with great sobriety, while others, like Norton Juster's punning piece or much of modern fantasy, rely on the quick linguistic reversals of irony and oxymoron. What do works of one style or another have in common?

One can read each story alone, of course, but our argument that fantastic reality is dependent on the reader's experience of the world implies as well that fantastic reality is dependent on the reader's prior training as a reader. Alice says that "when I used to read fairy tales, I fancied that kind of thing never happened, and now here I am in the middle of one!" To understand the significance of this passage one must know what fairy tales are, of course, but what is more important, one must recognize that in fairy tales no character ever doubts the fairy-tale reality and hence never makes such a comment as Alice's that reflects on the nature of the narrative. Such self-reflexive comments are stylistic reversals characteristic of development toward the fantastic within a given genre. Alice's comment would never be uttered in a true fairy tale and hence the comment is itself incorrect: Alice is *not* in a fairy tale but in something more fantastic yet. As we have seen, Alice is in a Fantasy. But to recognize this, to see that Alice's world is constantly shifting and hence does not offer the child-like security of fairy tales but rather the adult exploration of the nature of reality, requires that we make comparisons between Alice's style and, say, that of the brothers Grimm. Comparison is not an academic exercise but a continuing aspect of each reader's own education, a process of self-instruction which is essential for gaining a full sense of the technical achievement and human significance of a given story. Writers too learn technique by reading and so it is fitting that the selections here be arranged by types as those types emerged chronologically. The order of this collection is intended to prompt comparisons not just between adjacent stories but between a given story and all its predecessors in matters of plot, character, theme, and style. Taken together, these stories should be not "merely entertaining" but illuminatingly entertaining; they should reveal the techniques by which humankind has been able to deal with real and serious issues in the creation of fantastic worlds.

The Sources of the Fantastic

THE SOURCES OF THE FANTASTIC

The narrative sources of the fantastic fall into three interpenetrating categories: myth, folktale, and fairy tale. Myth is the oldest of these. Ernst Cassirer in *Language and Myth* (1925) went so far as to argue that the very origins of human language and of human myth were simultaneous. Even today we speak of casting a spell with words; the word *spell* itself comes from an Old High German word that means *tale*. If we can name something we may feel that much closer to controlling it. This obvious superstition has not died, though perhaps we rely on the magic of words less than people once did. Still, we ensure the fairness of choosing sides by saying "Eeny, meeny, miney, mo"; we require that a marriage be sanctified according to the proper formula of "With this ring I thee wed"; we admit and even welcome our community with all those who have also lost loved ones by saying, over a grave, "Rest in peace." There are huge and common life experiences that our language—and our myths—

have tried to handle for us since before history. It is easier to deal with those larger-than-human forces if we can name them: Eros, Thunder, Death, Sun. Once these are named, their power can be admitted by making them gods. And as gods, they can have stories told about them. The god stories that seem to a culture to explain the ways of the world are its myths.

In the thousands of years since our myths first formed, they have become less and less important as explanation and yet have more and more become embedded in our language. Especially in the later, written forms (which some scholars like to distinguish as *mythology* rather than *myth*) we find the sources of Herculean feats and Procrustean beds and the Oedipus complex. This last is especially important because it points to the reason myths have persisted: the narrative shapes of myths, the fantastic worlds which offered an ordered alternative to the real world of our prehistoric ancestors, are narrative shapes which still seem to offer important alternatives to the real worlds we seem to inhabit. The basic issue of father-son competition has not gone away, but we can individually begin to face father-guilt by the recital of a myth.

Myths, as the common property of a culture, serve as subjects of art long after the myths have been superseded as explanations. Even atheists observe the neutrality of the Red Cross; even grown-ups enjoy dressing as Santa Claus. As cultures become more sophisticated, more conscious of the artistry behind their myths, they begin to shape examples of those myths more consciously and offer them first as entertainment and only second as explanation. In this way, folktales are produced, the corporate productions of a whole culture, narratives that are common property, that are taken as significant but, unlike myths, are admitted man-made. An analogy might be helpful here: the so-called wolf whistle used to express physical appreciation has a special tone and interval and duration in our culture. No one knows the source of the wolf whistle. Similarly, no one knows the origin of the tunes of some children's chants (like the taunting one that goes "N*ya* nya, na, *nya* nya"), yet we all recognize the meanings of those chants, meanings that, for all we know, belong to prehistory. But in more sophisticated times, we find folk songs, corporate productions that may be thought of as important (think of certain work songs, for example, or songs of lost love) but are sung ostensibly for their entertainment value rather than their historical verity; folk songs are canonical, but, unlike myths, they are not sacred. In the same way, folktales deal with the same issues as do myths, but these more sophisticated narratives are not sacred.

Some stories, especially the sacred ones, are worth telling again and again, but others are not. The story of "Little Red Riding Hood," for example, is very nice for a child, but there is a limit to how many times an adult can hear it freshly. A special set of narrative conventions can grow up as a culture gets yet more sophisticated, and those conventions will attach to one class of stories—and its associated audience—or another. The most widely known such conventions are those of the fairy tale, with its audience of children and, in later life, adults who can enjoy the stories once again by watching or imagining the reaction the story fosters in a child's eyes. Myth, folktale, and fairy tale then form a sliding scale along which the stories become more conventionalized, the audience becomes more limited, the teller becomes more sophisticated, the truth value becomes more symbolic and less literal, but in all of which the issues remain the same. We open this section of *Fantastic Worlds* with Genesis and the story of the Fall; we close this section with Tolkien's "Leaf by Niggle," the conventionalized, sophisticated, allegorical, modern, man-authored fairy tale of Salvation. Although we have named three narrative sources of the fantastic—myth, folktale, and fairy tale—the single impulse behind the creation of those narratives is the need of people.

THE NEED FOR THE FANTASTIC

People have always wondered about their place in the scheme of things. Jean Piaget has argued that all infants, because their needs are met in ways that seem to them automatic, develop an

"illusion of central position." They think that the universe revolves around them. This must be a very nice feeling. It is little
wonder that we resist learning otherwise and that, even as
adults, we may cherish this illusion within us. Fantastic narratives often support this illusion of central position. The complete
selection of myths, and also "The Magic Swan Geese" and "Leaf
By Niggle," implicitly project a universe that cares about individual humans and responds to their needs and desires.

A special case of the illusion of central position is what Freud
called "the omnipotence of thought," the fantasy that, should
one think something, it will come to pass. Freudians trace much
of our feelings of guilt about wishing our parents dead to this
residual infantile sense that the thought might be as good as the
deed. It is clear that the real world does not conform to our
thoughts; it is not sunny simply because we want to have a
picnic. And yet we are not entirely free of a belief in the
potency of our thoughts; if it rains when we want to have a
picnic, we say, "Wouldn't you just know it!"—as if some greater
power resented the power of our thoughts and thwarted us.
Since we do not believe in the simple omnipotence of thought,
a narrative world that indulged this alternative to our world
would be fantastic; since we do, to some degree, accept a secondary potency for thought, the device of thoughts becoming
deeds is easily made believable to us in a narrative. Most fantastic narratives indulge the illusion of central position, and a
majority of these narratives do so by dramatizing the omnipotence of thought.

"Hansel and Grethel" is a good example of the way a fantastic
narrative accepts the omnipotence of thought, and it is a good
example of a number of other basic human issues as well. Let us
examine this story in some detail. As we recall, Hansel and
Grethel live alone with their father. He remarries. The stepmother hates the children and she arranges to have them left in
the forest. Although this fails at first because Hansel leaves a
trail, it finally succeeds. Wandering lost, the children find a
house made of goodies. Attracted by this, they are captured by a

witch who intends to eat Hansel after she fattens him. Grethel feeds Hansel and he offers a chicken bone instead of the finger that the myopic witch wants to squeeze to gauge his fattening. Finally Grethel kills the witch by pushing her into her own hot oven. The children then have no trouble finding their way home and there they discover that the stepmother has died. The last image is of the children each holding one of the father's hands. Let us look beneath the surface to see what human materials this story is dealing with.

First, one should observe, as Max Lüthi has in *Once Upon a Time* (1970), that no one ever says "I love you" in a fairy tale; instead, one character feeds another. Fantastic literature generally can make dramatically overt matters which normally remain within the feelings of a character or the implications of a situation. Mother-love is sustaining; it offers sustenance. Witches, Lüthi points out, are recognizable as inversions of this: they are cannibals. Instead of wanting to feed a child, a witch wants to eat it. Witches are symbolic anti-mothers. Food imagery is everywhere in "Hansel and Grethel." The children are in the woods to gather firewood for cooking. Hansel's trick of leaving a trail is a good one until he leaves breadcrumbs, a track the birds eat: the children must learn to take biological needs into account. They themselves are trapped by the temptation of goodies. Hansel is only spared because he can present a bone, a remnant of flesh already eaten. The witch wishes to eat Hansel. Grethel saves him by killing the witch, specifically, by putting her in the oven and cooking her as she would have cooked Hansel. Because the witch is an anti-mother, Grethel is morally allowed to kill her in the anti-mother way yet without herself being taken for a witch. When they return home, the hated stepmother is (as) dead (as the witch). The children return to their father's full protection. Thus the right use of love (food) has led from the initial situation of lack (the true mother dead) to a new stable situation in which Grethel can take over the role of cook.

If one projects the thoughts of the children, especially of Grethel, who is the active heroine, one sees not only a basic concern with food, but a related basic concern with sex. As we know from having read the story, Grethel and the stepmother are in competition for the father's affection. Since the stepmother is, after all, the father's wife (beloved), his daughter, Grethel, could not justifiably kill her. However, the witch may be killed, and that deed done, the stepmother is discovered to be dead. This is the omnipotence of thought. Lest even the thought appear unwarranted, the witch's guilt that flows from her desire to eat the children is foreshadowed by the stepmother's guilt that flows from her desire to kill them. An aggressive Freudian reading would also suggest that Grethel had been in competition for the father's affections since even before the true mother's death, and that her death, then, was a result of Grethel's omnipotent thought, her wish to have no competitor. In this reading, the proto-sexual desire of Grethel is the initial problem that is dramatized by the substitution of a stepmother for a true mother (a fairy-tale true mother, of course, could not respond negatively to Grethel even if the daughter were a competitor); Grethel's task, saving her brother from an anti-mother, morally allows Grethel to fulfill the role of true mother (symbolized by her cooking the witch). Having become the true mother, no competitive mother (true or step) is on the scene when Grethel returns to her now wifeless father. Hence, the fairy-tale plot, which revolves around food and the characters' relations to it, is a device for allowing Grethel—or a listener who can identify with her—to indulge the omnipotence of the normally forbidden thought that one may want to supplant one's parent.

The guilt that might attend competitive thoughts in the child auditor's mind is assuaged by the story. This saving of emotional energy is what Freud called "psychic economy." Freud believed that we read always to achieve this psychic economy. If "Hansel and Grethel" is "entertaining," this analysis would suggest that its entertainment value resides in its ability to deal symbolically with such basic human issues as parent/child competition. There are other such basic issues too, of course: fear of sex, the desire to die, the need to understand, the wish for power, and so on. In fantastic narratives, alternatives to the real world, these issues can be embodied. In the narratives of this section, the fear of sex can be confirmed in Actaeon's fate or removed in Sleeping Beauty's; the desire to die can be justified by the Fall or ameliorated in the Pawnee tale; the need to understand can be accepted by explanatory tales like that about the tortoise and can be applauded by moral tales like that about Mr. Rabbit; the wish for power can be chided in "The Magic Swan Geese" or fully accepted in "The Tinderbox." Fantastic worlds, confronting as they do issues that are often hidden in the real world, are created in the service of human need.

NOTES ON NARRATIVE STRUCTURES

One may well wonder, after such an analysis, how much of what we have observed is part of the intent of the storyteller. There are at least two important responses that need to be made to that question, one psychological and one structural.

The psychological response is a simple one: fantastic stories offer psychic economy by compensation; neither the reader nor the author need be consciously aware of the roots of this compensatory function. Compensation is the technical term for the substitution of one experience, symbol, behavior, or what have you for another which is desired but repressed. A dieter, repressing the behavior of eating, may find himself overindulging in exercise or sex or television by way of compensation; someone repressing his desire for sex may compensate for it by working that much harder to earn money. That an author or reader feels drawn to, entertained by, a narrative already indicates that the narrative in some way deals with a significant issue. Since this "dealing with" is vicarious only, occurring in the psychically economic world of art, the writing or reading must compensate for a dis-ease the reader or writer either feels or can project himself as feeling in the real world. Art, then (like dreams and Freudian slips, among other things), has a compensatory function.

In an essay called "The Uncanny" (1919), Freud made a special application of this principle of compensation to "uncanny" literature and experiences. His major literary example was Hoffmann's story called "The Sandman," which is reproduced in the middle section of this anthology. Freud suggested that the uncanny arises when the familiar occurs in an unfamiliar context; alternatively, the uncanny arises when a symbol "takes on the full function of the thing symbolized." The first part of Freud's formulation obviously accords with our somewhat broader notion that the fantastic is not simply the unreal, but the reversal of ground rules as one reads, the reversal of the context by the text; the second part of Freud's formulation suggests the function of dramatization which we have noticed, the externalization of a normally internal or implicit state, such as love symbolized through food. Freud's "uncanny," then, is an aspect of our "fantastic." Ghost stories belong to both camps, *Mary Poppins* only to the broader fantastic grouping. In both cases, however, this psychological thesis implies that the entertaining text must begin by engaging the reader in a vicarious—even if unconscious—sense of something important being repressed (Grethel's original wish to supplant her mother) and then dealing with this repressed material (food symbolism) in order to achieve a new reconciliation with the fact of repression (Grethel is now the only female in her father's life). This simple three-part structure, of course, becomes immensely complicated when one tries to discern in any given case how the sense of repression is generated and how it is manipulated and how it is finally quieted. Freud, and the conclusions that follow from his insights, give us only a start.

A second step toward an understanding of how much is known by the writer and reader is offered by a work by Vladimir Propp called *Morphology of the Folktale* (1928). This is a structural study of the order in which "functions" ("an act of a character defined from the point of view of its significance for the course of the action") take place in fairy tales. (One should note at this point that "fairy tale" and "folktale" are, as we said, interpenetrating categories. Propp's original title in Russian refers to *skázka*, which can mean either "folktale" or "fairy tale." In the same way, the German title of the Grimm brothers' collection refers to *Märchen,* which can mean "fairy tales," "fables," "legends," or even "fibs.") Propp exemplifies his method of analysis with Afanas'ev's version of "The Magic Swan Geese," which is reproduced in this section of the anthology; Propp's surprising conclusions have been tested many times in the last half-century, and they seem to hold. He found that in all truly oral folktales there were only thirty-one functions. Some of these functions, like absentation of the hero from his home (or, in its extreme form, the death of a parent), must occur. Other functions, such as falling under a spell, if they occur, must occur with a specified co-function, such as release from the spell. Some functions, like magical tests presented to the hero, are free to replicate: he may have one task or he may have three. (In some cultures, like those of the American Indians, replication comes in fours, as in the two tales reproduced here.) Whatever sample of obligatory and optional functions happens to be in a given tale, they must occur in their archetypal order. That is, if functions 4, 13, and 6 occur, they must be in the order 4, 6, 13. Although the full detail of Propp's discoveries is apparent only on reading his book, and although it is surely surprising that he could come up with apparently correct rules of such strictness, nonetheless his work seems to be true, and it gives us for oral folktales a much more detailed structure than the three-part compensation structure we derived earlier.

Propp's conclusions should give us faith that we can infer, even if only unconsciously, a sense of the right structure for a truly fairy tale. As cultures become more literate, tales get written down. Authors embellish them by changing the order of episodes or by inserting other minor stories into the main story. Sometimes a replicated function occurs four times or only twice. Sometimes a hero leaves home and fails to return, or he may return but the tale will go on for a bit. The more the basic oral structure is violated, the more literate the tale is likely to be. Hence Propp's demonstration of structural orthodoxy in oral tales gives us a way of judging the state of literacy in a culture from which we have a tale.

Although Afanas'ev collected his tales, as best he could, from illiterate peasants, the Grimm brothers worked quite differently. They employed a network of scribes who went into the field and wrote down, as best they could, stories from illiterate peasants. The scribes sent these transcriptions to Jakob who would sort of average them, trying to produce "typical" versions of each story. Wilhelm then took each synthesis and "refined" it so that it would read smoothly and offend few sensibilities. Although these Grimm stories began as oral folktales, they ended by helping to establish the conventions for the literate genre known as the fairy tale. In the wake of the Grimm brothers, other authors, such as Andersen, MacDonald, and Tolkien, could feel free to employ these literary conventions and, ignoring possible oral sources, construct wholly new so-called "fairy tales." We can see where each text stands in the developing literary tradition by noting its variation from earlier conventions, all the way back to the oral forms common in so many different cultures.

Just as the fact of a three-part structure of compensation argues for the perhaps unconscious but nonetheless real understanding on the part of reader and writer of a story's subtle structures, so the existence of the even more complex Proppian structure indicates that there is a stable and repeatable meaning to fairy tales and people know this when they construct and attend to them. The regular development of convention shows that even those writers who choose to violate conventions do so in full knowledge of what those conventions are and hence of what those structures can do, or once could do, in providing psychic economy. The fact that the structural study of the psychological aspects and functional aspects of tales can proceed in a regular way argues that the universal human concerns we have mentioned are being dealt with by people who in some way know what they are doing.

AUDIENCE ANALYSIS

Much of the preceding discussion has implied ways by which one could use a text to analyze its audience. The degree of structural variation from just prior norms indicates the degree to which the audience (and writers for that audience) are sophisticated in those norms. Although traditional fairy tales are intended for children, Hoffmann subtitled "The Golden Pot," his own favorite among his pointedly adult tales, "A Modern Fairy Tale." He realized that to interest his sophisticated audience he had to take known conventions and "modernize" them. Similarly, the nature of the fantasy or psychological problem structurally laid to rest by a tale gives us clues as to the concerns of the tale's audience. In the same way that some conventional information can be correlated with reading education, some psychological information can be correlated with approximate age (or, more logically, life experience).

"Little Red-cap," for example, is a story that, among other things, concerns a little girl's fear of approaching menarche. This thought may at first seem quite strange, but if we attempt the sort of analysis here that we employed with "Hansel and Grethel" we notice that the mantle of red velvet (blood, sensuality) is passed down from the (menopausal) grandmother to the pre-pubic granddaughter. The grandmother lives safely in the forest (inhabited by all sorts of things, like wolves, that become dangerous when a young girl like Red is about), while the mother lives in the socially controlled world of the town. The mother makes a social demand for propriety, telling Red not to tarry in the forest, but the wolf talks her into stopping to sniff the flowers (sex organs of plants) and she is drawn ever farther afield. The whole reason for her trip is to bring the grandmother, who is (obviously) waning, restorative (red) wine and cake (clearly a post-Christian version of the story). The wolf swallows the grandmother and then Red, but they are rescued by a passing hunter who magically knows to cut the belly open (a birth image) instead of shooting the beast. Out pops Red, out pops Grandma. Red, not the hunter, takes stones and sews them (woman's work) into the wolf's belly, so that he is killed by falling to (Mother) Earth. Red also administers the wine to Grandma and rejuvenates her. The danger of dabbling in the sensuous is real here. The mother, who is necessarily a sexually active female, is protected by virtue of her civilized habitation; the grandmother is protected by virtue of her infertility. Only Red is at stake. Mothers love and sustain. Red is bringing the sustenance from her mother to her grandmother while wearing the red mantle of love passed down to her from her grandmother, her mother's mother. The hunter, who mediates between the sensuous world of the forest and the civilized world of the town, saves Red, and she herself then knows how to dispatch the wolf. In our version, the story ends thusly: "Little Red-cap said to herself that she would never more stray about in the wood alone, but would mind what her mother told her." (What follows in the text is obviously an anti-Proppian accretion from the Grimm brothers.) This line expresses Red's knowledge that mother knows best. How old is Red? Metaphorically, we might say she is ten, quite aware that sexuality will be soon upon her (these are peasant stories, recall, from agricultural areas), but content to be reassured that she need not yet submit to her own guidance. In the Perrault version of the tale, however, the huntsman does not save Red. She stays eaten. The message of that story is not so much reassurance as warning. For the child listening to that version, keeping out of the woods is an even harsher lesson. Perhaps that Red is eight. And, finally, in the version of the story told in *Once Upon A Time: The Fairy Tale World of Arthur Rackham* (1972), the story ends with these lines: "Red Riding Hood thought: 'I will never wander off into the forest as long as I live, if my Mother forbids it.'" That last proviso is the giveaway: this Red is feeling her sexuality already, not enough to be willing to break out of her home, but enough to want to leave open a pathway into the woods. We might call her—and her ideal audience—twelve.

Thus we see that our knowledge of how the fantastic dramatizes basic human problems has led us not only to a fuller understanding of the texts, but of the people who appreciate them. Different narratives have peculiar importance for different people depending upon their experiences and education. Yet at the same time that we can use this knowledge to analyze an audience, we should recognize that the analysis depends first on our recognition of similarities. The three versions of Little Red Riding Hood attest to the widely shared apprehensions of girls approaching womanhood. And we must remember that all women have the memories of their girlhoods within them. Beyond this, the facts of apprehension need not be so specifically attached to the sexual or even the sensual. The wolf is a physical danger, after all, and the hunts*man* is the defense against it. Boys too can understand Red's predicament and are led to hope that they will grow up to meet their own crises successfully. And every man has the memory of *his* boyhood within *him*. And yet more broadly, we have the common Proppian structure of the fairy tale to give us a complex, yet palpable, aesthetic order as an alternative to our world. And we have the three-part structure of compensation to let us know at least that there is art to oppose life. Individuals will prefer one narrative or another, surely, but they all feel the attraction of narration. With all the differences among narratives, the creation of fantastic worlds places humanity more comfortably; no longer in the chaos of eternal night, we arise at God's caring behest in Genesis and live through to some vision, perhaps like Tolkien's, of a permanent realm of fantastic beauty.

MYTH

The First Book of Moses, called GENESIS
King James Version

CHAPTER I

*I*N THE BEGINNING GOD created the heaven and the earth.

2 And the earth was without form, and void; and darkness *was* upon the face of the deep. And the Spirit of God moved upon the face of the waters.

3 And God said, Let there be light: and there was light.

4 And God saw the light, that *it was* good: and God divided the light from the darkness.

5 And God called the light Day, and the darkness he called Night. And the evening and the morning were the first day.

6 And God said, Let there be a firmament in the midst of the waters, and let it divide the waters from the waters.

7 And God made the firmament, and divided the waters which *were* under the firmament from the waters which *were* above the firmament: and it was so.

8 And God called the firmament Heaven. And the evening and the morning were the second day.

9 And God said, Let the waters under the heaven be gathered together unto one place, and let the dry *land* appear: and it was so.

10 And God called the dry *land* Earth; and the gathering together of the waters called he Seas: and God saw that *it was* good.

11 And God said, Let the earth bring forth grass, the herb yielding seed, *and* the fruit tree yielding fruit after his kind, whose seed *is* in itself, upon the earth: and it was so.

12 And the earth brought forth grass, *and* herb yielding seed after his kind, and the tree yielding fruit, whose seed *was* in itself, after his kind: and God saw that *it was* good.

13 And the evening and the morning were the third day.

14 And God said, Let there be lights in the firmament of the heaven to divide the day from the night; and let them be for signs, and for seasons, and for days, and years:

15 And let them be for lights in the firmament of the heaven to give light upon the earth: and it was so.

16 And God made two great lights; the greater light to rule the day, and the lesser light to rule the night: *he made* the stars also.

17 And God set them in the firmament of the heaven to give light upon the earth,

18 And to rule over the day and over the night, and to divide the light from the darkness: and God saw that *it was* good.

19 And the evening and the morning were the fourth day.

20 And God said, Let the waters bring forth abundantly the moving creature that hath life, and fowl *that* may fly above the earth in the open firmament of heaven.

21 And God created great whales, and every living creature that moveth, which the waters brought forth abundantly, after their kind, and every winged fowl after his kind: and God saw that *it was* good.

22 And God blessed them, saying, Be fruitful, and multiply, and fill the waters in the seas, and let fowl multiply in the earth.

23 And the evening and the morning were the fifth day.

24 And God said, Let the earth bring forth the living creature after his kind, cattle, and creeping thing, and beast of the earth after his kind: and it was so.

25 And God made the beast of the earth after his kind, and cattle after their kind, and every thing that creepeth upon the earth after his kind: and God saw that *it was* good.

26 And God said, Let us make man in our image, after our likeness: and let them have dominion over the fish of the sea, and over the fowl of the air, and over the cattle, and over all the earth, and over every creeping thing that creepeth upon the earth.

27 So God created man in his *own* image, in the image of God created he him; male and female created he them.

28 And God blessed them, and God said unto them, Be fruitful, and multiply, and replenish the earth, and subdue it: and have dominion over the fish of the sea, and over the fowl of the air, and over every living thing that moveth upon the earth.

29 And God said, Behold, I have given you every herb bearing seed, which *is* upon the face of all the earth, and every tree, in the which *is* the fruit of a tree yielding seed; to you it shall be for meat.

30 And to every beast of the earth, and to every fowl of the air, and to every thing that creepeth upon the earth, wherein *there is* life, I *have given* every green herb for meat: and it was so.

31 And God saw every thing that he had made, and, behold, *it was* very good. And the evening and the morning were the sixth day.

CHAPTER 2

Thus the heavens and the earth were finished, and all the host of them.

2 And on the seventh day God ended his work which he had made; and he rested on the seventh day from all his work which he had made.

3 And God blessed the seventh day, and sanctified it: because that in it he had rested from all his work which God created and made.

4 These *are* the generations of the heavens and of the earth when they were created, in the day that the Lord God made the earth and the heavens.

5 And every plant of the field before it was in the earth, and every herb of the field before it grew: for the Lord God had not caused it to rain upon the earth, and *there was* not a man to till the ground.

6 But there went up a mist from the earth, and watered the whole face of the ground.

7 And the Lord God formed man *of* the dust of the ground, and breathed into his nostrils the breath of life; and man became a living soul.

8 And the Lord God planted a garden eastward in Eden; and there he put the man whom he had formed.

9 And out of the ground made the Lord God to grow every tree that is pleasant to the sight, and good for food; the tree of life also in the midst of the garden, and the tree of knowledge of good and evil.

10 And a river went out of Eden to water the garden; and from thence it was parted, and became into four heads.

11 The name of the first is Pi'-son: that *is* it which compasseth the whole land of Hav'-i-lah, where *there* is gold;

12 And the gold of that land *is* good: there *is* bdellium and the onyx stone.

13 And the name of the second river *is* Gi'-hon: the same *is* it that compasseth the whole land of E-thi-o'-pi-a.

14 And the name of the third river *is* Hid'-de-kel: that *is* it which goeth toward the east of Assyria. And the fourth river is Eu-phra'-tes.

15 And the Lord God took the man, and put him into the garden of Eden to dress it and to keep it.

16 And the Lord God commanded the man, saying, Of every tree of the garden thou mayest freely eat:

17 But of the tree of the knowledge of good and evil, thou shalt not eat of it: for in the day that thou eatest thereof thou shalt surely die.

18 And the Lord God said, *It is* not good that the man should be alone; I will make him an help meet for him.

19 And out of the ground the Lord God formed every beast of the field, and every fowl of the air; and brought *them* unto Adam to see what he would call them: and whatsoever Adam called every living creature, that *was* the name thereof.

20 And Adam gave names to all cattle, and to the fowl of the air, and to every beast of the field; but for Adam there was not found an help meet for him.

21 And the Lord God caused a deep sleep to fall upon Adam, and he slept: and he took one of his ribs, and closed up the flesh instead thereof;

22 And the rib, which the Lord God had taken from man, made he a woman, and brought her unto the man.

23 And Adam said, This *is* now bone of my bones, and flesh of

my flesh: she shall be called Woman, because she was taken out of Man.

24 Therefore shall a man leave his father and his mother, and shall cleave unto his wife: and they shall be one flesh.

25 And they were both naked, the man and his wife, and were not ashamed.

CHAPTER 3

Now the serpent was more subtil than any beast of the field which the LORD God had made. And he said unto the woman, Yea, hath God said, Ye shall not eat of every tree of the garden?

2 And the woman said unto the serpent, We may eat of the fruit of the trees of the garden:

3 But of the fruit of the tree which *is* in the midst of the garden, God hath said, Ye shall not eat of it, neither shall ye touch it, lest ye die.

4 And the serpent said unto the woman, Ye shall not surely die:

5 For God doth know that in the day ye eat thereof, then your eyes shall be opened, and ye shall be as gods, knowing good and evil.

6 And when the woman saw that the tree *was* good for food, and that it *was* pleasant to the eyes, and a tree to be desired to make *one* wise, she took of the fruit thereof, and did eat, and gave also unto her husband with her; and he did eat.

7 And the eyes of them both were opened, and they knew that they *were* naked; and they sewed fig leaves together, and made themselves aprons.

8 And they heard the voice of the LORD God walking in the garden in the cool of the day; and Adam and his wife hid themselves from the presence of the LORD God amongst the trees of the garden.

9 And the LORD God called unto Adam, and said unto him, Where *art* thou?

10 And he said, I heard thy voice in the garden, and I was afraid, because I *was* naked; and I hid myself.

11 And he said, Who told thee that thou *wast* naked? Hast thou eaten of the tree, whereof I commanded thee that thou shouldest not eat?

12 And the man said, The woman whom thou gavest *to be* with me, she gave me of the tree, and I did eat.

13 And the Lord God said unto the woman, What *is* this *that* thou hast done? And the woman said, The serpent beguiled me, and I did eat.

14 And the Lord God said unto the serpent, Because thou hast done this, thou *art* cursed above all cattle, and above every beast of the field; upon thy belly shalt thou go, and dust shalt thou eat all the days of thy life:

15 And I will put enmity between thee and the woman, and between thy seed and her seed; it shall bruise thy head, and thou shalt bruise his heel.

16 Unto the woman he said, I will greatly multiply thy sorrow and thy conception; in sorrow thou shalt bring forth children; and thy desire *shall be* to thy husband, and he shall rule over thee.

17 And unto Adam he said, Because thou hast hearkened unto the voice of thy wife, and hast eaten of the tree, of which I commanded thee, saying, Thou shalt not eat of it: cursed *is* the ground for thy sake; in sorrow shalt thou eat *of* it all the days of thy life;

18 Thorns also and thistles shall it bring forth to thee; and thou shalt eat the herb of the field;

19 In the sweat of thy face shalt thou eat bread, till thou return unto the ground; for out of it wast thou taken: for dust thou *art,* and unto dust shalt thou return.

20 And Adam called his wife's name Eve; because she was the mother of all living.

21 Unto Adam also and to his wife did the Lord God make coats of skins, and clothed them.

22 And the Lord God said, Behold, the man is become as one of us, to know good and evil: and now, lest he put forth his hand, and take also of the tree of life, and eat, and live for ever:

23 Therefore the Lord God sent him forth from the garden of Eden, to till the ground from whence he was taken.

24 So he drove out the man; and he placed at the east of the garden of Eden Cher'-u-bims, and a flaming sword which turned every way, to keep the way of the tree of life.

GEORGE BIRD GRINNELL, ED.

A LL ANIMALS OF THE PLAINS at one time heard
and knew him, and all birds of the air heard and knew
him. All things that he had made understood him, when
he spoke to them,—the birds, the animals, and the people.
Old Man was travelling about, south of here, making
the people. He came from the south, travelling north,
making animals and birds as he passed along. He made
the mountains, prairies, timber, and brush first. So he
went along, travelling northward, making things as he
went, putting rivers here and there, and falls on them,
putting red paint here and there in the ground,—fixing
up the world as we see it to-day. He made the Milk River
(the Teton) and crossed it, and, being tired, went up on
a little hill and lay down to rest. As he lay on his back,
stretched out on the ground, with arms extended, he
marked himself out with stones,—the shape of his body,
head, legs, arms, and everything. There you can see
those rocks to-day. After he had rested, he went on northward, and stumbled over a knoll and fell down on his
knees. Then he said, "You are a bad thing to be stumbling against"; so he raised up two large buttes there, and
named them the Knees, and they are called so to this
day. He went on further north, and with some of the
rocks he carried with him he built the Sweet Grass Hills.
Old Man covered the plains with grass for the animals
to feed on. He marked off a piece of ground, and in it he
made to grow all kinds of roots and berries,—camas, wild
carrots, wild turnips, sweet-root, bitter-root, sarvis berries,
bull berries, cherries, plums, and rosebuds. He put trees
in the ground. He put all kinds of animals on the ground.
When he made the bighorn with its big head and horns,
he made it out on the prairie. It did not seem to travel

easily on the prairie; it was awkward and could not go fast. So he took it by one of its horns, and led it up into the mountains, and turned it loose; and it skipped about among the rocks, and went up fearful places with ease. So he said, "This is the place that suits you; this is what you are fitted for, the rocks and the mountains." While he was in the mountains, he made the antelope out of dirt, and turned it loose, to see how it would go. It ran so fast that it fell over some rocks and hurt itself. He saw that this would not do, and took the antelope down on the prairie, and turned it loose; and it ran away fast and gracefully, and he said, "This is what you are suited to."

One day Old Man determined that he would make a woman and a child; so he formed them both—the woman and the child, her son—of clay. After he had moulded the clay in human shape, he said to the clay, "You must be people," and then he covered it up and left it, and went away. The next morning he went to the place and took the covering off, and saw that the clay shapes had changed a little. The second morning there was still more change, and the third still more. The fourth morning he went to the place, took the covering off, looked at the images, and told them to rise and walk; and they did so. They walked down to the river with their Maker, and then he told them that his name was *Nápi*, Old Man.

As they were standing by the river, the woman said to him, "How is it? will we always live, will there be no end to it?" He said: "I have never thought of that. We will have to decide it. I will take this buffalo chip and throw it in the river. If it floats, when people die, in four days they will become alive again; they will die for only four days. But if it sinks, there will be an end to them." He threw the chip into the river, and it floated. The woman turned and picked up a stone, and said: "No, I will throw this stone in the river; if it floats we will always live, if it sinks people must die, that they may always be sorry for each other."* The woman threw the stone into the water, and it sank. "There," said Old Man, "you have chosen. There will be an end to them."

---

* That is, that their friends who survive may always remember them.
[G.B.G.]

It was not many nights after, that the woman's child died, and she cried a great deal for it. She said to Old Man: "Let us change this. The law that you first made, let that be a law." He said: "Not so. What is made law must be law. We will undo nothing that we have done. The child is dead, but it cannot be changed. People will have to die."

That is how we came to be people. It is he who made us.

The first people were poor and naked, and did not know how to get a living. Old Man showed them the roots and berries, and told them that they could eat them; that in a certain month of the year they could peel the bark off some trees and eat it, that it was good. He told the people that the animals should be their food, and gave them to the people, saying, "These are your herds." He said: "All these little animals that live in the ground—rats, squirrels, skunks, beavers—are good to eat. You need not fear to eat of their flesh." He made all the birds that fly, and told the people that there was no harm in their flesh, that it could be eaten. The first people that he created he used to take about through the timber and swamps and over the prairies, and show them the different plants. Of a certain plant he would say, "The root of this plant, if gathered in a certain month of the year, is good for a certain sickness." So they learned the power of all herbs.

In those days there were buffalo. Now the people had no arms, but those black animals with long beards were armed; and once, as the people were moving about, the buffalo saw them, and ran after them, and hooked them, and killed and ate them. One day, as the Maker of the people was travelling over the country, he saw some of his children that he had made, lying dead, torn to pieces and partly eaten by the buffalo. When he saw this he was very sad. He said: "This will not do. I will change this. The people shall eat the buffalo."

He went to some of the people who were left, and said to them, "How is it that you people do nothing to these animals that are killing you?" The people said: "What can we do? We have no way to kill these animals, while they are armed and can kill us." Then said the Maker: "That is not hard. I will make you a weapon that will kill these animals." So he went out, and cut some sarvis berry shoots, and brought them in, and peeled the bark off them. He took a larger piece of wood, and flattened it, and tied a string to it, and made a bow. Now, as he was the master of all birds and could do with them as he wished, he went out and caught one, and took feathers from its wing, and split them, and tied them to the shaft of wood. He tied four feathers along the shaft, and tried the arrow at a mark, and found that it did not fly well. He took these feathers off, and put on three; and when he tried it again, he found that it was good. He went out and began to break sharp pieces off the stones. He tried them, and found that the black flint stones made the best arrow points, and some white flints. Then he taught the people how to use these things.

Then he said: "The next time you go out, take these things with you, and use them as I tell you, and do not run from these animals. When they run at you, as soon as they get pretty close, shoot the arrows at them, as I have taught you; and you will see that they will run from you or will run in a circle around you."

Now, as people became plenty, one day three men went out on to the plain to see the buffalo, but they had no arms. They saw the animals, but when the buffalo saw the men, they ran after them and killed two of them, but one got away. One day after this, the people went on a little hill to look about, and the buffalo saw them, and said, "*Saiyah*, there is some more of our food," and they rushed on them. This time the people did not run. They began to shoot at the buffalo with the bows and arrows *Nápi* had given them, and the buffalo began to fall; but in the fight a person was killed.

At this time these people had flint knives given them, and they cut up the bodies of the dead buffalo. It is not healthful to eat the meat raw, so Old Man gathered soft dry rotten driftwood and made punk of it, and then got a piece of hard wood, and drilled a hole in it with an arrow point, and gave them a pointed piece of hard wood, and taught them how to make a fire with fire sticks, and to cook the flesh of these animals and eat it.

They got a kind of stone that was in the land, and then took another harder stone and worked one upon the other, and hollowed out the softer one, and made a kettle of it. This was the fashion of their dishes.

Also Old Man said to the people: "Now, if you are overcome, you may go and sleep, and get power. Something will come to you in your dream, that will help you. Whatever these animals tell you to do, you must obey them, as they appear to you in your sleep. Be guided by them. If anybody wants help, if you are alone and travelling, and cry aloud for help, your prayer will be answered. It may be by the eagles, perhaps by the buffalo, or by the bears. Whatever animal answers your prayer, you must listen to him."

That was how the first people got through the world, by the power of their dreams.

After this, Old Man kept on, travelling north. Many of the animals that he had made followed him as he went. The animals understood him when he spoke to them, and he used them as his servants. When he got to the north point of the Porcupine Mountains, there he made some more mud images of people, and blew breath upon them, and they became people. He made men and women. They asked him, "What are we to eat?" He made many images of clay, in the form of buffalo. Then he blew breath on these, and they stood up; and when he made signs to them, they started to run. Then he said to the people, "Those are your food." They said to him, "Well, now, we have those animals; how are we to kill them?" "I will show you," he said. He took them to the cliff, and made them build rock piles like this, > ; and he made the people hide behind these piles of rock, and said, "When I lead the buffalo this way, as I bring them opposite to you, rise up."

After he had told them how to act, he started on toward a herd of buffalo. He began to call them, and the buffalo started to run toward him, and they followed him until they were inside the lines. Then he dropped back; and as the people rose up, the buffalo ran in a straight line and jumped over the cliff. He told the people to go and take the flesh of those animals. They tried to tear the limbs apart, but they could not. They tried to bite pieces out, and could not. So Old Man went to the edge of the cliff, and broke some pieces of stone with sharp edges, and told them to cut the flesh with these. When they had taken the skins from these animals, they set up some poles and put the hides on them, and so made a shelter to sleep under. There were some of these buffalo that went over the cliff that were not dead. Their legs were broken, but they were still alive. The people cut strips of green hide, and tied stones in the middle, and made large mauls, and broke in the skulls of the buffalo, and killed them.

After he had taught those people these things, he started off again, travelling north, until he came to where Bow and Elbow rivers meet. There he made some more people, and taught them the same things. From here he again went on northward. When he had come nearly to the Red Deer's River, he reached the hill where the Old Man sleeps. There he lay down and rested himself. The form of his body is to be seen there yet.

When he awoke from his sleep, he travelled further northward and came to a fine high hill. He climbed to the top of it, and there sat down to rest. He looked over the country below him, and it pleased him. Before him the hill was steep, and he said to himself, "Well, this is a fine place for sliding; I will have some fun," and he began to slide down the hill. The marks where he slid down are to be seen yet, and the place is known to all people as the "Old Man's Sliding Ground."

This is as far as the Blackfeet followed Old Man. The Crees know what he did further north.

In later times once, *Nápi* said, "Here I will mark you off a piece of ground," and he did so.* Then he said: "There is your land, and it is full of all kinds of animals, and many things grow in this land. Let no other people come into it. This is for you five tribes (Blackfeet, Bloods, Piegans, Gros Ventres, Sarcees). When people come to cross the line, take your bows and arrows, your lances. and your battle axes, and give them battle and keep them out. If they gain a footing, trouble will come to you."

Our forefathers gave battle to all people who came to cross these lines, and kept them out. Of late years we have let our friends, the white people, come in, and you know the result. We, his children, have failed to obey his laws.

---

* The boundaries of this land are given as running east from a point in the summit of the Rocky Mountains west of Fort Edmonton, taking in the country to the east and south, including the Porcupine Hills, Cypress Mountains, and Little Rocky Mountains, down to the mouth of the Yellowstone on the Missouri; then west to the head of the Yellowstone, and across the Rocky Mountains to the Beaverhead; thence to the summit of the Rocky Mountains and north along them to the starting-point. [G.B.G.]

*L*ONG, LONG AGO THERE was a great famine in the world, and a certain young man whilst wandering in search of food strayed into a part of the bush where he had never been before. Presently he perceived a strange mass lying on the ground. He approached and saw that it was the body of a giant whose hair resembled that of white men in that it was silky rather than woolly. It was of an incredible length and stretched as far as from Krachi to Salaga. The young man was properly awed at the spectacle, and wished to withdraw, but the giant noticing him asked what he wanted.

The young man explained and begged the giant to give him some food. The latter agreed on condition that the youth would serve him for a while. This matter having been arranged, the giant said his name was Owuo or Death, and then gave the boy some meat.

Never before had the latter tasted such fine food, and he was well pleased with his bargain. He served his master for a long time and received plenty of meat, but one day he grew homesick, and begged his master to give him a short holiday. The latter agreed if the youth would promise to bring another boy in his place. So the youth returned to his village and there persuaded his brother to go with him into the bush and gave him to Owuo.

In course of time the youth got hungry again and longed for the meat which Owuo had taught him to like so much. So one day he made up his mind to return to his master, and leaving the village made his way back to the giant's abode. The latter asked him what he wanted, and when the youth told him that he wanted to taste once more of the good meat, the giant told him to enter the hut and take as much as he liked, but he would have to work for him again.

The youth agreed and entered the hut. He ate as much as he could, and set to at the task his master set him. The work continued for a long time and the boy ate his fill every day. But to his surprise he never saw anything of his brother, and whenever he asked about him the giant told him that the lad was away on his business.

Once more the youth grew homesick and asked for leave to return to his village. The giant agreed on condition that he would bring a girl for him, Owuo, to wed. So the youth went home and there persuaded his sister to go into the bush and marry the giant. The girl agreed, and took with her a slave companion, and they all repaired to the giant's abode. There the youth left the two girls and went back to the village.

It was not very long after that he again grew hungry and longed for the taste of the meat. So he made his way once more into the bush and found the giant. The giant did not seem overpleased to see the boy and grumbled at being bothered a fourth time. However, he told the boy to go into the inner chamber of his hut and take what he wanted. The youth did so and took up a bone which he began to devour. To his horror he recognized it at once as being the bone of his sister. He looked around at all the rest of the meat and saw that it was that of his sister and her slave girl.

Thoroughly frightened he escaped from the house and ran back into the village. There he told the elders what he had done and the awful thing he had seen. At once the alarm was sounded and all the people went out into the bush to see for themselves the dread thing they had heard about. When they drew near to the giant, they grew afraid at the sight of so evil a monster. They went back to the village and consulted among themselves what best they should do. At least it was agreed to go to Salaga where the giant's hair finished and set light to it. This was done, and when the hair was burning well, they returned to the bush and watched the giant.

Presently the latter began to toss about and sweat. It was quite evident that he was beginning to feel the heat. The nearer the flames advanced the more he tossed and grumbled. At last the fire reached his head, and for the moment the giant was dead.

The villagers approached him cautiously, and the young man noticed "medicine" which had been concealed in the roots of the giant's hair. He took it and called the others to come and see what he had found. No one could say what power this medicine might have, but an old man suggested that no harm would be done if they took some and sprinkled it on the bones and meat in the hut. This idea was carried out, and to the surprise of every one, the girls and the boy returned to life at once.

The youth who had still some of the medicine left proposed to put it on the giant. But at this there was a great uproar, as the people feared Owuo might come to life again. The boy therefore by way of compromise sprinkled it into the eye of the dead giant. At once the eye opened and the people all fled away in terror. But it is from that eye that death comes; for every time that Owuo shuts that eye a man dies, and unfortunately for us he is for ever blinking and winking.

How I Brought Death into the World

AMOS TUTUOLA

ONE FINE MORNING, I took all my native juju and also my father's juju with me and I left my father's home-town to find out whereabouts was my tapster who had died.

But in those days, there were many wild animals and every place was covered by thick bushes and forests; again, towns and villages were not near each other as nowadays, and as I was travelling from bushes to bushes and from forests to forests and sleeping inside it for many days and months, I was sleeping on the branches of trees, because spirits etc. were just like partners, and to save my life from them; and again I could spend two or three months before reaching a town or a village. Whenever I reached a town or a village, I would spend almost four months there, to find out my palm-wine tapster from the inhabitants of that town or village and if he did not reach there, then I would leave there and continue my journey to another town or village. After the seventh month that I had left my home town, I reached a town and went to an old man, this old man was not a really man, he was a god and he was eating with his wife when I reached there. When I entered the house I saluted both of them, they answered me well, although nobody should enter his house like that as he was a god, but I myself was a god and juju-man. Then I told the old man (god) that I am looking for my palm-wine tap-ster who had died in my town some time ago, he did not answer to my question but asked me first what was my name? I replied that my name was "Father of gods" who could do everything in this world, then he said: "was that true" and I said yes; after that he told me to go to his native black-smith in an unknown place, or who was living in another town, and bring the right thing that he had told the black-smith to make for him. He said that if I could bring the right thing that he told the black-smith to make for him, then he would believe that I was the "Father of gods who could do everything in this world" and he would tell me where my tapster was.

Immediately this old man told or promised me so, I went away, but after I had travelled about one mile away then I used one of my juju and at once I changed into a very big bird and flew back to the roof of the old man's house; but as I stood on the roof of his house, many people saw me there. They came nearer and looked at me on the roof, so when the old man noticed that many had surrounded his house and were looking at the roof, he and his wife came out from the house and when he saw me (bird) on the roof, he told his wife that if he had not sent me to his native black-smith to bring the bell that he told the black-smith to make for him, he would tell me to mention the name of the bird. But at the same time that he said so, I knew what he wanted from the black-smith and I flew away to his black-smith, then when I reached there I told the black-smith that the old man (god) told me to bring his bell which he had told him to make for him. So the black-smith gave me the bell; after that, I returned to the old man with the bell and when he saw me with the bell, he and his wife were surprised and also shocked at that moment.

After that he told his wife to give me food, but after I had eaten the food, he told me again, that there remained another wonderful work to do for him, before he would tell me whereabouts my tapster was. When it was 6:30 a.m. of the following morning, he (god) woke me up, and gave me a wide and strong net which was the same in colour as the ground of that town. He told me to go and bring "Death" from his house with the net. When I left his house or the town about a mile, there I saw a junction of roads and I was doubtful when I reached the junction, I did not know which was Death's road among these roads, and when I thought within myself that as it was the market day, and all the market goers would soon be returning from the market—I lied down on the middle of the roads, I put my head to one of the roads, my left hand to one, right hand

to another one, and my both feet to the rest, after that I pretended
as I had slept there. But when all the market goers were returning
from the market, they saw me lied down there and shouted thus:—
"Who was the mother of this fine boy, he slept on the roads and
put his head towards Death's road."

Then I began to travel on Death's road, and I spent about eight
hours to reach there, but to my surprise I did not meet anybody on
this road until I reached there and I was afraid because of that.
When I reached his (Death's) house, he was not at home by that
time, he was in his yam garden which was very close to his house,
and I met a small rolling drum in his verandah, then I beat it to
Death as a sign of salutation. But when he (Death) heard the
sound of the drum, he said thus:—"Is that man still alive or dead?"
Then I replied "I am still alive and I am not a dead man."

But at the same time that he heard so from me, he was greatly
annoyed and he commanded the drum with a kind of voice that the
strings of the drum should tight me there; as a matter of fact, the
strings of the drum tighted me so that I was hardly breathing.

When I felt that these strings did not allow me to breathe and
again every part of my body was bleeding too much, then I myself
commanded the ropes of the yams in his garden to tight him there,
and the yams in his garden to tight him there, and the yam stakes
should begin to beat him also. After I had said so and at the same
time, all the ropes of the yams in his garden tighted him hardly,
and all the yam stakes were beating him repeatedly, so when he
(Death) saw that these stakes were beating him repeatedly, then
he commanded the strings of the drum which tighted me to release
me, and I was released at the same time. But when I saw that I
was released, then I myself commanded the ropes of the yams to
release him and the yam stakes to stop beating him, and he was released at once. After he was released by the ropes of yams and yam
stakes, he came to his house and met me at his verandah, then we
shook hands together, and he told me to enter the house, he put me
to one of his rooms, and after a while, he brought food to me and
we ate it together, after that we started conversations which went
thus:—He (Death) asked me from where did I come? I replied that

I came from a certain town which was not so far from his place. Then he asked what did I come to do? I told him that I had been hearing about him in my town and all over the world and I thought within myself that one day I should come and visit or to know him personally. After that he replied that his work was only to kill the people of the world, after that he got up and told me to follow him and I did so.

He took me around his house and his yam garden too, he showed me the skeleton bones of human-beings which he had killed since a century ago and showed me many other things also, but there I saw that he was using skeleton bones of human-beings as fuel woods and skull heads of human-beings as his basins, plates and tumblers etc.

Nobody was living near or with him there, he was living lonely, even bush animals and birds were very far away from his house. So when I wanted to sleep at night, he gave me a wide black cover cloth and then gave me a separate room to sleep inside, but when I entered the room, I met a bed which was made with bones of human-beings; but as this bed was terrible to look at or to sleep on it, I slept under it instead, because I knew his trick already. Even as this bed was very terrible, I was unable to sleep under as I lied down there because of fear of the bones of human-beings, but I lied down there awoke. To my surprise was that when it was about two o'clock in the mid-night, there I saw somebody enter into the room cautiously with a heavy club in his hands, he came nearer to the bed on which he had told me to sleep, then he clubbed the bed with all his power, he clubbed the centre of the bed thrice and he returned cautiously, he thought that I slept on that bed and he thought also that he had killed me.

But when it was 6 o'clock early in the morning, I first woke up and went to the room in which he slept, I woke him up, so when he heard my voice, he was frightened, even he could not salute me at all when he got up from his bed, because he thought that he had killed me last night.

But the second day that I slept there, he did not attempt to do anything again, but I woke up by two o'clock of that night, and went to the road which I should follow to the town and I travelled about a quarter of a mile to his house, then I stopped and dug a pit of his (Death's) size on the centre of that road, after that I spread the net which the old man gave me to bring him (Death) with on that pit, then I returned to his house, but he did not wake up as I was playing this trick.

When it was 6 o'clock in the morning, I went to his door and woke him up as usual, then I told him that I wanted to return to my town this morning, so that I wanted him to lead me a short distance; then he got up from his bed and he began to lead me as I told him, but when he led me to the place that I had dug, I told him to sit down, so I myself sat down on the road side, but as he sat down on the net, he fell into the pit, and without any ado I rolled up the net with him and put him on my head and I kept going to the old man's house who told me to go and bring him Death.

As I was carrying him along the road, he was trying all his efforts to escape or to kill me, but I did not give him a chance to do that. When I had travelled about eight hours, then I reached the town and went straight to the old man's house who told me to go and bring Death from his house. When I reached the old man's house, he was inside his room, then I called him and told him that I had brought Death that he told me to go and bring. But immediately he heard from me that I had brought Death and when he saw him on my head, he was greatly terrified and raised alarm that he thought nobody could go and bring Death from his house, then he told me to carry him (Death) back to his house at once, and he (old man) hastily went back to his room and started to close all his doors and windows, but before he could close two or three of his windows, I threw down Death before his door and at the same time that I threw him down, the net cut into pieces and Death found his way out.

Then the old man and his wife escaped through the windows and also the whole people in that town ran away for their lives and left their properties there. (The old man had thought that Death would kill me if I went to his house, because nobody could reach Death's house and return, but I had known the old man's trick already.)

So that since the day that I had brought Death out from his house, he has no permanent place to dwell or stay, and we are hearing his name about in the world. This was how I brought out Death to the old man who told me to go and bring him before he (old man) would tell me whereabouts my palm-wine tapster was that I was looking for before I reached that town and went to the old man.

*I*NDEED, ONE MUST EVER wait for the last day of a man's life, and call no one happy until he is dead and buried.

Amid so much prosperity, it was one of his grandsons, Actaeon, who first brought distress to Cadmus, when antlers, foreign to his human shape, sprouted from the youth's forehead, and his hounds gorged themselves on their master's blood. But calm reflection will show that destiny was to blame for Actaeon's misfortunes, not any guilt on his own part; for there is nothing sinful in losing one's way.

The scene of this event was a mountain where the ground was stained with the bloodshed of wild beasts of many kinds. The heat of mid-day had shortened the shadows, and the sun was midway between his eastern and his western goal, when the young Actaeon called to his comrades, as they roamed the lonely thickets, saying in a gentle tone: "My friends, our nets and swords are dripping with blood from the beasts we have taken—we have had enough success for one day. When tomorrow's dawn, riding in her saffron car, brings us another day, we shall return to our chosen task. But now the sun is at its highest, halfway on its course, cracking open the fields with its heat. For the present, then, put an end to your hunting, and gather in your knotted nets." The men did as he suggested and stopped, for a time, their strenuous activities.

There was a valley, thickly overgrown with pitchpine, and with sharp-needled cypress trees. It was called Gargaphie, and was sacred to Diana, the goddess of the hunt. Far in its depths lay a woodland cave, which no hand of man had wrought: but nature by her own devices had imitated art. She had carved a natural arch from the living stone and the soft tufa rocks. On the right hand was a murmuring spring of clear water, spreading out into a wide pool with grassy banks. Here the goddess, when she was tired with hunting in the woods, used to bathe her fastidious limbs in the pure water. When she entered the grotto she handed her javelin to one of the nymphs, who acted as her armour-bearer, along with her quiver and her bow, unstrung. Another nymph received her cloak and hung it across her arm, while two more took off her sandals. Yet another attendant, more skilled than the rest, Crocale, the daughter of Ismenus, gathered up the tresses which lay scattered on the goddess' shoulders, and bound them into a knot, though her own hair hung loose. Nephele, Hyale, Rhanis, Psecas, and Phiale drew up the water in capacious jars, and poured it over their mistress.

Now while Diana was bathing there in her stream, as usual, the grandson of Cadmus, who had for the present abandoned his hunting, came wandering with hesitant steps through this wood which he had never seen before. He reached the grove—so were the fates directing him—and entered the cave, which was moist with spray. The nymphs, discovered in their nakedness, beat their breasts at the sight of a man, and filled all the grove with their sudden outcry. Crowding round Diana, they sheltered her with their own bodies, but the goddess was taller than they, head and shoulders above them all. When she was caught unclad, a blush mantled her cheeks, as bright as when clouds reflect the sun's rays, as bright as rosy dawn. Though hidden by her comrades, who gathered closely round her, she stood turned aside, looking back over her shoulder. She wished she had her arrows ready to hand: instead, she caught up a handful of the water which she did have, and threw it in the young man's face. As she sprinkled his hair with the vengeful drops she also spoke these words, ominous of coming disaster. "Now, if you can, you may tell how you saw me when I was undressed." She uttered no more threats, but made the horns of a long-lived stag sprout where she had scattered water on his brow. She lengthened his neck, brought the tips of his ears to a point, changed his hands to feet, his arms to long legs, and covered his body with a dappled skin. Then she put panic fear in his heart as well. The hero fled, and even as he ran, marvelled to find himself so swift. When he glimpsed his face and his horns, reflected in the water, he tried to say "Alas!" but no words came. He groaned—that was all the voice he had—and tears ran down his changed cheeks. Only his mind remained the same as before. What was he to do? Return home to the royal palace, or hide in the woods? He was ashamed to do the first, afraid to do the second.

As he hesitated, his hounds caught sight of him. Melampus and the wise Ichnobates were the first to give tongue, Ichnobates of the Cretan breed, and Melampus of the Spartan. Then the others rushed to the chase, swifter than the wind, Pamphagus and Dorceus and Oribasus, all Arcadians, and strong Nebrophonus, fierce Theron and Laelaps too. Ptereclas, the swift runner, was there, and keen-scented Agre, Hylaeus who had lately been gored by a wild boar, Nape, offspring of a wolf, Poemenis, the shepherd dog, Harpyia with her two pups, Ladon from Sicyon, slender-flanked, and Dromas and Canace, Sticte and Tigris, Alce, white-coated Leucon, and black-haired Asbolus; with them was Lacon, a dog of outstanding strength, Aello the stout runner, Thous and swift Lycisce with her brother Cyprius, Harpalus, who had a white spot in the middle of his black forehead, and Melaneus and shaggy Lachne, Lebros and Agriodus, both cross-bred of a Cretan mother and a Spartan father, shrill-barking Hylactor, and others whom it would take long to name. The pack, eager for its prey, swept over the rocks and crags, over un-approachable cliffs, through places where the going was difficult, and where there was no way at all. Actaeon fled, where he had himself so often pursued his quarry, fled, alas, before his own faithful hounds. He longed to cry out: "I am Actaeon! Don't you know your own master?" but the words he wanted to utter would not come—the air echoed with barking. First Melanchaetes fastened his teeth in his master's back, then Theridamas and Oresitrophus clung to his shoulder. They had been slow to begin the chase, but had outstripped the others by taking a short cut over the mountains. While they held their master down, the rest of the pack gathered, and sank their teeth in his body, till there was no place left for tearing. Actaeon groaned, uttering a sound which, though not human, was yet such as no stag could produce. The ridges he knew so well were filled with his mournful cries. Falling to his knees, like a suppliant in prayer, he silently swayed his head this way and that, as if stretching out beseeching arms. But his friends, not knowing what they did, urged on the ravening mob with their usual encouragements and looked round for Actaeon, shouted for Actaeon, as if he were not there, each trying to call louder than the other. They lamented that their leader was absent, and that his slowness prevented him from seeing the booty chance had offered. Actaeon turned his head at the sound of his name. Well might he wish to be absent, but he was all too surely present. Well might he wish to see and not to feel the cruel deeds of his hounds. They surrounded him on every side, fastening their jaws on his body, and tore to pieces the seeming stag, which was in fact their master. Only when he had been dispatched by wounds innumerable, so men say, was the anger of Diana, the quiver-bearing goddess, appeased.

When the story was told, opinions were divided: some thought that the goddess had been too cruel, others praised her, and declared her act in keeping with her strict chastity. Both sides could justify their views.

*I*T IS NOT POSSIBLE for any god to undo the actions
of another god, but in return for his loss of sight, the
omnipotent father granted Tiresias the power to know
the future and softened his punishment by conferring
this honour upon him.

His fame spread throughout the Aonian cities,. and
when the people consulted him he gave replies with
which none could find fault.

The dark river nymph, Liriope, was the first to test his
reliability and truthfulness. She was the nymph whom
Cephisus once embraced with his curving stream, imprisoned in his waves, and forcefully ravished. When her
time was come, that nymph most fair brought forth a
child with whom one could have fallen in love even in
his cradle, and she called him Narcissus. When the
prophetic seer was asked whether this boy would live to
a ripe old age, he replied: "Yes, if he does not come to
know himself." For a long time this pronouncement
seemed to be nothing but empty words: however, it was
justified by the outcome of events: the strange madness
which afflicted the boy and the nature of his death proved
its truth.

Cephisus' child had reached his sixteenth year, and
could be counted as at once boy and man. Many lads and
many girls fell in love with him, but his soft young body
housed a pride so unyielding that none of those boys or
girls dared to touch him. One day, as he was driving
timid deer into his nets, he was seen by that talkative
nymph who cannot stay silent when another speaks, but
yet has not learned to speak first herself. Her name is
Echo, and she always answers back.

Echo still had a body then, she was not just a voice:
but although she was always chattering, her power of

speech was no different from what it is now. All she could do was to repeat the last words of the many phrases that she heard. Juno had brought this about because often, when she could have caught the nymphs lying with her Jupiter on the mountainside, Echo, knowing well what she did, used to detain the goddess with an endless flow of talk, until the nymphs could flee. When Juno realized what was happening, she said: "I shall curtail the powers of that tongue which has tricked me: you will have only the briefest possible use of your voice." And in fact she carried out her threats. Echo still repeats the last words spoken, and gives back the sounds she has heard.

So, when she saw Narcissus wandering through the lonely countryside, Echo fell in love with him, and followed secretly in his steps. The more closely she followed, the nearer was the fire which scorched her: just as sulphur, smeared round the tops of torches, is quickly kindled when a flame is brought near it. How often she wished to make flattering overtures to him, to approach him with tender pleas! But her handicap prevented this, and would not allow her to speak first; she was ready to do what it would allow, to wait for sounds which she might re-echo with her own voice.

The boy, by chance, had wandered away from his faithful band of comrades, and he called out: "Is there anybody here?" Echo answered: "Here!" Narcissus stood still in astonishment, looking round in every direction, and cried at the pitch of his voice: "Come!" As he called, she called in reply. He looked behind him, and when no one appeared, cried again: "Why are you avoiding me?" But all he heard were his own words echoed back. Still he persisted, deceived by what he took to be another's voice, and said, "Come here, and let us meet!" Echo answered: "Let us meet!" Never again would she reply more willingly to any sound. To make good her words she came out of the wood and made to throw her arms round the neck she loved: but he fled from her, crying as he did so, "Away with these embraces! I would die before I would have you touch me!" Her only answer was: "I would have you touch me!" Thus scorned, she concealed herself in the woods, hiding her shamed face in the shelter of the leaves, and ever since that day, she dwells in lonely caves. Yet still her love remained firmly rooted in her heart, and was increased by the pain of having been rejected. Her anxious thoughts kept her awake, and made her pitifully thin. She became wrinkled and wasted; all the freshness of her beauty withered into the air. Only her voice and her bones were left, till finally her voice alone remained; for her bones, they say, were turned to stone. Since then, she hides in the woods, and, though never seen on the mountains, is heard there by all: for her voice is the only part of her that still lives.

Narcissus had played with her affections, treating her as he had previously treated other spirits of the waters and the woods, and his male admirers too. Then one of those he had scorned raised up his hands to heaven and prayed: "May he himself fall in love with another, as we have done with him! May he too be unable to gain his loved one!" Nemesis heard and granted his righteous prayer.

There was a clear pool, with shining silvery waters, where shepherds had never made their way; no goats that pasture on the mountains, no cattle had ever come here. Its peace was undisturbed by bird or beast or falling branches. Around it was a grassy sward, kept ever green by the nearby waters; encircling woods sheltered the spot from the fierce sun, and made it always cool.

Narcissus, wearied with hunting in the heat of the day, lay down here: for he was attracted by the beauty of the place, and by the spring. While he sought to quench his thirst, another thirst grew in him, and as he drank, he was enchanted by the beautiful reflection that he saw. He fell in love with an insubstantial hope, mistaking a mere shadow for a real body. Spellbound by his own self, he remained there motionless, with fixed gaze, like a statue carved from Parian marble. As he lay on the bank, he gazed at the twin stars that were his eyes, at his flowing locks, worthy of Bacchus or Apollo, his smooth cheeks, his ivory neck, his lovely face where a rosy flush stained the snowy whiteness of his complexion, admiring all the features for which he was himself admired. Unwittingly, he desired himself, and was himself the object of his own approval, at once seeking and sought, himself kindling the flame with which he burned. How often did he vainly kiss the treacherous pool, how often plunge his arms deep in the waters, as he tried to clasp the neck he saw! But he could not lay hold upon himself. He did not know what he was looking at, but was fired by the sight, and excited by the very illusion that deceived his eyes. Poor foolish boy, why vainly grasp at the fleeting image that eludes you? The thing you are seeking does not exist: only turn aside and you will lose what you love. What you see is but the shadow cast by your reflection; in itself it is nothing. It comes with you, and lasts while you are there; it will go when you go, if go you can.

No thought of food or sleep could draw him from the spot. Stretched on the shady grass, he gazed at the shape that was no true shape with eyes that could never have their fill, and by his own eyes he was undone. Finally he raised himself a little. Holding out his arms to the surrounding woods: "Oh you woods," he cried, "has anyone ever felt a love more cruel? You surely know, for many lovers have found you an ideal haunt for secret meetings. You who have lived so many centuries, do you remember anyone, in all your long years, who has pined away as I do? I am in love, and see my loved one, but that form which I see and love, I cannot reach: so far am I deluded by my love. My distress is all the greater because it is not a mighty ocean that separates us, nor yet highways or mountains, or city walls with close-barred gates. Only a little water keeps us apart. My love himself desires to be embraced: for whenever I lean forward to kiss the clear waters he lifts up his face to mine and strives to reach me. You would think he could be reached — it is such a small thing that hinders our love. Whoever you are, come out to me! Oh boy beyond compare, why do you elude me? Where do you go, when I try to reach you? Certainly it is not my looks or my years which you shun, for I am one of those the nymphs have loved. With friendly looks you proffer me some hope. When I stretch out my arms to you, you stretch yours towards me in return: you laugh when I do, and often I have marked your tears when I was weeping. You answer my signs with nods, and, as far as I can guess from the movement of your lovely lips, reply to me in words that never reach my ears. Alas! I am myself the boy I see. I know it: my own reflection does not deceive me. I am on fire with love for my own self. It is I who kindle the flames which I must endure. What should I do? Woo or be wooed? But what then shall I seek by my wooing? What I desire, I have. My very plenty makes me poor. How I wish I could separate myself from my body! A new prayer this, for a lover, to wish the thing he loves away! Now grief is sapping my strength; little of life remains for me — I am cut off in the flower of my youth. I have no quarrel with death, for in death I shall forget my pain: but I could wish that the object of my love might outlive me: as it is, both of us will perish together, when this one life is destroyed."

When he had finished speaking, he returned to gazing distractedly at that same face. His tears disturbed the water, so that the pool rippled, and the image grew dim. He saw it disappearing, and cried aloud: "Where are you fleeing? Cruel creature, stay, do not desert one who loves you! Let me look upon you, if I cannot touch you. Let me, by looking, feed my ill-starred love." In his grief, he tore away the upper portion of his tunic, and beat his bared breast with hands as white as marble. His breast flushed rosily where he struck it, just as apples often shine red in part, while part gleams whitely, or as grapes, ripening in variegated clusters, are tinged with purple. When Narcissus saw this reflected in the water — for the pool had returned to its former calm — he could bear it no longer. As golden wax melts with gentle heat, as morning frosts are thawed by the warmth of the sun, so he was worn and wasted away with love, and slowly consumed by its hidden fire. His fair complexion with its rosy flush faded away, gone was his youthful strength, and all the beauties which lately charmed his eyes. Nothing remained of that body which Echo once had loved.

The nymph saw what had happened, and although she remembered her own treatment, and was angry at it, still she grieved for him. As often as the unhappy boy sighed "Alas," she took up his sigh, and repeated "Alas!" When he beat his hands against his shoulders she too gave back the same sound of mourning. His last words as he gazed into the familiar waters were: "Woe is me for the boy I loved in vain!" and the spot re-echoed the same words. When he said his last farewell, "Farewell!" said Echo too. He laid down his weary head on the green grass, and death closed the eyes which so admired their owner's beauty. Even then, when he was received into the abode of the dead, he kept looking at himself in the waters of the

Styx. His sisters, the nymphs of the spring, mourned for him, and cut off their hair in tribute to their brother. The wood nymphs mourned him too, and Echo sang her refrain to their lament.

The pyre, the tossing torches, and the bier, were now being prepared, but his body was nowhere to be found. Instead of his corpse, they discovered a flower with a circle of white petals round a yellow centre.

When this story became known, it brought well-deserved fame to the seer Tiresias. It was told throughout all the cities of Greece, and his reputation was boundless.

P ANDION, KING OF ATHENS, seeing that Tereus was rich and powerful, and a descendant of mighty Mars himself, gave him his daughter's hand in marriage. But neither the Graces nor Hymen nor Juno, who bestows her blessing upon brides, was present at that ceremony. Furies lit the bridal pair upon their way, with torches stolen from funeral processions, Furies prepared the marriage couch, and the cursed screech-owl brooded over their house, perched on the roof above their marriage chamber. Such were the omens when Procne and Tereus were married, such the omens when they became parents. Thrace, little knowing what impended, rejoiced with their king and queen, as the royal pair themselves gave thanks to the gods; proclamation was made that the day on which Pandion's daughter had married the noble king of Thrace, and the birthday of their son Itys, too, should be celebrated as public holidays. So blind are men, regarding what is truly to their advantage.

Now five autumns had passed away, as the sun rolled on his yearly course, when Procne spoke coaxingly to her husband: "If you love me at all, send me to see my sister, or else have my sister come here. You can promise my father that she will not be long away from home. A chance to see Philomela will be a magnificent gift for me." Tereus gave orders for ships to be launched and, with the help of sail and oars, came to the harbours of Cecrops' land, where he disembarked on the shore of Piraeus. As soon as he was admitted to the presence of of his father-in-law, the king, they shook each other by the hand, and exchanged the usual greetings. Then Tereus began to explain the reason for his coming, and to deliver his wife's message, promising that if her sister were allowed to visit her, she would not be kept away too long, when suddenly Philomela appeared, richly attired in gorgeous robes, but richer still in her own beauty. She was like the descriptions that one often hears of the naiads and dryads who haunt the depths of the woodlands, if only they wore ornaments and garments such as hers. A flame of desire was kindled in Tereus' heart when he saw her, flaring up as quickly as the fire that burns withered corn, or dry leaves, or stores of hay. Her beauty, indeed, was excuse enough, but he was further excited by his own passionate nature, for the people of his country are an emotional race. So, thanks to the fault of the national temperament and of his own, he burned with ardent passion. His impulse was to bribe the attendants who guarded her, to undermine her nurse's loyalty, to tempt the girl herself with magnificent gifts, lavishing his whole kingdom on her: or else to seize her and carry her off, and then to defend his prize by savage fighting. There was nothing that his unbridled passion would not dare. His heart could not contain the fires that burned within. He was impatient, now, of delay, and eagerly turned back to deliver Procne's message, and to put forward his own plea under cover of hers. Love made him eloquent, and whenever his request seemed too pressing, he declared that Procne would have it so. He enforced his arguments with tears, as if his wife had entrusted him with those as well.

O gods above, how blind we mortals are! The very acts which furthered his wicked scheme made people believe that he was a devoted husband, and he was praised for his criminal behaviour. Moreover, Philomela shared his eagerness. Throwing her arms round her father's neck, she coaxed him to let her go to visit her sister, and begged him, as he hoped for her welfare, to agree to a plan which was, in fact, entirely contrary to it. Tereus gazed at the princess and already, in anticipation, held her in his arms. As he watched her kissing Pandion, throwing her arms about his neck, the sight of all this goaded him to greater frenzy, and added food and fuel to his desire. When he saw her embrace the king, how he wished that *he* were the father! Yet even had he been so, his desires would still have been equally wicked. The king yielded to the wishes of his two daughters: Philomela, overjoyed, thanked her father and supposed, poor girl, that his decision was a victory for herself and her sister, when in fact it was to be the ruin of them both.

Now the sun had but a little way to go, and his horses were galloping down the slope of the evening sky: a kingly banquet was spread upon the tables, and the golden goblets were filled with wine. After the feast, the guests retired to peaceful slumbers. But the Thracian king, though he had gone to bed, was in a fever of love for the princess and lay, recalling her face, her movements, her hands, and imagining the parts he had not seen to be just as he would have them. So he fostered his love, too restless to sleep.

When the dawn came, and Tereus was on the point of departure, Pandion clasped his hand and, with tears in his eyes, begged him to look after his companion. "My dear son," he said, "since your affectionate pleading leaves me no choice, I entrust this child of mine to you, in accordance with your own wishes, Tereus, and those of my two daughters. I beg you, by your honour, by the gods above, and by the relationship that binds us, to watch over her like a father, and to send back to me, as soon as may be, this dear girl who is the comfort of my old age. The time will drag for me, all the while she is away. And you, Philomela, if you love me at all, come back to me as soon as you can. It is enough that your sister is so far from home." With these injunctions, he kissed his daughter good-bye, crying quietly as he did so. He asked them both to give him their hands as a pledge that they would keep their promise and then, joining their hands together, begged them to remember to convey his greetings to his absent daughter and to his grandson. Sobs choked him, so that he could scarcely manage to utter a last farewell: his mind was filled with anxious foreboding.

Once Philomela was on board the painted ship, when the sea was churned up under the oar-blades, and the land left behind, then the barbarous prince cried out: "I have won! I have on board with me the girl I prayed for!" In his triumph he could scarcely wait for the joys which he anticipated, could not tear his eyes away from his prize: as when an eagle, seizing a hare in its crooked talons, deposits the prize in its lofty eyrie — then the captor gazes gloatingly on the prisoner, for whom there is no escape.

They had accomplished their journey and, on reaching their own shores, disembarked from the travel-worn ship. The king dragged Pandion's daughter to a high-walled steading, hidden in the dark depths of an ancient forest, and there he shut her up. She, for her part, pale and trembling, frightened of everything, begged him with tears to tell her where her sister was. Instead, he told her of his guilty passion and, by sheer force, overcame the struggles of the lonely and defenceless girl, while she vainly called aloud to her father, to her sister, and above all to the gods, for help. She was quivering with fear, like some timid lamb which has been mauled and cast aside by a grey wolf, and cannot yet believe in its safety: or like a dove, its feathers matted with its own blood, still trembling and afraid of the greedy talons which held it fast.

Soon, when she came to herself again, she tore her disordered hair, clawed at her arms and beat them against her breast, as if she were in mourning. Then, stretching out her hands, she cried: "You horrible barbarian, you cruel scoundrel! Are you quite unmoved by the charges my father laid upon you, by the affectionate tears he shed as he let me go? Do you care nothing for my sister's anxiety, for my innocent youth, or for your own marriage? You have confounded all natural feelings: I am my sister's rival, you a husband twice over, and Procne ought, by rights, to be my enemy. You traitor, why not take my life from me as well, to complete your crime? How I wish that you had done so, before I was forced into that unspeakable union! Then my ghost would have been guiltless. Yet if the gods above take notice of these things, if the power of heaven is more than an empty name, if all has not been lost, though I am lost, then one day no matter when, you will pay the penalty for this. I myself will throw aside all modesty, and proclaim your deeds. If I have the chance, I shall come forward before your people, and tell my story. If I am to be kept shut up in the woods, I shall fill the forests with my voice, and win sympathy from the very rocks that witnessed my degradation. Heaven will hear my cries, and any god that dwells there!"

Her words roused the fierce tyrant to anger, and to fear no less. Goaded on by both these passions, he snatched his sword out of its scabbard where it hung at his waist, and seizing his victim by the hair, twisted her arms behind her back, and bound them fast. Philomela, filled with hopes of death when she saw the sword, offered him her throat. But even as she poured out her scorn, still calling upon her father, and struggling to speak, he grasped her tongue with a pair of forceps, and cut it out with his cruel sword. The remaining stump still quivered in her throat, while the tongue itself lay pulsing and murmuring incoherently to the dark earth. It writhed convulsively, like a snake's tail when it has newly been cut off and, dying, tried to reach its mistress' feet. Even after this atrocity, they say, though I can hardly bring myself to believe it, that the king in his guilty passion often took his pleasure with the body he had so mutilated.

After such behaviour, he had the audacity to go back to Procne. When the queen saw her husband, she inquired for her sister, and he then told her a tale of his own invention: he declared that Philomela was dead, groaning in pretended grief, and convincing the listeners by his tears. Procne tore from her shoulders her bright robes, with their broad golden hems, clothed herself in black, and set up an empty tomb, at which she made offerings to a ghost that was no ghost, and lamented the sad fate of her sister, whose sufferings were far other than she thought.

The sungod had driven his car through the twelve signs of heaven, and a full year had passed. What could Philomela do? She was closely guarded to prevent her escape, the walls of the steading were stout, built of solid stone, her dumb lips could not reveal what had happened. But grief and pain breed great ingenuity, and distress teaches us to be inventive. Cunningly she set up her threads on a barbarian loom, and wove a scarlet design on a white ground, which pictured the wrong she had suffered. When it was finished, she gave it to one of her servants and, by her gestures, conveyed to the girl that she wished her to take it to the queen. The servant did as she was asked, and carried the tapestry to Procne, without knowing what she was giving her.

When the cruel tyrant's wife unfolded the woven cloth, she read there the unhappy story of her own misfortunes. She uttered not a word: it was incredible how she restrained herself, but her grief was too great for speech and, when she sought for words, she could find none bitter enough. There was no time for tears. Instead, she concentrated on schemes for revenge, and rushed ahead with a plan that was to confound completely the issues of right and wrong.

It was the time of the solemn festival which the young women of Thrace celebrate every three years in honour of Bacchus. Their sacred rites are carried on by night, by night Rhodope rings with the clashing of shrill cymbals. By night, therefore, the queen left her home, all ready for the worship of the god, and carrying the ritual weapons of his frenzied followers. Her head was wreathed with the vine leaves, a deerskin was slung over her left side, and she carried a light spear resting on her shoulder. Then she went whirling through the woods, accompanied by her attendants, a figure that struck terror to the heart. She pretended that she was being driven by Bacchus' frenzy, but it was the fury of grief that drove her on. At length she came to the hidden steading. Amid howls and Bacchic cries the gates were broken down; then Procne seized her sister, dressed her in the costume of one of Bacchus' worshippers, concealing her face with ivy leaves, and led the bewildered girl back to the palace.

When Philomela realized that she had come to that accursed house, she shuddered in distress, and grew deathly pale: but Procne, having gained her home, removed the emblems of Bacchus' festival from her unhappy sister's brow, and uncovered her downcast face. She flung her arms around her, but Philomela did not dare to lift her head or meet her sister's eyes, considering herself the cause of the other's sorrow. She gazed steadfastly at the ground, and her gestures conveyed what her voice could not: for she was eager to swear by the gods that she had been forcefully assaulted and disgraced. Procne, blazing with uncontrollable anger, cut short her sister's sobs, saying: "This is no time for tears, but rather for the sword, or anything more effective than the sword, if such you have. I am prepared to go to any lengths of crime, my sister — either to set the palace alight, and trap that scheming Tereus in the flames, or to cut out his tongue and his eyes, to hew off the limbs which wronged you, and drive his guilty soul from his body, through a thousand gaping wounds. The revenge prepared must be something tremendous: but I am still in doubt as to what it should be."

While Procne was speaking, Itys came up to his mother. The sight of her son suggested what she could do and, looking at him with ruthless eyes, she murmured: "How like his father he is!" Without another word, seething with silent rage, she prepared for her terrible deed. Even so, when her son came close and greeted her, drawing down her head with his little arms, kissing her and prattling childish endearments, the mother was shaken. Her anger was checked and, against her will, tears gathered in her eyes. But as soon as she felt her excessive love for the child weakening her resolution, she turned away from him again, to look at her sister's face. As her eyes went from one to the other, she upbraided herself, saying: "Why does one of them speak to me lovingly, while the other has no tongue to speak at all? Why does he call me mother, when she cannot call me sister? See the kind of man you have married, you, Pandion's daughter! You are not worthy of your father! It is criminal to feel affection for a husband such as Tereus!"

She hesitated no longer, but dragged Itys away to a distant part of the lofty palace, like some tigress on the Ganges' banks, dragging an unweaned fawn through the thick forest. He realized what was in store for him and, stretching out his hands, cried "Mother, Mother!" and tried to throw his arms round her neck. But Procne drove a sword into his side, close to his breast, and did not even turn her face away. That wound alone was enough to kill him, but Philomela took the sword, and cut his throat as well. While his limbs were still warm, still retained some vestiges of life, the two sisters tore them apart: the room was dripping with blood. Then they cooked his flesh, boiling some in bronze pots, and roasting some on spits.

Next, Procne invited her husband, who knew nothing of what she had done, to partake of this feast. She pretended that it was a sacred ritual, practised in her own country, and that only her husband might be present at the meal. On this pretext, she got rid of their attendants, and the servants. So Tereus, all by himself, sat in state on his ancestral throne, and ate what was before him, swallowing down mouthfuls of flesh that was his own. He was so utterly blind to what was going on, that he called out: "Bring Itys here!" Procne could not conceal her cruel exultation. Eager to be the first to announce the catastrophe she had brought about, she told her husband: "The boy you are asking for is here, inside, with you." Tereus looked round, asking where his son was. As he inquired for him and called his name once more, Philomela leaped forward in all her disarray, her hair spattered with the blood of the boy she had madly murdered. She thrust Ity's head, dripping with gore, before his father's face. Never would she have been more glad to have been able to speak, to express her glee in fitting words. With a roar of fury the Thracian king pushed away the tables, invoking the snaky-haired sisters from the Stygian depths. Could he have done so, he would willingly have burst open his breast and disgorged from it the frightful banquet of human flesh which he had eaten. Then again he wept, calling himself the wretched tomb of his own son. Drawing his sword, he was rushing in pursuit of Pandion's daughters, when it almost seemed that the girls' bodies were hovering in the air, raised up on wings: in fact, they were hovering on wings. One of them flew off to the woods, the other flew under the eaves of the roof: traces of the murder were still visible on her breast, her feathers were still crimson with blood. The king, made swift by grief and longing for revenge, was also turned into a bird. He had a crest of feathers on his head and, in place of his long sword, wore a huge jutting beak. This bird is called the hoopoe, and it looks as if it were accoutred for battle.

FOLKTALE

The Ghost Wife   GEORGE BIRD GRINNELL, ED.

O NE TIME THERE WERE living together a man and
his wife. They had a young child. The woman died. The
man was very sad, and mourned for his wife.

One night he took the child in his arms, and went out
from the village to the place where his wife was buried,
and stood over the grave, and mourned for his wife. The
little child was very helpless, and cried all the time. The
man's heart was sick with grief and loneliness. Late in
the night he fell asleep, fainting and worn out with sorrow. After a while he awoke, and when he looked up,
there was a form standing by him. The form standing
there was the one who had died. She spoke to her husband, and said, "You are very unhappy here. There is a
place to go where we would not be unhappy. Where I
have been nothing bad happens to one. Here, you never
know what evil will come to you. You and the child had
better come to me."

The man did not want to die. He said to her, "No;
it will be better if you can come back to us. We love you.
If you were with us we would be unhappy no longer."

For a long time they discussed this, to decide which
one should go to the other. At length the man by his
persuasions overcame her, and the woman agreed to
come back. She said to the man, "If I am to come back
you must do exactly as I tell you for four nights. For
four days the curtain must remain let down before my
sleeping place; it must not be raised; no one must look
behind it."

The man did as he had been told, and after four days
had passed, the curtain was lifted, and the woman came
out from behind it. Then they all saw her, first her rela-

tions, and afterward the whole tribe. Her husband and her child were very glad, and they lived happily together.

A long time after this, the man took another wife. The first wife was always pleasant and good-natured, but the new one was bad-tempered, and after some time she grew jealous of the first woman, and quarreled with her. At length, one day the last married became angry with the other, and called her bad names, and finally said to her, "You ought not to be here. You are nothing but a ghost, any-way."

That night when the man went to bed, he lay down, as was his custom, by the side of his first wife. During the night he awoke, and found that his wife had disappeared. She was seen no more. The next night after this happened, the man and the child both died in sleep. The wife had called them to her. They had gone to that place where there is a living.

This convinced everybody that there is a hereafter.

The Magic Swan Geese

ALEXANDR AFANAS'EV, ED.

A N OLD MAN LIVED with his old wife; they had a daughter and a little son. "Daughter, daughter," said the mother, "we are going to work; we shall bring you back a bun, sew you a dress, and buy you a kerchief. Be careful, watch over your little brother, do not leave the house." The parents went away and the daughter forgot what they had told her; she put her brother on the grass beneath the window, ran out into the street, and became absorbed in games. Some magic swan geese came, seized the little boy, and carried him off on their wings.

The girl came back and found her brother gone. She gasped, and rushed to look in every corner, but could not find him. She called him, wept, and lamented that her father and mother would scold her severely; still her little brother did not answer. She ran into the open field; the swan geese flashed in the distance and vanished behind a dark forest. The swan geese had long had a bad reputation; they had done a great deal of damage and stolen many little children. The girl guessed that they had carried off her brother, and rushed after them. She ran and ran and saw a stove. "Stove, stove, tell me, whither have the geese flown?" "If you eat my cake of rye I will tell you." "Oh, in my father's house we don't even eat cakes of wheat!" The stove did not tell her. She ran farther and saw an apple tree. "Apple tree, apple tree, tell me, whither have the geese flown?" "If you eat one of my wild apples, I will tell you." "Oh, in my father's house we don't even eat sweet apples." She ran farther and saw a river of milk with shores of pudding. "River of milk, shores of pudding, whither have the geese flown?" "If you eat of my simple pudding with milk, I will tell you." "Oh, in my father's house we don't even eat cream."

She would have run in the fields and wandered in the woods for a long time, if she had not luckily met a hedgehog. She wanted to nudge him, but was afraid that he would prick her, and she asked: "Hedgehog, hedgehog, have you not seen whither the geese have flown?" "Thither," he said, and showed her. She ran and saw a little hut that stood on chicken legs and turned round and round. In the little hut lay Baba Yaga with veined snout and clay legs, and the little brother was sitting on a bench, playing with golden apples. His sister saw him, crept near him, seized him, and carried him away. But the geese flew after her: if the robbers overtook her, where would she hide?

There flowed the river of milk with shores of pudding. "Little mother river, hide me!" she begged. "If you eat my pudding." There was nothing to be done; she ate it, and the river hid her beneath the shore, and the geese flew by. She went out, said "Thank you," and ran on, carrying her brother; and the geese turned back and flew toward her. What could she do in this trouble? There was the apple tree. "Apple tree, apple tree, little mother, hide me!" she begged. "If you eat my wild apple." She ate it quickly. The apple tree covered her with branches and leaves; the geese flew by. She went out again and ran on with her brother. The geese saw her and flew after her. They came quite close, they began to strike her with their wings; at any moment they would tear her brother from her hands. Luckily there was the stove on her path. "Madam Stove, hide me!" she begged. "If you eat my cake of rye." The girl quickly stuck the cake in her mouth, went into the stove, and sat there. The geese whirred and whirred, quacked and quacked, and finally flew away without recovering their prey. And the girl ran home, and it was a good thing that she came when she did, for soon afterward her mother and father arrived.

Why Tortoise's Shell Is Not Smooth

CHINUA ACHEBE

L OW VOICES, BROKEN NOW and again by singing, reached Okonkwo from his wives' huts as each woman and her children told folk stories. Ekwefi and her daughter, Ezinma, sat on a mat on the floor. It was Ekwefi's turn to tell a story.

"Once upon a time," she began, "all the birds were invited to a feast in the sky. They were very happy and began to prepare themselves for the great day. They painted their bodies with red cam wood and drew beautiful patterns on them with *uli*.

"Tortoise saw all these preparations and soon discovered what it all meant. Nothing that happened in the world of the animals ever escaped his notice; he was full of cunning. As soon as he heard of the great feast in the sky his throat began to itch at the very thought. There was a famine in those days and Tortoise had not eaten a good meal for two moons. His body rattled like a piece of dry stick in his empty shell. So he began to plan how he would go to the sky."

"But he had no wings," said Ezinma.

"Be patient," replied her mother. "That is the story. Tortoise had no wings, but he went to the birds and asked to be allowed to go with them.

" 'We know you too well,' said the birds when they had heard them. 'You are full of cunning and you are ungrateful. If we allow you to come with us you will soon begin your mischief.'

" 'You do not know me,' said Tortoise. 'I am a changed man. I have learned that a man who makes trouble for others is also making it for himself.'

"Tortoise had a sweet tongue, and within a short time all the birds agreed that he was a changed man, and they each gave him a feather, with which he made two wings.

"At last the great day came and Tortoise was the first to arrive at the meeting place. When all the birds had gathered together, they set off in a body. Tortoise was very happy and voluble as he flew among the birds, and he was soon chosen as the man to speak for the party because he was a great orator.

" 'There is one important thing which we must not forget,' he said as they flew on their way. 'When people are invited to a great feast like this, they take new names for the occasion. Our hosts in the sky will expect us to honor this age-old custom.'

"None of the birds had heard of this custom but they knew that Tortoise, in spite of his failings in other directions, was a widely-traveled man who knew the customs of different peoples. And so they each took a new name. When they had all taken, Tortoise also took one. He was to be called *All of you*.

"At last the party arrived in the sky and their hosts were very happy to see them. Tortoise stood up in his many-colored plumage and thanked them for their invitation. His speech was so eloquent that all the birds were glad they had brought him, and nodded their heads in approval of all he said. Their hosts took him as the king of the birds, especially as he looked somewhat different from the others.

"After kola nuts had been presented and eaten, the people of the sky set before their guests the most delectable dishes Tortoise had even seen or dreamed of. The soup was brought out hot from the fire and in the very pot in which it had been cooked. It was full of meat and fish. Tortoise began to sniff aloud. There was pounded yam and also yam pottage cooked with palm-oil and fresh fish. There were also pots of palm-wine. When everything had been set before the guests, one of the people of the sky came forward and tasted a little from each pot. He then invited the birds to eat. But Tortoise jumped to his feet and asked: 'For whom have you prepared this feast?'

" 'For all of you,' replied the man.

"Tortoise turned to the birds and said: 'You remember that my name is *All of you*. The custom here is to serve the spokesman first and the others later. They will serve you when I have eaten.'

"He began to eat and the birds grumbled angrily. The people of the sky thought it must be their custom to leave all the food for their king. And so Tortoise ate the best part of the food and then drank two pots of palm-wine, so that he was full of food and drink and his body filled out in his shell.

"The birds gathered round to eat what was left and to peck at the bones he had thrown all about the floor. Some of them were too angry to eat. They chose to fly home on an empty stomach. But before they left each took back the feather he had lent to Tortoise. And there he stood in his hard shell full of food and wine but without any wings to fly home. He asked the birds to take a message for his wife, but they all refused. In the end Parrot, who had felt more angry than the others, suddenly changed his mind and agreed to take the message.

" 'Tell my wife,' said Tortoise, 'to bring out all the soft things in my house and cover the compound with them so that I can jump down from the sky without very great danger.'

"Parrot promised to deliver the message, and then flew away. But when he reached Tortoise's house he told his wife to bring out all the hard things in the house. And so she brought out her husband's hoes, machetes, spears, guns and even his cannon. Tortoise looked down from the sky and saw his wife bringing things out, but it was too far to see what they were. When all seemed ready he let himself go. He fell and fell and fell until he began to fear that he would never stop falling. And then like the sound of his cannon he crashed on the compound."

"Did he die?" asked Ezinma.

"No," replied Ekwefi. "His shell broke into pieces. But there was a great medicine man in the neighborhood. Tortoise's wife sent for him and he gathered all the bits of shell and stuck them together. That is why Tortoise's shell is not smooth."

How Mr. Rabbit Was
Too Sharp for Mr. Fox   *JOEL CHANDLER HARRIS*

U NCLE REMUS," said the little boy one evening, when he had found the old man with little or nothing to do, "did the fox kill and eat the rabbit when he caught him with the Tar-Baby?"

"Law, honey, ain't I tell you 'bout dat?" replied the old darkey, chuckling slyly. "I 'clar ter grashus I ought er tole you dat, but old man Nod wuz ridin' on my eyeleds 'twel a leetle mo'n I'd a dis'member'd my own name, en den on to dat here come yo' mammy hollerin' atter you.

"W'at I tell you w'en I fus' begin? I tole you Brer Rabbit wuz a monstus soon creetur; leas'ways dat's w'at I laid out fer ter tell you. Well, den, honey, don't you go en make no udder calkalashuns, kaze in dem days Brer Rabbit en his fambly wuz at de head er de gang w'en enny racket wuz on han', en dar dey stayed. 'Fo' you begins fer ter wipe yo' eyes 'bout Brer Rabbit, you wait en see whar'bouts Brer Rabbit gwineter fetch up at. But dat's needer yer ner dar.

"W'en Brer Fox fine Brer Rabbit mixt up wid de Tar-Baby, he feel mighty good, en he roll on de groun' en laff. Bimeby he up'n say, sezee:

" 'Well, I speck I got you dis time, Brer Rabbit,' sezee; 'maybe I ain't, but I speck I is. You been runnin' roun' here sassin' atter me a mighty long time, but I speck you done come ter de een' er de row. You bin cuttin' up yo' capers en bouncin' 'roun' in dis neighborhood ontwel you come ter b'leeve yo'se'f de boss er de whole gang. En den youer allers some'rs whar you got no bizness,' sez Brer Fox, sezee. 'Who ax you fer ter come en strike up a 'quaintance wid dish yer Tar-Baby? En who stuck you up dar whar you iz? Nobody in de roun' worril. You des tuck en jam yo'se'f on dat Tar-Baby widout waitin' fer

enny invite,' sez Brer Fox, sezee, 'en dar you is, en dar you'll stay twel
I fixes up a bresh-pile and fires her up, kaze I'm gwineter bobbycue
you dis day, sho,' sez Brer Fox, sezee.

"Den Brer Rabbit talk mighty 'umble.

" 'I don't keer w'at you do wid me, Brer Fox,' sezee, 'so you don't
fling me in dat brier-patch. Roas' me, Brer Fox,' sezee, 'but don't
fling me in dat brier-patch,' sezee.

" 'Hit's so much trouble fer ter kindle a fier,' sez Brer Fox, sezee,
'dat I speck I'll hatter hang you,' sezee.

" 'Hang me des ez high as you please, Brer Fox,' sez Brer Rabbit,
sezee, 'but do fer de Lord's sake don't fling me in dat brier-patch,'
sezee.

" 'I ain't got no string,' sez Brer Fox, sezee, 'en now I speck I'll
hatter drown you,' sezee.

" 'Drown me des ez deep ez you please, Brer Fox,' sez Brer Rabbit,
sezee, 'but do don't fling me in dat brier-patch,' sezee.

" 'Dey ain't no water nigh,' sez Brer Fox, sezee, 'en now I speck
I'll hatter skin you,' sezee.

" 'Skin me, Brer Fox,' sez Brer Rabbit, sezee, 'snatch out my eye-
balls, t'ar out my years by de roots, en cut off my legs,' sezee, 'but do
please, Brer Fox, don't fling me in dat brier-patch,' sezee.

"Co'se Brer Fox wanter hurt Brer Rabbit bad ez he kin, so he
cotch 'im by de behime legs en slung 'im right in de middle er de
brier-patch. Dar wuz a considerbul flutter whar Brer Rabbit struck
de bushes, en Brer Fox sorter hang 'roun' fer ter see w'at wuz gwineter happen. Bimeby he hear somebody call 'im, en way up de hill he
see Brer Rabbit settin' cross-legged on a chinkapin log koamin' de
pitch outen his har wid a chip. Den Brer Fox know dat he bin swop
off mighty bad. Brer Rabbit wuz bleedzed fer ter fling back some er his
sass, en he holler out:

" 'Bred en bawn in a brier-patch, Brer Fox—bred en bawn in a
brier-patch!' en wid dat he skip out des ez lively ez a cricket in de
embers."

*T*HERE'S MANY CONFLICTIN' stories about how Paul dug the Columbia River, but of course there's only one right one and that's the one I was just tellin' about the Inland Empire. I was right there and I saw how it was done. When Paul got his raft of logs finished and was ready to take 'em out he just went out there and plowed out the river. And there wasn't nothin' to it at all. He plowed it out first and then filled it up with water and evened it out so it would be nice and smooth for his logs to slide over. On a windy day in the Gorge when an east wind is blowin' you can see the hole yet in the water where Paul never put in the last bucketful when he was evenin' it out.

But some of them other stories is interestin' just to show how such stories grow up.

I know there's some that says it happened just by accident. Paul was havin' Babe pull a big log chain into a solid bar that he wanted, and the bar broke before it was finished, and Babe'd got such a start he couldn't stop, but run all the way to Astoria pullin' the piece of chain behind him. It cut up quite a scratch as it went along, and that scratch, they say, is the Columbia River.

I was in a little hotel up at Acme once, settin' at a table with some other loggers, and one of them settin' at the end eatin' pie, started in to tell how Paul dug the Columbia purposely, and how he used tamed mountain goats to do the work with. Proof of that is that there ain't no mountain goats south of the river now. Just at the time the water was turned in the teams of goats all happened to be workin' on the north side and that's why they haven't never got across.

It was partikkelarly interestin' to me, of course, because that fellow had the nerve to say that he was on that job

—Paul had him to trim the beards on his goats to keep 'em from gettin' all galled up. The beards used to grow long and get under the breast strap on the harness and rub until there was a sore there and then the goats wouldn't pull good.

Anyway, no matter what they say about it, the Columbia is a fine river to have a highway alongside of, the way they've got down there.

When he was loggin' in Oregon Paul built up Mt. Hood for a kind of lookout place, from where to watch his different camps; for he had a lot of foreigners workin' for him that year and they wouldn't work without somebody havin' to watch 'em all the time. Paul hired a kind of efficiency expert to help him on that, and that fellow, Gerber, used to walk around among the different camps and keep tab on the men and count up how they spent their time, and he certainly could make up some big figgurs, all right.

He always put down whenever anybody stopped to borrow a chew, and how long it took him, and counted up how long it took the men to light their pipes, or ask the time of day, or go for a drink, and kept tab on how much time was spent in talkin' baseball, or dodgin' the straw boss, or gettin' ready for quittin' time, and it always added up to a pretty considerable figgur, especially that last item. He used to try to make his accounts balance up with the time in the timekeeper's book, but he couldn't quite make that, though.

It was a hard job he had, all right, and he had to keep steppin' all the time.

He tried to increase his efficiency one time by swallowin' a watch and so makin' himself work automatic, but that didn't work out good, because the mainspring broke inside him and busted him.

The first watch he had, Paul had imported for him from Connecticut.

It was such a good watch it gained enough time in the first three days to pretty near pay for itself.

But when he bragged about it to Paul, Paul said he guessed he'd have to sell it. At that rate, he says, it might be Doomsday before he'd get his loggin' in Oregon done. And so Paul sold the watch afterwards to a fellow down in New Mexico. On account of the earth bein' bigger down there the watch wouldn't be able to gain so fast.

Paul made a good deal of lumber down in Oregon and most of it he shipped to Japan. He had a band saw in his mill and three different cutting floors, and a carriage on each one. The top band wheel was in the roof and the bottom one below the first floor. But when they started this mill runnin' the sawyer on the bottom begun kickin' because he was cuttin' with a dull saw all the time, and so then Paul punched teeth on the back side of the saw and pointed 'em upward and then ran the mill backwards every other day and that way they cut a lot of lumber, and everybody was satisfied.

Paul built one of the biggest steamships that was ever seen, to take his lumber to Japan. All the old steamboat men remember her. I know she had forty-two decks and not a single bottom and her boilers was all of rubber.

The way that happened, Paul wanted to load her mighty heavy and at the same time he wanted to make a great speed, and the engineer says to him:

"I can't go at any such rate as that," he says. "The boilers would bust if I tried to get up a pressure for a speed like that."

"Well, I tell you," says Paul, "make 'em of rubber then. That way they'll give, when we want 'em to, and then we can go just as fast as we've a mind to."

And so they made 'em of rubber, and they never had no accident with 'em. But of course the smokestack had to be awful big. I know one time Paul sent a man up to paint it, and a long time afterwards the man's grandson come down and asked if he could have some more paint.

Paul kept this lumber ship of his as long as he was loggin' in Oregon, but then he sold her. She was sunk afterwards, and the remainder of her is now called Catalina Island. The Wrigley Chewin' Gum Company salvaged the rubber boilers, and they're usin' some of the material yet for makin' their chewin' gum.

Paul liked Oregon all right, but one thing he sure didn't like and that was the fog. And it made him lose money too—the time they shingled the cook-shanty, f'rinstance, they shingled forty foot out on the fog before they noticed it, and there was all them perfectly good cedar shingles gone to waste, for when the fog lifted it was so thick it just took that part of the roof up with it.

Some of the people down in Oregon was always wantin' Paul to make somethin' for 'em, some place where tourists could go to spend their money before goin' to California, and they was after him all the time. And so finally he said he'd make Crater Lake for 'em—some of 'em had been sayin' they thought a lake like that would be nice—and he said, all right, he'd go ahead with it.

The snow left from the Winter of the Blue Snow was still layin' about fifty foot thick up on the tops of the Cascades and Paul went up with Babe to bring it down to make a lake of.

Babe got lost a number of times on the way up, by fallin' into drifts, and it made it hard to find him, because he was just about exactly the same color as the snow. And another thing was, his hoof-prints was so heavy—weighed pretty near a ton each—and if he got lost they was always so far apart it was a hard thing to carry 'em up and get the connection between 'em.

But Paul and Babe finally got there though, and Paul used a big scraper to haul out the snow, and he dumped all the loads in Crater Lake. Each load was 196 cubic tons, and there was 465 loads in all.

The snow meltin' in the lake the next summer made it blue, and it made it awful wintry cold too, at the same time, like it is. But it's a mighty pretty lake, though.

In fact the only job I ever knowed of Paul doin' that wasn't just up to snuff was the Palouse job, and that's one of them he done while he was loggin' in Oregon, too. He shouldn't of tackled it in the first place if he couldn't do it right, I always said.

The way it was: Old man Palouse hired him to come over and clear the Palouse country for him, and so then Paul went over there and logged it off and cleared the stumps out and scraped it up. But he had somethin' else on his mind all the time—another job he wanted to do—and so he didn't do a good job of it and never leveled it out smooth afterwards, the way he should of. Babe never liked that part of the work anyway. Always hated to lay on his side so long while Paul hauled him around to even out the bumps.

So Paul got in a hurry and wanted to get away from there, and so what he done was, he just got a couple of quarts of sagebrush whisky and went up to see old man Palouse, and gave him a drink or two, and then in the mornin' he took the old man up to the top of a high hill and showed him the country. Old man Palouse was pretty much gone from the drinks he'd had and anyway from where they was standin' the country looked real level and nice, so Paul got him to accept the contract and call it finished. And Paul tore away like a hurricane to his next job. He never could wait when he had a new job in sight, and so that's why the Palouse country is so hilly and rough like it is. Paul was always ashamed of himself for it, and they say he wept the Great Salt Lake full of tears because he was sorry, but I don't believe that. He made the lake, partly anyhow, to have salt on hand for Babe.

The job that Paul was goin' to when he left the Palouse country was one he'd invented himself, and took a notion of—not really new, of course, because it was somethin' the same as he'd done the time of the Underground Railroad.

He dug the Underground Railroad and let 'em use it for a time while they needed it, and then, afterwards, he made it over for the Standard Oil Company. The tube wasn't just in the right place and was a little too thick for a pipe-line, so he pulled it out long, and stretched it out all the way down to their oil fields in Texas for the Standard Oil people, and they was very well satisfied with the job he made of it.

The idea he had down in Oregon was, there was a good many holes in different parts of the state—prospectors' holes, where they'd been diggin' for gold, and oil wells they'd dug that hadn't never given no oil—and Paul thought if you could get all them holes together they'd be good to use for post-holes when the pioneers and farmers would come along afterwards. He could sell 'em at a profit maybe, or he might give 'em away to them that was needin' 'em. Anyway it was a shame to let 'em all go to waste.

So Paul took Babe, and they went out through the country and pulled up holes. It was light, easy work, because the holes didn't weigh much to speak of, and then Paul tied 'em all together in a string and took 'em to a mountain side to cache 'em—just made a hole in the mountain and pulled 'em through pretty near over to the other side, and then plugged up the hole.

And after he'd got it done he didn't think no more about it, but just went away and left 'em there.

Well, I don't know if Paul ever went back to look for them postholes or not, or if he ever means to go back again and try to locate 'em. Anyway, he wasn't there when they was found.

For when the Union Pacific was puttin' their railroad through there, the engineers was makin' surveys and, without knowin' it, they started in to put their tunnel right in the identical spot where Paul had hid all the holes.

The chief engineer set a gang of men to work diggin', and then he went away to tend to some other work, and the very first pick that was put in the mountain, they struck the holes, and the air that was in there started to come out. The heat of the friction from havin' been crowded in there so close blowed the whole crew of men off to nowheres so's they was never seen again. Just a little boy who they had for water carrier was left. He told the chief engineer what had happened, and the engineer seen the tunnel was all through and finished up in fine shape. So he didn't have to use no crew of men to dig the tunnel, but he collected for full time from the railroad company just the same—same as if he'd had a full company workin' all the time.

One time Paul'd went in for a little minin' himself.

The claim Paul staked out—and now I got to be careful, for minin' ain't in my line neither no more than it was Paul's—was from an old stump that was a landmark in that part of the country where he was then, just due southwest of where Mars cuts the Milky Way, then north 80 chains, 3 links and a swivel, then east 40 paces stepped off with the Blue Ox to a blue spot in the sky, then proceedin' South 38 chains 4 links, thence southwest to the stump where was the place of beginnin'—Paul'd had a lawyer help him make it out in the first place. It was a gold mine, and it had started out to be a placer deposit but had changed its mind afterwards. But of course on the outside it looked the same as it had always done.

Paul worked the mine for two months, he doin' all the work and furnishin' the provisions, and the lawyer sellin' the stock and collectin' the money. Paul said that lawyer wanted to borrow the Blue Ox, too, so's he could water the stock, but Paul drawed the line on that.

After workin' for a while, Paul took a little of the gravel to an assayer's office to have it tested—and now let me see if I can remember the right words for that. It was—igneous—prehistoric—and erroneous, that's what it was. Paul's mine was reported to be igneous, prehistoric, and erroneous.

And that was the first and last of Paul's minin' experiments, for he was sure plum disgusted. And from there he went back to his loggin' again, up near Astoria.

FAIRY TALE

Little Red-cap   *JAKOB AND WILHELM GRIMM*

*T*HERE WAS ONCE a sweet little maid, much beloved by everybody, but most of all by her grandmother, who never knew how to make enough of her. Once she sent her a little cap of red velvet, and as it was very becoming to her, and she never wore anything else, people called her Little Red-cap. One day her mother said to her,

"Come, Little Red-cap, here are some cakes and a flask of wine for you to take to grandmother; she is weak and ill, and they will do her good. Make haste and start before it grows hot, and walk properly and nicely, and don't run, or you might fall and break the flask of wine, and there would be none left for grandmother. And when you go into her room, don't forget to say, Good morning, instead of staring about you."

"I will be sure to take care," said Little Red-cap to her mother, and gave her hand upon it. Now the grandmother lived away in the wood, half-an-hour's walk from the village; and when Little Red-cap had reached the wood, she met the wolf; but as she did not know what a bad sort of animal he was, she did not feel frightened.

"Good day, Little Red-cap," said he.

"Thank you kindly, Wolf," answered she.

"Where are you going so early, Little Red-cap?"

"To my grandmother's."

"What are you carrying under your apron?"

"Cakes and wine; we baked yesterday; and my grandmother is very weak and ill, so they will do her good, and strengthen her."

"Where does your grandmother live, Little Red-cap?"

"A quarter of an hour's walk from here; her house stands beneath the three oak trees, and you may know it by the hazel bushes," said Little Red-cap. The wolf thought to himself,

"That tender young thing would be a delicious morsel, and would taste better than the old one; I must manage somehow to get both of them."

Then he walked by Little Red-cap a little while, and said,

"Little Red-cap, just look at the pretty flowers that are growing all round you, and I don't think you are listening to the song of the birds; you are posting along just as if you were going to school, and it is so delightful out here in the wood."

Little Red-cap glanced round her, and when she saw the sunbeams darting here and there through the trees, and lovely flowers everywhere, she thought to herself,

"If I were to take a fresh nosegay to my grandmother she would be very pleased, and it is so early in the day that I shall reach her in plenty of time"; and so she ran about in the wood, looking for flowers. And as she picked one she saw a still prettier one a little farther off, and so she went farther and farther into the wood. But the wolf went straight to the grandmother's house and knocked at the door.

"Who is there?" cried the grandmother.

"Little Red-cap," he answered, "and I have brought you some cake and wine. Please open the door."

"Lift the latch," cried the grandmother; "I am too feeble to get up."

So the wolf lifted the latch, and the door flew open, and he fell on the grandmother and ate her up without saying one word. Then he drew on her clothes, put on her cap, lay down in her bed, and drew the curtains.

Little Red-cap was all this time running about among the flowers, and when she had gathered as many as she could hold, she remembered her grandmother, and set off to go to her. She was surprised to find the door standing open, and when she came inside she felt very strange, and thought to herself,

"Oh dear, how uncomfortable I feel, and I was so glad this morning to go to my grandmother!"

And when she said, "Good morning," there was no answer. Then she went up to the bed and drew back the curtains; there lay the grandmother with her cap pulled over her eyes, so that she looked very odd.

"O grandmother, what large ears you have got!"

"The better to hear with."

"O grandmother, what great eyes you have got!"

"The better to see with."

"O grandmother, what large hands you have got!"

"The better to take hold of you with."

"But, grandmother, what a terrible large mouth you have got!"

"The better to devour you!" And no sooner had the wolf said it than he made one bound from the bed, and swallowed up poor Little Red-cap.

Then the wolf, having satisfied his hunger, lay down again in the bed, went to sleep, and began to snore loudly. The huntsman heard him as he was passing by the house, and thought,

"How the old woman snores—I had better see if there is anything the matter with her."

Then he went into the room, and walked up to the bed, and saw the wolf lying there.

"At last I find you, you old sinner!" said he; "I have been looking for you a long time." And he made up his mind that the wolf had swallowed the grandmother whole, and that she might yet be saved. So he did not fire, but took a pair of shears and began to slit up the wolf's body. When he made a few snips Little Red-cap appeared, and after a few more snips she jumped out and cried, "Oh dear, how frightened I have been! it is so dark inside the wolf." And then out came the old grandmother, still living and breathing. But Little Red-cap went and quickly fetched some large stones, with which she filled the wolf's body, so that when he waked up, and was going to rush away, the stones were so heavy that he sank down and fell dead.

They were all three very pleased. The huntsman took off the wolf's skin, and carried it home. The grandmother ate the cakes, and drank the wine, and held up her head again, and Little Red-cap said to herself that she would never more stray about in the wood alone, but would mind what her mother told her.

It must also be related how a few days afterwards, when Little

Red-cap was again taking cakes to her grandmother, another wolf spoke to her, and wanted to tempt her to leave the path; but she was on her guard, and went straight on her way, and told her grandmother how that the wolf had met her, and wished her good-day, but had looked so wicked about the eyes that she thought if it had not been on the high road he would have devoured her.

"Come," said the grandmother, "we will shut the door, so that he may not get in."

Soon after came the wolf knocking at the door, and calling out, "Open the door, grandmother, I am Little Red-cap, bringing you cakes." But they remained still, and did not open the door. After that the wolf slunk by the house, and got at last upon the roof to wait until Little Red-cap should return home in the evening; then he meant to spring down upon her, and devour her in the darkness. But the grandmother discovered his plot. Now there stood before the house a great stone trough, and the grandmother said to the child, "Little Red-cap, I was boiling sausages yesterday, so take the bucket, and carry away the water they were boiled in, and pour it into the trough."

And Little Red-cap did so until the great trough was quite full. When the smell of the sausages reached the nose of the wolf he snuffed it up, and looked round, and stretched out his neck so far that he lost his balance and began to slip, and he slipped down off the roof straight into the great trough, and was drowned. Then Little Red-cap went cheerfully home, and came to no harm.

I N TIMES PAST there lived a king and queen, who said
to each other every day of their lives, "Would that we
had a child!" and yet they had none. But it happened
once that when the queen was bathing, there came a frog
out of the water, and he squatted on the ground, and said
to her,

"Thy wish shall be fulfilled; before a year has gone by,
thou shalt bring a daughter into the world."

And as the frog foretold, so it happened; and the queen
bore a daughter so beautiful that the king could not contain himself for joy, and he ordained a great feast. Not
only did he bid to it his relations, friends, and acquaintances, but also the wise women, that they might be kind
and favourable to the child. There were thirteen of them
in his kingdom, but as he had only provided twelve
golden plates for them to eat from, one of them had to be
left out. However, the feast was celebrated with all
splendour; and as it drew to an end, the wise women
stood forward to present to the child their wonderful
gifts: one bestowed virtue, one beauty, a third riches,
and so on, whatever there is in the world to wish for. And
when eleven of them had said their say, in came the un-
invited thirteenth, burning to revenge herself, and without greeting or respect, she cried with a loud voice,

"In the fifteenth year of her age the princess shall
prick herself with a spindle and shall fall down dead."

And without speaking one more word she turned away
and left the hall. Every one was terrified at her saying,
when the twelfth came forward, for she had not yet bestowed her gift, and though she could not do away with
the evil prophecy, yet she could soften it, so she said,

"The princess shall not die, but fall into a deep sleep
for a hundred years."

Now the king, being desirous of saving his child even from this misfortune, gave commandment that all the spindles in his kingdom should be burnt up.

The maiden grew up, adorned with all the gifts of the wise women; and she was so lovely, modest, sweet, and kind and clever, that no one who saw her could help loving her.

It happened one day, she being already fifteen years old, that the king and queen rode abroad, and the maiden was left behind alone in the castle. She wandered about into all the nooks and corners, and into all the chambers and parlours, as the fancy took her, till at last she came to an old tower. She climbed the narrow winding stair which led to a little door, with a rusty key sticking out of the lock; she turned the key, and the door opened, and there in the little room sat an old woman with a spindle, diligently spinning her flax.

"Good day, mother," said the princess, "what are you doing?"

"I am spinning," answered the old woman, nodding her head.

"What thing is that that twists round so briskly?" asked the maiden, and taking the spindle into her hand she began to spin; but no sooner had she touched it than the evil prophecy was fulfilled, and she pricked her finger with it. In that very moment she fell back upon the bed that stood there, and lay in a deep sleep. And this sleep fell upon the whole castle; the king and queen, who had returned and were in the great hall, fell fast asleep, and with them the whole court. The horses in their stalls, the dogs in the yard, the pigeons on the roof, the flies on the wall, the very fire that flickered on the hearth, became still, and slept like the rest; and the meat on the spit ceased roasting, and the cook, who was going to pull the scullion's hair for some mistake he had made, let him go, and went to sleep. And the wind ceased, and not a leaf fell from the trees about the castle.

Then round about that place there grew a hedge of thorns thicker every year, until at last the whole castle was hidden from view, and nothing of it could be seen but the vane on the roof. And a rumour went abroad in all that country of the beautiful sleeping Rosamond, for so was the princess called; and from time to time many kings' sons came and tried to force their way through the hedge; but it was impossible for them to do so, for the thorns held fast together like strong hands, and the young men were caught by them, and not being able to get free, there died a lamentable death.

Many a long year afterwards there came a king's son into that country, and heard an old man tell how there should be a castle standing behind the hedge of thorns, and that there a beautiful enchanted princess named Rosamond had slept for a hundred years, and with her the king and queen, and the whole court. The old man had been told by his grandfather that many king's sons had sought to pass the thorn-hedge, but had been caught and pierced by the thorns, and had died a miserable death. Then said the young man, "Nevertheless, I do not fear to try; I shall win through and see the lovely Rosamond." The good old man tried to dissuade him, but he would not listen to his words.

For now the hundred years were at an end, and the day had come when Rosamond should be awakened. When the prince drew near the hedge of thorns, it was changed into a hedge of beautiful large flowers, which parted and bent aside to let him pass, and then closed behind him in a thick hedge. When he reached the castle-yard, he saw the horses and brindled hunting-dogs lying asleep, and on the roof the pigeons were sitting with their heads under their wings. And when he came indoors, the flies on the wall were asleep, the cook in the kitchen had his hand uplifted to strike the scullion, and the kitchen-maid had the black fowl on her lap ready to pluck. Then he mounted higher, and saw in the hall the whole court lying asleep, and above them, on their thrones, slept the king and the queen. And still he went farther, and all was so quiet that he could hear his own breathing; and at last he came to the tower, and went up the winding stair, and opened the door of the little room where Rosamond lay. And when he saw her looking so lovely in her sleep, he could not turn away his eyes; and presently he stooped and kissed her, and she awaked, and opened her eyes, and looked very kindly on him. And she rose, and they went forth together, and the king and the queen and whole court waked up, and gazed on each other with great eyes of wonderment. And the horses in the yard got up and shook themselves, the hounds sprang up and wagged their tails, the pigeons on the roof drew their heads from under their wings, looked around, and flew into the field, the flies on the wall crept on a little farther, the kitchen fire leapt up and blazed, and cooked the meat, the joint on the spit began to roast, the cook gave the scullion such a box on the ear that he roared out, and the maid went on plucking the fowl.

Then the wedding of the Prince and Rosamond was held with all splendour, and they lived very happily together until their lives' end.

Hansel
and Grethel   *JAKOB AND WILHELM GRIMM*

NEAR A GREAT FOREST there lived a poor woodcutter
and his wife, and his two children; the boy's name was
Hansel and the girl's Grethel. They had very little to
bite or to sup, and once, when there was great dearth in
the land, the man could not even gain the daily bread.
As he lay in bed one night thinking of this, and turning
and tossing, he sighed heavily, and said to his wife,

"What will become of us? we cannot even feed our
children; there is nothing left for ourselves."

"I will tell you what, husband," answered the wife;
"we will take the children early in the morning into the
forest, where it is thickest; we will make them a fire, and
we will give each of them a piece of bread, then we will
go to our work and leave them alone; they will never find
the way home again, and we shall be quit of them."

"No, wife," said the man, "I cannot do that; I cannot
find in my heart to take my children into the forest and
to leave them there alone; the wild animals would soon
come and devour them."

"O you fool," said she, "then we will all four starve;
you had better get the coffins ready,"—and she left him no
peace until he consented.

"But I really pity the poor children," said the man.

The two children had not been able to sleep for hunger, and had heard what their step-mother had said to
their father. Grethel wept bitterly, and said to Hansel,

"It is all over with us."

"Do be quiet, Grethel," said Hansel, "and do not fret;
I will manage something." And when the parents had
gone to sleep he got up, put on his little coat, opened the
back door, and slipped out. The moon was shining
brightly, and the white flints that lay in front of the

house glistened like pieces of silver. Hansel stooped and filled the little pocket of his coat as full as it would hold. Then he went back again, and said to Grethel,

"Be easy, dear little sister, and go to sleep quietly; God will not forsake us," and laid himself down again in his bed.

When the day was breaking, and before the sun had risen, the wife came and awakened the two children, saying,

"Get up, you lazy bones; we are going into the forest to cut wood."

Then she gave each of them a piece of bread, and said,

"That is for dinner, and you must not eat it before then, for you will get no more."

Grethel carried the bread under her apron, for Hansel had his pockets full of the flints. Then they set off all together on their way to the forest. When they had gone a little way Hansel stood still and looked back towards the house, and this he did again and again, till his father said to him,

"Hansel, what are you looking at? take care not to forget your legs."

"O father," said Hansel, "I am looking at my little white kitten, who is sitting up on the roof to bid me good-bye."

"You young fool," said the woman, "that is not your kitten, but the sunshine on the chimney-pot."

Of course Hansel had not been looking at his kitten, but had been taking every now and then a flint from his pocket and dropping it on the road.

When they reached the middle of the forest the father told the children to collect wood to make a fire to keep them warm; and Hansel and Grethel gathered brushwood enough for a little mountain; and it was set on fire, and when the flame was burning quite high the wife said,

"Now lie down by the fire and rest yourselves, you children, and we will go and cut wood; and when we are ready we will come and fetch you."

So Hansel and Grethel sat by the fire, and at noon they each ate their pieces of bread. They thought their father was in the wood all the time, as they seemed to hear the strokes of the axe: but really it was only a dry branch hanging to a withered tree that the wind moved to and fro. So when they had stayed there a long time their eyelids closed with weariness, and they fell fast asleep. When at last they woke it was night, and Grethel began to cry, and said,

"How shall we ever get out of this wood?" But Hansel comforted her, saying,

"Wait a little while longer, until the moon rises, and then we can easily find the way home."

And when the full moon got up Hansel took his little sister by the hand, and followed the way where the flint stones shone like silver, and showed them the road. They walked on the whole night through, and at the break of day they came to their father's house. They knocked at the door, and when the wife opened it and saw that it was Hansel and Grethel she said,

"You naughty children, why did you sleep so long in the wood? we thought you were never coming home again!"

But the father was glad, for it had gone to his heart to leave them both in the woods alone.

Not very long after that there was again great scarcity in those parts, and the children heard their mother say at night in bed to their father,

"Everything is finished up; we have only half a loaf, and after that the tale comes to an end. The children must be off; we will take them farther into the wood this time, so that they shall not be able to find the way back again; there is no other way to manage."

The man felt sad at heart, and he thought,

"It would better to share one's last morsel with one's children."

But the wife would listen to nothing that he said, but scolded and reproached him. He who says A must say B too, and when a man has given in once he has to do it a second time.

But the children were not asleep, and had heard all the talk. When the parents had gone to sleep Hansel got up to go out and get more flint stones, as he did before, but the wife had locked the door, and Hansel could not get out; but he comforted his little sister, and said,

"Don't cry, Grethel, and go to sleep quietly, and God will help us."

Early the next morning the wife came and pulled the children out of bed. She gave them each a little piece of bread—less than before; and on the way to the wood Hansel crumbled the bread in his pocket, and often stopped to throw a crumb on the ground.

"Hansel, what are you stopping behind and staring for?" said the father.

"I am looking at my little pigeon sitting on the roof, to say good-bye to me," answered Hansel.

"You fool," said the wife, "that is no pigeon, but the morning sun shining on the chimney pots."

Hansel went on as before, and strewed bread crumbs all along the road.

The woman led the children far into the wood, where they had never been before in all their lives. And again there was a large fire made, and the mother said,

"Sit still there, you children, and when you are tired you can go to sleep; we are going into the forest to cut wood, and in the evening, when we are ready to go home we will come and fetch you."

So when noon came Grethel shared her bread with Hansel, who had strewed his along the road. Then they went to sleep, and the evening passed, and no one came for the poor children. When they awoke it was dark night, and Hansel comforted his little sister, and said,

"Wait a little, Grethel, until the moon gets up, then we shall be able to see the way home by the crumbs of bread that I have scattered along it."

So when the moon rose they got up, but they could find no crumbs of bread, for the birds of the woods and of the fields had come and picked them up. Hansel thought they might find the way all the same, but they could not. They went on all that night, and the next day from the morning until the evening, but they could not find the way out of the wood, and they were very hungry, for they had nothing to eat but the few berries they could pick up. And when they were so tired that they could no longer drag themselves along, they lay down under a tree and fell asleep.

It was now the third morning since they had left their father's house. They were always trying to get back to it, but instead of that they only found themselves farther in the wood, and if help had not soon come they would have been starved. About noon they saw a pretty snow-white bird sitting on a bough, and singing so sweetly that they stopped to listen. And when he had finished the bird spread his wings and flew before them, and they followed after him until they came to a little house, and the bird perched on the roof, and when they came nearer they saw that the house was built of bread, and roofed with cakes; and the window was of transparent sugar.

"We will have some of this," said Hansel, "and make a fine meal. I will eat a piece of the roof, Grethel, and you can have some of the window—that will taste sweet."

So Hansel reached up and broke off a bit of the roof, just to see how it tasted, and Grethel stood by the window and gnawed at it. Then they heard a thin voice call out from inside,

> *"Nibble, nibble, like a mouse,*
> *Who is nibbling at my house?"*

And the children answered,

> *"Never mind,*
> *It is the wind."*

And they went on eating, never disturbing themselves. Hansel, who found that the roof tasted very nice, took down a great piece of it, and Grethel pulled out a large round windowpane, and sat her down and began upon it. Then the door opened, and an aged woman came out, leaning upon a crutch. Hansel and Grethel felt very frightened, and let fall what they had in their hands. The old woman, however, nodded her head, and said,

"Ah, my dear children, how come you here? you must come indoors and stay with me, you will be no trouble."

So she took them each by the hand, and led them into her little house. And there they found a good meal laid out, of milk and pancakes, with sugar, apples, and nuts. After that she showed them two little white beds, and Hansel and Grethel laid themselves down on them, and thought they were in heaven.

The old woman, although her behaviour was so kind, was a wicked witch, who lay in wait for children, and had built the little house on purpose to entice them. When they were once inside she used to kill them, cook them, and eat them, and then it was a feast-day with her. The witch's eyes were red, and she could not see very far, but she had a keen scent, like the beasts, and knew very well when human creatures were near. When she knew that Hansel and Grethel were coming, she gave a spiteful laugh, and said triumphantly,

"I have them, and they shall not escape me!"

Early in the morning, before the children were awake, she got up to look at them, and as they lay sleeping so peacefully with round rosy cheeks, she said to herself,

"What a fine feast I shall have!"

Then she grasped Hansel with her withered hand, and led him into a little stable, and shut him up behind a grating; and call and scream as he might, it was no good. Then she went back to Grethel and shook her, crying,

"Get up, lazy bones; fetch water, and cook something nice for your brother; he is outside in the stable, and must be fattened up. And when he is fat enough I will eat him."

Grethel began to weep bitterly, but it was of no use, she had to do what the wicked witch bade her.

And so the best kind of victuals was cooked for poor Hansel, while Grethel got nothing but crab-shells. Each morning the old woman visited the little stable, and cried,

"Hansel, stretch out your finger, that I may tell if you will soon be fat enough."

Hansel, however, used to hold out a little bone, and the old woman, who had weak eyes, could not see what it was, and supposing it to be Hansel's finger, wondered very much that it was not getting fatter. When four weeks had passed and Hansel seemed to remain so thin, she lost patience and could wait no longer.

"Now then, Grethel," cried she to the little girl; "be quick and draw water; be Hansel fat or be he lean, to-morrow I must kill and cook him."

Oh what a grief for the poor little sister to have to fetch water, and how the tears flowed down over her cheeks!

"Dear God, pray help us!" cried she; "if we had been devoured by wild beasts in the wood at least we should have died together."

"Spare me your lamentations," said the old woman; "they are of no avail."

Early next morning Grethel had to get up, make the fire, and fill the kettle.

"First we will do the baking," said the old woman; "I have heated the oven already, and kneaded the dough."

She pushed poor Grethel towards the oven, out of which the flames were already shining.

"Creep in," said the witch, "and see if it is properly hot, so that the bread may be baked."

And Grethel once in, she meant to shut the door upon her and let her be baked, and then she would have eaten her. But Grethel perceived her intention, and said,

"I don't know how to do it: how shall I get in?"

"Stupid goose," said the old woman, "the opening is big enough, do you see? I could get in myself!" and she stooped down and put her head in the oven's mouth. Then Grethel gave her a push, so that she went in farther, and she shut the iron door upon her, and put up the bar. Oh how frightfully she howled! but Grethel ran away, and left the wicked witch to burn miserably. Grethel went straight to Hansel, opened the stable door, and cried,

"Hansel, we are free! the old witch is dead!"

Then out flew Hansel like a bird from its cage as soon as the door is opened. How rejoiced they both were! how they fell each on the other's neck! and danced about, and kissed each other! And as they had nothing more to fear they went over all the old witch's house, and in every corner there stood chests of pearls and precious stones.

"This is something better than flint stones," said Hansel, as he filled his pockets, and Grethel, thinking she also would like to carry something home with her, filled her apron full.

"Now, away we go," said Hansel;—"if we only can get out of the witch's wood."

When they had journeyed a few hours they came to a great piece of water.

"We can never get across this," said Hansel, "I see no stepping-stones and no bridge."

"And there is no boat either," said Grethel; "but here comes a white duck; if I ask her she will help us over." So she cried,

> *"Duck, duck, here we stand,*
> *Hansel and Grethel, on the land,*
> *Stepping-stones and bridge we lack,*
> *Carry us over on your nice white back."*

And the duck came accordingly, and Hansel got upon her and told his sister to come too.

"No," answered Grethel, "that would be too hard upon the duck; we can go separately, one after the other."

And that was how it was managed, and after that they went on happily, until they came to the wood, and the way grew more and more familiar, till at last they saw in the distance their father's house. Then they ran till they came up to it, rushed in at the door, and fell on their father's neck. The man had not had a quiet hour since he left his children in the wood; but the wife was dead. And when Grethel opened her apron the pearls and precious stones were scattered all over the room, and Hansel took one handful after another out of his pocket. Then was all care at an end, and they lived in great joy together.

A SOLDIER CAME MARCHING down the road: Left . . . right! Left . . . right! He had a pack on his back and a sword at his side. He had been in the war and he was on his way home. Along the road he met a witch. She was a disgusting sight, with a lower lip that hung all the way down to her chest.

"Good evening, young soldier," she said. "What a handsome sword you have and what a big knapsack. I can see that you are a real soldier! I shall give you all the money that you want."

"Thank you, old witch," he said.

"Do you see that big tree?" asked the witch, and pointed to the one they were standing next to. "The trunk is hollow. You climb up to the top of the tree, crawl into the hole, and slide deep down inside it. I'll tie a rope around your waist, so I can pull you up again when you call me."

"What am I supposed to do down in the tree?" asked the soldier.

"Get money!" answered the witch and laughed. "Now listen to me. When you get down to the very bottom, you'll be in a great passageway where you'll be able to see because there are over a hundred lamps burning. You'll find three doors; and you can open them all because the keys are in the locks. Go into the first one; and there on a chest, in the middle of the room, you'll see a dog with eyes as big as teacups. Don't let that worry you. You will have my blue checkered apron; just spread it out on the floor, put the dog down on top of it, and it won't do you any harm. Open the chest and take as many coins as you wish, they are all copper. If it's silver you're after, then go into the next room. There you'll find a dog with eyes as big as millstones; but don't let that worry you, put him on the apron and take the money. If you'd rather have gold, you can have that too; it's in the third room. Wait till you see that dog, he's got eyes as big as the Round Tower in Copenhagen; but don't let that worry you. Put him down on my apron and he won't hurt you; then you can take as much gold as you wish."

"That doesn't sound bad!" said the soldier. "But what am I to do for you, old witch? I can't help thinking that you must want something too."

"No," replied the witch. "I don't want one single coin. Just bring me the old tinderbox that my grandmother forgot the last time she was down there."

"I'm ready, tie the rope around my waist!" ordered the soldier.

"There you are, and here is my blue checkered apron," said the witch.

The soldier climbed the tree, let himself fall into the hole, and found that he was in the passageway, where more than a hundred lights burned.

He opened the first door. Oh! There sat the dog with eyes as big as teacups glaring at him.

"You are a handsome fellow!" he exclaimed as he put the dog down on the witch's apron. He filled his pockets with copper coins, closed the chest, and put the dog back on top of it.

He went into the second room. Aha! There sat the dog with eyes as big as millstones. "Don't keep looking at me like that," said the soldier good-naturedly. "It isn't polite and you'll spoil your eyes." He put the dog down on the witch's apron and opened the chest. When he saw all the silver coins, he emptied the copper out of his pockets and filled both them and his knapsack with silver.

Now he entered the third room. That dog was big enough to frighten anyone, even a soldier. His eyes were as large as the Round Tower in Copenhagen and they turned around like wheels.

"Good evening," said the soldier politely, taking off his cap, for such a dog he had never seen before. For a while he just stood looking at it; but finally he said to himself, "Enough of this!" Then he put the dog down on the witch's apron and opened up the chest.

"God preserve me!" he cried. There was so much gold that there was enough to buy the whole city of Copenhagen; and all the ginger-bread men, rocking horses, riding whips, and tin soldiers in the whole world.

Quickly the soldier threw away all the silver coins that he had in his pockets and knapsack and put gold in them instead; he even filled his boots and his cap with money. He put the dog back on the chest, closed the door behind him, and called up through the hollow tree.

"Pull me up, you old witch!"

"Have you got the tinderbox?" she called back.

"Right you are, I have forgotten it," he replied honestly, and went back to get it. The witch hoisted him up and again he stood on the road; but now his pockets, knapsack, cap, and boots were filled with gold and he felt quite differently.

"Why do you want the tinderbox?" he asked.

"Mind your own business," answered the witch crossly. "You have got your money, just give me the tinderbox."

"Blah! Blah!" said the soldier. "Tell me what you are going to use it for, right now; or I'll draw my sword and cut off your head."

"No!" replied the witch firmly; but that was a mistake, for the soldier chopped her head off. She lay there dead. The soldier put all his gold in her apron, tied it up into a bundle, and threw it over his shoulder. The tinderbox he dropped into his pocket; and off to town he went.

The town was nice, and the soldier went to the nicest inn, where he asked to be put up in the finest room and ordered all the things he liked to eat best for his supper, because now he had so much money that he was rich.

The servant who polished his boots thought it was very odd that a man so wealthy should have such worn-out boots. But the soldier hadn't had time to buy anything yet; the next day he bought boots and clothes that fitted his purse. And the soldier became a refined gentleman. People were eager to tell him all about their town and their king, and what a lovely princess his daughter was.

"I would like to see her," said the soldier.

"But no one sees her," explained the townfolk. "She lives in a copper castle, surrounded by walls, and towers, and a moat. The king doesn't dare allow anyone to visit her because it has been foretold that she will marry a simple soldier, and the king doesn't want that to happen."

"If only I could see her," thought the soldier, though it was unthinkable.

The soldier lived merrily, went to the theater, kept a carriage so he could drive in the king's park, and gave lots of money to the poor. He remembered well what it felt like not to have a penny in his purse.

He was rich and well dressed. He had many friends; and they all said that he was kind and a real cavalier; and such things he liked to hear. But since he used money every day and never received any, he soon had only two copper coins left.

He had to move out of the beautiful room downstairs, up to a tiny one in the garret, where he not only polished his boots himself but also mended them with a large needle. None of his friends came to see him, for they said there were too many stairs to climb.

It was a very dark evening and he could not even buy a candle. Suddenly he remembered that he had seen the stub of a candle in the tinderbox that he had brought up from the bottom of the hollow tree. He found the tinderbox and took out the candle. He struck the flint. There was a spark, and in through the door came the dog with eyes as big as teacups.

"What does my master command?" asked the dog.

"What's this all about?" exclaimed the soldier. "That certainly was an interesting tinderbox. Can I have whatever I want? Bring me some money," he ordered. In less time than it takes to say thank you, the dog was gone and back with a big sack of copper coins in his mouth.

Now the soldier understood why the witch had thought the tinderbox so valuable. If he struck it once, the dog appeared who sat on the chest full of copper coins; if he struck it twice, then the dog came who guarded the silver money; and if he struck it three times, then came the one who had the gold.

The soldier moved downstairs again, wore fine clothes again, and had fine friends, for now they all remembered him and cared for him as they had before.

One night, when he was sitting alone after his friends had gone, he thought, "It is a pity that no one can see that beautiful princess. What is the good of her beauty if she must always remain behind the high walls and towers of a copper castle? Will I never see her? . . . Where is my tinderbox?"

He made the sparks fly and the dog with eyes as big as teacups came. "I know it's very late at night," he said, "but I would so like to see the beautiful princess, if only for a minute."

Away went the dog; and faster than thought he returned with the sleeping princess on his back. She was so lovely that anyone would have known that she was a real princess. The soldier could not help kissing her, for he was a true soldier.

The dog brought the princess back to her copper castle; but in the morning while she was having tea with her father and mother, the king and queen, she told them that she had had a very strange dream that night. A large dog had come and carried her away to a soldier who kissed her.

"That's a nice story," said the queen, but she didn't mean it.

The next night one of the older ladies in waiting was sent to watch over the princess while she slept, and find out whether it had only been a dream, and not something worse.

The soldier longed to see the princess so much that he couldn't bear it, so at night he sent the dog to fetch her. The dog ran as fast as he could, but the lady in waiting had her boots on and she kept up with him all the way. When she saw which house he had entered, she took out a piece of chalk and made a big white cross on the door.

"Now we'll be able to find it in the morning," she thought, and went home to get some sleep.

When the dog returned the princess to the castle, he noticed the cross on the door of the house where his master lived; so he took a piece of white chalk and put crosses on all the doors of all the houses in the whole town. It was a very clever thing to do, for now the lady in waiting would never know which was the right door.

The next morning the king and queen, the old lady in waiting, and all the royal officers went out into town to find the house where the princess had been.

"Here it is!" exclaimed the king, when he saw the first door with a cross on it.

"No, my sweet husband, it is here," said his wife, who had seen the second door with a cross on it.

"Here's one!"

"There's one!"

Everyone shouted at once, for it didn't matter where anyone looked: there he would find a door with a cross on it; and so they all gave up.

Now the queen was so clever, she could do more than ride in a golden carriage. She took out her golden scissors and cut out a large piece of silk and sewed it into a pretty little bag. This she filled with the fine grain of buckwheat, and tied the bag around the princess' waist. When this was done, she cut a little hole in the bag just big enough for the little grains of buckwheat to fall out, one at a time, and show the way to the house where the princess was taken by the dog.

During the night the dog came to fetch the princess and carry her on his back to the soldier, who loved her so much that now he had only one desire, and that was to be a prince so that he could marry her.

The dog neither saw nor felt the grains of buckwheat that made a little trail all the way from the copper castle to the soldier's room at the inn. In the morning the king and queen had no difficulty in finding where the princess had been, and the soldier was thrown into jail.

There he sat in the dark with nothing to do; and what made matters worse was that everyone said, "Tomorrow you are going to be hanged!"

That was not amusing to hear. If only he had had his tinderbox, but he had forgotten it in his room. When the sun rose, he watched the people, through the bars of his window, as they hurried toward the gates of the city, for the hanging was to take place outside the walls. He heard the drums and the royal soldiers marching. Everyone was running. He saw a shoemaker's apprentice, who had not bothered to take off his leather apron and was wearing slippers. The boy lifted his legs so high, it looked as though he were galloping. One of his slippers flew off and landed near the window of the soldier's cell.

"Hey!" shouted the soldier. "Listen, shoemaker, wait a minute, nothing much will happen before I get there. But if you will run to the inn and get the tinderbox I left in my room, you can earn four copper coins. But you'd better use your legs or it will be too late."

The shoemaker's apprentice, who didn't have one copper coin, was eager to earn four; and he ran to get the tinderbox as fast as he could; and gave it to the soldier.

And now you shall hear what happened after that!

Outside the gates of the town, a gallows had been built; around it stood the royal soldiers and many hundreds of thousands of people. The king and the queen sat on their lovely throne, and across from them sat the judge and the royal council.

The soldier was standing on the plaftorm, but as the noose was put around his neck, he declared that it was an ancient custom to grant a condemned man his last innocent wish. The only thing he wanted was to be allowed to smoke a pipe of tobacco.

The king couldn't refuse; and the soldier took out his tinderbox and struck it: once, twice, three times! Instantly, the three dogs were before him: the one with eyes as big as teacups, the one with eyes as big as millstones, and the one with eyes as big as the Round Tower in Copenhagen.

"Help me! I don't want to be hanged!" cried the soldier.

The dogs ran toward the judge and the royal council. They took one man by the leg and another by the nose, and threw them up in the air, so high that when they hit the earth again they broke into little pieces.

"Not me!" screamed the king; but the biggest dog took both the king and the queen and sent them flying up as high as all the others had been.

The royal guards got frightened; and the people began to shout: "Little soldier, you shall be our king and marry the princess!"

The soldier rode in the king's golden carriage; and the three dogs danced in front of it and barked: "Hurrah!"

The little boys whistled and the royal guards presented arms. The princess came out of her copper castle and became queen, which she liked very much. The wedding feast lasted a week; and the three dogs sat at the table and made eyes at everyone.

"I saw a ship sailing upon the sea,
Deeply laden as ship could be;
But not so deep as in love I am,
For I care not whether I sink or swim."
Old Ballad

"But Love is such a Mystery
I cannot find it out:
For when I think I'm best resolv'd,
I then am in most doubt."
SIR JOHN SUCKLING

O NE STORY I WILL try to reproduce. But, alas! it is like trying to reconstruct a forest out of broken branches and withered leaves. In the fairy book, everything was just as it should be, though whether in words or something else, I cannot tell. It glowed and flashed the thoughts upon the soul, with such a power that the medium disappeared from the consciousness, and it was occupied only with the things themselves. My representation of it must resemble a translation from a rich and powerful language, capable of embodying the thoughts of a splendidly developed people, into the meagre and half-articulate speech of a savage tribe. Of course, while I read it, I was Cosmo, and his history was mine. Yet, all the time, I seemed to have a kind of double consciousness, and the story a double meaning. Sometimes it seemed only to represent a simple story of ordinary life, perhaps almost of universal life; wherein two souls, loving each other and longing to come nearer do, after all, but behold each other as in a glass darkly.

As through the hard rock go the branching silver veins; as into the solid land run the creeks and gulfs from the unresting sea; as the lights and influences of the upper worlds sink silently through the earth's atmosphere; so doth Faerie invade the world of men, and sometimes startle the common eye with an association as of cause and effect, when between the two no connecting links can be traced.

Cosmo von Wehrstahl was a student at the University of Prague. Though of a noble family, he was poor, and prided himself upon the independence that poverty gives; for what will not a man pride himself upon, when he cannot get rid of it? A favourite with his fellow-students, he yet had no companions; and none of them had ever crossed the threshold of his lodging in the top of one of the highest houses in the old town. Indeed, the secret of much of that complaisance which recommended him to his fellows, was the thought of his unknown retreat, whither in the evening he could betake himself and indulge undisturbed in his own studies and reveries. These studies, besides those subjects necessary to his course at the University, embraced some less commonly known and approved; for in a secret drawer lay the works of Albertus Magnus and Cornelius Agrippa, along with others less read and more abstruse. As yet, however, he had followed these researches only from curiosity, and had turned them to no practical purpose.

His lodging consisted of one large low-ceiled room, singularly bare of furniture; for besides a couple of wooden chairs, a couch which served for dreaming on both by day and night, and a great press of black oak, there was very little in the room that could be called furniture. But curious instruments were heaped in the corners; and in one stood a skeleton, half-leaning against the wall, half-supported by a string about its neck. One of its hands, all of fingers, rested on the heavy pommel of a great sword that stood beside it. Various weapons were scattered about over the floor. The walls were utterly bare of adornment; for the few strange things, such as a large dried bat with wings dispread, the skin of a porcupine, and a stuffed sea-mouse, could hardly be reckoned as such. But although his fancy delighted in vagaries like these, he indulged his imagination with far different fare. His mind had never yet been filled with an absorbing passion; but it lay like a still twilight open to any wind, whether the low breath that wafts but odours, or the storm that bows the great trees till they strain and creak. He saw everything as through a rose-coloured glass. When he looked from his window on the street below, not a maiden passed but she moved as in a story, and drew his thoughts after her till she disappeared in the vista. When he walked in the streets, he always felt as if reading a tale, into which he sought to weave every face of interest that went by; and every sweet voice swept his soul as with the wing of a passing angel. He was in fact a poet without words; the more absorbed and endangered, that the springing waters were dammed back into his soul, where, finding no utterance, they grew, and swelled, and undermined. He used to lie on his hard couch, and read a tale or a poem, till the book dropped from his hand; but he dreamed on, he knew not whether awake or asleep, until the opposite roof grew upon his sense, and turned golden in the sunrise. Then he arose too; and the impulses of vigorous youth kept him ever active, either in study or in sport, until again the close of the day left him free; and the world of night, which had lain drowned in the cataract of the day, rose up in his soul, with all its stars, and dim-seen phantom shapes. But this could hardly last long. Some one form must sooner or later step within the charmed circle, enter the house of life, and compel the bewildered magician to kneel and worship.

One afternoon, towards dusk, he was wandering dreamily in one of the principal streets, when a fellow-student roused him by a slap on the shoulder, and asked him to accompany him into a little back alley to look at some old armour which he had taken a fancy to possess. Cosmo was considered an authority in every matter pertaining to arms, ancient or modern. In the use of weapons, none of the students could come near him; and his practical acquaintance with some had principally contributed to establish his authority in reference to all. He accompanied him willingly. They entered a narrow alley, and thence a dirty little court, where a low arched door admitted them into a heterogeneous assemblage of everything musty, and dusty, and old, that could well be imagined. His verdict on the armour was satisfactory, and his companion at once concluded the purchase. As they were leaving the place, Cosmo's eye was attracted by an old mirror of an elliptical shape, which leaned against the wall, covered with dust. Around it was some curious carving, which he could see but very indistinctly by the glimmering light which the owner of the shop carried in his hand. It was this carving that attracted his attention; at least so it appeared to him. He left the place, however, with his friend, taking no further notice of it. They walked together to the main street, where they parted and took opposite directions.

No sooner was Cosmo left alone, than the thought of the curious old mirror returned to him. A strong desire to see it more plainly arose within him, and he directed his steps once more towards the shop. The owner opened the door when he knocked, as if he had expected him. He was a little, old, withered man, with a hooked nose, and burning eyes constantly in a slow restless motion, and looking here and there as if after something that eluded them. Pretending to examine several other articles, Cosmo at last approached the mirror, and requested to have it taken down.

"Take it down yourself, master; I cannot reach it," said the old man.

Cosmo took it down carefully, when he saw that the carving was indeed delicate and costly, being both of admirable design and execution; containing withal many devices which seemed to embody some meaning to which he had no clue. This, naturally, in one of his tastes and temperament, increased the interest he felt in the old mirror; so much, indeed, that he now longed to possess it, in order to study its frame at his leisure. He pretended, however, to want it only for use; and saying he feared the plate could be of little service, as it was rather old, he brushed away a little of the dust from its face, expecting to see a dull reflection within. His surprise was great when he found the reflection brilliant, revealing a glass not only uninjured by age, but wondrously clear and perfect (should the whole correspond to this part) even for one newly from the hands of the maker. He asked carelessly what the owner wanted for the thing. The old man replied by mentioning a sum of money far beyond the reach of poor Cosmo, who proceeded to replace the mirror where it had stood before.

"You think the price too high?" said the old man.

"I do not know that it is too much for you to ask," replied Cosmo; "but it is far too much for me to give."

The old man held up his light towards Cosmo's face. "I like your look," said he.

Cosmo could not return the compliment. In fact, now he looked closely at him for the first time, he felt a kind of repugnance to him, mingled with a strange feeling of doubt whether a man or a woman stood before him.

"What is your name?" he continued.

"Cosmo von Wehrstahl."

"Ah, ah! I thought as much. I see your father in you. I knew your father very well, young sir. I dare say in some odd corners of my house, you might find some old things with his crest and cipher upon them still. Well, I like you: you shall have the mirror at the fourth part of what I asked for it; but upon one condition."

"What is that?" said Cosmo; for, although the price was still a great deal for him to give, he could just manage it; and the desire to possess the mirror had increased to an altogether unaccountable degree, since it had seemed beyond his reach.

"That if you should ever want to get rid of it again, you will let me have the first offer."

"Certainly," replied Cosmo, with a smile; adding, "a moderate condition indeed."

"On your honour?" insisted the seller.

"On my honour," said the buyer; and the bargain was concluded.

"I will carry it home for you," said the old man, as Cosmo took it in his hands.

"No, no; I will carry it myself," said he; for he had a peculiar dislike to revealing his residence to any one, and more especially to this person, to whom he felt every moment a greater antipathy.

"Just as you please," said the old creature, and muttered to himself as he held his light at the door to show him out of the court: "Sold for the sixth time! I wonder what will be the upshot of it this time. I should think my lady had enough of it by now!"

Cosmo carried his prize carefully home. But all the way he had an uncomfortable feeling that he was watched and dogged. Repeatedly he looked about, but saw nothing to justify his suspicions. Indeed, the streets were too crowded and too ill lighted to expose very readily a careful spy, if such there should be at his heels. He reached his lodging in safety, and leaned his purchase against the wall, rather relieved, strong as he was, to be rid of its weight; then, lighting his pipe, threw himself on the couch, and was soon lapt in the folds of one of his haunting dreams.

He returned home earlier than usual the next day, and fixed the mirror to the wall, over the hearth, at one end of his long room. He then carefully wiped away the dust from its face, and clear as the water of a sunny spring, the mirror shone out from beneath the envious covering. But his interest was chiefly occupied with the curious carving of the frame. This he cleaned as well as he could with a brush; and then he proceeded to a minute examination of its various parts, in the hope of discovering some index to the intention of the carver. In this however, he was unsuccessful; and, at length, pausing with some weariness and disappointment, he gazed vacantly for a few moments into the depth of the reflected room. But ere long he said, half aloud: "What a strange thing a mirror is! and what a wondrous affinity exists between it and a man's imagination! For this room of mine, as I behold it in the glass, is the same, and yet not the same. It is not the mere representation of the room I live in, but it looks just as if I were reading about it in a story I like. All its commonness has disappeared. The mirror has lifted it out of the region of fact into the realm of art; and the very representing of it to me has clothed with interest that which was otherwise hard and bare; just as one sees with delight upon the stage the representation of a character from which one would escape in life as from something unendurably wearisome. But is it not rather that art rescues nature from the weary and sated regards of our senses, and the degrading injustice of our anxious every-day life, and, appealing to the imagination, which dwells apart, reveals Nature in some degree as she really is, and as she represents herself to the eye of the child, whose every-day life, fearless and unambitious, meets the true import of the wonder-teeming world around him, and rejoices therein without questioning? That skeleton, now—I almost fear it, standing there so still, with eyes only for the unseen, like a watch-tower looking across all the waste of this busy world into the quiet regions of rest beyond. And yet I know every bone and every joint in it as well as my own fist. And that old battle-axe looks as if any moment it might be caught up by a mailed hand, and, borne forth by the mighty arm, go crashing through casque, and skull, and brain, invading the Unknown with yet another bewildered ghost. I should like to live in *that* room if I could only get into it."

Scarcely had the half-moulded words floated from him, as he stood gazing into the mirror, when, striking him as with a flash of amazement that fixed him in his posture, noiseless and unannounced, glided suddenly through the door into the reflected room, with stately motion, yet reluctant and faltering step, the graceful form of a woman, clothed all in white. Her back only was visible as she walked slowly up to the couch in the further end of the room, on which she laid herself wearily, turning towards him a face of unutterable loveliness, in which suffering, and dislike, and a sense of compulsion, strangely mingled with the beauty. He stood without the power of motion for some moments, with his eyes irrecoverably fixed upon her; and even after he was conscious of the ability to move, he could not summon up courage to turn and look on her, face to face, in the veritable chamber in which he stood. At length, with a sudden effort, in which the exercise of the will was so pure, that it seemed involuntary, he turned his face to the couch. It was vacant. In bewilderment, mingled with terror, he turned again to the mirror: there, on the reflected couch, lay the exquisite lady-form. She lay with closed eyes, whence two large tears were just welling from beneath the veiling lids; still as death, save for the convulsive motion of her bosom.

Cosmo himself could not have described what he felt. His emotions were of a kind that destroyed consciousness, and could never be clearly recalled. He could not help standing yet by the mirror, and keeping his eyes fixed on the lady, though he was painfully aware of his rudeness, and feared every moment that she would open hers, and meet his fixed regard. But he was, ere long, a little relieved; for, after a while, her eyelids slowly rose, and her eyes remained uncovered, but unemployed for a time; and when, at length, they began to wander about the room, as if languidly seeking to make some acquaintance with her environment, they were never directed towards him: it seemed nothing but what was in the mirror could affect her vision; and, therefore, if she saw him at all, it could only be his back, which, of necessity, was turned towards her in the glass. The two figures in the mirror could not meet face to face, except he turned and looked at her, present in his room; and, as she was not there, he concluded that if he were to turn towards the part in his room corresponding to that in which she lay, his reflection would either be invisible to her altogether, or at least it must appear to her to gaze vacantly towards her, and no meeting of the eyes would produce the impression of spiritual proximity. By and by her eyes fell upon the skeleton, and he saw her shudder and close them. She did not open them again, but signs of repugnance continued evident on her countenance. Cosmo would have removed the obnoxious thing at once, but he feared to discompose her yet more by the assertion of his presence, which the act would involve. So he stood and watched her. The eyelids yet shrouded the eyes, as a costly case the jewels within; the troubled expression gradually faded from the countenance, leaving only a faint sorrow behind; the feautres settled into an unchanging expression of rest; and by these signs, and the slow regular motion of her breathing, Cosmo knew that she slept. He could now gaze on her without embarrassment. He saw that her figure, dressed in the simplest robe of white, was worthy of her face; and so harmonious, that either the delicately-moulded foot, or any finger of the equally delicate hand, was an index to the whole. As she lay, her whole form manifested the relaxation of perfect repose. He gazed till he was weary, and at last seated himself near the new-found shrine, and mechanically took up a book, like one who watches by a sick-bed. But his eyes gathered no thoughts from the page before him. His intellect had been stunned by the bold contradiction, to its face, of all its experience, and now lay passive, without assertion, or speculation, or even conscious astonishment; while his imagination sent one wild dream of blessedness after another coursing through his soul. How long he sat he knew not; but at length he roused himself, rose, and, trembling in every portion of his frame, looked again into the mirror. She was gone. The mirror reflected faithfully what his room presented, and nothing more. It stood there like a golden setting whence the central jewel has been stolen away; like a night-sky without the glory of its stars. She had carried with her all the strangeness of the reflected room. It had sunk to the level of the one without. But when the first pangs of his disappointment had passed, Cosmo began to comfort himself with the hope that she might return, perhaps the next evening, at the same hour. Resolving that if she did, she should not at least be scared by the hateful skeleton, he removed that and several other articles of questionable appearance into a recess by the side of the hearth, whence they could not possibly cast any reflection into the mirror; and having made his poor room as tidy as he could, sought the solace of the open sky and of a night wind that had begun to blow; for he could not rest where he was. When he returned, somewhat composed, he could hardly prevail with himself to lie down on his bed; for he could not help feeling as if she had lain upon it; and for him to lie there now would be something like sacrilege. However, weariness prevailed; and laying himself on the couch, dressed as he was, he slept till day.

With a beating heart, beating till he could hardly breathe, he stood in dumb hope before the mirror, on the following evening. Again the reflected room shone as through a purple vapour in the gathering twilight. Everything seemed waiting like himself for a coming splendour to glorify its poor earthliness wih the presence of a heavenly joy. And just as the room vibrated with the strokes of the neighbouring church bell, announcing the hour of six, in glided the pale beauty, and again laid herself on the couch. Poor Cosmo nearly lost his senses with delight. She was there once more! Her eyes sought the corner where the skeleton had stood, and a faint gleam of satisfaction crossed her face, apparently at seeing it empty. She looked suffering still, but there was less of discomfort expressed in her countenance than there had been the night before. She took more notice of the things about her, and seemed to gaze with some curiosity on the strange apparatus standing here and there in her room. At length, however, drowsiness seemed to overtake her, and again she fell asleep. Resolved not to lose sight of her this time, Cosmo watched the sleeping form. Her slumber was so deep and absorbing, that a fascinating repose seemed to pass contagiously from her to him, as he gazed upon her; and he started as if awaking from a dream, when the lady moved, and, without opening her eyes, rose, and passed from the room with the gait of a somnambulist.

Cosmo was now in a state of extravagant delight. Most men have a secret treasure somewhere. The miser has his golden hoard; the virtuoso his pet ring; the student his rare book; the poet his favourite haunt; the lover his secret drawer; but Cosmo had a mirror with a lovely lady in it. And now that he knew by the skeleton, that she was affected by the things around her, he had a new object in life: he would turn the bare chamber in the mirror into a room such as no lady need disdain to call her own. This he could effect only by furnishing and adorning his. And Cosmo was poor. Yet he possessed accomplishments that could be turned to account; although, hitherto, he had preferred living on his slender allowance, to increasing his means by what his pride considered unworthy of his rank. He was the best swordsman in the University; and now he offered to give lessons in fencing and similar exercises, to such as chose to pay him well for the trouble. His proposal was heard with surprise by the students; but it was eagerly accepted by many; and soon his instructions were not confined to the richer students, but were anxiously sought by many of the young nobility of Prague and its neighbourhood. So that very soon he had a good deal of money at his command. The first thing he did was to remove his apparatus and oddities into a closet in the room. Then he placed his bed and a few other necessaries on each side of the hearth, and parted them from the rest of the room by two screens of Indian fabric. Then he put an elegant couch for the lady to lie upon, in the corner where his bed had formerly stood; and, by degrees, every day adding some article of luxury, converted it, at length, into a rich boudoir.

Every night, about the same time, the lady entered. The first time she saw the new couch, she started with a half-smile; then her face grew very sad, the tears came to her eyes, and she laid herself upon the couch, and pressed her face into the silken cushions, as if to hide from everything. She took notice of each addition and each change as the work proceeded; and a look of acknowledgment, as if she knew that some one was ministering to her, and was grateful for it, mingled with the constant look of suffering. At length, after she had laid down as usual one evening, her eyes fell upon some paintings with which Cosmo had just finished adorning the walls. She rose, and to his great delight, walked across the room, and proceeded to examine them carefully, testifying much pleasure in her looks as she did so. But again the sorrowful, tearful expression returned, and again she buried her face in the pillows of her couch. Gradually, however, her countenance had grown more composed; much of the suffering manifest on her first appearance had vanished, and a kind of quiet, hopeful expression had taken its place; which, however, frequently gave way to an anxious, troubled look, mingled with something of sympathetic pity.

Meantime, how fared Cosmo? As might be expected in one of his temperament, his interest had blossomed into love, and his love—shall I call it *ripened,* or—*withered* into passion? But, alas! he loved a shadow. He could not come near her, could not speak to her, could not hear a sound from those sweet lips, to which his longing eyes would cling like bees to their honey-founts. Ever and anon he sang to himself:

"I shall die for love of the maiden";

and ever he looked again, and died not, though his heart seemed ready to break with intensity of life and longing. And the more he did for her, the more he loved her; and he hoped that, although she never appeared to see him, yet she was pleased to think that an unknown would give his life to her. He tried to comfort himself over his separation from her, by thinking that perhaps some day she would see him and make signs to him, and that would satisfy him; "for," thought he, "is not this all that a loving soul can do to enter into communion with another! Nay, how many who love never come nearer than to behold each other as in a mirror; seem to know and yet never know the inward life; never enter the other soul; and part at last, with but the vaguest notion of the universe on the borders of which they have been hovering for years? If I could but speak to her, and knew that she heard me, I should be satisfied." Once he contemplated painting a picture on the wall, which should, of necessity, convey to the lady a thought of himself; but, though he had some skill with the pencil, he found his hand tremble so much when he began the attempt, that he was forced to give it up.

. . .

"Who lives, he dies; who dies, he is alive."

One evening, as he stood gazing on his treasure, he thought he saw a faint expression of self-consciousness on her countenance, as if she surmised that passionate eyes were fixed upon her. This grew; till at last the red blood rose over her neck, and cheek, and brow. Cosmo's longing to approach her became almost delirious. This night she was dressed in an evening costume, resplendent with diamonds. This could add nothing to her beauty, but it presented it in a new aspect; enabled her loveliness to make a new manifestation of itself in a new embodiment. For essential beauty is infinite; and, as the soul of Nature needs an endless succession of varied forms to embody her loveliness, countless faces of beauty springing forth, not any two the same, at every one of her heart-throbs; so the individual form needs an infinite change of its environments, to enable it to uncover all the phases of its loveliness. Diamonds glittered from amidst her hair, half-hidden in its luxuriance, like stars through dark rain-clouds; and the bracelets on her white arms flashed all the colours of a rainbow of lightnings, as she lifted her snowy hands to cover her burning face. But her beauty shone down all its adornment. "If I might have but one of her feet to kiss," thought Cosmo, "I should be content." Alas! he deceived himself, for passion is never content. Nor did he know that there are *two* ways out of her enchanted house. But, suddenly, as if the pang had been driven into his heart from without, revealing itself first in pain, and afterwards in definite form, the thought darted into his mind, "She has a lover somewhere. Remembered words of his bring the colour on her face now. I am nowhere to her. She lives in another world all day, and all night, after she leaves me. Why does she come and make me love her, till I, a strong man, am too faint to look upon her more?" He looked again, and her face was pale as a lily. A sorrowful compassion seemed to rebuke the glitter of the restless jewels, and the slow tears rose in her eyes. She left her room sooner this evening than was her wont. Cosmo remained alone, with a feeling as if his bosom had been suddenly left empty and hollow, and the weight of the whole world was crushing in its walls. The next evening, for the first time since she began to come, she came not.

And now Cosmo was in wretched plight. Since the thought of a rival had occurred to him, he could not rest for a moment. More than ever he longed to see the lady face to face. He persuaded himself that if he but knew the worst he would be satisfied; for then he could abandon Prague, and find that relief in constant motion, which is the hope of all active minds when invaded by distress. Meantime he waited with unspeakable anxiety for the next night, hoping she would return: but she did not appear. And now he fell really ill. Rallied by his fellow-students on his wretched looks, he ceased to attend the lectures. His engagements were neglected. He cared for nothing. The sky, with the great sun in it, was to him a heartless, burning desert. The men and women in the streets were mere puppets, without motives in themselves, or interest to him. He saw them all as on the ever-changing field of a *camera obscura*. She—she alone and altogether—was his universe, his well of life, his incarnate good. For six evenings she came not. Let his absorbing passion, and the slow fever that was consuming his brain, be his excuse for the resolution which he had taken and begun to execute, before that time had expired.

Reasoning with himself, that it must be by some enchantment connected with the mirror, that the form of the lady was to be seen in it, he determined to attempt to turn to account what he had hitherto studied principally from curiosity. "For," said he to himself, "if a spell can force her presence in that glass (and she came unwillingly at first), may not a stronger spell, such as I know, especially with the aid of her half-presence in the mirror, if ever she appears again, compel her living form to come to me here? If I do her wrong, let love be my excuse. I want only to know my doom from her own lips." He never doubted, all the time, that she was a real earthly woman; or, rather, that there was a woman, who, somehow or other, threw this reflection of her form into the magic mirror.

He opened his secret drawer, took out his books of magic, lighted his lamp, and read and made notes from midnight till three in the morning, for three successive nights. Then he replaced his books;

and the next night went out in quest of the materials necessary for the conjuration. These were not easy to find; for, in love-charms and all incantations of this nature, ingredients are employed scarcely fit to be mentioned, and for the thought even of which, in connection with her, he could only excuse himself on the score of his bitter need. At length he succeeded in procuring all he required; and on the seventh evening from that on which she had last appeared, he found himself prepared for the exercise of unlawful and tyrannical power.

He cleared the centre of the room; stooped and drew a circle of red on the floor, around the spot where he stood; wrote in the four quarters mystical signs, and numbers which were all powers of seven or nine; examined the whole ring carefully, to see that no smallest break had occurred in the circumference; and then rose from his bending posture. As he rose, the church clock struck seven; and, just as she had appeared the first time, reluctant, slow, and stately, glided in the lady. Cosmo trembled; and when, turning, she revealed a countenance worn and wan, as with sickness or inward trouble, he grew faint, and felt as if he dared not proceed. But as he gazed on the face and form which now possessed his whole soul, to the exclusion of all other joys and griefs, the longing to speak to her, to know that she heard him, to hear from her one word in return, became so unendurable, that he suddenly and hastily resumed his preparations. Stepping carefully from the circle, he put a small brazier into its centre. He then set fire to its contents of charcoal, and while it burned up, opened his window and seated himself, waiting, beside it.

It was a sultry evening. The air was full of thunder. A sense of luxurious depression filled the brain. The sky seemed to have grown heavy, and to compress the air beneath it. A kind of purplish tinge pervaded the atmosphere, and through the open window came the scents of the distant fields, which all the vapours of the city could not quench. Soon the charcoal glowed. Cosmo sprinkled upon it the incense and other substances which he had compounded, and, stepping within the circle, turned his face from the brazier and towards the mirror. Then, fixing his eyes upon the face of the lady, he began with a trembling voice to repeat a powerful incantation. He had not gone far, before the lady grew pale; and then, like a returning wave, the blood washed all its banks with its crimson tide, and she hid her face in her hands. Then he passed to a conjuration stronger yet. The lady rose and walked uneasily to and fro in her room. Another spell; and she seemed seeking with her eyes for some object on which they wished to rest. At length it seemed as if she suddenly espied him; for her eyes fixed themselves full and wide upon his, and she drew gradually, and somewhat unwillingly, close to her side of the mirror, just as if his eyes had fascinated her. Cosmo had never seen her so near before. Now at least, eyes met eyes; but he could not quite understand the expression of hers. They were full of tender entreaty, but there was something more that he could not interpret. Though his heart seemed to labour in his throat, he would allow no delight or agitation to turn him from his task. Looking still in her face, he passed on to the mightiest charm he knew. Suddenly the lady turned and walked out of the door of her reflected chamber. A moment after, she entered his room with veritable presence; and, forgetting all his precautions, he sprang from the charmed circle, and knelt before her. There she stood, the living lady of his passionate visions, alone beside him, in a thundery twilight, and the glow of a magic fire.

"Why," said the lady, with a trembling voice, "didst thou bring a poor maiden through the rainy streets alone?"

"Because I am dying for love of thee; but I only brought thee from the mirror there."

"Ah, the mirror!" and she looked up at it, and shuddered. "Alas! I am but a slave, while that mirror exists. But do not think it was the power of thy spells that drew me; it was thy longing desire to see me, that beat at the door of my heart, till I was forced to yield."

"Canst thou love me then?" said Cosmo, in a voice calm as death, but almost inarticulate with emotion.

"I do not know," she replied sadly; "that I cannot tell, so long as I am bewildered with enchantments. It were indeed a joy too great, to lay my head on thy bosom and weep to death; for I think thou lovest me, though I do not know;—but——"

Cosmo rose from his knees.

"I love thee as—nay, I know not what—for since I have loved thee, there is nothing else."

He seized her hand: she withdrew it.

"No, better not; I am in thy power, and therefore I may not."

She burst into tears, and, kneeling before him in her turn, said—

"Cosmo, if thou lovest me, set me free, even from thyself: break the mirror."

"And shall I see thyself instead?"

"That I cannot tell, I will not deceive thee; we may never meet again."

A fierce struggle arose in Cosmo's bosom. Now she was in his power. She did not dislike him at least; and he could see her when he would. To break the mirror would be to destroy his very life, to banish out of his universe the only glory it possessed. The whole world would be but a prison, if he annihilated the one window that looked into the paradise of love. Not yet pure in love, he hesitated.

With a wail of sorrow, the lady rose to her feet. "Ah! he loves me not; he loves me not even as I love him; and alas! I care more for his love than even for the freedom I ask."

"I will not wait to be willing," cried Cosmo; and sprang to the corner where the great sword stood.

Meantime it had grown very dark; only the embers cast a red glow through the room. He seized the sword by the steel scabbard, and stood before the mirror; but as he heaved a great blow at it with the heavy pommel, the blade slipped half-way out of the scabbard, and the pommel struck the wall above the mirror. At that moment, a terrible clap of thunder seemed to burst in the very room beside them; and ere Cosmo could repeat the blow, he fell senseless on the hearth. When he came to himself, he found that the lady and the mirror had both disappeared. He was seized with a brain fever, which kept him to his couch for weeks.

When he recovered his reason, he began to think what could have become of the mirror. For the lady, he hoped she had found her way back as she came; but as the mirror involved her fate with its own, he was more immediately anxious about that. He could not think she had carried it away. It was much too heavy, even if it had not been too firmly fixed in the wall, for her to remove it. Then again, he remembered the thunder; which made him believe that it was not the lightning, but some other blow that had struck him down. He concluded that, either by supernatural agency, he having exposed himself to the vengeance of the demons in leaving the circle of safety, or in some other mode, the mirror had probably found its way back to its former owner; and, horrible to think of, might have been by this time once more disposed of, delivering up the lady into the power of another man; who, if he used his power no worse than he himself had done, might yet give Cosmo abundant cause to curse the selfish indecision which prevented him from shattering the mirror at once. Indeed, to think that she whom he loved, and who had prayed to him for freedom, should be still at the mercy, in some degree, of the possessor of the mirror, and was at least exposed to his constant observation, was in itself enough to madden a chary lover.

Anxiety to be well retarded his recovery; but at length he was able to creep abroad. He first made his way to the old broker's, pretending to be in search of something else. A laughing sneer on the creature's face convinced him that he knew all about it; but he could not see it amongst his furniture, or get any information out of him as to what had become of it. He expressed the utmost surprise at hearing it had been stolen; a surprise which Cosmo saw at once to be counterfeited; while, at the same time, he fancied that the old wretch was not at all anxious to have it mistaken for genuine. Full of distress, which he concealed as well as he could, he made many searches, but with no avail. Of course he could ask no questions; but he kept his ears awake for any remotest hint that might set him in a direction of search. He never went out without a short heavy hammer of steel about him, that he might shatter the mirror the moment he was made happy by the sight of his lost treasure, if ever that blessed moment should arrive. Whether he should see the lady again, was now a thought altogether secondary, and postponed to the achievement of her freedom. He wandered here and there, like an anxious ghost, pale and haggard; gnawed ever at the heart, by the thought of what she might be suffering—all from his fault.

One night, he mingled with a crowd that filled the rooms of one of the most distinguished mansions in the city; for he accepted every invitation, that he might lose no chance, however poor, of obtaining some information that might expedite his discovery. Here he wandered about, listening to every stray word that he could catch, in the hope of a revelation. As he approached some ladies who were talking quietly in a corner, one said to another: "Have you heard of the strange illness of the Princess von Hohenweiss?"

"Yes; she has been ill for more than a year now. It is very sad for so fine a creature to have such a terrible malady. She was better for some weeks lately, but within the last few days the same attacks have returned, apparently accompanied with more suffering than ever. It is altogether an inexplicable story."

"Is there a story connected with her illness?"

"I have only heard imperfect reports of it; but it is said that she gave offence some eighteen months ago to an old woman who had held an office of trust in the family, and who, after some incoherent threats, disappeared. This peculiar affection followed soon after. But the strangest part of the story is its association with the loss of an antique mirror, which stood in her dressing-room, and of which she constantly made use."

Here the speaker's voice sank to a whisper; and Cosmo, although his very soul sat listening in his ears, could hear no more. He trembled too much to dare to address the ladies, even if it had been advisable to expose himself to their curiosity. The name of the Princess was well known to him, but he had never seen her; except indeed it was she, which now he hardly doubted, who had knelt before him on that dreadful night. Fearful of attracting attention, for, from the weak state of his health, he could not recover an appearance of calmness, he made his way to the open air, and reached his lodgings; glad in this, that he at least knew where she lived, although he never dreamed of approaching her openly, even if he should be happy enough to free her from her hateful bondage. He hoped, too, that as he had unexpectedly learned so much, the other and far more important part might be revealed to him ere long.

.   .   .

"Have you seen Steinwald lately?"

"No, I have not seen him for some time. He is almost a match for me at the rapier, and I suppose he thinks he needs no more lessons."

"I wonder what has become of him. I want to see him very much. Let me see; the last time I saw him he was coming out of that old broker's den, to which, if you remember, you accompanied me once, to look at some armour. That is fully three weeks ago."

This hint was enough for Cosmo. Von Steinwald was a man of influence in the court, well known for his reckless habits and fierce passions. The very possibility that the mirror should be in his possession was hell itself to Cosmo. But violent or hasty measures of any sort were most unlikely to succeed. All that he wanted was an opportunity of breaking the fatal glass; and to obtain this he must bide his time. He revolved many plans in his mind, but without being able to fix upon any.

At length, one evening, as he was passing the house of Von Steinwald, he saw the windows more than usually brilliant. He watched for a while, and seeing that company began to arrive, hastened home, and dressed as richly as he could, in the hope of mingling with the guests unquestioned: in effecting which, there could be no difficulty for a man of his carriage.

.   .   .

In a lofty, silent chamber, in another part of the city, lay a form more like marble than a living woman. The loveliness of death seemed frozen upon her face, for her lips were rigid, and her eyelids closed. Her long white hands were crossed over her breast, and no breathing disturbed their repose. Beside the dead, men speak in whispers, as if the deepest rest of all could be broken by the sound of a living voice. Just so, though the soul was evidently beyond the reach of all intimations from the senses, the two ladies, who sat beside her, spoke in the gentlest tones of subdued sorrow.

"She has lain so for an hour."

"This cannot last long, I fear."

"How much thinner she has grown within the last few weeks! If she would only speak, and explain what she suffers, it would be better for her. I think she has visions in her trances, but nothing can induce her to refer to them when she is awake."

"Does she ever speak in these trances?"

"I have never heard her; but they say she walks sometimes, and once put the whole household in a terrible fright by disappearing for a whole hour, and returned drenched with rain, and almost dead with exhaustion and fright. But even then she would give no account of what had happened."

A scarce audible murmur from the yet motionless lips of the lady here startled her attendants. After several ineffectual attempts at articulation, the word *"Cosmo!"* burst from her. Then she lay still as before; but only for a moment. With a wild cry, she sprang from the couch erect on the floor, flung her arms above her head, with clasped and straining hands, and, her wide eyes flashing with light, called aloud, with a voice exultant as that of a spirit bursting from a sepulchre, "I am free! I am free! I thank thee!" Then she flung herself on the couch, and sobbed; then rose, and paced wildly up and down the room, with gestures of mingled delight and anxiety. Then turning to her motionless attendants—"Quick, Lisa, my cloak and hood!" Then lower—"I must go to him. Make haste, Lisa! You may come with me, if you will."

In another moment they were in the street, hurrying along towards one of the bridges over the Moldau. The moon was near the zenith, and the streets were almost empty. The Princess soon outstripped her attendant, and was half-way over the bridge, before the other reached it.

"Are you free, lady? The mirror is broken: are you free?"

The words were spoken close beside her, as she hurried on. She turned; and there, leaning on the parapet in a recess of the bridge, stood Cosmo, in a splendid dress, but with a white and quivering face.

"Cosmo!—I am free—and thy servant for ever. I was coming to you now."

"And I to you, for Death made me bold; but I could get no further. Have I atoned at all? Do I love you a little—truly?"

"Ah, I know now that you love me, my Cosmo; but what do you say about death?"

He did not reply. His hand was pressed against his side. She looked more closely: the blood was welling from between the fingers. She flung her arms around him with a faint bitter wail.

When Lisa came up, she found her mistress kneeling above a wan dead face, which smiled on in the spectral moonbeams.

And now I will say no more about these wondrous volumes; though I could tell many a tale out of them, and could, perhaps, vaguely represent some entrancing thoughts of a deeper kind which I found within them. From many a sultry noon till twilight, did I sit in that grand hall, buried and risen again in these old books. And I trust I have carried away in my soul some of the exhalations of their undying leaves. In after hours of deserved or needful sorrow, portions of what I read there have often come to me again, with an unexpected comforting; which was not fruitless, even though the comfort might seem in itself groundless and vain.

*T*HERE WAS ONCE a little man called Niggle, who had a long journey to make. He did not want to go, indeed the whole idea was distasteful to him; but he could not get out of it. He knew he would have to start some time, but he did not hurry with his preparations.

Niggle was a painter. Not a very successful one, partly because he had many other things to do. Most of these things he thought were a nuisance; but he did them fairly well, when he could not get out of them: which (in his opinion) was far too often. The laws in his country were rather strict. There were other hindrances, too. For one thing, he was sometimes just idle, and did nothing at all. For another, he was kind-hearted, in a way. You know the sort of kind heart: it made him uncomfortable more often than it made him do anything; and even when he did anything, it did not prevent him from grumbling, losing his temper, and swearing (mostly to himself). All the same, it did land him in a good many odd jobs for his neighbour, Mr. Parish, a man with a lame leg. Occasionally he even helped other people from further off, if they came and asked him to. Also, now and again, he remembered his journey, and began to pack a few things in an ineffectual way: at such times he did not paint very much.

He had a number of pictures on hand; most of them were too large and ambitious for his skill. He was the sort of painter who can paint leaves better than trees. He used to spend a long time on a single leaf, trying to catch its shape, and its sheen, and the glistening of dew-drops on its edges. Yet he wanted to paint a whole tree, with all of its leaves in the same style, and all of them different.

There was one picture in particular which bothered him. It had begun with a leaf caught in the wind, and it became a tree; and the tree grew, sending out innumerable branches, and thrusting out the most fantastic roots. Strange birds came and settled on the twigs and had to be attended to. Then all round the Tree, and behind it, through the gaps in the leaves and boughs, a country began to open out; and there were glimpses of a forest marching over the land, and of mountains tipped with snow. Niggle lost interest in his other pictures; or else he took them and tacked them on to the edges of his great picture. Soon the canvas became so large that he had to get a ladder; and he ran up and down it, putting in a touch here, and rubbing out a patch there. When people came to call, he seemed polite enough, though he fiddled a little with the pencils on his desk. He listened to what they said, but underneath he was thinking all the time about his big canvas, in the tall shed that had been built for it out in his garden (on a plot where once he had grown potatoes).

He could not get rid of his kind heart. "I wish I was more strongminded!" he sometimes said to himself, meaning that he wished other people's troubles did not make him feel uncomfortable. But for a long time he was not seriously perturbed. "At any rate, I shall get this one picture done, my real picture, before I have to go on that wretched journey," he used to say. Yet he was beginning to see that he could not put off his start indefinitely. The picture would have to stop just growing and get finished.

One day, Niggle stood a little way off from his picture and considered it with unusual attention and detachment. He could not make up his mind what he thought about it, and wished he had some friend who would tell him what to think. Actually it seemed to him wholly unsatisfactory, and yet very lovely, the only really beautiful picture in the world. What he would have liked at that moment would have been to see himself walk in, and slap him on the back, and say (with obvious sincerity): "Absolutely magnificent! I see exactly what you are getting at. Do get on with it, and don't bother about anything else! We will arrange for a public pension, so that you need not."

However, there was no public pension. And one thing he could see: it would need some concentration, some *work*, hard uninterrupted work, to finish the picture, even at its present size. He rolled up his sleeves, and began to concentrate. He tried for several days not to bother about other things. But there came a tremendous crop of interruptions. Things went wrong in his house; he had to go and serve on a jury in the town; a distant friend fell ill; Mr. Parish was laid up with lumbago; and visitors kept on coming. It was springtime, and they wanted a free tea in the country: Niggle lived in a pleasant little house, miles away from the town. He cursed them in his heart, but he could not deny that he had invited them himself, away back in the winter, when he had not thought it an "interruption" to visit the shops and have tea with acquaintances in the town. He tried to harden his heart; but it was not a success. There were many things that he had not the face to say *no* to, whether he thought them duties or not; and there were some things he was compelled to do, whatever he thought. Some of his visitors hinted that his garden was rather neglected, and that he might get a visit from an Inspector. Very few of them knew about his picture, of course; but if they had known, it would not have made much difference. I doubt if they would have thought that it mattered much. I dare say it was not really a very good picture, though it may have had some good passages. The Tree, at any rate, was curious. Quite unique in its way. So was Niggle; though he was also a very ordinary and rather silly little man.

At length Niggle's time became really precious. His acquaintances in the distant town began to remember that the little man had got to make a troublesome journey, and some began to calculate how long at the latest he could put off starting. They wondered who would take his house, and if the garden would be better kept.

The autumn came, very wet and windy. The little painter was in his shed. He was up on the ladder, trying to catch the gleam of the westering sun on the peak of a snow-mountain, which he had glimpsed just to the left of the leafy tip of one of the Tree's branches. He knew that he would have to be leaving soon: perhaps early next year. He could only just get the picture finished, and only so so, at that: there were some corners where he would not have time now to do more than hint at what he wanted.

There was a knock on the door. "Come in!" he said sharply, and climbed down the ladder. He stood on the floor twiddling his brush. It was his neighbour, Parish: his only real neighbour, all other folk lived a long way off. Still, he did not like the man very much: partly because he was so often in trouble and in need of help; and also because he did not care about painting, but was very critical about gardening. When Parish looked at Niggle's garden (which was often) he saw mostly weeds; and when he looked at Niggle's pictures (which was seldom) he saw only green and grey patches and black lines, which seemed to him nonsensical. He did not mind mentioning the weeds (a neighbourly duty), but he refrained from giving any opinion of the pictures. He thought this was very kind, and he did not realize that, even if it was kind, it was not kind enough. Help with the weeds (and perhaps praise for the pictures) would have been better.

"Well, Parish, what is it?" said Niggle.

"I oughtn't to interrupt you, I know," said Parish (without a glance at the picture). "You are very busy, I'm sure."

Niggle had meant to say something like that himself, but he had missed his chance. All he said was: "Yes."

"But I have no one else to turn to," said Parish.

"Quite so," said Niggle with a sigh: one of those sighs that are a private comment, but which are not made quite inaudible. "What can I do for you?"

"My wife has been ill for some days, and I am getting worried," said Parish. "And the wind has blown half the tiles off my roof, and water is pouring into the bedroom. I think I ought to get the doctor. And the builders, too, only they take so long to come. I was wondering if you had any wood and canvas you could spare, just to patch me up and see me through for a day or two." Now he did look at the picture.

"Dear, dear!" said Niggle. "You *are* unlucky. I hope it is no more than a cold that your wife has got. I'll come round presently, and help you move the patient downstairs."

"Thank you very much," said Parish, rather coolly. "But it is not a cold, it is a fever. I should not have bothered you for a cold. And my wife is in bed downstairs already. I can't get up and down with trays, not with my leg. But I see you are busy. Sorry to have troubled you. I had rather hoped you might have been able to spare the time to go for the doctor, seeing how I'm placed; and the builder too, if you really have no canvas you can spare."

"Of course," said Niggle; though other words were in his heart, which at the moment was merely soft without feeling at all kind. "I could go. I'll go, if you are really worried."

"I am worried, very worried. I wish I was not lame," said Parish.

So Niggle went. You see, it was awkward. Parish was his neighbour, and everyone else a long way off. Niggle had a bicycle, and Parish had not, and could not ride one. Parish had a lame leg, a genuine lame leg which gave him a good deal of pain: that had to be remembered, as well as his sour expression and whining voice. Of course, Niggle had a picture and barely time to finish it. But it seemed that this was a thing that Parish had to reckon with and not Niggle. Parish, however, did not reckon with pictures; and Niggle could not alter that. "Curse it!" he said to himself, as he got out his bicycle.

It was wet and windy, and daylight was waning. "No more work for me today!" thought Niggle, and all the time that he was riding, he was either swearing to himself, or imagining the strokes of his brush on the mountain, and on the spray of leaves beside it, that he had first imagined in the spring. His fingers twitched on the handlebars. Now he was out of the shed, he saw exactly the way in which to treat that shining spray which framed the distant vision of the mountain. But he had a sinking feeling in his heart, a sort of fear that he would never now get a chance to try it out.

Niggle found the doctor, and he left a note at the builder's. The office was shut, and the builder had gone home to his fireside. Niggle got soaked to the skin, and caught a chill himself. The doctor did not set out as promptly as Niggle had done. He arrived next day, which was quite convenient for him, as by that time there were two patients to deal with, in neighbouring houses. Niggle was in bed, with a high temperature, and marvellous patterns of leaves and involved branches forming in his head and on the ceiling. It did not comfort him to learn that Mrs. Parish had only had a cold, and was getting up. He turned his face to the wall and buried himself in leaves.

He remained in bed some time. The wind went on blowing. It

took away a good many more of Parish's tiles, and some of Niggle's as well: his own roof began to leak. The builder did not come. Niggle did not care; not for a day or two. Then he crawled out to look for some food (Niggle had no wife). Parish did not come round: the rain had got into his leg and made it ache; and his wife was busy mopping up water, and wondering if "that Mr. Niggle" had forgotten to call at the builder's. Had she seen any chance of borrowing anything useful, she would have sent Parish round, leg or no leg; but she did not, so Niggle was left to himself.

At the end of a week or so Niggle tottered out to his shed again. He tried to climb the ladder, but it made his head giddy. He sat and looked at the picture, but there were no patterns of leaves or visions of mountains in his mind that day. He could have painted a far-off view of a sandy desert, but he had not the energy.

Next day he felt a good deal better. He climbed the ladder, and began to paint. He had just begun to get into it again, when there came a knock on the door.

"Damn!" said Niggle. But he might just as well have said "Come in!" politely, for the door opened all the same. This time a very tall man came in, a total stranger.

"This is a private studio," said Niggle. "I am busy. Go away!"

"I am an Inspector of Houses," said the man, holding up his appointment-card, so that Niggle on his ladder could see it.

"Oh!" he said.

"Your neighbour's house is not satisfactory at all," said the Inspector.

"I know," said Niggle. "I took a note to the builders a long time ago, but they have never come. Then I have been ill."

"I see," said the Inspector. "But you are not ill now."

"But I'm not a builder. Parish ought to make a complaint to the Town Council, and get help from the Emergency Service."

"They are busy with worse damage than any up here," said the Inspector. "There has been a flood in the valley, and many families are homeless. You should have helped your neighbour to make temporary repairs and prevent the damage from getting more costly to mend than necessary. That is the law. There is plenty of material here: canvas, wood, waterproof paint."

"Where?" asked Niggle indignantly.

"There!" said the Inspector, pointing to the picture.

"My picture!" exclaimed Niggle.

"I dare say it is," said the Inspector. "But houses come first. That is the law."

"But I can't . . ." Niggle said no more, for at that moment another man came in. Very much like the Inspector he was, almost his double: tall, dressed all in black.

"Come along!" he said. "I am the Driver."

Niggle stumbled down from the ladder. His fever seemed to have come on again, and his head was swimming; he felt cold all over.

"Driver? Driver?" he chattered. "Driver of what?"

"You, and your carriage," said the man. "The carriage was ordered long ago. It has come at last. It's waiting. You start today on your journey, you know."

"There now!" said the Inspector. "You'll have to go; but it's a bad way to start on your journey, leaving your jobs undone. Still, we can at least make some use of this canvas now."

"Oh, dear!" said poor Niggle, beginning to weep. "And it's not, not even finished!"

"Not finished?" said the Driver. "Well, it's finished with, as far as you're concerned, at any rate. Come along!"

Niggle went, quite quietly. The Driver gave him no time to pack, saying that he ought to have done that before, and they would miss the train; so all Niggle could do was to grab a little bag in the hall. He found that it contained only a paint-box and a small book of his own sketches: neither food nor clothes. They caught the train all right. Niggle was feeling very tired and sleepy; he was hardly aware of what was going on when they bundled him into his compartment. He did not care much: he had forgotten where he was supposed to be going, or what he was going for. The train ran almost at once into a dark tunnel.

Niggle woke up in a very large, dim railway station. A Porter went along the platform shouting, but he was not shouting the name of the place; he was shouting *Niggle!*

Niggle got out in a hurry, and found that he had left his little bag behind. He turned back, but the train had gone away.

"Ah, there you are!" said the Porter. "This way! What! No luggage? You will have to go to the Workhouse."

Niggle felt very ill, and fainted on the platform. They put him in an ambulance and took him to the Workhouse Infirmary.

He did not like the treatment at all. The medicine they gave him was bitter. The officials and attendants were unfriendly, silent, and strict; and he never saw anyone else, except a very severe doctor, who visited him occasionally. It was more like being in a prison than in a hospital. He had to work hard, at stated hours: at digging, carpentry, and painting bare boards all one plain colour. He was never allowed outside, and the windows all looked inwards. They kept him in the dark for hours at a stretch, "to do some thinking," they said. He lost count of time. He did not even begin to feel better, not if that could be judged by whether he felt any pleasure in doing anything. He did not, not even in getting into bed.

At first, during the first century or so (I am merely giving his impressions), he used to worry aimlessly about the past. One thing he kept on repeating to himself, as he lay in the dark: "I wish I had called on Parish the first morning after the high winds began. I meant to. The first loose tiles would have been easy to fix. Then Mrs. Parish might never have caught cold. Then I should not have caught cold either. Then I should have had a week longer." But in time he forgot what it was that he had wanted a week longer for. If he worried at all after that, it was about his jobs in the hospital. He planned them out, thinking how quickly he could stop that board creaking, or rehang that door, or mend that table-leg. Probably he really became rather useful, though no one ever told him so. But that, of course, cannot have been the reason why they kept the poor little man so long. They may have been waiting for him to get better, and judging "better" by some odd medical standard of their own.

At any rate, poor Niggle got no pleasure out of life, not what he had been used to call pleasure. He was certainly not amused. But it could not be denied that he began to have a feeling of—well, satisfaction: bread rather than jam. He could take up a task the moment one bell rang, and lay it aside promptly the moment the next one went, all tidy and ready to be continued at the right time. He got through quite a lot in a day, now; he finished small things off neatly. He had no "time of his own" (except alone in his bed-cell), and yet he was becoming master of his time; he began to know just what he could do with it. There was no sense of rush. He was quieter inside now, and at resting-time he could really rest.

Then suddenly they changed all his hours; they hardly let him go to bed at all; they took him off carpentry altogether and kept him at plain digging, day after day. He took it fairly well. It was a long while before he even began to grope in the back of his mind for the curses that he had practically forgotten. He went on digging, till his back seemed broken, his hands were raw, and he felt that he could not manage another spadeful. Nobody thanked him. But the doctor came and looked at him.

"Knock off!" he said. "Complete rest—in the dark."

Niggle was lying in the dark, resting completely; so that, as he had not been either feeling or thinking at all, he might have been lying there for hours or for years, as far as he could tell. But now he heard Voices: not voices that he had ever heard before. There seemed to be a Medical Board, or perhaps a Court of Inquiry, going on close at hand, in an adjoining room with the door open, possibly, though he could not see any light.

"Now the Niggle case," said a Voice, a severe voice, more severe than the doctor's.

"What was the matter with him?" said a Second Voice, a voice that you might have called gentle, though it was not soft—it was a voice of authority, and sounded at once hopeful and sad. "What was the matter with Niggle? His heart was in the right place."

"Yes, but it did not function properly," said the First Voice. "And his head was not screwed on tight enough: he hardly ever thought at all. Look at the time he wasted, not even amusing himself! He never got ready for his journey. He was moderately well-off, and yet he arrived here almost destitute, and had to be put in the paupers' wing. A bad case, I am afraid. I think he should stay some time yet."

"It would not do him any harm, perhaps," said the Second Voice. "But, of course, he is only a little man. He was never meant to be anything very much; and he was never very strong. Let us look at the Records. Yes. There are some favourable points, you know."

"Perhaps," said the First Voice; "but very few that will really bear examination."

"Well," said the Second Voice, "there are these. He was a painter by nature. In a minor way, of course; still, a Leaf by Niggle has a charm of its own. He took a great deal of pains with leaves, just for their own sake. But he never thought that that made him important. There is no note in the Records of his pretending, even to himself, that it excused his neglect of things ordered by the law."

"Then he should not have neglected so many," said the First Voice.

"All the same, he did answer a good many Calls."

"A small percentage, mostly of the easier sort, and he called those Interruptions. The Records are full of the word, together with a lot of complaints and silly imprecations."

"True; but they looked like interruptions to him, of course, poor little man. And there is this: he never expected any Return, as so many of his sort call it. There is the Parish case, the one that came in later. He was Niggle's neighbour, never did a stroke for him, and seldom showed any gratitude at all. But there is no note in the Records that Niggle expected Parish's gratitude; he does not seem to have thought about it."

"Yes, that is a point," said the First Voice; "but rather small. I think you will find Niggle often merely forgot. Things he had to do for Parish he put out of his mind as a nuisance he had done with."

"Still, there is this last report," said the Second Voice, "that wet bicycle-ride. I rather lay stress on that. It seems plain that this was a genuine sacrifice: Niggle guessed that he was throwing away his last chance with his picture, and he guessed, too, that Parish was worrying unnecessarily."

"I think you put it too strongly," said the First Voice. "But you have the last word. It is your task, of course, to put the best interpretation on the facts. Sometimes they will bear it. What do you propose?"

"I think it is a case for a little gentle treatment now," said the Second Voice.

Niggle thought that he had never heard anything so generous as that Voice. It made Gentle Treatment sound like a load of rich gifts, and the summons to a King's feast. Then suddenly Niggle felt ashamed. To hear that he was considered a case for Gentle Treatment overwhelmed him, and made him blush in the dark. It was like being publicly praised, when you and all the audience knew that the praise was not deserved. Niggle hid his blushes in the rough blanket.

There was a silence. Then the First Voice spoke to Niggle, quite close. "You have been listening," it said.

"Yes," said Niggle.

"Well, what have you to say?"

"Could you tell me about Parish?" said Niggle. "I should like to see him again. I hope he is not very ill? Can you cure his leg? It used to give him a wretched time. And please don't worry about him and me. He was a very good neighbour, and let me have excellent potatoes very cheap, which saved me a lot of time."

"Did he?" said the First Voice. "I am glad to hear it."

There was another silence. Niggle heard the Voices receding. "Well, I agree," he heard the First Voice say in the distance. "Let him go on to the next stage. Tomorrow, if you like."

Niggle woke up to find that his blinds were drawn, and his little cell was full of sunshine. He got up, and found that some comfortable clothes had been put out for him, not hospital uniform. After breakfast the doctor treated his sore hands, putting some salve on them that healed them at once. He gave Niggle some good advice, and a bottle of tonic (in case he needed it). In the middle of the morning they gave Niggle a biscuit and a glass of wine; and then they gave him a ticket.

"You can go to the railway station now," said the doctor. "The Porter will look after you. Good-bye."

Niggle slipped out of the main door, and blinked a little. The sun was very bright. Also he had expected to walk out into a large town, to match the size of the station; but he did not. He was on the top of a hill, green, bare, swept by a keen invigorating wind.

Nobody else was about. Away down under the hill he could see the roof of the station shining.

He walked downhill to the station briskly, but without hurry. The Porter spotted him at once.

"This way!" he said, and led Niggle to a bay, in which there was a very pleasant little local train standing: one coach, and a small engine, both very bright, clean, and newly painted. It looked as if this was their first run. Even the track that lay in front of the engine looked new: the rails shone, the chairs were painted green, and the sleepers gave off a delicious smell of fresh tar in the warm sunshine. The coach was empty.

"Where does this train go, Porter?" asked Niggle.

"I don't think they have fixed its name yet," said the Porter. "But you'll find it all right." He shut the door.

The train moved off at once. Niggle lay back in his seat. The little engine puffed along in a deep cutting with high green banks, roofed with blue sky. It did not seem very long before the engine gave a whistle, the brakes were put on, and the train stopped. There was no station, and no signboard, only a flight of steps up the green embankment. At the top of the steps there was a wicket-gate in a trim hedge. By the gate stood his bicycle; at least, it looked like his, and there was a yellow label tied to the bars with NIGGLE written on it in large black letters.

Niggle pushed open the gate, jumped on the bicycle, and went bowling downhill in the spring sunshine. Before long he found that the path on which he had started had disappeared, and the bicycle was rolling along over a marvellous turf. It was green and close; and yet he could see every blade distinctly. He seemed to remember having seen or dreamed of that sweep of grass somewhere or other. The curves of the land were familiar somehow. Yes: the ground was becoming level, as it should, and now, of course, it was beginning to rise again. A great green shadow came between him and the sun. Niggle looked up, and fell off his bicycle.

Before him stood the Tree, his Tree, finished. If you could say that of a Tree that was alive, its leaves opening, its branches growing and bending in the wind that Niggle had so often felt or guessed, and had so often failed to catch. He gazed at the Tree, and slowly he lifted his arms and opened them wide.

"It's a gift!" he said. He was referring to his art, and also to the result; but he was using the word quite literally.

He went on looking at the Tree. All the leaves he had ever laboured at were there, as he had imagined them rather than as he had made them; and there were others that had only budded in his mind, and many that might have budded, if only he had had time. Nothing was written on them, they were just exquisite leaves, yet they were dated as clear as a calendar. Some of the most beautiful—and the most perfect examples of the Niggle style—were seen to have been produced in collaboration with Mr. Parish: there was no other way of putting it.

The birds were building in the Tree. Astonishing birds: how they sang! They were mating, hatching, growing wings, and flying away singing into the Forest, even while he looked at them. For now he saw that the Forest was there too, opening out on either side, and marching away into the distance. The Mountains were glimmering far away.

After a time Niggle turned towards the Forest. Not because he was tired of the Tree, but he seemed to have got it all clear in his mind now, and was aware of it, and of its growth, even when he was not looking at it. As he walked away, he discovered an odd thing: the Forest, of course, was a distant Forest, yet he could approach it, even enter it, without its losing that particular charm. He had never before been able to walk into the distance without turning it into mere surroundings. It really added a considerable attraction to walking in the country, because, as you walked, new distances opened out; so that you now had double, treble, and quadruple distances, doubly, trebly, and quadruply enchanting. You could go on and on, and have a whole country in a garden, or in a picture (if you preferred to call it that). You could go on and on, but not perhaps for ever. There were the Mountains in the background. They did get nearer, very slowly. They did not seem to belong to the picture, or only as a link to something else, a glimpse through the trees of something different, a further stage: another picture.

Niggle walked about, but he was not merely pottering. He was looking round carefully. The Tree was finished, though not finished with—"Just the other way about to what it used to be," he thought—but in the Forest there were a number of inconclusive regions, that still needed work and thought. Nothing needed altering any longer, nothing was wrong, as far as it had gone, but it needed continuing up to a definite point. Niggle saw the point precisely, in each case.

He sat down under a very beautiful distant tree—a variation of the Great Tree, but quite individual, or it would be with a little more attention—and he considered where to begin work, and where to end it, and how much time was required. He could not quite work out his scheme.

"Of course!" he said. "What I need is Parish. There are lots of things about earth, plants, and trees that he knows and I don't. This place cannot be left just as my private park. I need help and advice: I ought to have got it sooner."

He got up and walked to the place where he had decided to begin work. He took off his coat. Then, down in a little sheltered hollow hidden from a further view, he saw a man looking round rather bewildered. He was leaning on a spade, but plainly did not know what to do. Niggle hailed him. "Parish!" he called.

Parish shouldered his spade and came up to him. He still limped a little. They did not speak, just nodded as they used to do, passing in the lane; but now they walked about together, arm in arm. Without talking, Niggle and Parish agreed exactly where to make the small house and garden, which seemed to be required.

As they worked together, it became plain that Niggle was now the better of the two at ordering his time and getting things done. Oddly enough, it was Niggle who became most absorbed in building and gardening, while Parish often wandered about looking at trees, and especially at the Tree.

One day Niggle was busy planting a quickset hedge, and Parish was lying on the grass near by, looking attentively at a beautiful and shapely little yellow flower growing in the green turf. Niggle had put a lot of them among the roots of his Tree long ago. Suddenly Parish looked up: his face was glistening in the sun, and he was smiling.

"This is grand!" he said. "I oughtn't to be here, really. Thank you for putting in a word for me."

"Nonsense," said Niggle. "I don't remember what I said, but anyway it was not nearly enough."

"Oh yes, it was," said Parish. "It got me out a lot sooner. That Second Voice, you know: he had me sent here; he said you had asked to see me. I owe it to you."

"No. You owe it to the Second Voice," said Niggle. "We both do."

They went on living and working together: I do not know how long. It is no use denying that at first they occasionally disagreed, especially when they got tired. For at first they did sometimes get tired. They found that they had both been provided with tonics. Each bottle had the same label: *A few drops to be taken in water from the Spring, before resting.*

They found the Spring in the heart of the Forest; only once long ago had Niggle imagined it, but he had never drawn it. Now he perceived that it was the source of the lake that glimmered, far away and the nourishment of all that grew in the country. The few drops made the water astringent, rather bitter, but invigorating; and it cleared the head. After drinking they rested alone; and then they got up again and things went on merrily. At such times Niggle would think of wonderful new flowers and plants, and Parish always knew exactly how to set them and where they would do best. Long before the tonics were finished they had ceased to need them. Parish lost his limp.

As their work drew to an end they allowed themselves more and more time for walking about, looking at the trees, and the flowers, and the lights and shapes, and the lie of the land. Sometimes they sang together; but Niggle found that he was now beginning to turn his eyes, more and more often, towards the Mountains.

The time came when the house in the hollow, the garden, the grass, the forest, the lake, and all the country was nearly complete, in its own proper fashion. The Great Tree was in full blossom.

"We shall finish this evening," said Parish one day. "After that we will go for a really long walk."

They set out next day, and they walked until they came right through the distances to the Edge. It was not visible, of course: there was no line, or fence, or wall; but they knew that they had come to the margin of that country. They saw a man, he looked like a shepherd; he was walking towards them, down the grass-slopes that led up into the Mountains.

"Do you want a guide?" he asked. "Do you want to go on?"

For a moment a shadow fell between Niggle and Parish, for Niggle knew that he did now want to go on, and (in a sense) ought to go on; but Parish did not want to go on, and was not yet ready to go.

"I must wait for my wife," said Parish to Niggle. "She'd be lonely. I rather gathered that they would send her after me, some time or other, when she was ready, and when I had got things for her. The house is finished now, as well as we could make it; but I should like to show it to her. She'll be able to make it better, I expect: more homely. I hope she'll like this country, too." He turned to the shepherd. "Are you a guide?" he asked. "Could you tell me the name of this country?"

"Don't you know?" said the man. "It is Niggle's Country. It is Niggle's Picture, or most of it: a little of it is now Parish's Garden."

"Niggle's Picture!" said Parish in astonishment. "Did *you* think of all this, Niggle? I never knew you were so clever. Why didn't you tell me?"

"He tried to tell you long ago," said the man; "but you would not look. He had only got canvas and paint in those days, and you wanted to mend your roof with them. This is what you and your wife used to call Niggle's Nonsense, or That Daubing."

"But it did not look like this then, not *real*," said Parish.

"No, it was only a glimpse then," said the man; "but you might have caught the glimpse, if you had ever thought it worth while to try."

"I did not give you much chance," said Niggle. "I never tried to explain. I used to call you Old Earthgrubber. But what does it matter? We have lived and worked together now. Things might have been different, but they could not have been better. All the same, I am afraid I shall have to be going on. We shall meet again, I expect: there must be many more things we can do together. Good-bye!" He shook Parish's hand warmly: a good, firm, honest hand it seemed. He turned and looked back for a moment. The blossom on the Great Tree was shining like flame. All the birds were flying in the air and singing. Then he smiled, and nodded to Parish, and went off with the shepherd.

He was going to learn about sheep, and the high pasturages, and look at a wider sky, and walk ever further and further towards the Mountains, always uphill. Beyond that I cannot guess what became of him. Even little Niggle in his old home could glimpse the Mountains far away, and they got into the borders of his picture; but what they are really like, and what lies beyond them, only those can say who have climbed them.

"I think he was a silly little man," said Councillor Tompkins. "Worthless, in fact; no use to Society at all."

"Oh, I don't know," said Atkins, who was nobody of importance, just a schoolmaster. "I am not so sure: it depends on what you mean by *use*."

"No practical or economic use," said Tompkins. "I dare say he could have been made into a serviceable cog of some sort, if you schoolmasters knew your business. But you don't, and so we get useless people of his sort. If I ran this country I should put him and his like to some job that they're fit for, washing dishes in a communal kitchen or something, and I should see that they did it properly. Or I would put them away. I should have put *him* away long ago."

"Put him away? You mean you'd have made him start on the journey before his time?"

"Yes, if you must use that meaningless old expression. Push him through the tunnel into the great Rubbish Heap: that's what I mean."

"Then you don't think painting is worth anything, not worth preserving, or improving, or even making use of?"

"Of course, painting has uses," said Tompkins. "But you couldn't make use of his painting. There is plenty of scope for bold young men not afraid of new ideas and new methods. None for this old-fashioned stuff. Private day-dreaming. He could not have designed a telling poster to save his life. Always fiddling with leaves and flowers.

I asked him why, once. He said he thought they were pretty! Can you believe it? He said *pretty!* 'What, digestive and genital organs of plants?' I said to him; and he had nothing to answer. Silly footler."

"Footler," sighed Atkins. "Yes, poor little man, he never finished anything. Ah well, his canvases have been put to 'better uses,' since he went. But I am not sure, Tompkins. You remember that large one, the one they used to patch the damaged house next door to his, after the gales and floods? I found a corner of it torn off, lying in a field. It was damaged, but legible: a mountain-peak and a spray of leaves. I can't get it out of my mind."

"Out of your what?" said Tompkins.

"Who are you two talking about?" said Perkins intervening in the cause of peace: Atkins had flushed rather red.

"The name's not worth repeating," said Tompkins. "I don't know why we are talking about him at all. He did not live in town."

"No," said Atkins; "but you had your eye on his house, all the same. That is why you used to go and call, and sneer at him while drinking his tea. Well, you've got his house now, as well as the one in town, so you need not grudge him his name. We were talking about Niggle, if you want to know, Perkins."

"Oh, poor little Niggle!" said Perkins. "Never knew he painted."

That was probably the last time Niggle's name ever came up in conversation. However, Atkins preserved the odd corner. Most of it crumbled; but one beautiful leaf remained intact. Atkins had it framed. Later he left it to the Town Museum, and for a long while "Leaf: by Niggle" hung there in a recess, and was noticed by a few eyes. But eventually the Museum was burnt down, and the leaf, and Niggle, were entirely forgotten in his old country.

"It is proving very useful indeed," said the Second Voice. "As a holiday, and a refreshment. It is splendid for convalescence; and not only for that, for many it is the best introduction to the Mountains. It works wonders in some cases. I am sending more and more there. They seldom have to come back."

"No, that is so," said the First Voice. "I think we shall have to give the region a name. What do you propose?"

"The Porter settled that some time ago," said the Second Voice. "*Train for Niggle's Parish in the bay*: he has shouted that for a long while now. Niggle's Parish. I sent a message to both of them to tell them."

"What did they say?"

"They both laughed. Laughed—the Mountains rang with it!"

The Diversity
of Fantastic Literature

THE CONTINUUM OF THE FANTASTIC

Individual narratives may be more or less fantastic. Having located the technical stimulus for the affect we associate with the fantastic in the interactive process by which a reader engages a text, we must recognize that the perception of the fantastic in the text is to some extent dependent on the reader, on his experience of life and letters, on his frame of mind, and so on. A text may seem more or less fantastic to different readers or even to the same reader at different times or during different readings of the same text. But even if we postulate some ideal reader who is maximally aware of the subtleties of manipulation and reversal in a text, some texts will simply offer more fantastic reversal than others. This conclusion follows from our initial recognition that even realistic narratives are minimally fantastic, while even thorough-going Fantasies are minimally realistic. We can express these observations by a spatial metaphor, conceiving of narratives as arranged along a continuum stretching from Realism on the left to Fantasy on the right.

Since none of us is, in fact, an ideal reader, it would not pay to be overly precise in assigning works a place on this scale, which theoretically admits of infinite variation. For the sake of discussion, let me suggest that we give the scale ten cardinal points and that we recognize that any given reader's assignment of a text to one or another of these is not so much an assertion about the exact and unavoidable nature of the text but about the reader's best perceptions of it as he remembers a given reading. Understanding these provisions, a more precise delineation of the continuum of the fantastic may well provide us with a handy device for analyzing the relationships among fantastic narratives.

Cardinal points 1 and 2 should be reserved for Realism, whatever that means. In some times and to some people books like Henry James's *The Ambassadors* have been considered to be as realistic as one could get, but at other times James's concentration on individual psychology has made it seem that he unrealistically plays down social forces; in that case, more panoramic books, like Émile Zola's *Germinal*, would be thought to be as realistic as one could get. If James is a 1, Zola is probably a 2, and vice versa. Both can quite arguably be called Realism. 3 and 4 would not be Realism, but still would be realistic. Comic novels like those of Jane Austen, which often depend on lucky coincidence and invariably lead to a happy marriage, are much more fundamentally alternative to our real world than a novel of Realism would be. A Dickens novel, while still realistic, is yet more thoroughly alternative than is an Austen novel, because Dickens has his plots depend upon whole strings of marvelous coincidences and he thinks nothing of indulging at least some omnipotence of thought, say by letting Oliver Twist discover the real family for which he has always longed. If James and Zola are 1 and 2 on the scale, then Austen and Dickens are 3 and 4, and together these four categories make up the realistic branch of the continuum.

Fairy tales, as we have already noted, offer a highly conventionalized alternative to the real world; they are truly fantastic literature. However, once within the world of a traditional fairy tale, one experiences no more fantastic reversals. Hence, one can easily imagine narratives that are more fantastic than are fairy tales, works like those of heroic fantasy, which use a fairy-tale-like world but continually invade the normally golden and crystalline world of Faërie with explicit human passions and actual human blood. Each invasion, if one is sensitive to the continuing shift of ground rules from the fairy-tale-like to the realistic, offers another shock of the fantastic. Still, a text could be even more fantastic than that without yet becoming a thoroughgoing Fantasy. For example, the thematic development could depend upon some notion which itself is subject to continuing reversal. If a tale like "The Magic Swan Geese" belongs at one cardinal point, a self-conscious fairy tale like that by MacDonald should be at the point next on the right, while Poe's "The Black Cat," with its constantly reversing development of the theme of the supernatural belongs yet one point further right on the scale. If we find a narrative that is yet more fantastic, say made stylistically fantastic by employing, in addition to matters of setting, plot, and theme, the linguistic reversals characteristic of puns or self-reflexivity or oxymoron, as we do find in the selections from Juster and Carroll, then that work may properly be called a Fantasy. Whether such a work is as fantastic as one can imagine, of course, depends upon one's imagination, but one could safely assign Juster and Carroll to the 9 and 10 range. The works to their left, then, while not Fantasies, are truly fantastic literature. Our examples would then make "The Magic Swan Geese" a 6, "The Tale of Cosmo" a 7, and "The Black Cat" an 8.

In using the continuum, the exact number chosen is not nearly so important, of course, as the explication of one's reading response that led to the choice. In constructing our scale I have not yet used 5—works that are more fantastic than Dickens but less fantastic than fairy tales. My reason is that I sense there to be a large body of books which deserve to be distinguished as falling between those two other ranges on the continuum. Such works would offer a fantastic narrative world, more fantastic indeed than Dickens's world, but not one so flagrantly alternative to our own as to be inhabited by witches and dragons. Such a work would offer as much security as fairy-tale worlds do, would have clearly defined conventions and reward reader expectation positively, but the security—no matter how magical in fact—would seem to be explicable in ways that, again, are not flagrantly alternative to our world. One genre that fits these parameters is the Tale of the Great Detective.

Consider: in such a tale we almost invariably find a puzzle that is guaranteed insoluble and a Great Detective who will solve it, a police Inspector (or Magistrate or Prefect) who is good enough at his job but limited to thinking in terms of that job and hence incapable of dealing with that other essential ingredient, the imaginative criminal; justice, in the classic versions, always distributed to the proper parties and the world made right again; the story usually beginning in a quiet, isolated, civilized atmosphere (like Holmes's apartment), requiring someone to barge in with a problem that necessitates leaving the apartment for somewhere uncivilized (London at night, or the moors) in order to solve the crime and allow the Great Detective to return to his quiet, isolated, civilized atmosphere. In short, the Tale of the Great Detective is a fairy tale for adults. Absentation, testing, return. Security is the watchword, and all is secure once (and this is alternative to our world) guilt has been properly brought to light and the innocent saved, the evil punished. The Tale of the Great Detective, as opposed to police procedural novels or spy thrillers, shares even the cleanliness of the fairy tale. The corpse is no gorier in a Holmes story than the witch is in "Hansel and Grethel." Such adult stories, then, although clearly not true Fantasies, are obviously and significantly fantastic. There are certain other genres, like the dime Western, that also fall at point 5 on our approximate continuum.

To summarize, then, for the sake of convenience: all literature is to some extent fantastic and we can try to indicate the extent by reading each text and deciding how much use it makes of fundamental reversal. We might remember cardinal points of comparison on the continuum of the fantastic by thinking of specific examples.

1. Henry James, *The Ambassadors*	Realism
2. Émile Zola, *Germinal*	
3. Jane Austen	Realistic literature
4. Charles Dickens	
5. Tales of the Great Detective	Fantastic literature
6. "The Magic Swan Geese"	
7. "The Tale of Cosmo"	
8. "The Black Cat"	
9. "The Royal Banquet"	Fantasy
10. *Alice in Wonderland*	

Even such a cursory exploration of the continuum of the fantastic suggests that if we took Fantasy and Fantastic literature together we would be confronting a rich diversity of narrative texts.

THE DIVERSITY OF FANTASTIC LITERATURE

This section of the anthology is designed to offer a broad range of works that will help one gain some sense of the diversity of fantastic literature. Those works gathered in the section called "Fantasy" exemplify much of what we have said, but may do so only if read in certain ways. The piece by Addison contains a self-conscious, fairy-tale-like story, and hence might be thought of as falling at the 7 or 8 point on our continuum. However, at least two matters need to be noted in addition. First, that narrative is set within a straight essay. Essays, of course, make different claims for the truth of their arguments than do fictions; the two forms implicitly suggest two different relations with the reader's real world. The reversals that we feel as we are reminded of the relationship between the story and the essay frame around it make the total piece feel somewhat more fantastic. Second, the theme of the piece—the nature of time and the sense of duration —has obvious implications for understanding the reading process itself. Thus, the piece is also implicitly self-reflexive. My own sense is that the structural and thematic shocks added to the already fantastic and self-conscious tale make Addison's piece about as fantastic as "The Royal Banquet." This, of course, is one reader's judgment. Every reader will judge for himself.

"Ritter Gluck" and "The Oval Portrait" explore a common motif in the fantastic, the separation and interpenetration of life and art. Since art is necessarily to some extent fantastic, one should expect a concern with the nature of the art/life boundary to be common in fantastic narratives. In addition, since the discussion of that boundary itself exists in a work of art which must masquerade as presenting reality, such narratives are also self-reflexive. "The Oval Portrait," incidentally, deserves comparison with Lovecraft's "The Picture in the House" because of their common concern with graphic art, and with the Addison piece because of a common attention to the importance of framing narratives (as well as framing pictures). "The Secret Life of Walter Mitty" is not as thoroughly fantastic a narrative as the others, but it is more pointedly obvious than almost any other in identifying a psychological source for fantasy and showing dramatically at least one reason why fantasy and the fantastic are so important to people. And, finally, the section contains the excerpts from Carroll and Juster, which we have already remarked on. Taken as a group, these six selections demonstrate that even in trying to exemplify the most common and obvious characteristics of Fantasy, one finds oneself dealing with materials that in some ways are terribly disparate. The many fantastic worlds, after all, are much roomier than the one poor real world.

Each of the next four sections collects narratives that fall within a single conventional world, just as all fairy tales or all Tales of the Great Detective share a single base in literary conventions. These four sections hardly exhaust the universe of fantastic worlds, but they are the worlds most popular today. Science fiction is especially important and so has gotten a double dose to make internal comparisons (say, between the two stories called "The Star") richer. These four sections are arranged roughly in the chronological order in which they achieved prominence and hence can be thought to have influenced their successors. Each section presents tales taken from across a significant period of time so that one can assess both the ways in which a type of narrative has changed and the common elements that have been retained. "Horror fiction" is perhaps the broadest term of the four and might be thought to include, say, "ghost stories." Ghost stories have a rhetoric peculiarly their own and as a narrative type flourished over a comparatively short period. Nowadays we see another type of horror fiction as the successor to ghost stories: occult fiction exemplified by *Rosemary's Baby, The Exorcist, The Other,* and so forth. Occult fiction, like ghost stories, has its own conventions and rhetoric and, so far at least, is significant over a comparatively short time span. Heroic fantasy, also characterized by a special rhetoric and set of conventions, has had a longer run. It should be clear in reading this section that Warner's selection could be written as it is only by virtue of the author's ability to presume an audience familiar with the conventions established by Morris and the mood made famous by Lord Dunsany. Science fiction too, by covering so long a time span in this collection, provides the materials for studying both how a set of literary conventions can come to be seen as constituting a genre and also how the conventions of that genre can develop.

THE FANTASTIC AND LITERARY HISTORY

Most of us were entertained by fairy tales as children; most of us, when caring for children, enjoy recounting for them those same fairy tales. Nonetheless, the transition from happy hearer to happy teller may take twenty years, years in which we show no interest in fairy tales whatever. How can this be? There are two answers. First, our happiness at telling the stories is not the same as was our happiness in hearing them, no more than the pleasures of getting a present are the same as those of giving one. The more adult pleasures of giving require an ability to participate in another person's experience and an ability to remember one's own experience. Second, the primary enjoyment of receiving fairy tales dissolves for us as we grow up and begin to reject the stories as just more of the same. The sameness we note is not, however, mere repetition. Little children who enjoy fairy tales also enjoy hearing the same tale time and again and require that each retelling appear to be a word-perfect repetition. Part of the security of the land of Faërie is enacted in the audience situation by this exact repetition. The sameness that pales is rather the sameness of the very structure of fairy tales, that marvelously universal—and finally boring—Proppian structure which we count on unconsciously to force everything to come out right. When this narrative structure begins to seem just too simple to be relevant—even as alternative—to our real world, then we seek narratives of increasing complexity and leave fairy tales behind. George Kubler has called this sort of enervation due to artistic experience "aesthetic fatigue." As adults reciting fairy tales, we are grateful for the sparkle of young eyes that conquers aesthetic fatigue and gives us back our youth. The reading of children's literature to children is, like fantastic literature itself, an indulgence in our atavistic desires.

Children, fortunately, are not the only expedients for sensitizing our jaded responses. Authors often seek out new materials to cut into suits of the same old design; thus American psychological novels of this century have been working their way through a cast of characters drawn from different ethnic backgrounds and races. These are significant developments, to be sure, for using blacks, say, as protagonists in the formerly white domain of serious fiction, has important political implications for both whites and blacks. An equally important technique for enlivening our response to narrative is highlighting some of those generic conventions which normally affect us only unconsciously but nonetheless define the genre itself. Highlighting thus makes us conscious of those conventions. This is obviously the case, in differing ways, with parody, satire, and farce. Ghost stories, being relative latecomers to horror fiction, almost uniformly contain some commentary about the fact that one, naturally, does not believe in ghosts. This sort of self-reflection makes the typical ghost story just that much more fantastic than a traditional horror story. The device of self-reflection, by virtue of highlighting the narrative situation, has the same fantastic effect as the entrance into a fairy tale of a plumber named Sid. Most of the devices by which a genre develops work from the assumption that the reader of the newer text knows the conventions that defined the older text, and hence those older conventions can be treated as an art world for which the newer text offers an alternative. In the case of Clarke's "The Star," the reference is not merely to earlier science fiction but specifically to Wells's story of that same title. Thus Clarke's tale must be read with double sight, both in its own right and as a commentary on the earlier piece. As with the other highlighting devices we have noted, such double sight creates effects clearly akin in the double vision we have in reading a fairy tale to a child.

A modern piece of heroic fantasy like "The Five Black Swans" doubtless has some resonance with the old fairy tale called "The Magic Swan Geese," but the most direct source for Warner's writing is the narrower tradition of heroic fantasy itself, such works as "Golden Wings." Both Morris and Warner are concerned with lost love, among other things, but while Morris sees the literary world itself in which those conventions were supposed to have functioned as problematic and while Morris tries to lose himself in that world, Warner consciously opposes that world to a more mundane world that resembles our own. Her technique forces our attention to shift repeatedly from one world to the other, and each shift, potentially, constitutes a new reversal of the locally operating narrative ground rules. Thus Warner's piece is more fantastic than Morris's, although they are both recognizably part of the same genre. Applied to theme, style, plot, character, or setting, or some combination of these, the fantastic has been one of the strongest forces combating aesthetic fatigue and thereby forging the development of literary genres. The pressures to create fantastic worlds come not only from the so-called real world; they come as well from the world of art.

THE FANTASTIC AND GENRE CRITICISM

Comparison and contrast are complementary aspects of a fundamental tool of human inquiry. In order to make fruitful contrasts and comparisons we choose objects of inquiry that seem somewhat alike and yet somewhat different. If one wants to know about auto engines, one compares engines from different types of autos but not internal combustion engines from airplanes or starter motors from cars. The objects of the real world do not fall necessarily into any particular set of categories; rather, human beings put them into classes in ways that serve human needs. There is no single botanical feature, or set of features, that objectively distinguishes a weed from other plants; weed is the class of plants we do not want. In art, the classes are called genres (ultimately from the Latin word for class), and they have been recognized through time by their continuing utility. Even though we seem to have trouble defining, say, comedy and tragedy, those genres, both in themselves and as an opposing pair, have amply demonstrated their utility in prompting inquiry and insights that people have found useful.

If our conception of the fantastic offers a useful way of looking at narrative, then perhaps we can use the fantastic to suggest non-traditional types of genres that might lead to non-traditional types of insights. The most obvious possibility is that we compare works that fall at similar points on our continuum of the fantastic. We have noticed, for example, that Tales of the Great Detective are somewhat less fantastic than fairy tales. However, we have also noticed that the increasing use of the fantastic is a normal part of the historical development of any given genre. Many Tales of the Great Detective are made into, say, class 6 tales, by their use of self-reflection. Ellery Queen, for example, is the pseudonymous author of tales about a Great Detective named Ellery Queen; Agatha Christie's fictional Hercule Poirot is always claiming superiority to Sherlock Holmes on the ground that Holmes is only a fictional character. In that sort of literary environment, one in which we are as aware of convention as we are with the words "Once upon a time," we may truly be dealing with fairy tales for adults. Once this comparison comes to mind, we may see that it leads to some rather significant connections: both class 6 types offer the comfort of extreme stability, both resolve the threat to stability by a return to the original value system (rather than the learning of a new one, as in novels of personal development), and both are highly formulaic. This last quality implies that a given reader may enjoy the type more than any particular example of it, and this is true: just as children will clamor for a story with witches, an adult will stop by his local bookstore to see if there's an Agatha Christie he's missed.

This sort of comparison also leads us to ask questions that might not otherwise arise. For example, why are fairy tales for children, while Tales of the Great Detective are for adults? In part, one supposes, because adults will reject the magic of Faërie as irrelevant to the real world, while children will accept it. The adults prefer the "science" of the Holmes figure. However, as anyone who has ever read a Holmes story knows, the science he employs may sound possible, but for a human being it is impossible. For example, in one story Holmes's suspicions depend upon his just happening to know the time high tide had occurred at some particular seaside town months in the past. Holmes's use of "science," then—and its associated jargon, artifacts, and so on—is a literary convention designed to justify the reader's belief in a perfectly controlled world. Children, perhaps because grown-ups do in fact control their worlds to so great a degree, do not seem to need these trappings, but adults obviously do. By seeing fairy tales and Tales of the Great Detective both as class 6 narratives, we have come to see that both offer similar psychic economy, but in detail they are different in order to reach different audiences. We can go further and suggest that "science" could become a sufficient justification only after the adult reading public had developed a sense of the usefulness of science. In other words, the mere existence of science was insufficient. The development of these tales in the second third of the nineteenth century accords with this guess. Further, once science stops appearing to offer an emblem for rational control, the genre will lose its appeal. This is a process we may be observing at the moment.

Of course, the fantastic may be used by authors to develop a given genre so that it retains interest. We would expect there to be fairy tales and Tales of the Great Detective that show ever more fantastic devices, including works so rich in these that one would want to call them Fantasies. In fact, this is the case. Fairy tales have gone to Fantasy with the Alice books, as we have noted; detective fiction has done ͻe same with a work like Robbe-Grillet's *The Erasers;* dime Westerns get more and more fantastic, until we find such true Fantasies as Ishmael Reed's *Yellow Back Radio Broke-Down;* picaresque novels stretch from a work in the 4 range, like the anonymous *Lazarillo de Tormes,* all the way to a work in the 10 range, like *Options,* by Robert Sheckley; and science fiction varies from range 5 novels like Wells's *The Time Machine* to range 10 works like David Lindsay's *A Voyage to Arcturus.* In other words, for each traditional genre we should be able to find a minimal degree of the fantastic that it requires to serve some need (range 5 for Tales of the Great Detective and science fiction, range 6 for fairy tales and ghost stories) and then discover what that common need might be in the total range. In addition, we can watch each genre develop—and thus find out how aesthetic fatigue set in—by looking specifically at the increase of the fantastic, at examples of the genre from higher-numbered ranges.

Finally, we should note that by the time the fantastic has been used enough to make a work range 9 or 10, readers ordinarily no longer call the work by the name of the genre it arose from (fairy tale, science fiction) but instead simply call it Fantasy. The fact that Fantasy, at least when encountered in its thoroughgoing forms, has a common feel has led people, intelligently enough, to treat Fantasy as a genre. Traditional genres are comparatively easy to distinguish from each other; although there are borderline works, of course, we can pretty much tell whether a given story is a Tale of a Great Detective or a True Romance. But as works become more fantastic our responses to them are ever more dominated by this fact, and so the genres feel convergent. Thus we often find ourselves wondering if we really can distinguish between, say, science fiction and Fantasy. The problem lies not in the field of literature but in our ways of looking at that field.

We can all make generic distinctions between "The Birthmark" and Hoffmann's "Ritter Gluck," but can we distinguish the latter from "The Sandman"? This story, also by Hoffmann, is certainly science fiction, concerning as it does the story of a man who falls in love with a robot; but it is clearly horror fiction, concerning as it does the invasion of the real world by the devil; and still again, it is a true Fantasy, shocking us repeatedly by the alternation of ground rules—first sensible psychology, then black magic, then warmed-over physics, and, finally, demonology. The solution to this problem in genre theory lies in the initial question: by supposing that Fantasy is the same *type* of genre as fairy tale or ghost story, people have fallen into a situation that invites dispute. "The Sandman" is science fiction *and* Fantasy, just as *Alice in Wonderland* is fairy tale *and* Fantasy while "Our Ideas of Time" is a philosophic essay *and* Fantasy. Our use of the continuum of the fantastic and our recognition of the importance of the fantastic as a force in literary history has led us to a revised understanding of the role of the fantastic in genre criticism. This new role does not compete with traditional genre theory but does complement it by offering the reader a unified theory that can cross traditional generic boundaries in order to see how common human needs have been addressed by the rich diversity of fantastic literature.

FANTASY

Our Ideas of Time   *JOSEPH ADDISON*

*T*HE LAST METHOD which I proposed in my *Saturday's* Paper, for filling up those empty Spaces of Life which are so tedious and burthensome to idle People, is the employing our selves in the Pursuit of Knowledge. I remember Mr. *Boyle,* speaking of a certain Mineral, tells us, That a Man may consume his whole Life in the Study of it, without arriving at the Knowledge of all its Qualities. The Truth of it is, there is not a single Science, or any Branch of it, that might not furnish a Man with Business for Life, though it were much longer than it is.

I shall not here engage on those beaten Subjects of the Usefulness of Knowledge, nor of the Pleasure and Perfection it gives the Mind, nor on the Methods of attaining it, nor recommend any particular Branch of it, all which have been the Topicks of many other Writers: but shall indulge my self in a Speculation that is more uncommon, and may therefore perhaps be more entertaining.

I have before shewn how the unemployed Parts of Life appear long and tedious, and shall here endeavour to shew how those Parts of Life which are exercised in Study, Reading, and the Pursuits of Knowledge, are long but not tedious; and by that Means discover a Method of lengthening our Lives, and at the same Time of turning all the Parts of them to our Advantage.

Mr. *Lock* observes, "That we get the Idea of Time, or Duration, by reflecting on that Train of Ideas which succeed one another in our Minds: That for this Reason, when we sleep soundly without dreaming, we have no Perception of Time, or the Length of it, whilst we sleep; and that the Moment wherein we leave off to think, till the Moment we begin to think again, seem to have no

Distance." To which the Author adds: "And so, I doubt not, but it would be to a waking Man, if it were possible for him to keep only one *Idea* in his Mind, without Variation, and the Succession of others: And we see, that one who fixes his Thoughts very intently on one thing, so as to take but little Notice of the Succession of *Ideas* that pass in his Mind whilst he is taken up with that earnest Contemplation, lets slip out of his Account a good Part of that Duration, and thinks that Time shorter than it is.

We might carry this Thought further, and consider a Man as, on one Side, shortening his Time by thinking on nothing, or but a few things; so, on the other, as lengthening it, by employing his Thoughts on many Subjects, or by entertaining a quick and constant Succession of Ideas. Accordingly Monsieur *Mallebranche,* in his *Enquiry after Truth,* (which was published several Years before Mr. *Lock's Essay on Humane Understanding*) tells us, That it is possible some Creatures may think Half an Hour as long as we do a thousand Years; or look upon that Space of Duration which we call a Minute, as an Hour, a Week, a Month, or an whole Age.

This Notion of Monsieur *Mallebranche,* is capable of some little Explanation from what I have quoted out of Mr. *Lock;* for if our Notion of Time is produced by our reflecting on the Succession of Ideas in our Mind, and this Succession may be infinitely accelerated or retarded, it will follow, that different Beings may have different Notions of the same Parts of Duration, according as their Ideas, which we suppose are equally distinct in each of them, follow one another in a greater or less Degree of Rapidity.

There is a famous Passage in the *Alcoran,* which looks as if *Mahomet* had been possessed of the Notion we are now speaking of. It is there said, That the Angel *Gabriel* took *Mahomet* out of his Bed one Morning to give him a Sight of all things in the seven Heavens, in Paradise, and in Hell, which the Prophet took a distinct View of; and after having held ninety thousand Conferences with God, was brought back again to his Bed. All this, says the *Alcoran,* was transacted in so small a Space of Time, that *Mahomet,* at his Return, found his Bed still warm, and took up an Earthen Pitcher (which was thrown down at the very Instant that the Angel *Gabriel* carried him away) before the Water was all spilt.

There is a very pretty Story in the *Turkish* Tales which relates to this Passage of that famous Impostor, and bears some Affinity to the Subject we are now upon. A Sultan of *Ægypt*, who was an Infidel, used to laugh at this Circumstance in *Mahomet's* Life, as what was altogether impossible and absurd: But conversing one Day with a great Doctor in the Law, who had the Gift of working Miracles, the Doctor told him, he would quickly convince him of the Truth of this Passage in the History of *Mahomet,* if he would consent to do what he should desire of him. Upon this the Sultan was directed to place himself by an huge Tub of Water, which he did accordingly; and as he stood by the Tub amidst a Circle of his great Men, the holy Man bid him plunge his Head into the Water, and draw it up again: The King accordingly thrust his Head into the Water, and at the same time found himself at the Foot of a Mountain on a Sea-shore. The King immediately began to rage against his Doctor for this Piece of Treachery and Witchcraft; but at length, knowing it was in vain to be angry, he set himself to think on proper Methods for getting a Livelihood in this strange Country: Accordingly he applied himself to some People whom he saw at work in a neighbouring Wood; these People conducted him to a Town that stood at a little Distance from the Wood, where after some Adventures he married a Woman of great Beauty and Fortune. He lived with this Woman so long till he had by her seven Sons and seven Daughters: He was afterwards reduced to great Want, and forced to think of plying in the Streets as a Porter for his Livelyhood. One Day as he was walking alone by the Sea-Side, being seized with many melancholy Reflections upon his former and his present State of Life, which had raised a Fit of Devotion in him, he threw off his Cloaths with a Design to wash himself, according to the Custom of the *Mahometans,* before he said his Prayers.

After his first Plunge into the Sea, he no sooner raised his Head above the Water, but he found himself standing by the Side of the Tub, with the great Men of his Court about him, and the holy Man at his Side: He immediately upbraided his Teacher for having sent him on such a Course of Adventures, and betray'd him into so long a State of Misery and Servitude; but was wonderfully surprized when he heard that the State he talked of was only a Dream and

Delusion; that he had not stirred from the Place where he then stood; and that he had only dipped his Head into the Water, and immediately taken it out again.

The *Mahometan* Doctor took this Occasion of instructing the Sultan, that nothing was impossible with God; and that *He,* with whom a Thousand Years are but as one Day, can if he pleases make a single Day, nay a single Moment, appear to any of his Creatures as a thousand Years.

I shall leave my Reader to compare these Eastern Fables with the Notions of those two great Philosophers whom I have quoted in this Paper; and shall only, by way of Application, desire him to consider how we may extend Life beyond its natural Dimensions, by applying ourselves diligently to the Pursuits of Knowledge.

The Hours of a wise Man are lengthened by his Ideas, as those of a Fool are by his Passions: The Time of the one is long, because he does not know what to do with it: so is that of the other, because he distinguishes every Moment of it with useful or amusing Thought; or in other Words, because the one is always wishing it away, and the other always enjoying it.

How different is the View of past Life, in the Man who is grown old in Knowledge and Wisdom, from that of him who is grown old in Ignorance and Folly? The latter is like the Owner of a barren Country, that fills his Eye with the Prospect of naked Hills and Plains which produce nothing either profitable or ornamental: the other beholds a beautiful and spacious Landskip, divided into delightful Gardens, green Meadows, fruitful Fields, and can scarce cast his Eye on a single Spot of his Possessions, that is not covered with some beautiful Plant or Flower.

Ritter Gluck:
A Recollection from the Year 1809
                                        E. T. A. HOFFMANN

U SUALLY THERE ARE still several lovely days in the late fall in Berlin. The cheerful sun breaks out of the clouds, and the moisture in the soft breezes that drift through the streets quickly evaporates. A gaudy stream of people wanders along the Lindenstrasse to the Zoological Gardens—dandies, solid citizens with their wives and adored children, all dressed in their Sunday best, clergymen, Jewesses, junior barristers, prostitutes, professors, milliners, dancers, officers, etc. Soon all the tables at Klaus's and at Weber's are occupied; the coffee steams, the dandies light their thin cigars; everyone chats, quarrels about war and peace, about Mademoiselle Bethmann's shoes, whether they were recently gray or green, about the closed commercial state and the bad pennies, etc., until everything dissolves into an aria from *Fanchon,* in which a harp that is out of tune, a couple of untuned violins, a consumptive flute, and a spastic bassoon torment themselves and the people nearby. Close to the railing that separates the crowds at Weber's from the Heerstrasse are several small round tables and garden chairs. One can breathe fresh air here, observe those coming and going; one is remote from the cacaphonic racket of that execrable orchestra. That is where I sit, abandoning myself to playful reveries in which sympathetic figures appear with whom I chat about learning, art, everything that is supposedly dearest to man. The crowd of strollers weaves past me more and more gayly, but nothing disturbs me, nothing can scatter my imaginary companions. Only the damned trio from an extremely vile waltz drags me from my dream world. I hear only the screeching upper register of the violins and flute and the snoring bass of the bassoon; the sounds rise and fall, keeping firmly to octaves that lacerate the ear, and I cry out involuntarily like a person seized by a burning pain, "What insane music! What abominable octaves!" Someone murmurs next to me, "Accursed fate! Another octave-chaser!"

I looked up and only then became aware that a man had sat down at the same table, his eyes riveted on me; I could not take my eyes off him.

I had never seen a face, a figure, which had made such an impression on me so quickly. A gently curved nose was attached to a wide, open forehead, which had noticeable swellings above the bushy, partly gray eyebrows, beneath which eyes blazed forth with an almost youthful fire (the man was probably over fifty). The delicately formed chin was a strange contrast to the closed mouth, and a ludicrous smile produced by the curious play of muscles in his sunken cheeks seemed to rebel against the deep, melancholy seriousness which rested on his forehead. There were only a few gray locks of hair behind his large ears which stuck straight out from his head. A very wide, modern frock coat enveloped his large gaunt frame. Just as my glance met his, he cast down his eyes and continued the occupation that my exclamation had evidently interrupted. With evident satisfaction, he was shaking out some tobacco from various little paper bags into a large tin can that was in front of him and was dampening it with red wine from a quarter liter bottle. The music had stopped; I felt compelled to address him.

"It is a relief that the music has stopped," I said. "It was unendurable."

The old man cast a fleeting glance at me and shook out the last paper bag.

"It would be better not to play at all," I continued. "Isn't that your opinion?"

"I don't have an opinion," he said. "You are a musician and connoisseur by profession—"

"You are mistaken. I am neither. I once learned how to play the piano and the thorough bass, as one must as part of a good education; and at that time I was told, among other things, that nothing pro-

duced a more unpleasant effect than having the bass pace the so-
prano in octave intervals. I accepted that at that time as authoritative
and I have since found it always verified."

"Really?" he interrupted me, as he stood up and strode slowly and
thoughtfully towards the musicians while frequently striking his
forehead with the flat of his hand, his face upturned, like someone
trying to awaken a recollection. I saw him speaking to the musicians
whom he treated with lordly dignity. He returned and had scarcely
sat down when they began to play the overture to *Iphigenia in Aulis*.

With half-closed eyes, his folded arms resting on the table, he listened to the *andante*. Tapping his left foot gently, he signaled the
entrance of the voices; then he raised his head—quickly casting a
glance around—he rested his left hand with fingers spread apart on
the table as if he were playing a chord on a piano, and he raised his
right hand up high. He was the Kapellmeister signalling the orchestra the start of a new tempo—his right hand dropped and the *allegro*
began! A burning glow flushed his pale cheeks; his eyebrows met on
his wrinkled forehead; an inner storm inflamed his wild expression
with a fire that increasingly consumed the smile that still hovered
around his half-opened mouth. Then he leaned back and raised his
eyebrows; the play of muscles around his mouth began again; his
eyes shone; a deep inner pain was released in a voluptuous pleasure
that convulsively shook his inner being. He drew a breath from deep
within his lungs; drops formed on his forehead; he signalled for the
entrance of the *tutti* and other major places; his right hand kept the
beat, and with his left he pulled out a handkerchief and wiped his
face. Thus he clothed with flesh and color the skeleton of the overture played by the pair of violins. I heard the soft, melting elegy
which the flute utters when the storm of the violins and the bass
viols has exhausted itself and the thunder of the drums is silent; I
heard the softly played tones of the cello and the bassoon which
filled the heart with ineffable sadness; the *tutti* returned, the *unisono*
strode on like a sublime and lofty giant, the somber lament died away
under his crushing tread.

The overture was over; he let his arms fall, and he sat there with
his eyes closed like a person exhausted by excessive exertion. His bot-

tle was empty; I filled his glass with Burgundy, which I had meanwhile ordered. He sighed deeply and seemed to be awaking from a dream. I urged him to drink, which he did without ceremony, and while he dashed off the glass in one swallow, he cried, "I am satisfied with the performance! The orchestra performed very nicely!"

"And yet," I interrupted, "and yet, only the pale outline of a masterpiece that has been composed with vivid colors was presented."

"Do I judge rightly? You are not a Berliner!"

"Quite right. I only stay here from time to time."

"The Burgundy is good. But it is getting cold here."

"Let's go inside and finish the bottle."

"A good suggestion. I don't know you; but on the other hand, you don't know me either. We will not ask each other's name; names are sometimes a nuisance. I will drink the Burgundy; it costs me nothing and we are comfortable together and that is enough."

He said all this with a good-natured cordiality. We had entered the room. When he sat down, he opened his frock coat and I noticed with surprise that he was wearing under it an embroidered waistcoat, long coattails, black velvet britches, and a quite small dagger. He buttoned the coat again carefully.

"Why did you ask me if I was a Berliner?" I began.

"Because in that case I would have been obliged to leave you."

"That sounds mysterious."

"Not in the least, as soon as I tell you that I—well, that I am a composer."

"I still can't guess what you mean."

"Then forgive my remark, for I see you do not understand anything about Berlin and Berliners."

He rose and paced violently up and down a few times; then he stepped to the window and scarcely audibly sang the chorus of the priestesses from *Iphigenia in Tauris,* while tapping on the window pane from time to time at the entrance of the *tutti* passage. With astonishment I noticed that he gave certain different directions to the melody that were striking in their power and novelty. I let him go on. He finished and returned to his seat. Quite taken by the man's strange behavior and the extraordinary signs of a rare musical talent, I remained silent. After a while he began.

"Have you never composed?"

"Yes. I have tried my skill; only I found that everything which I had written in moments of inspiration afterwards seemed to be flat and boring. So I gave it up."

"You acted wrongly. The very fact that you rejected your own attempts is no bad sign of your talent. One learns music as a boy because father and mother wish it. So one fiddles and bangs away; but without noticing it, one's senses become more receptive to melody. Perhaps it was the half-forgotten theme of a little song which one now sang differently, the first thought of one's own; and this embryo, laboriously nourished by strange powers, grew to be a giant which consumed everything around and was transformed into your blood and marrow. Ah—how to suggest the thousand ways by which one can come to composing! It is a wide highway: everyone romps around on it and exults and shouts, 'We are the sacred people! We have attained the goal!' One enters the kingdom of dreams through the ivory gate: only a few even see the gate, even fewer pass through! It looks strange here. Absurd figures hover here and there, but they have character—one more than the other. They cannot be seen on the highway; they can only be found behind the ivory gate. It is difficult to get out of this kingdom; monsters block the way as they do in front of Alzinen's castle—everything spins, turns—many dream away the dream in the kingdom of dreams—they dissolve in dreams—they do not cast a shadow any longer, for otherwise, by the shadow, they would know about the ray of light that passes through this kingdom; but only a few, awakened from the dream, arise and stride through the kingdom of dreams—they attain the truth—the highest moment is there: contact with the eternal, the ineffable! Look at the sun; it is the triad from which the chords, like stars, shoot out and entwine you with threads of fire. You lie as in a cocoon of fire until the soul swings up to the sun."

He jumped up at the last words, cast his eyes upward and raised his hand. Then he sat down again and quickly emptied his refilled glass. A silence arose which I did not want to break for fear of getting the extraordinary man off the track. Finally he continued more calmly.

"When I was in the kingdom of dreams, a thousand aches and

worries tortured me. It was night and I was terrified by the grinning larvae of the monsters who dashed out at me and sometimes dragged me into the ocean's abyss, sometimes carried me high into the sky. Rays of light shot through the night and these rays of light were tones which encircled me with delightful clarity. I awoke from my pains and saw a large, bright eye that was looking into an organ; and as it looked, tones sounded forth and shimmered and entwined themselves in marvelous chords that had never before been conceived. Melodies streamed back and forth, and I swam in this stream and was about to drown. Then the eye looked at me and sustained me above the roaring waves. It became night again; two colossi in gleaming armor strode towards me: the Tonic and the Dominant. They snatched me up, but the eye said smiling, 'I know what fills your heart with yearning. The gentle, soft youth Tierce will walk among the colossi; you will hear his sweet voice; you will see me again and my melodies will be yours.' "

He stopped.

"And you saw the eye again?"

"Yes, I saw it again. For many years I sighed in the kingdom of dreams—there—indeed, there—I sat in a marvelous valley and listened to the flowers singing together. Only a sunflower was silent and sadly bowed her closed calyx to the ground. Invisible bonds drew me to her—she raised her head—the calyx opened and shone toward me from within the eye. Now tones, like rays of light, flowed from my head to the flowers, which greedily drank them. The leaves of the sunflower grew bigger and bigger—fire streamed from them—encompassed me—the eye had vanished and I was in the calyx."

With the last words he sprang up and hurried out of the room with a quick, youthful stride. I awaited his return in vain; I decided, therefore, to go back to the city.

When I was near the Brandenburg Gate, I saw a lanky figure striding along in the darkness and immediately recognized my odd friend. I spoke to him.

"Why did you leave me so quickly?"

"It got too hot and THE 'EUPHON' began to sound."

"I don't understand you!"

"All the better."

"All the worse, for I would like to understand you completely."

"Don't you hear anything?"

"No."

"It is gone! Let us go. Usually I don't like company, but—you do not compose—you are not a Berliner."

"I cannot fathom why you are so prejudiced against Berliners. Here, where art is respected and practiced widely, I would think a man with your artistic soul would feel happy."

"You are mistaken! I am damned to wander here as my torment in barren space, like a departed spirit."

"In barren space, here, in Berlin?"

"Yes, it is barren around me, for no kindred spirit joins me. I am alone."

"But the artists! The composers!"

"Away with them! They carp and niggle—refine everything to the smallest measure; rake through everything just to find one wretched thought. From chattering so much about art and artistic sensitivity and what have you—they never get around to creating, and if they do happen to feel as if they had to bring a few wretched thoughts to light, the fearful coldness reveals their great distance from the sun— it is Laplandish work."

"Your criticism seems much too harsh to me. At least the splendid productions in the theater must satisfy you."

"Once I prevailed upon myself to go to the theater to hear the opera of my young friend—what is it called? Oh, the whole world is in this opera! The spirits of hell stride through the bright crowd of elegant people—everything in it has a voice and an all-powerful sound—the devil, I mean *Don Juan!* But I couldn't last through the overture, which was spewed forth *prestissimo*, without meaning or understanding; and I had prepared myself for it with fasting and prayer because I know that the 'Euphon' is much too moved by these masses and has an impure appeal."

"Even if I have to admit that Mozart's masterpieces are mostly neglected here in a way scarcely explicable, still Gluck's works certainly enjoy a dignified performance."

"You think so? I wanted to hear *Iphigenia in Tauris* once. As I entered the theater, I heard how the overture of *Iphigenia in Tauris* was being played. Hm—I think, a mistake. *This Iphigenia* is being given! I am astonished when the *andante* with which Iphigenia is received in Tauris begins and the storm follows. Twenty years lie in between! The whole effect, the tragedy's whole well-planned exposition is lost. A quiet set—a storm—the Greeks are cast on land, the opera is there! Well, do you think the composer tossed out the overture so that one can blow it how and where one wants to, like a little trumpet piece?"

"I admit the blunder. Still, everything is done to promote Gluck's works."

"Oh, yes indeed!" he said curtly and then smiled bitterly and ever more bitterly. Suddenly he rose, and nothing could stay him. He vanished in a moment, and for several days I sought him in vain in the Zoological Gardens.

Several months had passed. One cold rainy night I had been delayed in a remote section of the city and was hurrying to my home in the Friedrichstrasse. I had to pass the theater. The sound of music, of trumpets and drums, reminded me that Gluck's *Armida* was being performed, and I was on the point of going in when a strange soliloquy by the windows, where almost every tone of the orchestra could be heard, aroused my attention.

"Now the king is coming—they are playing the March—Drum away! Just drum away! That's very gay! Yes, they have to do it eleven times today—otherwise the parade isn't enough of a parade. Ah ha!— *maestoso*—poke along, boys. Look, there's a super with a shoelace dragging. Right, for the twelfth time and always striking the dominant. O ye eternal powers! It is never going to end! Now he is making a bow—Armida very humbly acknowledges the applause—. Once again? Right. Two soldiers are still missing. Now they are banging into the recitative. What evil spirit holds me here in his spell?"

"The spell is dissolved," I cried. "Come along!"

I quickly seized my odd friend from the Zoological Gardens—for the soliloquist was none other—by the arm and dragged him off with me. He seemed surprised and followed me in silence. We had already reached the Friedrichstrasse when he suddenly stopped.

"I know you," said he. "You were in the Zoological Gardens. We did a lot of talking—I drank wine—and became heated—afterwards the 'Euphon' rang for two days. I endured a great deal—it is past!"

"I am delighted that chance has led me to you again. Let us become better acquainted with one another. I don't live very far from here. How would it be—"

"I cannot and may not go to another's house."

"No. You won't escape me. I will come to you."

"Then you will still have to walk a few hundred steps with me. But didn't you want to go to the theater?"

"I wanted to hear *Armida*, but now—"

"You shall hear *Armida* right *now!* Come along!"

We walked along the Friedrichstrasse in silence; he suddenly turned into a cross-street, and I was scarcely able to follow him, because he ran down the street so quickly until he finally stopped in front of a modest house. He knocked for rather a long time before the door was finally opened. Feeling our way in the dark, we found the stairs and then a room in the upper floor, the door of which my guide carefully locked behind us. I heard another door being opened. Soon he came back with a light, and the appearance of the strangely furnished room surprised me not a little. Chairs ornamented with an old-fashioned richness, a wall clock with a gilded case, and a broad, cumbersome mirror gave everything the gloomy appearance of a past splendor. In the middle stood a small piano on which were a porcelain inkstand and several sheets of paper lined for music. A closer glance at these materials convinced me, however, that nothing had been written for a long time, for the paper was quite yellowed, and thick spiderwebs covered the inkstand. The man stepped over to a cupboard in the corner of the room which I had not noticed before, and when he pulled aside the curtain, I saw a row of beautifully bound books with golden letters: *Orfeo, Armida, Alceste, Iphigenia,* etc.; in brief, I saw Gluck's masterpieces standing together.

"You have Gluck's complete works?" I cried.

He did not answer; but his mouth twisted in a convulsive smile, and in a flash the play of muscles in his sunken cheeks distorted his face to a fearful mask. His somber glance directed fixedly at me, he seized one of the books—it was *Armida*—and strode solemnly toward the piano. I opened it quickly and set up the music stand. He seemed pleased with that. He opened the book and—who can describe my astonishment—I saw music paper, but without a single note written on it.

He said, "Now I will play the overture. Turn the pages at the right moments!" I promised to do so; then he played marvelously and masterfully, with complete chords, the majestic *tempo di marcia* with which the overture begins, almost completely true to the original. The *allegro,* however, merely had Gluck's main thoughts woven into it. He introduced so many new and inspired twists that my astonishment grew and grew. His modulations were especially striking without becoming harsh, and he knew how to add so many melodic *melismas* that they seemed to be recurring in ever-rejuvenated form. His face glowed; sometimes his eyebrows were drawn together and a long restrained anger seemed about to burst forth; sometimes his eyes swam in tears of deepest melancholy. At times he sang the theme with a pleasant tenor voice while both hands were working at artistic *melismas.* Then, in a quite special way, he knew how to imitate the hollow sound of the drum. I turned the pages industriously by watching his glance. The overture was over and he fell back in his chair exhausted, his eyes closed. But soon he leaned forward again and said in a hollow voice, while hastily turning more empty pages of the book, "I wrote all this, my good sir, when I came from the kingdom of dreams. But I betrayed that which is holy to the unholy and an ice cold hand reached into my glowing heart! It did not break. Then I was damned to wander among the unholy like a departed spirit—formless, so that no one would recognize me until the sunflower should raise me again to the eternal. Ah—now let us sing Armida's scene!"

Then he sang the final scene of *Armida* with an expression that penetrated my soul. Here too he deviated noticeably from the true original; but the transformed music was the Gluck scene in a higher power. He recapitulated powerfully in sound, and in the highest measure, everything that hate, love, despair, madness can express. His voice seemed to be that of a young man, for it swelled up from the deepest groan to a penetrating power. All my fibers trembled—I was beside myself. When he had finished, I hurled myself into his arms and cried in a strained voice, "What is it? Who are you?"

He stood up and measured me with an earnest, penetrating glance; but when I wanted to ask more, he had vanished with the light through the door and left me in the darkness. Almost a quarter of an hour passed; I had despaired of ever seeing him again and was seeking to open the door, oriented by the position of the piano, when he suddenly returned in an embroidered court dress, with a rich waistcoat, his dagger at his side and the light in his hand.

I was paralyzed. Solemnly he strode towards me, seized me gently by the hand, and said, smiling strangely, *"I am Ritter Gluck!"*

*T*HE CHATEAU into which my valet had ventured to
make forcible entrance, rather than permit me, in my
desperately wounded condition, to pass a night in the
open air, was one of those piles of commingled gloom and
grandeur which have so long frowned among the Apen-
nines, not less in fact than in the fancy of Mrs. Radcliffe.
To all appearance it had been temporarily and very lately
abandoned. We established ourselves in one of the smallest and least sumptuously furnished apartments. It lay in
a remote turret of the building. Its decorations were rich,
yet tattered and antique. Its walls were hung with tapestry and bedecked with manifold and multiform ar-
morial trophies, together with an unusually great number
of very spirited modern paintings in frames of rich golden
arabesque. In these paintings, which depended from the
walls not only in their main surfaces, but in very many
nooks which the bizarre architecture of the château rendered necessary—in these paintings my incipient delir-
ium, perhaps, had caused me to take deep interest; so
that I bade Pedro to close the heavy shutters of the
room—since it was already night,—to light the tongues of
a tall candelabrum which stood by the head of my bed,
and to throw open far and wide the fringed curtains of
black velvet which enveloped the bed itself. I wished all
this done that I might resign myself, if not to sleep, at
least alternately to the contemplation of these pictures,
and the perusal of a small volume which had been found
upon the pillow, and which purported to criticise and describe them.

Long, long I read—and devoutly, devoutly I gazed.
Rapidly and gloriously the hours flew by and the deep
midnight came. The position of the candelabrum displeased me, and outreaching my hand with difficulty,

rather than disturb my slumbering valet, I placed it so as to throw its rays more fully upon the book.

But the action produced an effect altogether unanticipated. The rays of the numerous candles (for there were many) now fell within a niche of the room which had hitherto been thrown into deep shade by one of the bedposts. I thus saw in vivid light a picture all unnoticed before. It was the portrait of a young girl just ripening into womanhood. I glanced at the painting hurriedly, and then closed my eyes. Why I did this was not at first apparent even to my own perception. But while my lids remained thus shut, I ran over in mind my reason for so shutting them. It was an impulsive movement to gain time for thought—to make sure that my vision had not deceived me—to calm and subdue my fancy for a more sober and more certain gaze. In a very few moments I again looked fixedly at the painting.

That I now saw aright I could not and would not doubt; for the first flashing of the candles upon that canvas had seemed to dissipate the dreamy stupor which was stealing over my senses, and to startle me at once into waking life.

The portrait, I have already said, was that of a young girl. It was a mere head and shoulders, done in what is technically termed a *vignette* manner; much in the style of the favorite heads of Sully. The arms, the bosom, and even the ends of the radiant hair melted imperceptibly into the vague yet deep shadow which formed the background of the whole. The frame was oval, richly gilded and filigreed in *Moresque*. As a thing of art nothing could be more admirable than the painting itself. But it could have been neither the execution of the work, nor the immortal beauty of the countenance, which had so suddenly and so vehemently moved me. Least of all, could it have been that my fancy, shaken from its half slumber, had mistaken the head for that of a living person. I saw at once that the peculiarities of the design, of the *vignetting*, and of the frame, must have instantly dispelled such idea—must have prevented even its momentary entertainment. Thinking earnestly upon these points, I remained, for an hour perhaps, half sitting, half reclining, with my vision riveted upon the portrait. At length, satisfied with the true secret of its effect, I fell back within the bed. I had found the spell of the picture in an absolute *lifelikeliness* of expression, which, at first startling, finally confounded, subdued, and appalled me. With deep and reverent awe I replaced the candelabrum in its former position. The cause of my deep agitation being thus shut from view, I sought eagerly the volume which discussed the paintings and their histories. Turning to the number which designated the oval portrait, I there read the vague and quaint words which follow:

"She was a maiden of rarest beauty, and not more lovely than full of glee. And evil was the hour when she saw, and loved, and wedded the painter. He, passionate, studious, austere, and having already a bride in his Art: she a maiden of rarest beauty, and not more lovely than full of glee; all light and smiles, and frolicsome as the young fawn; loving and cherishing all things; hating only the Art which was her rival; dreading only the pallet and brushes and other untoward instruments which deprived her of the countenance of her lover. It was thus a terrible thing for this lady to hear the painter speak of his desire to portray even his young bride. But she was humble and obedient, and sat meekly for many weeks in the dark high turret-chamber where the light dripped upon the pale canvas only from overhead. But he, the painter, took glory in his work, which went on from hour to hour, and from day to day. And he was a passionate, and wild, and moody man, who became lost in reveries; so that he *would* not see that the light which fell so ghastly in that lone turret withered the health and the spirits of his bride, who pined visibly to all but him. Yet she smiled on and still on, uncomplainingly, because she saw that the painter (who had high renown) took a fervid and burning pleasure in his task, and wrought day and night to depict her who so loved him, yet who grew daily more dispirited and weak. And in sooth some who beheld the portrait spoke of its resemblance in low words, as of a mighty marvel, and a proof not less of the power of the painter than of his deep love for her whom he depicted so surpassingly well. But at length, as the labor drew nearer to its conclusion, there were admitted none into the turret; for the painter had grown wild with the ardor of his work, and turned his eyes from the canvas rarely, even to regard the countenance of his wife. And he *would* not see that the tints which he spread upon the canvas were drawn from the cheeks of her who sat beside him. And when many weeks had passed, and but little remained to do, save one brush upon the mouth and one tint upon the eye, the spirit of the lady again flickered up as the flame within the socket of the lamp. And then the brush was given, and then the tint was placed; and, for one moment, the painter stood entranced before the work which he had wrought; but in the next, while he yet gazed, he grew tremulous and very pallid, and aghast, and crying with a loud voice, 'This is indeed *Life* itself!' turned suddenly to regard his beloved:—*She was dead!*"

I SHOULD SEE the garden far better," said Alice to herself, "if I could get to the top of that hill: and here's a path that leads straight to it—at least, no, it doesn't do *that*—" (after going a few yards along the path, and turning several sharp corners), "but I suppose it will at last. But how curiously it twists! It's more like a corkscrew than a path! Well, *this* turn goes to the hill, I suppose— no, it doesn't! This goes straight back to the house! Well then, I'll try it the other way."

And so she did: wandering up and down, and trying turn after turn, but always coming back to the house, do what she would. Indeed, once, when she turned a corner rather more quickly than usual, she ran against it before she could stop herself.

"It's no use talking about it," Alice said, looking up at the house and pretending it was arguing with her. "I'm *not* going in again yet. I know I should have to get through the Looking-glass again—back into the old room—and there'd be an end of all my adventures!"

So, resolutely turning her back upon the house, she set out once more down the path, determined to keep straight on till she got to the hill. For a few minutes all went on well, and she was just saying "I really *shall* do it this time—" when the path gave a sudden twist and shook itself (as she described it afterwards), and the next moment she found herself actually walking in at the door.

"Oh, it's too bad!" she cried. "I never saw such a house for getting in the way! Never!"

However, there was the hill full in sight, so there was nothing to be done but start again. This time she came upon a large flower-bed, with a border of daisies, and a willow-tree growing in the middle.

"O Tiger-lily!" said Alice, addressing herself to one

that was waving gracefully about in the wind, "I *wish* you could talk!"

"We *can* talk," said the Tiger-lily, "when there's anybody worth talking to."

Alice was so astonished that she couldn't speak for a minute: it quite seemed to take her breath away. At length, as the Tiger-lily only went on waving about, she spoke again, in a timid voice—almost in a whisper. "And can *all* the flowers talk?"

"As well as *you* can," said the Tiger-lily. "And a great deal louder."

"It isn't manners for us to begin, you know," said the Rose, "and I really was wondering when you'd speak! Said I to myself, 'Her face has got *some* sense in it, though it's not a clever one!' Still, you're the right colour, and that goes a long way."

"I don't care about the colour," the Tiger-lily remarked. "If only her petals curled up a little more, she'd be all right."

Alice didn't like being criticized, so she began asking questions. "Aren't you sometimes frightened at being planted out here, with nobody to take care of you?"

"There's the tree in the middle," said the Rose. "What else is it good for?"

"But what could it do, if any danger came?" Alice asked.

"It could bark," said the Rose.

"It says 'Bough-wough!'" cried a Daisy. "That's why its branches are called boughs!"

"Didn't you know *that?*" cried another Daisy. And here they all began shouting together, till the air seemed quite full of little shrill voices. "Silence, every one of you!" cried the Tiger-lily, waving itself passionately from side to side, and trembling with excitement. "They know I can't get at them!" it panted, bending its quivering head towards Alice, "or they wouldn't dare to do it!"

"Never mind!" Alice said in a soothing tone, and, stooping down to the daisies, who were just beginning again, she whispered, "If you don't hold your tongues, I'll pick you!"

There was silence in a moment, and several of the pink daisies turned white.

"That's right!" said the Tiger-lily. "The daisies are worst of all.

When one speaks, they all begin together, and it's enough to make one wither to hear the way they go on!"

"How is it you can all talk so nicely?" Alice said, hoping to get it into a better temper by a compliment. "I've been in many gardens before, but none of the flowers could talk."

"Put your hand down, and feel the ground," said the Tiger-lily. "Then you'll know why."

Alice did so. "It's very hard," she said; "but I don't see what that has to do with it."

"In most gardens," the Tiger-lily said, "they make the beds too soft—so that the flowers are always asleep."

This sounded a very good reason, and Alice was quite pleased to know it. "I never thought of that before!" she said.

"It's *my* opinion that you never think *at all,*" the Rose said, in a rather severe tone.

"I never saw anybody that looked stupider," a Violet said, so suddenly, that Alice quite jumped; for it hadn't spoken before.

"Hold *your* tongue!" cried the Tiger-lily. "As if *you* ever saw anybody! You keep your head under the leaves, and snore away there, till you know no more what's going on in the world, than if you were a bud!"

"Are there any more people in the garden besides me?" Alice said, not choosing to notice the Rose's last remark.

"There's one other flower in the garden that can move about like you," said the Rose. "I wonder how you do it—" ("You're always wondering," said the Tiger-lily), "but she's more bushy than you are."

"Is she like me?" Alice asked eagerly, for the thought crossed her mind, "There's another little girl in the garden, somewhere!"

"Well, she has the same awkward shape as you," the Rose said: "but she's redder—and her petals are shorter, I think."

"They're done up close, like a dahlia," said the Tiger-lily: "not tumbled about, like yours."

"But that's not *your* fault," the Rose added kindly. "You're beginning to fade, you know—and then one can't help one's petals getting a little untidy."

Alice didn't like this idea at all: so, to change the subject, she asked "Does she ever come out here?"

"I daresay you'll see her soon," said the Rose. "She's one of the kind that has nine spikes, you know."

"Where does she wear them?" Alice asked with some curiosity.

"Why, all round her head, of course," the Rose replied. "I was wondering *you* hadn't got some too. I thought it was the regular rule."

"She's coming!" cried the Larkspur. "I hear her footstep, thump, thump, along the gravel-walk."

Alice looked round eagerly and found that it was the Red Queen. "She's grown a good deal!" was her first remark. She had indeed: when Alice first found her in the ashes, she had been only three inches high—and here she was, half a head taller than Alice herself!

"It's the fresh air that does it," said the Rose: "wonderfully fine air it is, out here."

"I think I'll go and meet her," said Alice, for, though the flowers were interesting enough, she felt that it would be far grander to have a talk with a real Queen.

"You can't possibly do that," said the Rose: "*I* should advise you to walk the other way."

This sounded nonsense to Alice, so she said nothing, but set off at once towards the Red Queen. To her surprise she lost sight of her in a moment, and found herself walking in at the front-door again.

A little provoked, she drew back, and, after looking everywhere for the Queen (whom she spied out at last, a long way off), she thought she would try the plan, this time, of walking in the opposite direction.

It succeeded beautifully. She had not been walking a minute before she found herself face to face with the Red Queen, and full in sight of the hill she had been so long aiming at.

"Where do you come from?" said the Red Queen. "And where are you going? Look up, speak nicely, and don't twiddle your fingers all the time."

Alice attended to all these directions, and explained, as well as she could, that she had lost her way.

"I don't know what you mean by *your* way," said the Queen: "all the ways about here belong to *me*—but why did you come out here at all?" she added in a kinder tone. "Curtsey while you're thinking what to say. It saves time."

Alice wondered a little at this, but she was too much in awe of the Queen to disbelieve it. "I'll try it when I go home," she thought to herself, "the next time I'm a little late for dinner."

"It's time for you to answer now," the Queen said, looking at her watch: "open your mouth a *little* wider when you speak, and always say 'your Majesty.'"

"I only wanted to see what the garden was like, your Majesty—"

"That's right," said the Queen, patting her on the head, which Alice didn't like at all: "though, when you say 'garden'—*I've* seen gardens, compared with which this would be a wilderness."

Alice didn't dare to argue the point, but went on: "—and I thought I'd try and find my way to the top of that hill—"

"When you say 'hill,'" the Queen interrupted, "*I* could show you hills, in comparison with which you'd call that a valley."

"No, I shouldn't," said Alice, surprised into contradicting her at last: "a hill *can't* be a valley, you know. That would be nonsense—"

The Red Queen shook her head. "You may call it 'nonsense' if you like," she said, "but *I've* heard nonsense, compared with which that would be as sensible as a dictionary!"

Alice curtseyed again, as she was afraid from the Queen's tone that she was a *little* offended: and they walked on in silence till they got to the top of the little hill.

For some minutes Alice stood without speaking, looking out in all directions over the country—and a most curious country it was. There were a number of tiny little brooks running straight across it from side to side, and the ground between was divided up into squares by a number of little green hedges, that reached from brook to brook.

"I declare it's marked out just like a large chess-board!" Alice said at last. "There ought to be some men moving about somewhere—and so there are!" she added in a tone of delight, and her heart began to beat quick with excitement as she went on. "It's a great huge game of chess that's being played—all over the world—if this *is* the world at all, you know. Oh, what fun it is! How I *wish* I was one of them! I wouldn't mind being a Pawn, if only I might join—though of course I should *like* to be a Queen, best."

She glanced rather shyly at the real Queen as she said this, but her companion only smiled pleasantly, and said "That's easily managed. You can be the White Queen's Pawn, if you like, as Lily's too young to play; and you're in the Second Square to begin with: when you get to the Eighth Square you'll be a Queen—" Just at this moment, somehow or other, they began to run.

Alice never could quite make out, in thinking it over afterwards, how it was that they began: all she remembers is, that they were running hand in hand, and the Queen went so fast that it was all she could do to keep up with her: and still the Queen kept crying "Faster! Faster!" but Alice felt she *could not* go faster, though she had no breath left to say so.

The most curious part of the thing was, that the trees and the other things round them never changed their places at all: however fast they went, they never seemed to pass anything. "I wonder if all the things move along with us?" thought poor puzzled Alice. And the Queen seemed to guess her thoughts, for she cried "Faster! Don't try to talk!"

Not that Alice had any idea of doing *that*. She felt as if she would never be able to talk again, she was getting so much out of breath: and still the Queen cried "Faster! Faster!" and dragged her along. "Are we nearly there?" Alice managed to pant out at last.

"Nearly there!" the Queen repeated. "Why, we passed it ten minutes ago! Faster!" And they ran on for a time in silence, with the wind whistling in Alice's ears, and almost blowing her hair off her head, she fancied.

"Now! Now!" cried the Queen. "Faster! Faster!" And they went so fast that at last they seemed to skim through the air, hardly touching the ground with their feet, till suddenly, just as Alice was getting quite exhausted, they stopped, and she found herself sitting on the ground, breathless and giddy.

The Queen propped her up against a tree, and said kindly, "You may rest a little, now."

Alice looked round her in great surprise. "Why, I do believe we've been under this tree the whole time! Everything's just as it was!"

"Of course it is," said the Queen. "What would you have it?"

"Well, in *our* country," said Alice, still panting a little, "you'd generally get to somewhere else—if you ran very fast for a long time as we've been doing."

"A slow sort of country!" said the Queen. "Now, *here*, you see, it takes all the running *you* can do, to keep in the same place. If you want to get somewhere else, you must run at least twice as fast as that."

"I'd rather not try, please!" said Alice. "I'm quite content to stay here—only I *am* so hot and thirsty!"

"I know what *you'd* like!" the Queen said good-naturedly, taking a little box out of her pocket. "Have a biscuit?"

Alice thought it would not be civil to say "No," though it wasn't at all what she wanted. So she took it, and ate it as well as she could: and it was *very* dry: and she thought she had never been so nearly choked in all her life.

"While you're refreshing yourself," said the Queen, "I'll just take the measurements." And she took a ribbon out of her pocket, marked in inches, and began measuring the ground, and sticking little pegs in here and there.

"At the end of two yards," she said, putting in a peg to mark the distance, "I shall give you your directions—have another biscuit?"

"No, thank you," said Alice: "one's *quite* enough!"

"Thirst quenched, I hope?" said the Queen.

Alice did not know what to say to this, but luckily the Queen did not wait for an answer, but went on. "At the end of *three* yards I shall repeat them—for fear of your forgetting them. At the end of *four,* I shall say good-bye. And at the end of *five,* I shall go!"

She had got all the pegs put in by this time, and Alice looked on with great interest as she returned to the tree, and then began slowly walking down the row.

At the two-yard peg she faced round, and said "A pawn goes two squares in its first move, you know. So you'll go *very* quickly through the Third Square—by railway, I should think—and you'll find yourself in the Fourth Square in no time. Well, *that* square belongs to Tweedledum and Tweedledee—the Fifth is mostly water—the Sixth belongs to Humpty Dumpty—But you make no remark?"

"I—I didn't know I had to make one—just then," Alice faltered out.

"You *should* have said," the Queen went on in a tone of grave reproof, " 'It's extremely kind of you to tell me all this'—however, we'll suppose it said—the Seventh Square is all forest—however, one of the Knights will show you the way—and in the Eighth Square we shall be Queens together, and it's all feasting and fun!" Alice got up and curtseyed, and sat down again.

At the next peg the Queen turned again, and this time she said "Speak in French when you can't think of the English for a thing—turn out your toes as you walk—and remember who you are!" She did not wait for Alice to curtsey, this time, but walked on quickly to the next peg, where she turned for a moment to say "Good-bye," and then hurried on to the last.

How it happened, Alice never knew, but exactly as she came to the last peg, she was gone. Whether she vanished into the air, or whether she ran quickly into the wood ("and she *can* run very fast!" thought Alice), there was no way of guessing, but she was gone, and Alice began to remember that she was a Pawn, and that it would soon be time for her to move.

The Secret Life of Walter Mitty   *JAMES THURBER*

"WE'RE GOING THROUGH!" The Commander's voice was like thin ice breaking. He wore his full-dress uniform, with the heavily braided white cap pulled down rakishly over one cold gray eye. "We can't make it, sir. It's spoiling for a hurricane, if you ask me." "I'm not asking you, Lieutenant Berg," said the Commander. "Throw on the power lights! Rev her up to 8,500! We're going through!" The pounding of the cylinders increased: ta-pocketa-pocketa-pocketa-*pocketa-pocketa*. The Commander stared at the ice forming on the pilot window. He walked over and twisted a row of complicated dials. "Switch on No. 8 auxiliary!" he shouted. "Switch on No. 8 auxiliary!" repeated Lieutenant Berg. "Full strength in No. 3 turret!" shouted the Commander. "Full strength in No. 3 turret!" The crew, bending to their various tasks in the huge, hurtling eight-engined Navy hydroplane, looked at each other and grinned. "The Old Man'll get us through," they said to one another. "The Old Man ain't afraid of Hell!" . . .

"Not so fast! You're driving too fast!" said Mrs. Mitty. "What are you driving so fast for?"

"Hmm?" said Walter Mitty. He looked at his wife, in the seat beside him, with shocked astonishment. She seemed grossly unfamiliar, like a strange woman who had yelled at him in a crowd. "You were up to fifty-five," she said. "You know I don't like to go more than forty. You were up to fifty-five." Walter Mitty drove on toward Waterbury in silence, the roaring of the SN202 through the worst storm in twenty years of Navy flying fading in the remote, intimate airways of his mind. "You're tensed up again," said Mrs. Mitty. "It's one of your days. I wish you'd let Dr. Renshaw look you over."

Walter Mitty stopped the car in front of the building

where his wife went to have her hair done. "Remember to get those overshoes while I'm having my hair done," she said. "I don't need overshoes," said Mitty. She put her mirror back into her bag. "We've been all through that," she said, getting out of the car. "You're not a young man any longer." He raced the engine a little. "Why don't you wear your gloves? Have you lost your gloves?" Walter Mitty reached in a pocket and brought out the gloves. He put them on, but after she had turned and gone into the building and he had driven on to a red light, he took them off again. "Pick it up, brother!" snapped a cop as the light changed, and Mitty hastily pulled on his gloves and lurched ahead. He drove around the streets aimlessly for a time, and then he drove past the hospital on his way to the parking lot.

. . . "It's the millionaire banker, Wellington McMillan," said the pretty nurse. "Yes?" said Walter Mitty, removing his gloves slowly. "Who has the case?" "Dr. Renshaw and Dr. Benbow, but there are two specialists here, Dr. Remington from New York and Mr. Pritchard-Mitford from London. He flew over." A door opened down a long, cool corridor and Dr. Renshaw came out. He looked distraught and haggard. "Hello, Mitty," he said. "We're having the devil's own time with McMillan, the millionaire banker and close personal friend of Roosevelt. Obstreosis of the ductal tract. Tertiary. Wish you'd take a look at him." "Glad to," said Mitty.

In the operating room there were whispered introductions: "Dr. Remington, Dr. Mitty. Mr. Pritchard-Mitford, Dr. Mitty." "I've read your book on streptothricosis," said Pritchard-Mitford, shaking hands. "A brilliant performance, sir." "Thank you," said Walter Mitty. "Didn't know you were in the States, Mitty," grumbled Remington. "Coals to Newcastle, bringing Mitford and me up here for a tertiary." "You are very kind," said Mitty. A huge, complicated machine, connected to the operating table, with many tubes and wires, began at this moment to go pocketa-pocketa-pocketa. "The new anesthetizer is giving way!" shouted an interne. "There is no one in the East who knows how to fix it!" "Quiet, man!" said Mitty, in a low, cool voice. He sprang to the machine, which was now going pocketa-pocketa-queep-pocketa-queep. He began fingering delicately a row of glistening dials. "Give me a fountain pen!" he snapped. Someone handed him a fountain pen. He pulled a faulty piston out of the machine and inserted the pen in its place. "That will hold for ten minutes," he said. "Get on with the operation." A nurse hurried over and whispered to Renshaw, and Mitty saw the man turn pale. "Coreopsis has set in," said Renshaw nervously. "If you would take over, Mitty?" Mitty looked at him and at the craven figure of Benbow, who drank, and at the grave, uncertain faces of the two great specialists. "If you wish," he said. They slipped a white gown on him; he adjusted a mask and drew on thin gloves; nurses handed him shining . . .

"Back it up, Mac! Look out for that Buick!" Walter Mitty jammed on the brakes. "Wrong lane, Mac," said the parking-lot attendant, looking at Mitty closely. "Gee. Yeh," muttered Mitty. He began cautiously to back out of the lane marked "Exit Only." "Leave her sit there," said the attendant. "I'll put her away." Mitty got out of the car. "Hey, better leave the key." "Oh," said Mitty, handing the man the ignition key. The attendant vaulted into the car, backed it up with insolent skill, and put it where it belonged.

They're so damn cocky, thought Walter Mitty, walking along Main Street; they think they know everything. Once he had tried to take his chains off, outside New Milford, and he had got them wound around the axles. A man had had to come out in a wrecking car and unwind them, a young, grinning garageman. Since then Mrs. Mitty always made him drive to a garage to have the chains taken off. The next time, he thought, I'll wear my right arm in a sling; they won't grin at me then. I'll have my right arm in a sling and they'll see I couldn't possibly take the chains off myself. He kicked at the slush on the sidewalk. "Overshoes," he said to himself, and he began looking for a shoe store.

When he came out into the street again, with the overshoes in a box under his arm, Walter Mitty began to wonder what the other thing was his wife had told him to get. She had told him twice, before they set out from their house for Waterbury. In a way he hated these weekly trips to town—he was always getting something wrong. Kleenex, he thought, Squibb's, razor blades? No. Toothpaste, toothbrush, bicarbonate, carborundum, initiative and referendum? He gave it up. But she would remember it. "Where's the what's-its-name?" she would ask. "Don't tell me you forgot the what's-its-name." A newsboy went by shouting something about the Waterbury trial.

. . . "Perhaps this will refresh your memory." The District Attorney suddenly thrust a heavy automatic at the quiet figure on the witness stand. "Have you ever seen this before?" Walter Mitty took the gun and examined it expertly. "This is my Webley-Vickers 50.80," he said calmly. An excited buzz ran around the courtroom. The judge rapped for order. "You are a crack shot with any sort of firearms, I believe?" said the District Attorney, insinuatingly. "Objection!" shouted Mitty's attorney. "We have shown that the defendant could not have fired the shot. We have shown that he wore his right arm in a sling on the night of the fourteenth of July." Walter Mitty raised his hand briefly and the bickering attorneys were stilled. "With any known make of gun," he said evenly, "I could have killed Gregory Fitzhurst at three hundred feet *with my left hand.*" Pandemonium broke loose in the courtroom. A woman's scream rose above the bedlam and suddenly a lovely, dark-haired girl was in Walter Mitty's arms. The District Attorney struck at her savagely. Without rising from his chair, Mitty let the man have it on the point of the chin. "You miserable cur!" . . .

"Puppy biscuit," said Walter Mitty. He stopped walking and the buildings of Waterbury rose up out of the misty courtroom and surrounded him again. A woman who was passing laughed. "He said 'Puppy biscuit,'" she said to her companion. "That man said 'Puppy biscuit' to himself." Walter Mitty hurried on. He went into an A. & P., not the first one he came to but a smaller one farther up the street. "I want some biscuit for small, young dogs," he said to the clerk. "Any special brand, sir?" The greatest pistol shot in the world thought a moment. "It says 'Puppies Bark for It' on the box," said Walter Mitty.

His wife would be through at the hairdresser's in fifteen minutes, Mitty saw in looking at his watch, unless they had trouble drying it; sometimes they had trouble drying it. She didn't like to get to the hotel first; she would want him to be there waiting for her as usual. He found a big leather chair in the lobby, facing a window, and he put the overshoes and the puppy biscuit on the floor beside it. He picked up an old copy of *Liberty* and sank down into the chair. "Can Germany Conquer the World Through the Air?" Walter Mitty looked at the pictures of bombing planes and of ruined streets.

. . . "The cannonading has got the wind up in young Raleigh, sir," said the sergeant. Captain Mitty looked up at him through tousled hair. "Get him to bed," he said wearily. "With the others. I'll fly alone." "But you can't, sir," said the sergeant anxiously. "It takes two men to handle that bomber and the Archies are pounding hell out of the air. Von Richtman's circus is between here and Saulier." "Somebody's got to get that ammunition dump," said Mitty. "I'm going over. Spot of brandy?" He poured a drink for the sergeant and one for himself. War thundered and whined around the dugout and battered at the door. There was a rending of wood and splinters flew through the room. "A bit of a near thing," said Captain Mitty carelessly. "The box barrage is closing in," said the sergeant. "We only live once, Sergeant," said Mitty, with his faint, fleeting smile. "Or do we?" He poured another brandy and tossed it off. "I never see a man could hold his brandy like you, sir," said the sergeant. "Begging your pardon, sir." Captain Mitty stood up and strapped on his huge Webley-Vickers automatic. "It's forty kilometers through hell, sir," said the sergeant. Mitty finished one last brandy. "After all," he said softly, "what isn't?" The pounding of the cannon increased; there was the rat-tat-tatting of machine guns, and from somewhere came the menacing pocketa-pocketa-pocketa of the new flame-throwers. Walter Mitty walked to the door of the dugout humming "Auprès de Ma Blonde." He turned and waved to the sergeant. "Cheerio!" he said. . . .

Something struck his shoulder. "I've been looking all over this hotel for you," said Mrs. Mitty. "Why do you have to hide in this old chair? How did you expect me to find you?" "Things close in," said Walter Mitty vaguely. "What?" Mrs. Mitty said. "Did you get the what's-its-name? The puppy biscuit? What's in that box?" "Overshoes," said Mitty. "Couldn't you have put them on in the store?" "I was thinking," said Walter Mitty. "Does it ever occur to you that I am sometimes thinking?" She looked at him. "I'm going to take your temperature when I get you home," she said.

They went out through the revolving doors that made a faintly derisive whistling sound when you pushed them. It was two blocks to the parking lot. At the drugstore on the corner she said, "Wait here for me. I forgot something. I won't be a minute." She was more than a minute. Walter Mitty lighted a cigarette. It began to rain, rain with sleet in it. He stood up against the wall of the drugstore, smoking. . . . He put his shoulders back and his heels together. "To hell with the handkerchief," said Walter Mitty scornfully. He took one last drag on his cigarette and snapped it away. Then, with that faint, fleeting smile playing about his lips, he faced the firing squad; erect and motionless, proud and disdainful, Walter Mitty the Undefeated, inscrutable to the last.

R IGHT THIS WAY."

"Follow us."

"Come along."

"Step lively."

"Here we go," they shouted, hopping from the wagon and bounding up the broad marble stairway. Milo and Tock followed close behind. It was a strange-looking palace, and if he didn't know better he would have said that it looked exactly like an enormous book, standing on end, with its front door in the lower part of the binding just where they usually place the publisher's name.

Once inside, they hurried down a long hallway, which glittered with crystal chandeliers and echoed with their footsteps. The walls and ceiling were covered with mirrors, whose reflections danced dizzily along with them, and the footmen bowed coldly.

"We must be terribly late," gasped the earl nervously as they reached the tall doors of the banquet hall.

It was a vast room, full of people loudly talking and arguing. The long table was carefully set with gold plates and linen napkins. An attendant stood behind each chair, and at the center, raised slightly above the others, was a throne covered in crimson cloth. Directly behind, on the wall, was the royal coat of arms, flanked by the flags of Dictionopolis.

Milo noticed many of the people he had seen in the market place. The letter man was busy explaining to an interested group the history of the W, and off in a corner the Humbug and the Spelling Bee were arguing fiercely about nothing at all. Officer Shrift wandered through the crowd, suspiciously muttering, "Guilty, guilty, they're all guilty," and, on noticing Milo, brightened visibly and commented in passing, "Is it six million years already? My, how time flies."

Everyone seemed quite grumpy about having to wait for lunch, and they were all relieved to see the tardy guests arrive.

"Certainly glad you finally made it, old man," said the Humbug, cordially pumping Milo's hand. "As guest of honor you must choose the menu of course."

"Oh, my," he thought, not knowing what to say.

"Be quick about it," suggested the Spelling Bee. "I'm famished— f-a-m-i-s-h-e-d."

As Milo tried to think, there was an ear-shattering blast of trumpets, entirely off key, and a page announced to the startled guests: "KING AZAZ THE UNABRIDGED."

The king strode through the door and over to the table and settled his great bulk onto the throne, calling irritably, "Places, everyone. Take your places."

He was the largest man Milo had ever seen, with a great stomach, large piercing eyes, a gray beard that reached to his waist, and a silver signet ring on the little finger of his left hand. He also wore a small crown and a robe with the letters of the alphabet beautifully embroidered all over it.

"What have we here?" he said, staring down at Tock and Milo as everyone else took his place.

"If you please," said Milo, "my name is Milo and this is Tock. Thank you very much for inviting us to your banquet, and I think your palace is beautiful."

"Exquisite," corrected the duke.

"Lovely," counseled the minister.

"Handsome," recommended the count.

"Pretty," hinted the earl.

"Charming," submitted the undersecretary.

"SILENCE," suggested the king. "Now, young man, what can you do to entertain us? Sing songs? Tell stories? Compose sonnets? Juggle plates? Do tumbling tricks? Which is it?"

"I can't do any of those things," admitted Milo.

"What an ordinary little boy," commented the king. "Why, my cabinet members can do all sorts of things. The duke here can make mountains out of molehills. The minister splits hairs. The count makes hay while the sun shines. The earl leaves no stone unturned.

And the undersecretary," he finished ominously, "hangs by a thread. Can't you do anything at all?"

"I can count to a thousand," offered Milo.

"A-A-R-G-H, numbers! Never mention numbers here. Only use them when we absolutely have to," growled Azaz disgustedly. "Now, why don't you and Tock come up here and sit next to me, and we'll have some dinner?"

"Are you ready with the menu?" reminded the Humbug.

"Well," said Milo, remembering that his mother had always told him to eat lightly when he was a guest, "why don't we have a light meal?"

"A light meal it shall be," roared the bug, waving his arms.

The waiters rushed in carrying large serving platters and set them on the table in front of the king. When he lifted the covers, shafts of brilliant-colored light leaped from the plates and bounced around the ceiling, the walls, across the floor, and out the windows.

"Not a very substantial meal," said the Humbug, rubbing his eyes, "but quite an attractive one. Perhaps you can suggest something a little more filling."

The king clapped his hands, the platters were removed, and, without thinking, Milo quickly suggested, "Well, in that case, I think we ought to have a square meal of ———".

"A square meal it is," shouted the Humbug again. The king clapped his hands once more and the waiters reappeared carrying plates heaped high with steaming squares of all sizes and colors.

"Ugh," said the Spelling Bee, tasting one, "these are awful."

No one else seemed to like them very much either, and the Humbug got one caught in his throat and almost choked.

"Time for the speeches," announced the king as the plates were again removed and everyone looked glum. "You first," he commanded, pointing to Milo.

"Your Majesty, ladies and gentlemen," started Milo timidly, "I would like to take this opportunity to say that in all the ———"

"That's quite enough," snapped the king. "Mustn't talk all day."

"But I'd just begun," objected Milo.

"NEXT!" bellowed the king.

"Roast turkey, mashed potatoes, vanilla ice cream," recited the Humbug, bouncing up and down quickly.

"What a strange speech," thought Milo, for he'd heard many in the past and knew that they were supposed to be long and dull.

"Hamburgers, corn on the cob, chocolate pudding—p-u-d-d-i-n-g," said the Spelling Bee in his turn.

"Frankfurters, sour pickles, strawberry jam," shouted Officer Shrift from his chair. Since he was taller sitting than standing, he didn't bother to get up.

And so down the line it went, with each guest rising briefly, making a short speech, and then resuming his place. When everyone had finished, the king rose.

"Pâté de foie gras, soupe à l'oignon, faisan sous cloche, salade endive, fromages et fruits et demi-tasse," he said carefully and clapped his hands again.

The waiters reappeared immediately, carrying heavy, hot trays, which they set on the table. Each one contained the exact words spoken by the various guests, and they all began eating immediately with great gusto.

"Dig in," said the king, poking Milo with his elbow and looking disapprovingly at his plate. "I can't say that I think much of your choice."

"I didn't know that I was going to have to eat my words," objected Milo.

"Of course, of course, everyone here does," the king grunted. "You should have made a tastier speech."

Milo looked around at everyone busily stuffing himself and then back at his own unappetizing plate. It certaintly didn't look worth eating, and he was so very hungry.

"Here, try some somersault," suggested the duke. "It improves the flavor."

"Have a rigmarole," offered the count, passing the breadbasket.

"Or a ragamuffin," seconded the minister.

"Perhaps you'd care for a synonym bun," suggested the duke.

"Why not wait for your just desserts?" mumbled the earl indistinctly, his mouth full of food.

"How many times must I tell you not to bite off more than you can chew?" snapped the undersecretary, patting the distressed earl on the back.

"In one ear and out the other," scolded the duke, attempting to stuff one of his words through the earl's head.

"If it isn't one thing, it's another," chided the minister.

"Out of the frying pan into the fire," shouted the count, burning himself badly.

"Well, you don't have to bite my head off," screamed the terrified earl, and flew at the others in a rage.

The five of them scuffled wildly under the table.

"STOP THAT AT ONCE," thundered Azaz, "or I'll banish the lot of you!"

"Sorry."

"Excuse me."

"Forgive us."

"Pardon."

"Regrets," they apologized in turn, and sat down glaring at each other.

The rest of the meal was finished in silence until the king, wiping the gravy stains from his vest, called for dessert. Milo, who had not eaten anything, looked up eagerly.

"We're having a special treat today," said the king as the delicious smells of homemade pastry filled the banquet hall. "By royal command the pastry chefs have worked all night in the half bakery to make sure that ———"

"The half bakery?" questioned Milo.

"Of course, the half bakery," snapped the king. "Where do you think half-baked ideas come from? Now, please don't interrupt. By royal command the pastry chefs have worked all night to ———"

"What's a half-baked idea?" asked Milo again.

"Will you be quiet?" growled Azaz angrily; but, before he could begin again, three large serving carts were wheeled into the hall and everyone jumped up to help himself.

"They're very tasty," explained the Humbug, "but they don't always agree with you. Here's one that's very good." He handed it to

Milo and, through the icing and nuts, Milo saw that it said "THE EARTH IS FLAT."

"People swallowed that one for years," commented the Spelling Bee, "but it's not very popular these days—d-a-y-s." He picked up a long one that stated "THE MOON IS MADE OF GREEN CHEESE" and hungrily bit off the part that said "CHEESE." "Now *there's* a half-baked idea," he said, smiling.

Milo looked at the great assortment of cakes, which were being eaten almost as quickly as anyone could read them. The count was munching contentedly on "IT NEVER RAINS BUT IT POURS" and the king was busy slicing one that stated "NIGHT AIR IS BAD AIR."

"I wouldn't eat too many of those if I were you," advised Tock. "They may look good, but you can get terribly sick of them."

"Don't worry," Milo replied; "I'll just wrap one up for later," and he folded his napkin around "EVERYTHING HAPPENS FOR THE BEST."

HORROR FICTION

The Sandman   *E. T. A. HOFFMANN*

NATHANAEL TO LOTHAR

YOU CERTAINLY MUST be disturbed because I have not written for such a long, long time. Mother, I am sure, is angry, and Klara will imagine that I am spending my time in dissipation, having completely forgotten my pretty angel whose image is so deeply imprinted on my heart. But it's not so; I think of you all every day and every hour, and my lovely Klärchen appears to me in my sweet dreams, her bright eyes smiling at me as charmingly as when I was with you. Alas, how could I write to you in the tormented frame of mind which has disrupted all my thoughts! Something horrible has entered my life! Dark forebodings of some impending doom loom over me like black clouds which are impervious to every ray of friendly sunshine. I will now tell you what happened to me. I must tell you, but the mere thought of it makes me laugh like a madman. Oh, my dearest Lothar, how can I begin to make you realize, even vaguely, that what happened a few days ago really could have so fatal and disruptive an effect on my life? If you were here you could see for yourself; but now you will certainly think I am a crazy man who sees ghosts. In brief, this horrible thing I have experienced, the fatal effects of which I am vainly trying to shake off, is simply this: A few days ago, on October 30th, at twelve noon, a barometer dealer came into my room and offered me his wares. I bought nothing and threatened to kick him down the stairs, whereupon he left of his own accord.

You will surmise that only associations of the strangest kind that are profoundly entangled in my life could have made this incident significant, and that the character of this wretched dealer must have had an evil influence on me. In fact, this is the case. I will, with all my strength, pull myself together and calmly and patiently tell you enough about my early youth so that everything will appear clearly and distinctly to your keen mind. But just as I am about to begin, I can hear you laugh, and I can hear Klara say: "This is all childish nonsense!" Laugh! I beg you, have a good laugh! But, my God, my hair is standing on end, and it is in mad despair that I ask you to laugh at me—as Franz Moor asked Daniel. But back to my story.

Except at the noon meal, my brothers and sisters and I saw little of our father during the day. His work must have kept him very busy. After supper, which was served at seven in the old-fashioned way, we all went into father's workroom and sat at a round table. Father smoked and drank a large glass of beer. He often told us marvelous stories, and he would get so carried away that his pipe would keep going out and I would relight it for him with a piece of burning paper, which I thought was great fun. But there were occasions when he'd put picture books in our hands and sit silently in his armchair, blowing out billows of smoke till we all seemed to be swimming in clouds. Mother was very sad on such evenings, and hardly had the clock struck nine when she would say: "Now, children, off to bed with you! The Sandman is coming, I can already hear him." And at these times I always really did hear something clumping up the stairs with a heavy, slow step; it must have been the Sandman. Once, this dull trampling step was especially frightening; and as my mother led us away, I asked her: "Oh, Mama, who is this nasty Sandman who always drives us away from Papa? What does he look like?"

"My dear child, there is no Sandman," my mother answered. "When I tell you that the Sandman is coming, it only means that you are sleepy and can't keep your eyes open any longer, as though someone had sprinkled sand into them."

Mother's answer did not satisfy me, for in my childish mind I was certain that she denied that there was a Sandman only to keep us from being afraid of him—I had surely always heard him coming up the stairs. Full of curiosity to learn more about this Sandman and what his connection was with us children, I finally asked the old woman who took care of my youngest sister what kind of man the Sandman was.

"Oh, dear Thanael," she replied, "don't you know that yet? He is a wicked man who comes to children when they refuse to go to bed and throws handfuls of sand in their eyes till they bleed and pop out of their heads. Then he throws the eyes into a sack and takes them to the half-moon as food for his children, who sit in a nest and have crooked beaks like owls with which they pick up the eyes of human children who have been naughty."

A horrible picture of the cruel Sandman formed in my mind, and in the evenings, when I heard stumbling steps on the stairs, I trembled with fear and dread. My mother could get nothing out of me but the stammered, tearful cry: "The Sandman! The Sandman!" Then I ran into the bedroom and was tortured all night by the horrible apparition of the Sandman. I was old enough to realize that the nurse's tale of the Sandman and his children's nest in the half-moon couldn't be altogether true; nevertheless, the Sandman remained a frightful specter; and I was seized with utmost horror when I heard him not only mount the stairs, but violently tear open the door to my father's room and enter. Frequently, he stayed away for a long time; then he came many times in succession. This continued for years, and I never got used to this terrible phantom. My image of the horrible Sandman grew no paler. His intimacy with my father occupied my imagination more and more. An insurmountable reluctance prevented me from asking my father about him; but if only I—if only I could solve the mystery and get to *see* this fantastic Sandman with my own eyes—that was the desire which increased in me year by year. The Sandman had directed my thoughts toward marvels and wonders which can so easily take hold of a childish mind. I liked nothing better than to hear or read horrible tales about goblins, witches, dwarfs, and such; but at the head of them all was the Sandman, of whom I was always drawing hideous pictures, in charcoal, in chalk, on tables, cupboards, and walls.

When I was ten my mother moved me from the nursery into a small room which opened off the corridor and was close to my father's room. As always, on the stroke of nine, when the mysterious step could be heard in the house, we had to scurry out. From my room I could hear him enter my father's, and soon thereafter I seemed to detect a thin, strange-smelling vapor spreading through the house. As my curiosity to know the Sandman grew, so did my courage. When my mother had left, I would sneak out of my room into the corridor; but I could never discover anything, because the Sandman had already gone through the door by the time I got to a spot from which he would have been visible. Finally, driven by an uncontrollable impulse, I determined to hide in my father's room itself to await the Sandman.

I could tell one evening from my father's silence and my mother's sadness that the Sandman was coming. I pretended, therefore, to be very tired, left the room before nine o'clock, and hid in a dark corner close to the door. The front door groaned. Slow, heavy, resounding steps crossed the hall to the stairs. My mother hurried past me with the rest of the children. Softly, softly I opened the door of my father's room. He was sitting as usual, silent and rigid, his back to the door; he didn't notice me. I slipped quickly behind the curtain which covered an open cupboard in which my father's clothes were hanging. Closer, ever closer resounded the steps—there was a strange coughing, scraping, and mumbling outside. My heart quaked with fear and expectation. Close, close to the door, there was a sharp step; a powerful blow on the latch and the door sprang open with a bang! Summoning up every drop of my courage, I cautiously peeped out. The Sandman was standing in the middle of my father's room, the bright candlelight full on his face. The Sandman, the horrible Sandman, was the old lawyer Coppelius who frequently had dinner with us!

But the most hideous figure could not have filled me with deeper horror than this very Coppelius. Picture a large, broad-shouldered man with a fat, shapeless, head, an ochre-yellow face, bushy grey eyebrows from beneath which a pair of greenish cat's eyes sparkled piercingly, and with a large nose that curved over the upper lip. The crooked mouth was frequently twisted in a malignant laugh, at which time a pair of dark red spots would appear on his cheeks and a strange hissing sound would escape from between clenched teeth. Coppelius invariably appeared in an old-fashioned coat of ash grey, with trousers and vest to match, but with black stockings and shoes with small agate buckles. His little wig barely extended past the crown of his head, his pomaded curls stood high over his big red ears, and a broad hair bag stood stiffly out from his neck so that the silver clasp which held his folded cravat was visible. His whole appearance was loathsome and repulsive; but we children were most revolted by his huge, gnarled, hairy hands, and we would never eat anything they had touched. He noticed this and took pleasure in touching, under some pretext or other, some piece of cake or delicious fruit which mother had slipped on our plates, so that, tears welling up in our eyes, we were unable to enjoy the tidbit intended for us because of the disgust and abhorrence we felt. He did the same thing on holidays when each of us received a glass of sweet wine from our father. He would pass his hand over it or would even raise the glass to his blue lips and laugh demoniacally, and we could only express our indignation by sobbing softly. He always called us "the little beasts"; and when he was present, we were not to make a sound. How we cursed this horrible man who deliberately and malevolently ruined our slightest pleasure! Mother seemed to loathe the repulsive Coppelius as much as we did; the moment he appeared, her gaiety, her lightheartedness, and her natural manner were transformed into dejected brooding. Father behaved toward him as if he were a superior being whose bad manners must be endured and who must be humored at any cost. Coppelius needed only to hint, and his favorite dishes were cooked and rare wines were served.

When I now saw this Coppelius, then, the terrible conviction that he alone was the Sandman possessed me; but the Sandman was no longer the hobgoblin of the nurse's tale, the one who brought the eyes of children for his brood to feed upon in the owl's nest in the half-moon. No! He was a horrible and unearthy monster who wreaked grief, misery, and destruction—temporal and eternal—wherever he appeared.

I was riveted to the spot, spellbound. At the risk of being discovered and, as I could clearly anticipate, severely punished, I remained watching, my head stretched out through the curtain. My father greeted Coppelius ceremoniously. "To work!" Coppelius cried in a hoarse, jarring voice, throwing off his coat. Silently and gloomily my father took off his dressing gown, and both of them dressed in long black smocks. I did not see where these came from. My father opened the folding door of a wall cupboard, but what I had always believed was a cupboard was not. It was rather a black recess which housed a little hearth. Coppelius went to the hearth, and a blue flame crackled up from it. All kinds of strange utensils were about. God! As my old father now bent over the fire, he looked completely different. His mild and honest features seemed to have been distorted into a repulsive and diabolical mask by some horrible convulsive pain. He looked like Coppelius, who was drawing sparkling lumps out of the heavy smoke with the red-hot tongs he wielded and then hammering the coals furiously. It seemed as if I saw human faces on all sides—but eyeless faces, with horrible deep black cavities instead.

"Give me eyes! Give me eyes!" Coppelius ordered in a hollow booming voice. Overcome by the starkest terror, I shrieked and tumbled from my hiding place to the floor. Coppelius seized me. "Little beast! Little beast!" he bleated, baring his teeth. He dragged me to my feet and flung me on the hearth, where the flames began singeing my hair. "Now we have eyes, eyes, a beautiful pair of children's eyes!" he whispered. Pulling glowing grains from the fire with his naked hands, he was about to sprinkle them in my eyes when my father raised his hands entreatingly: "Master! Master!" he cried, "leave my Nathanael his eyes!" "Let the child keep his eyes and do his share of the world's weeping," Coppelius shrieked with a shrill laugh, "but now we must carefully observe the mechanism of the hands and feet." He thereupon seized me so violently that my joints cracked, unscrewed my hands and feet, then put them back, now this way, then another way. "There's something wrong here! It's better the way they were! The Old Man knew his business!" Coppelius hissed and muttered. But everything around me went pitch black; a sudden convulsive pain flashed through my nerves and bones—I felt nothing more.

A gentle, warm breath passed across my face, and I awoke as from the sleep of death, my mother bending over me.

"Is the Sandman still here?" I stammered.

"No, my dearest child, he left long ago and will do you no harm," my mother said, kissing and cuddling her reclaimed darling.

Why should I bore you, my dear Lothar? Why should I go into such copious detail when so much remains to be said? Suffice it to say that I had been caught spying and had been manhandled by Coppelius. My fear and terror had brought on a violent fever, which kept me ill for many weeks. "Is the Sandman still here?" were my first words after regaining consciousness, the first sign of my recovery, my deliverance. I have only to tell you now about the most horrible moment in all the years of my youth: then you will be convinced that it is not because of faulty vision that everything seems devoid of color to me, but that a somber destiny has really hung a murky veil over my life, which I will perhaps tear through only when I die.

Coppelius was not seen again; it was said that he had left the town.

It was about a year later, when we were once more sitting at the round table as was our custom. Father was very cheerful and was telling us entertaining stories about his youthful travels. As the clock struck nine, we suddenly heard the front door groan on its hinges and slow, leaden steps resounded across the hall and up the stairs.

"It's Coppelius," my mother said, growing pale.

"Yes, it is Coppelius," father repeated in a faint, broken voice. Tears welled in mother's eyes.

"But Father, Father!" she cried, "must it be like this?"

"It is the last time!" he answered, "I promise you this is the last time he will come here. Now go, take the children with you. Go, go to bed! Good night!"

I felt as if I had been turned into cold heavy stone—I couldn't catch my breath! But as I stood there, motionless, my mother seized me by the arm. "Come, Nathanael, do come!" I let myself be led to my room. "Calm yourself, calm yourself and go to bed!" my mother cried to me. "Go to bed and go to sleep. Sleep!" But tormented by an indescribable fear, I couldn't close my eyes. The destestable and loathsome Coppelius stood before me with fiery eyes, laughing at me malevolently. I tried in vain to obliterate his image from my mind. It must have been about midnight when there was a terrifying explosion—like the firing of a cannon. The entire house resounded with the detonation; there was a rattling and clattering past my door. The front door slammed shut violently.

"That is Coppelius!" I cried in terror, springing out of bed. Then there was a shriek, a wail of heart-rending grief. I rushed to my father's room. The door was open, and suffocating smoke rolled towards me. The maid shrieked: "Oh, the master! Oh, the master!" My father lay dead in front of the smoking hearth, his face charred black and his features hideously contorted; my brothers and sisters were sobbing and moaning around him—my mother unconscious beside him! "Coppelius, you vile Satan, you've murdered my father!" I cried, and lost consciousness.

When my father was placed in his coffin two days later, his features were once more serene and gentle, as they had been in life. My soul drew consolation from the thought that his alliance with the satanic Coppelius could not have thrust him into everlasting perdition.

The explosion had awakened the neighbors; the tragedy was talked about and reached the ears of the authorities, who wanted to proceed against Coppelius and hold him accountable. But Coppelius had vanished from town without leaving a trace.

So, my dear friend, when I now tell you that his barometer dealer was the infamous Coppelius himself, you will not blame me for regarding this apparition as foreboding some frightful disaster. He was dressed differently, but Coppelius's figure and face are too deeply etched on my mind for me possibly to make a mistake. In addition, Coppelius has hardly changed his name. I have been told that he claims to be a Piedmontese skilled craftsman, Giuseppe Coppola.

I am determined, regardless of the consequences, to deal with him and to avenge my father's death.

Do not tell my mother anything of this loathsome monster's presence here. Give my love to dear, sweet Klara. I will write to her when I am in a calmer frame of mind. Farewell, etc., etc.

KLARA TO NATHANAEL

Despite it's being true that you have not written for a long time, I believe that I am still in your thoughts. You surely had me most vividly in mind when you intended sending your last letter to Lothar, because you addressed it to me instead. I opened the letter with delight and did not realize my error until I read: "Oh, my dearest Lothar." I should have stopped reading and given the letter to your brother. Even though you have often reproached me, in your innocent, teasing manner, for being so serene and womanly in disposition that if the house were about to collapse I would quickly smooth a misplaced crease out of a curtain—like the woman in the story—before escaping; nevertheless, I can hardly tell you how deeply the beginning of your letter shocked me. I could barely breathe; everything swam before my eyes. Oh, my dearest Nathanael, what horrible thing has entered your life? To be parted from you, never again to see you—the thought pierced my breast like a red-hot dagger. I read on and on. Your description of the repulsive Coppelius horrifies me. For the first time I learned about the terrible, violent way your dear old father died. My brother Lothar, to whom I gave this letter, tried with little success to calm me. The horrid barometer dealer Giuseppe Coppola followed my every step, and I am almost ashamed to admit that he even disturbed my normally sound and restful sleep with all kinds of horrible dream images. Soon, however—by the very next day, in fact—I saw everything differently. Do not be angry with me, my dearest one, if Lothar tells you that despite your strange presentiment that Coppelius will harm you, I am still cheerful and calm.

I will frankly confess that in my opinion all the fears and terrors of which you speak took place only in your mind and had very little to do with the true, external world. A loathsome character old Coppelius may have been, but what really lead to the abhorrence you children felt stemmed from his hatred of children.

Naturally, your childish mind associated the dreadful Sandman of the nurse's tale with old Coppelius—who would have been a monster particularly threatening to children even if you had not believed in the Sandman. The sinister business conducted at night with your father was probably nothing other than secret alchemical experiments, which would have displeased your mother because not only was a great deal of money being squandered, but, as is always the case with such experimenters, your father's mind was so imbued with an illusory desire for higher knowledge that he may have become alienated from his family. Your father, no doubt, was responsible for his own death through some carelessness or other, and Coppelius is not guilty of it. Let me tell you that yesterday I asked our neighbor, an experienced chemist, whether experiments of this kind could possibly lead to such a sudden lethal explosion. "Absolutely," he replied, and continued, at length and in detail, to tell me how such an accident could occur, mentioning so many strange-sounding names that I can't recall any of them. Now, you will be annoyed with your Klara and will say: "Such a cold nature is impervious to any ray of the mysterious which often embraces man with invisible arms. Like the simple child who rejoices over some glittering golden fruit which conceals a fatal poison, she sees only the bright surface of the world."

Oh, my dearest Nathanael, do you not believe that even in gay, easygoing, and carefree minds there may exist a presentiment of dark powers within ourselves which are bent upon our own destruction? But forgive me, simple girl that I am, if I presume to tell you what my thoughts really are about such inner conflicts. I will not, to be sure, find the right words; and you will laugh at me—not because what I say is foolish, but because I express my ideas so clumsily.

If there is a dark power which treacherously attaches a thread to our heart to drag us along a perilous and ruinous path that we would not otherwise have trod; if there is such a power, it must form inside us, from part of us, must be identical with ourselves; only in this way can we believe in it and give it the opportunity it needs if it is to accomplish its secret work. If our mind is firm enough and adequately fortified by the joys of life to be able to recognize alien and hostile influences as such, and to proceed tranquilly along the path of our own choosing and propensities, then this mysterious power will perish in its futile attempt to assume a shape that is supposed to be a reflection of ourselves. "It is also a fact," Lothar adds, "that if we have once voluntarily surrendered to this dark physical power, it frequently introduces in us the strange shapes which the external world throws in our way, so that we ourselves engender the spirit which in our strange delusion we believe speaks to us from that shape. It is the phantom of our own ego, whose intimate relationship, combined with its profound effect on our spirits, either flings us into hell or transports us to heaven." You see, dear Nathanael, that my brother Lothar and I have fully discussed the matter of dark powers and forces—a subject which I have outlined for you not without difficulty and which seems very profound to me. I do not completely understand Lothar's last words; I have only an inkling of his meaning, and yet it seems to be very true. I beg you to cast the hateful lawyer Coppelius and the barometer man Giuseppe Coppola from your thoughts. Be convinced that these strange figures are powerless; only your belief in their hostile influence can make them hostile in reality. If profound mental agitation did not speak out from every line in your letter, if your frame of mind did not distress me so deeply, I could joke about Sandman the lawyer and barometer dealer Coppelius. Cheer up, please! I have decided to be your guardian angel, and if ugly Coppola takes it into his head to plague you in your dreams, I will exorcise him with loud laughter. Neither he nor his revolting fists frighten me at all; as a lawyer he is not going to spoil my tidbits, nor, as a Sandman, harm my eyes.

Ever yours, my dearest beloved Nathanael, etc., etc., etc.

NATHANAEL TO LOTHAR

I am very sorry that Klara recently opened and read my letter to you through a mistake occasioned by my distraction. She has written me a very thoughtful and philosophical letter in which she proves, in great detail, that Coppelius and Coppola exist only in my mind and are phantoms of my ego that will vanish in a moment if I accept them as such. As a matter of fact, one would not think that Klara, with her bright, dreamy, child-like eyes, could analyze with such intelligence and pendantry. She refers to your views. The two of you have discussed me. No doubt you are giving her lessons in logic so that she is learning to sift and analyze everything very neatly. Do stop that! By the way, it is probably quite certain that the barometer dealer Giuseppe Coppola cannot possibly be the old lawyer Coppelius. I am attending lectures by the physics professor who just came here recently and who, like the famous naturalist, is called Spalanzani and is of Italian origin. He has known Coppola for many years; besides which, one can tell from his accent that he is really a Piedmontese. Coppelius was a German, but, it seems to me, not an honest one. I am still a little uneasy. You and Klara may still consider me a morbid dreamer; however, I cannot get rid of the impression that Coppelius's damned face makes on me. I am very happy that he has left the city, as Spalanzani told me. This professor is an eccentric fellow. A small, chubby man with big cheekbones, a thin nose, protruding lips, and small piercing eyes. But better than from any description, you can get a picture of him if you look at a picture of Cagliostro as painted by Chodowiecki in any Berlin pocket-almanac. Spalanzani looks just like that.

Recently, when I went up the steps, I noticed that the curtain which usually covers the glass door was not completely drawn across. I do not even know why I was curious enough to peek, but I did. A tall, very slender, beautifully dressed, beautifully proportioned young lady was sitting in the room in front of a small table, on which she had placed her outstretched arms, with hands clasped. She was sitting opposite the door, so I could see her divinely beautiful face. She did not seem to notice me; indeed, her eyes seemed fixed, I might almost say without vision. It seemed to me as if she were sleeping with her eyes open. I became very uneasy and therefore stole quietly away to the neighboring lecture room. Later, I discovered that the figure which I had seen is Spalanzani's daughter, Olympia, whom he, for some strange reason, always keeps locked up so that no one can come near her. Perhaps, after all, there is something wrong with her; maybe she is an idiot, or something like that. But why do I write you about all this? I can tell you better and in greater detail when I see you. By the way, I am planning to visit you in two weeks. I must see my dear, sweet, lovely Klara again. The irritation which, I must confess, possessed me after the arrival of that disagreeable analytical letter will have vanished by then. For this reason I am not writing to her today. A thousand greetings, etc., etc., etc.

Gentle reader, nothing can be imagined that is stranger and more extraordinary than the fate which befell my poor friend, the young student Nathanael, which I have undertaken to relate to you. Have you, gentle reader, ever experienced anything that totally possessed your heart, your thoughts, and your senses to the exclusion of all else? Everything seethed and roiled within you; heated blood surged through your veins and inflamed your cheeks. Your gaze was peculiar, as if seeking forms in empty space invisible to other eyes, and speech dissolved into gloomy sighs. Then your friends asked you: "What is it, dear friend? What is the matter?" And wishing to describe the picture in your mind with all its vivid colors, the light and the shade, you struggled vainly to find words. But it seemed to you that you had to gather together all that had occurred—the wonderful, the magnificent, the heinous, the joyous, the ghastly—and express it in the very first word so that it would strike like lightning. Yet, every word, everything within the realm of speech, seemed colorless, frigid, dead. You tried, tried again, stuttered and stammered, while the insipid questions asked by friends struck your glowing passion like icy blasts until it was almost extinguished. If, like an audacious painter, you had initially sketched the outline of the picture within you in a few bold strokes, you would have easily been able to make the colors deeper and more intense until the multifarious crowd of living shapes swept your friends away and they saw themselves, as you see yourself, in the midst of the scene that had issued from your soul.

Sympathetic reader, no one, I must confess, asked me about the history of young Nathanael; you are, however, surely aware that I belong to that remarkable species of authors who, when they carry something within themselves as I have just described it, feels as if everyone who approaches—indeed, everyone in the whole world—is asking "What is it? Do tell us, dear sir!"

I was most strongly compelled to tell you about Nathanael's disastrous life. The marvelous and the extraordinary aspects of his life entirely captivated my soul; but precisely for this reason and because, my dear reader, it was essential at the beginning to dispose you favorably towards the fantastic—which is no mean matter—I tormented myself to devise a way to begin Nathanael's story in a manner at once creative and stirring: "Once upon a time," the nicest way to begin a story, seemed too prosaic. "In the small provincial town of S———, there lived"—was somewhat better, at least providing an opportunity for development towards the climax. Or, immediately, *in medias res:* " 'Go to hell!' the student Nathanael cried, his eyes wild with rage and terror, when the barometer dealer Giuseppe Coppola—" In fact, that is what I had written when I thought I noticed something humorous in Nathanael's wild look—but the story is not at all comic. There were no words I could find which were appropriate to describe, even in the most feeble way, the brilliant colors of my inner vision. I resolved not to begin at all. So, gentle reader, do accept the three letters, which my friend Lothar has been kind enough to communicate, as the outline of the picture to which I will endeavor to add ever more color as I continue with the story. As a good portrait painter, I may possibly succeed in making Nathanael recognizable even if the original is unknown to you; and you may feel as if you had seen him with your own eyes on very many occasions. Possibly, also, you will come to believe that real life is more singular and more fantastic than anything else and that all a writer can really do is present it as "in a glass, darkly."

To supply information necessary for the beginning, these letters must be supplemented by noting that soon after the death of Nathanael's father, Klara and Lothar, children of a distant relative who had likewise died and left them orphans, were taken in by Nathanael's mother. Klara and Nathanael soon grew strongly attached to each other, to which no one in the world could object; hence, when Nathanael left home to continue his studies at G———, they were engaged. His last letter is written from G———, where he is attending the lectures of the famous professor of physics Spalanzani.

I could now confidently continue with my story, but even at this moment Klara's face is so vividly before me that I cannot avert my eyes, just as I never could when she gazed at me with one of her lovely smiles. Klara could not be considered beautiful; all who profess to be judges of beauty agreed on that. Nevertheless, architects praised the perfect proportions of her figure, and painters considered her neck, shoulders, breasts almost too chastely formed. Yet on the other hand, they adored her glorious hair and raved about her coloring, which reminded them of Battoni's Magdalen. One of them, a veritable romantic, elaborated an old comparison between her eyes and a lake by Ruïsdael, in which the pure azure of a cloudless sky, the woodlands and flower-bedecked fields, and the whole bright and varied life of a lush landscape are reflected. Poets and musicians went even further and said: "That is nonsense about a lake and a mirror! Can we look at the girl without sensing heavenly music which flows into us from her glance and penetrates to the very soul until everything within us stirs awake and pulsates with emotion? And if we cannot then sing splendid tunes, we are not worth much; the smile flitting about her lips will tell us this clearly enough when we have the courage to squeak out in her presence something which we profess to be a song when, in fact, it is only a disconnected jumble of notes strung together."

And this really was the case. Klara had the spirited imagination of a gay, innocent, unaffected child, the deep sympathetic feelings of a woman, and an understanding which was clear and discriminating. Dreamers and visionaries had bad luck with her; for despite the fact that she said little—she was not disposed to be talkative—her clear glance and her rare ironical smile asked: "Dear friends, how can you suppose that I will accept these fleeting and shadowy images for true shapes which are alive and breathe?" For this reason, many chided Klara for being cold, without feeling, and unimaginative; but others, those whose conception of life was clearer and deeper, were singularly enamored of this tenderhearted, intelligent, and child-like girl, though no one cared for her so much as Nathanael, who had a strong proclivity for learning and art. Klara clung to her lover with all of her soul, and when he parted from her, the first clouds passed over her life. With what delight she flew into his arms when he returned to his native town (as he had promised he would in his last letter to Lothar) and entered his mother's room. It turned out as Nathanael had believed it would: the instant he saw Klara again thoughts about the lawyer Coppelius or Klara's pedantic letter—all his depression vanished.

Nevertheless, Nathanael was right when he wrote to his friend Lothar that the abhorrent barometer dealer Coppola had exercised a disastrous influence on his life. This was evident to everyone for even in the first few days of his visit Nathanael seemed completely changed; he surrendered to gloomy brooding and behaved in a manner more strange than they had known before. All of life, everything, had become only a dream and a presentiment; he was always saying that any man, although imagining himself to be free, was in fact only the horrible plaything of dark powers, which it was vain to resist. Man must humbly submit to whatever fate has in store for him. He went so far as to insist that it was foolish to believe that man's creative achievements in art or science resulted from the expression of free will; rather, he claimed that the inspiration requisite for creation comes not from within us but results from the influence of a higher external principle.

To the clear-thinking Klara all this mystical nonsense was repugnant in the extreme, but it seemed pointless to attempt any refutation. It was only when Nathanael argued that Coppelius was the evil principle that had entered him and possessed him at the moment he was listening behind the curtain, and that this loathsome demon would in some terrible way destroy their happiness, that Klara grew very serious and said, "Yes, Nathanael, you are right; Coppelius is an evil and malignant principle. His effect can be no less diabolical than the very powers of hell if they assume living form, but only if you fail to banish him from your mind and thoughts. He will exist and work on you only so long as you believe in him; it is only your belief which gives him power."

Nathanael was greatly angered because Klara said that the demon existed only in his own mind, and he wanted to begin a disquisition on the whole mystic doctrine of devils and sinister powers, but Klara terminated the conversation abruptly by making a trivial remark, much to Nathanael's great annoyance. He thought that profound secrets were inaccessible to those with cold, unreceptive hearts, without being clearly aware that he included Klara among these inferior natures; and therefore he did not cease trying to initiate her into these secrets. Early in the morning, when Klara was helping to prepare breakfast, he would stand beside her and read to her from various occult books until she begged: "But my dear Nathanael, what if I have to accuse you of being the evil principle which is fatally influencing my coffee? For if I please you and drop everything to look into your eyes as you read, my coffee will boil over and no one will have breakfast." Nathanael slammed his book shut and rushed to his room indignantly.

Nathanael had formerly possessed a notable talent for writing delightful and amusing stories, to which Klara would listen with enormous pleasure; now, however, his tales were gloomy, unintelligible, and shapeless so that although Klara spared his feelings and did not say so, he probably felt how little they interested her. Above all, Klara disliked the tedious; and her uncontrollable drowsiness of spirit was betrayed by her glance and by her word. In truth, Nathanael's stories were really very boring. His resentment of Klara's cold, prosaic disposition increased; she could not conquer her dislike of his dark, gloomy, and dreary occultism; and so they drifted farther and farther apart without being conscious of it. Nathanael was forced to confess to himself that the ugly image of Coppelius had faded in his imagination, and it often cost him great effort to present Coppelius in adequate vividness in his writing where he played the part of the sinister bogeyman. Finally it occurred to him to make his gloomy presentiment that Coppelius would destroy his happiness the subject of a poem. He portrayed himself and Klara as united in true love but plagued by some dark hand which occasionally intruded into their lives, snatching away incipient joy. Finally, as they stood at the altar, the sinister Coppelius appeared and touched Klara's lovely eyes, which sprang into Nathanael's own breast, burning and scorching like bleeding sparks. Then Coppelius grabbed him and flung him into a blazing circle of fire which spun round with the speed of a whirlwind and, with a rush, carried him away. The awesome noise was like a hurricane furiously whipping up the waves so that they rose up like white-headed black giants in a raging inferno. But through this savage tumult he could hear Klara's voice: "Can't you see me, dear one? Coppelius has deceived you. That which burned in your breast was not my eyes. Those were fiery drops of the blood from your own heart. Look at me. I have still got my own eyes." Nathanael thought: "It is Klara: I am hers forever." Then it was as though this thought had grasped the fiery circle and forced it to stop turning, while the raging noise died away in the black abyss. Nathanael looked into Klara's eyes; but it was death that, with Klara's eyes, looked upon him kindly. While Nathanael was composing his poem he was very calm and serene; he reworked and polished every line, and since he fettered himself with meter, he did not pause until everything in the poem was perfect and euphonious. But when it was finally completed and he read the poem aloud to himself, he was stricken with fear and a wild horror and he cried out: "Whose horrible voice is that?" Soon, however, he once more came to understand that it was really nothing more than a very successful poem, and he felt certain that it would arouse Klara's cold nature, although he did not clearly understand why Klara should be aroused by it or what would be accomplished by frightening her with these hideous visions which augured a terrible fate and the destruction of their love.

They were sitting in his mother's little garden. Klara was extremely cheerful because Nathanael had not plagued her with his dreams and foreboding for the three days he had devoted to writing the poem. Nathanael also chatted gaily about things which amused her, as he had in the past, so that Klara remarked: "Now I really do have you back again. Do you see how we have driven out the hateful Coppelius?"

Nathanael suddenly remembered that the poem which he had intended to read to Klara was in his pocket. He took the sheets from his pocket and started reading while Klara, anticipating something boring as usual and resigning herself to the situation, calmly began knitting. But as the dark cloud of the poem grew ever blacker, the knitting in her hand sank and she stared fixedly into Nathanael's eyes. But Nathanael was carried inexorably away by his poem; passion flushed his cheeks a fiery red, and tears flowed from his eyes.

When he finally finished, he uttered a groan of absolute exhaustion; he grasped Klara's hand and sighed, as though dissolving in inconsolable grief: "Alas! Klara, Klara!"

Klara pressed him tenderly to her bosom and said in a voice at once soft but very slow and somber: "Nathanael, my darling Nathanael, throw that mad, insane, stupid tale into the fire." Nathanael then sprang indignantly to his feet, thrust Klara away, and cried, "You damned, lifeless automaton"; and ran off. Klara, deeply hurt, wept bitter tears, sobbing, "He has never loved me because he does not understand me."

Lothar came into the arbor; Klara had to tell him everything that had happened. He loved his sister with all his soul, and every word of her complaint fell like a fiery spark upon his heart so that the indignation which he had long felt toward the visionary Nathanael flared into furious rage. He ran to find Nathanael and in harsh words reproached him for his insane behavior towards his beloved sister. Nathanael, incensed, answered in kind, "Crazy, conceited fool," and was answered by "Miserable commonplace idiot." A duel was inevitable, and they agreed to meet on the following morning behind the garden and to fight, in accordance with the local student custom, with sharpened foils. They stalked about in silence and gloom. Klara, who had overheard and seen the violent argument, and who had seen the fencing masters bring the foils at dusk, suspected what was to happen. They both reached the dueling ground and cast off their coats in foreboding silence, and with their eyes aglow with the lust of combat, they were about to attack when Klara burst through the garden door. Through her sobs she cried: "You ferocious, cruel beasts! Strike me down before you attack each other. How am I to live when my lover has slain my brother, or my brother has slain my lover?"

Lothar lowered his weapon and gazed in silence at the ground, but in Nathanael's heart the affection he had once felt for lovely Klara in the happiest days of youth reawoke with a lacerating sorrow. The murderous weapon fell from his hand, and he threw himself at Klara's feet: "Can you ever forgive me, my one and only, beloved Klara? Can you ever forgive me, my dear brother Lothar?" Lothar was touched by his friend's profound grief, and all three embraced in reconciliation, with countless tears, vowing eternal love and fidelity.

Nathanael felt as if a heavy burden which had weighted him to the ground had been lifted, as if by resisting the dark powers that had gripped him he had saved his whole being from the threat of utter ruin. He spent three blissful days with his dear friends and then returned to G——, where he intended to remain for another year before returning to his native town forever.

Everything that referred to Coppelius was kept from Nathanael's mother, for they knew that it was impossible for her to think of him without horror, since like Nathanael, she believed him to be guilty of her husband's death.

Upon returning to his lodgings, Nathanael was completely astonished to find that the whole house had been burned down; nothing remained amid the ruins but the bare outer walls. Although the fire had started in the laboratory of the chemist living on the ground floor and had then spread upwards, some of Nathanael's courageous and energetic friends had managed, by breaking into his room on the upper floor, to save his books and manuscripts and instruments. They had carried them undamaged to another house and had rented a room there, into which Nathanael immediately moved. It did not strike him as singular that he now lived opposite Professor Spalanzani, nor did it seem particularly strange to him when he discovered that by looking out of his window he could see where Olympia often sat alone, so that he could clearly recognize her figure, although her features were blurred and indistinct. It did finally occur to him that Olympia often sat for hours at a small table in the same position in which he had seen her when he had first discovered her through the glass door, doing nothing and incessantly gazing across in his direction. He was forced to confess to himself that he had never seen a lovelier figure, although, with Klara in his heart, he remained perfectly indifferent to the stiff and rigid Olympia: only occasionally did he glance up from his book at the beautiful statue—that was all.

He was writing to Klara when there was a soft tap at the door. At his call, the door opened and Coppola's repulsive face peered in. Nathanael was shaken to the roots. Remembering, however, what Spalanzani had said to him about his compatriot Coppola and what he had solemnly promised his sweetheart regarding the Sandman Coppelius, he felt ashamed of his childish fear of ghosts and forceably pulled himself together and said as calmly as possible, "I don't want a barometer, my good friend, do go away."

Coppola, however, came right into the room and said in a hoarse voice, his mouth twisted in a hideous laugh, his little eyes flashing piercingly from beneath his long, grey eyelashes, "Oh, no barometer? No barometer! I gotta da eyes too. I gotta da nice eyes!" Horrified, Nathanael cried, "Madman, how can you have eyes? Eyes?" But Coppola instantly put away his barometers and, thrusting his hands in his wide coat pockets, pulled out lorgnettes and eyeglasses and put them on the table. "So, glasses—put on nose, see! These are my eyes, nice-a eyes!" Saying this, he brought forth more and more eyeglasses from his pockets until the whole table began to gleam and sparkle. Myriad eyes peered and blinked and stared up at Nathanael, who could not look away from the table, while Coppola continued putting down more and more eyeglasses; and flaming glances crisscrossed each other ever more wildly and shot their blood-red rays into Nathanael's breast.

Overcome by an insane horror, Nathanael cried, "Stop, stop, you fiend!" He seized Coppola by the arm even as Coppola was once more searching in his pocket for more eyeglasses, although the table was already covered with them. Coppola gently shook him off with a hoarse revolting laugh and with the words "Oh! None for you? But here are nice spyglasses." He swept the eyeglasses together and returned them to the pocket from which they had come and then produced from a side pocket a number of telescopes of all sizes. As soon as the eyeglasses were gone Nathanael grew calm again, and focusing his thoughts on Klara, he clearly saw that this gruesome illusion had been solely the product of his own mind and that Coppola was an honest optician and maker of instruments and far removed from being the ghostly double and revenant of the accursed Coppelius. Besides, there was nothing at all remarkable about the spyglasses that Coppola was placing on the table now, or at least nothing so weird about them as about the eyeglasses. To make amends for his behavior, Nathanael decided actually to buy something, picked up a small, very beautifully finished pocket spy-glass, and in order to test it, looked through the window. Never in his life had he come across a glass which brought objects before his eyes with such clarity and distinctness. He involuntarily looked into Spalanzani's room. Olympia, as usual, sat before the little table, her arms upon it, her hands folded. For the first time now he saw her exquisitely formed face. Only her eyes seemed peculiarly fixed and lifeless. But as he continued to look more and more intently through the glass, it seemed as though moist moonbeams were beginning to shine in Olympia's eyes. It seemed as if the power of vision were only now starting to be kindled; her glances were inflamed with ever-increasing life.

Nathanael leaned on the window as if enchanted, staring steadily upon Olympia's divine beauty. The sound of a throat being cleared and a shuffling of feet awakened him from his enchantament. Coppola was standing behind him. "*Tre zechini—*three ducats," Coppola said. Nathanael had completely forgotten the optician. He quickly paid the sum requested. "Nice-a glass, no? Nice-a glass?" Coppola asked in his hoarse and revolting voice, smiling maliciously. "Yes, yes, yes," Nathanael answered irritably. "Goodbye, my friend." But only after casting many peculiar sidelong glances at Nathanael did Coppola leave the room. Nathanael heard him laughing loudly on the stairs. "Ah," thought Nathanael, "he's laughing at me because I overpaid him for this little spyglass." But as he quietly voiced these words he seemed to hear a deep sigh, like a dying man's, echoing through the room. Terror stopped his breath. To be sure, it was he who had deeply sighed; that was obvious. "Klara is absolutely right," he said to himself, "in calling me an absurd visionary, yet it is ridiculous—more than ridiculous—that I am so strangely distressed by the thought of having overpaid Coppola for the spyglass. I see no reason for it." Then Nathanael sat down to finish his letter to Klara, but a glance through the window showed him that Olympia still sat as before, and as though impelled by an irresistible power, he jumped up, seized Coppola's spyglass, and could not tear himself away from the alluring vision of Olympia until his friend Siegmund called for him to go to Professor Spalanzani's lecture. The curtain was tightly drawn across the fateful door so that he could not see Olympia; nor could he see her for the next two days from his own room, despite the fact that he scarcely ever left his window and, almost without interruption, gazed into her room through Coppola's glass. Moreover, on the third day curtains were drawn across the window, and Nathanael, in despair, driven by longing and ardent passion, rushed out beyond the city gates. Olympia's image hovered before him in the air, emerged from the bushes, and peered up at him with great and lustrous eyes from the shining brook. Klara's image had completely faded from his soul. He thought of nothing but Olympia, and he lamented aloud, in a tearful voice, "Oh! My loftly and lovely star of love, have you arisen only to disappear again and leave me in the gloomy night of dark despair?"

As he was about to return home, he became aware of great noise and activity in Spalanzani's house. The doors were open and various kinds of gear were being carried in. The first floor windows had been removed from their hinges, maids with large dust mops were busily rushing about, sweeping and dusting, while inside the house carpenters and upholsterers were banging and hammering. Nathanael stood absolutely still in the street, struck with amazement. Siegmund then joined him and asked with a laugh: "Well what do you think of our old Spalanzani now?" Nathanael assured him that he could say nothing, since he knew absolutely nothing about the professor, but that, much to his astonishment, he had noticed the feverish activity which was taking place in the silent and gloomy house. Siegmund told him that Spalanzani was going to give a great party, a concert and a ball, the next day and that half the university had been invited. Rumor had it that Spalanzani was going to present his daughter Olympia to the public for the first time, after so long having carefully guarded her from every human eye.

Nathanael received an invitation, and at the appointed hour, when carriages were driving up and lights gleamed in the decorated rooms, he went to the professor's house with palpitating heart. The gathering was large and dazzling. Olympia appeared, elegantly and tastefully dressed. No one could help but admire her beautifully shaped face and her figure. On the other hand, there was something peculiarly curved about her back, and the wasplike thinness of her waist also appeared to result from excessively tight lacing. There was, further, something stiff and measured about her walk and bearing which struck many unfavorably, but it was attributed to the constraint she felt in society. The concert began. Olympia played the piano with great talent and also skillfully sang a *bravura* aria in a voice that was high pitched, bell-like, almost shrill. Nathanael was completely enchanted; he was standing in the back row and could not precisely distinguish Olympia's features in the dazzling candlelight. Surreptitiously, he took Coppola's glass from his pocket and looked at her. Oh! Then he perceived the yearning glance with which she looked at him, and he saw how every note achieved absolute purity in the loving glance that scorched him to his very soul. Her skillful roulades appeared to him to be the heavenly exaltations of a soul transfigured by love; and, finally, when the cadenza was concluded, the long trill echoed shrilly through the hall and he felt as if he were suddenly embraced by burning arms. No longer able to contain himself, rapture and pain mingling within him, he cried: "Olympia!" Everyone looked at him; many laughed. The cathedral organist pulled a gloomier face than before and simply said, "Now, now!"

The concert was over. The ball began. Oh, to dance with her! That was his one desire. But how could he summon up the courage to ask her, the queen of the ball, to dance with him? And yet, without really knowing how it happened, just as the dance began he found himself standing close to her and she had not yet been asked to dance. Barely able to stammer a few words, he grasped her hand. It was cold as ice. A deathly chill passed through him. Gazing into Olympia's eyes he saw that they shone at him with love and longing; and at that moment the pulse seemed to beat again in her cold hand, and warm life-blood to surge through her veins. In Nathanael's heart, too, passion burned with greater intensity. He threw his arms around the lovely Olympia and whirled her through the dance. He had thought that he usually followed the beat of the music well, but from the peculiar rhythmical evenness with which she danced and which often confused him, he was aware of how faulty his own sense of time really was. Yet he would dance with no other partner, and he felt that he would murder anyone else who approached Olympia to ask her to dance. But this occurred only twice; to his amazement Olympia remained seated on each occasion until the next dance, when he did not fail to lead her out to the dance floor. If Nathanael had had eyes for anything but the lovely Olympia, there would inevitably have been a number of disagreeable quarrels; for it was obvious that the carefully smothered laughter which broke out among the young people in this corner and that, was directed towards the lovely Olympia, whom they were watching curiously for an unknown reason. Heated by the quantity of wine he had drunk and by the dancing, Nathanael had cast off his characteristic shyness. He sat beside Olympia, her hand in his, and with fervor and passion he spoke of his love in words that no one could understand, neither he nor Olympia. But perhaps she did, for she sat with her eyes fixed upon his, sighing again and again, "Ah, ah, ah!" Whereupon Nathanael answered: "Oh, you magnificent and heavenly woman! You ray shining from the promised land of love! You deep soul, in which my whole being is reflected," and more of the same. But Olympia did nothing but continue to sigh, "Ah, ah!"

Professor Spalanzani passed the happy couple several times and smiled at them with a look of strange satisfaction. It seemed to Nathanael, although he was in a very different, higher world, that it was suddenly getting noticeably darker down here at Professor Spalanzani's. When he looked around him, it was with great consternation that he saw that only two lights were burning in the empty room and that they were about to go out. The music and the dancing had ceased long ago. "We must part, we must part!" he cried in wild despair, then kissed Olympia's hand. He bent down to her mouth; icy lips met his burning ones. Just as when, touching her cold hand, he had felt a shudder seize him, the legend of the dead bride flashed suddenly through his mind. But Olympia drew him close to her, and the kiss seemed to warm her lips into life. Professor Spalanzani walked slowly through the empty room, his steps echoing hollowly, and in the flickering light cast by the candles, his figure assumed a sinister and ghostly appearance.

"Do you love me? Do you love me, Olympia? Just one word! Do you love me?" Nathanael whispered.

But as she rose, Olympia only sighed, "Ah, ah!"

"Yes, you, my lovely, wonderful evening star," said Nathanael, "you have risen for me and will illuminate and transfigure my soul forever."

"Ah, ah!" Olympia replied as she walked away. Nathanael followed her; they stood before the professor.

"You had a most lively conversation with my daughter," the professor said with a smile. "If you enjoy talking with this silly girl you are welcome to come and do so."

Nathanael left, his heart ablaze with all of heaven.

Spalanzani's ball was the talk of the town for the next few days. Despite the fact that the professor had done everything to put on a splendid show, the wags found plenty of fantastic and peculiar things to talk about. Their favorite target was the rigid and silent Olympia, who, her beautiful appearance notwithstanding, was assumed to be hopelessly stupid, which was thought to be the reason Spalanzani had so long kept her concealed. Nathanael heard all this, not without inner fury, but he said nothing. "What would be the use," he thought, "of proving to these fellows that it was their own stupidity which precluded them from appreciating Olympia's profound and beautiful mind."

"Do me a favor, brother," Siegmund said to him one day, "and tell me how it is possible for an intelligent fellow like you to have fallen for that wax-faced, wooden puppet across the way?"

Nathanael was about to lose his temper, but he quickly gained control of himself and replied: "Tell me, Siegmund, how do you account for the fact that a man who is able so readily to discern beauty has not seen the heavenly charms of Olympia? Yet, thank heaven you are not my rival, for if you were a rival, the blood of one of us would be spilled."

Siegmund, seeing how things were with his friend, adroitly switched tactics, and after commenting that there was no point in arguing about the object of a person's love, he added: "It's very strange, however, that many of us have come to the same conclusion about Olympia. She seems to us—don't take this badly, my brother—

strangely stiff and soulless. Her figure is symmetrical, so is her face, that's true enough, and if her eyes were not so completely devoid of life—the power of vision, I mean—she might be considered beautiful. Her step is peculiarly measured; all of her movements seem to stem from some kind of clockwork. Her playing and her singing are unpleasantly perfect, being as lifeless as a music box; it is the same with her dancing. We found Olympia to be rather weird, and we wanted to have nothing to do with her. She seems to us to be playing the part of a human being, and it's as if there really were something hidden behind all of this."

Nathanael did not surrender to the bitterness aroused in him by Siegmund's words; rather, mastering his resentment, he merely said, very gravely: "Olympia may indeed appear weird to you cold and unimaginative mortals. The poetical soul is accessible only to the poetical nature. Her adoring glances fell only upon *me* and irradiated my feelings and thoughts. I discover myself again only in Olympia's love. That she does not indulge in jabbering banalities like other shallow people may not seem right to you. It's true that she says little; but the few words she does utter are in a sacred language which expresses an inner world imbued with love, with the higher, spiritual knowledge gathered from a vision of the world beyond. But you have no feeling for these things; I am wasting my breath."

"God protect you, brother," said Siegmund very gently, almost sadly. "It does seem to me that you are moving in an evil direction. You may depend upon me if—no, I'll say nothing more." It suddenly dawned upon Nathanael that his cold, unimaginative friend Siegmund sincerely wished him very well, and so he warmly shook his outstretched hand.

Nathanael had completely forgotten that there was in the world a Klara whom he had once loved; his mother, Lothar—all had disappeared from his mind. He lived only for Olympia, beside whom he sat every day, hour after hour, carrying on about his love, about mutual sympathy kindled into life, and about their psychic affinity—and Olympia listened to all of this with great reverence. From deep within his desk, Nathanael dug up everything he had ever written—poems, fantasies, visions, romances, tales—and the number was in-

creased daily by a plethora of hyperbolic sonnets, verses, and canzo-
nets; and all of this he read to Olympia tirelessly for hours at a time.
Never before had he had such a splendid listener. She neither embroidered nor knitted; she did not look out of the window nor feed a
bird nor play with a lapdog or kitten; she did not twist slips of paper
or anything else around her fingers; she had no need to disguise a
yawn by forcing a cough. In brief, she sat for hours on end without
moving, staring directly into his eyes, and her gaze grew ever more
ardent and animated. Only when Nathanael at last stood up and
kissed her hand and then her lips did she say, "Ah, ah!" and then
add, "Goodnight, my dearest."

When Nathanael returned to his own room, he cried, "How
beautiful, how profound is her mind! Only you, only you truly understand me." He trembled with rapture when he thought of the
marvelous harmony which daily grew between him and Olympia; it
seemed to him as if she expressed thoughts about his work and about
all of his poetic gifts from the very depth of his own soul, as though
she spoke from within him. This must, to be sure, have been the
case, for Olympia never spoke any word other than those already recorded. But even in clear and sober moments, those, for example,
which followed his awaking in the morning, when Nathanael was
conscious of Olympia's utter passivity and taciturnity, he merely
said: "What are words? Mere words! The glance of her heavenly
eyes expresses more than any commonplace speech. Besides, how is
it possible for a child of heaven to confine herself to the narrow circle demanded by wretched, mundane life?"

Professor Spalanzani appeared to be most pleased by the intimacy
which had developed between his daughter and Nathanael, and he
gave Nathanael many unmistakable signs of his delight. When, at
great length, Nathanael ventured to hint delicately at a possible
marriage with Olympia, the professor's face broke into a smile and
he said that he would allow his daughter to make a perfectly free
choice. Emboldened by these words, and with passion inflaming his
heart, Nathanael determined to implore Olympia the very next day
to put into plain words what her sweet and loving glances had long
told him—that she would be his forever. He searched for the ring his

mother had given him when he had left. He intended to present it to Olympia as a symbol of his devotion and the joyous life with her that had flowered. While looking for the ring he came upon his letters from Klara and Lothar; he cast them aside indifferently, found the ring, put it in his pocket, and hurried with it across to Olympia.

While still on the stairs, he heard a singular hubbub that seemed to come from Spalanzani's study. There was a stamping, a rattling, pushing, a banging against the door, and, intermingled, curses and oaths: "Let go! Let go! Monster! Villain! Risking body and soul for it? Ha! Ha! Ha! Ha! That wasn't our arrangement! I, I made the eyes! I made the clockwork! Damned idiot, you and your damned clockwork! Dog of a clockmaker! Out! Let me go!" The voices causing this uproar belonged to Spalanzani and the abominable Coppelius. Nathanael rushed in, seized by a nameless dread. The professor was grasping a female figure by the shoulders, the Italian Coppola had her by the feet, and they were twisting and tugging her this way and that, contending furiously for possession of her. Nathanael recoiled in horror upon recognizing the figure as Olympia's. Flaring up in a wild rage, he was about to tear his beloved from the grasp of these madmen when Coppola, wrenching the figure from the professor's hand with the strength of a giant, struck the professor such a fearful blow with it that he toppled backwards over the table on which vials, retorts, flasks, and glass test tubes were standing— everything shattered into a thousand fragments. Then Coppola threw the figure over his shoulder and with a horrible, shrill laugh, ran quickly down the stairs, the figure's grotesquely dangling feet bumping and rattling woodenly on every step. Nathanael stood transfixed; he had only too clearly seen that in the deathly pale waxen face of Olympia there were no eyes, but merely black holes. She was a lifeless doll. Spalanzani was writhing on the floor; his head and chest and arm had been cut by the glass fragments and blood gushed from him as if from a fountain. But he summoned up all his strength: "After him, after him! What are you waiting for! Coppelius—Coppelius has stolen my best automaton. Worked at it for twenty years—put everything I had into it—mechanism—speech— movement—all mine. The eyes—the eyes stolen from you! Damn him!

Curse him! After him! Get me Olympia! Bring back Olympia! There are the eyes!"

And now Nathanael saw something like a pair of bloody eyes staring up at him from the floor. Spalanzani seized them with his uninjured hand and flung them at Nathanael so that they hit his breast. Then madness racked Nathanael with scorching claws, ripping to shreds his mind and senses.

"Whirl, whirl, whirl! Circle of fire! Circle of fire! Whirl round, circle of fire! Merrily, merrily! Aha, lovely wooden doll, whirl round!"

With these words Nathanael hurled himself upon the professor and clutched at his throat. He would have strangled him if several people who had been attracted by the noise had not rushed in and torn the raging Nathanael away, thus saving the professor, whose wounds were then bandaged. As strong as he was, Siegmund was unable to subdue the madman, who continued to scream in a horrible voice, "Wooden doll, whirl round!" and to flail about with clenched fists. Finally, several men combined their strength and flung Nathanael to the ground and tied him up. Nathanael's words turned into a heinous bellow, and in a raging frenzy, he was taken away to the madhouse.

Before continuing my narration, gentle reader, of what further happened to the unhappy Nathanael, I can assure you, in case you are interested in Spalanzani, that skillful craftsman and maker of automatons, that his recovery from his wounds was complete. He was, however, forced to leave the university because Nathanael's story had caused a considerable scandal and because opinion generally held that it was an inexcusable deceit to have smuggled a wooden doll into proper tea circles, where Olympia had been such a success, and to have palmed it off as a human. In fact, lawyers held that it was a subtle imposture and considered it felonious because it had been so craftily devised and was directed against the public so that, except for some astute students, it had gone undetected, notwithstanding the fact that everyone now claimed wisdom and pointed to various details which they said had struck them as suspicious. They did not, however, bring any clues to light. Why, for example, would anyone have had his suspicions aroused by the fact that Olympia, according to an elegant tea party-goer, had sneezed more often than she had yawned? This elegant gentleman was of the opinion that the sneezing had really been the sound of the concealed clockwork winding itself up—concomitantly, there had always been an audible creaking—and so on. The professor of poetry and rhetoric took a pinch of snuff, snapped the lid shut, cleared his throat, and solemnly declared: "Most honorable ladies and gentlemen, do you not see the point of it all? It is all an allegory, an extended metaphor. Do you understand? *Sapienti sat.*"

But many honorable gentlemen were not reassured by this. The story of the automaton had very deeply impressed them, and a horrible distrust of human figures in general arose. Indeed, many lovers insisted that their mistresses sing and dance unrythmically and embroider, knit, or play with a lapdog or something while being read to, so that they could assure themselves that they were not in love with a wooden doll, above all else, they required the mistresses not only to listen, but to speak frequently in such a way that it would prove that they really were capable of thinking and feeling. Many lovers, as a result, grew closer than ever before; but others gradually drifted apart. "One really can't be sure about this," said one or another. At tea parties, people yawned with incredible frequency and never sneezed, in order to ward off all suspicion. Spalanzani, as has been noted, had to leave the place in order to escape criminal charges of having fraudulently introduced an automaton into human society. Coppola had also disappeared.

Nathanael awoke as from a deep and frightful dream, opened his eyes, and experienced an indescribable sensation of bliss warmly permeating his body. He lay on his own bed in his own room at home, Klara bending over him, his mother and Lothar standing nearby.

"At last, at last, my darling Nathanael, you have recovered from your terrible illness and are once more mine!" cried Klara with deep emotion, clasping him in her arms. Bright scalding tears streamed from his eyes, so overcome with mingled feelings of sorrow and delight was he, and he gasped, "Klara, my Klara!"

Then Siegmund, who had faithfully stood by his friend in his hour of need, entered the room; and Nathanael shook his hand. "My faithful brother, you have not deserted me."

Every vestige of insanity had disappeared and Nathanael soon re-covered his strength again under the tender care of his mother, sweetheart, and friends. Good luck had, in the meantime, visited the house—an old miserly uncle, from whom they had expected noth-ing, had died and left not only a considerable fortune but a small es-tate which was pleasantly situated not far from the town. And there they resolved to go and live, Nathanael and Klara, whom he was to marry, and his mother and Lothar. Nathanael had grown more gen-tle and child-like than ever before, and for the first time could fully appreciate the heavenly purity of Klara's noble spirit. No one ever reminded him, even most remotely, of what had taken place. But when Siegmund said goodbye to him, he remarked, "By heaven, brother, I was on the wrong road. But an angel guided me to the path of light just in time. It was Klara." Siegmund would let him say nothing else for fear that the wounding memories of the past might flare up in him too vividly.

The time came when these four lucky people were to move into their property, and as they were walking through the streets at noon, after having made many purchases, the high tower of the town hall cast its huge shadow over the market place. "Oh!" said Klara, "Let us climb to the top once more and look at the distant mountains!" No sooner said than done. Nathanael and Klara climbed the tower; his mother and the servant went home. Lothar, not wishing to climb so many steps, remained below. There the two lovers stood arm in arm on the topmost gallery of the tower looking down into the fragrant woods beyond which the blue mountains rose up like a giant city.

"Just look at that strange little grey bush," Klara cried. "It really seems to be coming towards us." Nathanael automatically felt his side pocket, where he found Coppola's spyglass, and looked to one side. Klara was standing in front of the glass. Then there was a con-vulsive throbbing in his pulse. Deathly pale, he stared at Klara; but soon streams of fire flashed and spurted from his rolling eyes. He roared horrendously, like a hunted beast, leaped high into the air, and bursting with horrible laughter, he shrieked in a piercing voice, "Whirl wooden doll! Whirl wooden doll!" And seizing Klara with superhuman strength he tried to hurl her from the tower, but Klara, with a strength born of the agony of desperation, clung tightly to the railing. Lothar heard the madman raving, and he heard Klara's cry of terror. He was seized with a terrible foreboding and raced up the stairs. The door leading to the second flight was shut. Klara's cries were growing fainter and fainter. Mad with rage and fear, he pushed against the door, which finally burst open. "Help! Save me, save me!" Her voice faded in the air. "She is dead, murdered by that madman," Lothar cried. The door leading to the gallery was also locked, but his desperation endowed him with the strength of a giant and he tore it from its hinges. Good God! Klara was in the grasp of Nathanael the madman, hanging in the air over the gallery railing, to which she barely clung with one hand. Quick as lightning, Lothar seized his sister and pulled her back, at the same instant smashing the madman in the face with his fist so hard that he reeled back and let go of his victim.

Lothar raced down the stairs with his unconscious sister in his arms. She was saved. Nathanael dashed around the gallery, leaping up in the air and shouting, "Circle of fire! Whirl round, circle of fire! Whirl round!" A crowd gathered quickly, attracted by the wild screaming; and in the midst of them there towered the gigantic figure of the lawyer Coppelius, who had just arrived in town and had come directly to the market place. Some wanted to go up and overpower the madman, but Coppelius laughed and said, "Ha, ha! Just wait; he'll come down on his own." And he looked up with the rest. Nathanael suddenly froze, leaned forward, caught sight of Coppelius, and with a shattering scream of "Ah, nice-a eyes, nice-a eyes!" jumped over the railing.

Nathanael lay on the pavement with his head shattered, but Coppelius had vanished in the crowd.

Many years later it was reported that Klara had been seen in a remote district sitting hand in hand with a pleasant-looking man in front of the door of a splendid country house, two merry boys playing around her. Thus it may be concluded that Klara eventually found that quiet, domestic happiness which her cheerful nature required and which Nathanael, with his lacerated soul, could never have provided her.

F OR THE MOST WILD yet most homely narrative which I am about to pen, I neither expect nor solicit belief. Mad indeed would I be to expect it, in a case where my very senses reject their own evidence. Yet, mad am I not—and very surely do I not dream. But to-morrow I die, and to-day I would unburden my soul. My immediate purpose is to place before the world, plainly, succinctly, and without comment, a series of mere household events. In their consequences, these events have terrified—have tortured—have destroyed me. Yet I will not attempt to expound them. To me, they have presented little but horror—to many they will seem less terrible than *baroques.* Hereafter, perhaps, some intellect may be found which will reduce my phantasm to the commonplace—some intellect more calm, more logical, and far less excitable than my own, which will perceive, in the circumstances I detail with awe, nothing more than an ordinary succession of very natural causes and effects.

From my infancy I was noted for the docility and humanity of my disposition. My tenderness of heart was even so conspicuous as to make me the jest of my companions. I was especially fond of animals, and was indulged by my parents with a great variety of pets. With these I spent most of my time, and never was so happy as when feeding and caressing them. This peculiarity of character grew with my growth, and, in my manhood, I derived from it one of my principal sources of pleasure. To those who have cherished an affection for a faithful and sagacious dog, I need hardly be at the trouble of explaining the nature or the intensity of the gratification thus derivable. There is something in the unselfish and self-sacrificing love of a brute, which goes directly to the heart of him who has had frequent occasion to test the paltry friendship and gossamer fidelity of mere *Man.*

I married early, and was happy to find in my wife a disposition not uncongenial with my own. Observing my partiality for domestic pets, she lost no opportunity of procuring those of the most agreeable kind. We had birds, gold-fish, a fine dog, rabbits, a small monkey, and a *cat.*

This latter was a remarkably large and beautiful animal, entirely black, and sagacious to an astonishing degree. In speaking of his intelligence, my wife, who at heart was not a little tinctured with superstition, made frequent allusion to the ancient popular notion, which regarded all black cats as witches in disguise. Not that she was ever *serious* upon this point—and I mention the matter at all for no better reason than that it happens, just now, to be remembered.

Pluto—this was the cat's name—was my favorite pet and playmate. I alone fed him, and he attended me wherever I went about the house. It was even with difficulty that I could prevent him from following me through the streets.

Our friendship lasted, in this manner, for several years, during which my general temperament and character—through the instrumentality of the Fiend Intemperance—had (I blush to confess it) experienced a radical alteration for the worse. I grew, day by day, more moody, more irritable, more regardless of the feelings of others. I suffered myself to use intemperate language to my wife. At length, I even offered her personal violence. My pets, of course, were made to feel the change in my disposition. I not only neglected, but ill-used them. For Pluto, however, I still retained sufficient regard to restrain me from maltreating him, as I made no scruple of maltreating the rabbits, the monkey, or even the dog, when, by accident, or through affection, they came in my way. But my disease grew upon me—for what disease is like Alcohol!—and at length even Pluto, who was now becoming old, and consequently somewhat peevish—even Pluto began to experience the effects of my ill temper.

One night, returning home, much intoxicated, from one of my haunts about town, I fancied that the cat avoided my presence. I seized him; when, in his fright at my violence, he inflicted a slight wound upon my hand with his teeth. The fury of a demon instantly possessed me. I knew myself no longer. My original soul seemed, at

once, to take its flight from my body; and a more than fiendish malevolence, gin-nurtured, thrilled every fibre of my frame. I took from
my waistcoat-pocket a penknife, opened it, grasped the poor beast
by the throat, and deliberately cut one of its eyes from the socket! I
blush, I burn, I shudder, while I pen the damnable atrocity.

When reason returned with the morning—when I had slept off
the fumes of the night's debauch—I experienced a sentiment half of
horror, half of remorse, for the crime of which I had been guilty; but
it was, at best, a feeble and equivocal feeling, and the soul remained
untouched. I again plunged into excess, and soon drowned in wine
all memory of the deed.

In the meantime the cat slowly recovered. The socket of the lost
eye presented, it is true, a frightful appearance, but he no longer appeared to suffer any pain. He went about the house as usual, but, as
might be expected, fled in extreme terror at my approach. I had so
much of my old heart left, as to be at first grieved by this evident
dislike on the part of a creature which had once so loved me. But this
feeling soon gave place to irritation. And then came, as if to my final
and irrevocable overthrow, the spirit of PERVERSENESS. Of this spirit
philosophy takes no account. Yet I am not more sure that my soul
lives, than I am that perverseness is one of the primitive impulses of
the human heart—one of the indivisible primary faculties, or senti-
ments, which give direction to the character of Man. Who has not,
a hundred times, found himself committing a vile or a stupid action,
for no other reason than because he knows he should *not*? Have we
not a perpetual inclination, in the teeth of our best judgment, to violate that which is *Law*, merely because we understand it to be such?
This spirit of perverseness, I say, came to my final overthrow. It was
this unfathomable longing of the soul *to vex itself*—to offer violence
to its own nature—to do wrong for the wrong's sake only—that urged
me to continue and finally to consummate the injury I had inflicted
upon the unoffending brute. One morning, in cold blood, I slipped a
noose about its neck and hung it to the limb of a tree;—hung it with
the tears streaming from my eyes, and with the bitterest remorse at
my heart;—hung it *because* I knew that it had loved me, and *because*
I felt it had given me no reason of offence;—hung it *because* I knew

that in so doing I was committing a sin—a deadly sin that would so jeopardize my immortal soul as to place it—if such a thing were possible—even beyond the reach of the infinite mercy of the Most Merciful and Most Terrible God.

On the night of the day on which this most cruel deed was done, I was aroused from sleep by the cry of fire. The curtains of my bed were in flames. The whole house was blazing. It was with great difficulty that my wife, a servant, and myself, made our escape from the conflagration. The destruction was complete. My entire worldly wealth was swallowed up, and I resigned myself thenceforward to despair.

I am above the weakness of seeking to establish a sequence of cause and effect, between the disaster and the atrocity. But I am detailing a chain of facts—and wish not to leave even a possible link imperfect. On the day succeeding the fire, I visited the ruins. The walls, with one exception, had fallen in. This exception was found in a compartment wall, not very thick, which stood about the middle of the house, and against which had rested the head of my bed. The plastering had here, in great measure, resisted the action of the fire—a fact which I attributed to its having been recently spread. About this wall a dense crowd were collected, and many persons seemed to be examining a particular portion of it with very minute and eager attention. The words "strange!" "singular!" and other similar expressions, excited my curiosity. I approached and saw, as if graven in *bas-relief* upon the white surface, the figure of a gigantic *cat*. The impression was given with an accuracy truly marvellous. There was a rope about the animal's neck.

When I first beheld this apparition—for I could scarcely regard it as less—my wonder and my terror were extreme. But at length reflection came to my aid. The cat, I remembered, had been hung in a garden adjacent to the house. Upon the alarm of fire, this garden had been immediately filled by the crowd—by some one of whom the animal must have been cut from the tree and thrown, through an open window, into my chamber. This had probably been done with the view of arousing me from sleep. The falling of other walls had compressed the victim of my cruelty into the substance of the freshly-spread plaster; the lime of which, with the flames, and the *ammonia* from the carcass, had then accomplished the portraiture as I saw it.

Although I thus readily accounted to my reason, if not altogether to my conscience, for the startling fact just detailed, it did not the less fail to make a deep impression upon my fancy. For months I could not rid myself of the phantasm of the cat; and, during this period, there came back into my spirit a half-sentiment that seemed, but was not, remorse. I went so far as to regret the loss of the animal, and to look about me, among the vile haunts which I now habitually frequented, for another pet of the same species, and of somewhat similar appearance, with which to supply its place.

One night as I sat, half stupefied, in a den of more than infamy, my attention was suddenly drawn to some black object, reposing upon the head of one of the immense hogsheads of gin, or of rum, which constituted the chief furniture of the apartment. I had been looking steadily at the top of this hogshead for some minutes, and what now caused me surprise was the fact that I had not sooner perceived the object thereupon. I approached it, and touched it with my hand. It was a black cat—a very large one—fully as large as Pluto, and closely resembling him in every respect but one. Pluto had not a white hair upon any portion of his body; but this cat had a large, although indefinite splotch of white, covering nearly the whole region of the breast.

Upon my touching him, he immediately arose, purred loudly, rubbed against my hand, and appeared delighted with my notice. This, then, was the very creature of which I was in search. I at once offered to purchase it of the landlord; but this person made no claim to it—knew nothing of it—had never seen it before.

I continued my caresses, and when I prepared to go home, the animal evinced a disposition to accompany me. I permitted it to do so; occasionally stooping and patting it as I proceeded. When it reached the house it domesticated itself at once, and became immediately a great favorite with my wife.

For my own part, I soon found a dislike to it arising within me. This was just the reverse of what I had anticipated; but—I know not how or why it was—its evident fondness for myself rather disgusted and annoyed me. By slow degrees these feelings of disgust and annoyance rose into the bitterness of hatred. I avoided the creature; a certain sense of shame, and the remembrance of my former deed of cruelty, preventing me from physically abusing it. I did not, for some weeks, strike, or otherwise violently ill use it; but gradually—very gradually—I came to look upon it with unutterable loathing, and to flee silently from its odious presence, as from the breath of a pestilence.

What added, no doubt, to my hatred of the beast, was the discovery, on the morning after I brought it home, that, like Pluto, it also had been deprived of one of its eyes. This circumstance, however, only endeared it to my wife, who, as I have already said, possessed, in a high degree, that humanity of feeling which had once been my distinguishing trait, and the source of many of my simplest and purest pleasures.

With my aversion to this cat, however, its partiality for myself seemed to increase. It followed my footsteps with a pertinacity which it would be difficult to make the reader comprehend. Whenever I sat, it would crouch beneath my chair, or spring upon my knees, covering me with its loathsome caresses. If I arose to walk it would get between my feet and thus nearly throw me down, or, fastening its long and sharp claws in my dress, clamber, in this manner, to my breast. At such times, although I longed to destroy it with a blow, I was yet withheld from so doing, partly by a memory of my former crime, but chiefly—let me confess it at once—by absolute *dread* of the beast.

This dread was not exactly a dread of physical evil—and yet I should be at a loss how otherwise to define it. I am almost ashamed to own—yes, even in this felon's cell, I am almost ashamed to own—that the terror and horror with which the animal inspired me, had been heightened by one of the merest chimeras it would be possible to conceive. My wife had called my attention, more than once, to the character of the mark of white hair, of which I have spoken, and which constituted the sole visible difference between the strange beast and the one I had destroyed. The reader will remember that this mark, although large, had been originally very indefinite; but, by slow degrees—degrees nearly imperceptible, and which for a long time my reason struggled to reject as fanciful—it had, at length, assumed a rigorous distinctness of outline. It was now the representation of an object that I shudder to name—and for this, above all, I loathed, and dreaded, and would have rid myself to the monster *had I dared*—it was now, I say, the image of a hideous—of a ghastly thing—of the GALLOWS!—oh, mournful and terrible engine of Horror and of Crime—of Agony and of Death!

And now was I indeed wretched beyond the wretchedness of mere Humanity. And *a brute beast*—whose fellow I had contemptuously destroyed—*a brute beast* to work out for *me*—for me, a man fashioned in the image of the High God—so much of insufferable woe! Alas! neither by day nor by night knew I the blessing of rest any more! During the former the creature left me no moment alone, and in the latter I started hourly from dreams of unutterable fear to find the hot breath of *the thing* upon my face, and its vast weight—an incarnate nightmare that I had no power to shake off—incumbent eternally upon my *heart!*

Beneath the pressure of torments such as these the feeble remnant of the good within me succumbed. Evil thoughts became my sole intimates—the darkest and most evil of thoughts. The moodiness of my usual temper increased to hatred of all things and of all mankind; while from the sudden, frequent, and ungovernable outbursts of a fury to which I now blindly abandoned myself, my uncomplaining wife, alas, was the most usual and the most patient of sufferers.

One day she accompanied me, upon some household errand, into the cellar of the old building which our poverty compelled us to inhabit. The cat followed me down the steep stairs, and, nearly throwing me headlong, exasperated me to madness. Uplifting an axe, and forgetting in my wrath the childish dread which had hitherto stayed my hand, I aimed a blow at the animal, which, of course, would have proved instantly fatal had it descended as I wished. But this blow was arrested by the hand of my wife. Goaded by the interference into a rage more than demoniacal, I withdrew my arm from her grasp and buried the axe in her brain. She fell dead upon the spot without a groan.

This hideous murder accomplished, I set myself forthwith, and with entire deliberation, to the task of concealing the body. I knew that I could not remove it from the house, either by day or by night, without the risk of being observed by the neighbors. Many projects entered my mind. At one period I thought of cutting the corpse into minute fragments, and destroying them by fire. At another, I resolved to dig a grave for it in the floor of the cellar. Again, I deliberated about casting it in the well in the yard—about packing it in a box, as if merchandise, with the usual arrangements, and so getting a porter to take it from the house. Finally I hit upon what I considered a far better expedient than either of these. I determined to wall it up in the cellar, as the monks of the Middle Ages are recorded to have walled up their victims.

For a purpose such as this the cellar was well adapted. Its walls were loosely constructed, and had lately been plastered throughout with a rough plaster, which the dampness of the atmosphere had prevented from hardening. Moreover, in one of the walls was a projection, caused by a false chimney, or fireplace, that had been filled up and made to resemble the rest of the cellar. I made no doubt that I could readily displace the bricks at this point, insert the corpse, and wall the whole up as before, so that no eye could detect any thing suspicious.

And in this calculation I was not deceived. By means of a crowbar I easily dislodged the bricks, and, having carefully deposited the body against the inner wall, I propped it in that position, while with little trouble I relaid the whole structure as it originally stood. Having procured mortar, sand, and hair, with every possible precaution, I prepared a plaster which could not be distinguished from the old, and with this I very carefully went over the new brick-work. When I had finished, I felt satisfied that all was right. The wall did not present the slightest appearance of having been disturbed. The rubbish on the floor was picked up with the minutest care. I looked around triumphantly, and said to myself: "Here at least, then, my labor has not been in vain."

My next step was to look for the beast which had been the cause of so much wretchedness; for I had, at length, firmly resolved to put it to death. Had I been able to meet with it at the moment, there could have been no doubt of its fate; but it appeared that the crafty animal had been alarmed at the violence of my previous anger, and forbore to present itself in my present mood. It is impossible to describe or to imagine the deep, the blissful sense of relief which the absence of the detested creature occasioned in my bosom. It did not make its appearance during the night; and thus for one night, at least, since its introduction into the house, I soundly and tranquilly slept; aye, *slept* even with the burden of murder upon my soul.

The second and the third day passed, and still my tormentor came not. Once again I breathed as a freeman. The monster, in terror, had fled the premises for ever! I should behold it no more! My happiness was supreme! The guilt of my dark deed disturbed me but little. Some few inquiries had been made, but these had been readily answered. Even a search had been instituted—but of course nothing was to be discovered. I looked upon my future felicity as secured.

Upon the fourth day of the assassination, a party of the police came, very unexpectedly, into the house, and proceeded again to make rigorous investigation of the premises. Secure, however, in the inscrutability of my place of concealment, I felt no embarrassment whatever. The officers bade me accompany them in their search. They left no nook or corner unexplored. At length, for the third or fourth time, they descended into the cellar. I quivered not in a muscle. My heart beat calmly as that of one who slumbers in innocence. I walked the cellar from end to end. I folded my arms upon my bosom, and roamed easily to and fro. The police were thoroughly satisfied and prepared to depart. The glee at my heart was too strong to be restrained. I burned to say if but one word, by way of triumph, and to render doubly sure their assurance of my guiltlessness.

"Gentlemen," I said at last, as the party ascended the steps, "I delight to have allayed your suspicions. I wish you all health and a little more courtesy. By the bye, gentlemen, this—this is a very well-constructed house," (in the rabid desire to say something easily, I scarcely knew what I uttered at all),—"I may say an *excellently* well-constructed house. These walls—are you going, gentlemen?—these walls are solidly put together"; and here, through the mere frenzy of bravado, I rapped heavily with a cane which I held in my hand, upon that very portion of the brick-work behind which stood the corpse of the wife of my bosom.

But may God shield and deliver me from the fangs of the Arch-Fiend! No sooner had the reverberation of my blows sunk into silence, than I was answered by a voice from within the tomb!—by a cry, at first muffled and broken, like the sobbing of a child, and then quickly swelling into one long, loud, and continuous scream, utterly anomalous and inhuman—a howl—a wailing shriek, half of horror and half of triumph, such as might have arisen only out of hell, conjointly from the throats of the damned in their agony and of the demons that exult in the damnation.

Of my own thoughts it is folly to speak. Swooning, I staggered to the opposite wall. For one instant the party on the stairs remained motionless, through extremity of terror and awe. In the next a dozen stout arms were toiling at the wall. It fell bodily. The corpse, already greatly decayed and clotted with gore, stood erect before the eyes of the spectators. Upon its head, with red extended mouth and solitary eye of fire, sat the hideous beast whose craft had seduced me into murder, and whose informing voice had consigned me to the hangman. I had walled the monster up within the tomb.

S EARCHERS AFTER HORROR haunt strange, far places. For them are the catacombs of Ptolemais, and the carven mausolea of the nightmare countries. They climb to the moonlit towers of ruined Rhine castles, and falter down black cobwebbed steps beneath the scattered stones of forgotten cities in Asia. The haunted wood and the desolate mountain are their shrines, and they linger around the sinister monoliths on uninhabited islands. But the true epicure in the terrible, to whom a new thrill of unutterable ghastliness is the chief end and justification of existence, esteems most of all the ancient, lonely farmhouses of backwoods New England; for there the dark elements of strength, solitude, grotesqueness and ignorance combine to form the perfection of the hideous.

Most horrible of all sights are the little unpainted wooden houses remote from travelled ways, usually squatted upon some damp, grassy slope or leaning against some gigantic outcropping of rock. Two hundred years and more they have leaned or squatted there, while the vines have crawled and the trees have swelled and spread. They are almost hidden now in lawless luxuriances of green and guardian shrouds of shadow; but the small-paned windows still stare shockingly, as if blinking through a lethal stupor which wards off madness by dulling the memory of unutterable things.

In such houses have dwelt generations of strange people, whose like the world has never seen. Seized with a gloomy and fanatical belief which exiled them from their kind, their ancestors sought the wilderness for freedom. There the scions of a conquering race indeed flourished free from the restrictions of their fellows, but cowered in an appalling slavery to the dismal phantasms of their own minds. Divorced from the enlightenment of civilization, the strength of these Puritans turned into singular channels; and in their isolation, morbid self-repression, and struggle for life with relentless Nature, there came to them dark furtive traits from the prehistoric depths of their cold Northern heritage. By necessity practical and by philosophy stern, these folks were not beautiful in their sins. Erring as all mortals must, they were forced by their rigid code to seek concealment above all else; so that they came to use less and less taste in what they concealed. Only the silent, sleepy, staring houses in the backwoods can tell all that has lain hidden since the early days, and they are not communicative, being loath to shake off the drowsiness which helps them forget. Sometimes one feels that it would be merciful to tear down these houses, for they must often dream.

It was to a time-battered edifice of this description that I was driven one afternoon in November, 1896, by a rain of such chilling copiousness that any shelter was preferable to exposure. I had been travelling for some time amongst the people of the Miskatonic Valley in quest of certain genealogical data; and from the remote, devious, and problematical nature of my course, had deemed it convenient to employ a bicycle despite the lateness of the season. Now I found myself upon an apparently abandoned road which I had chosen as the shortest cut to Arkham, overtaken by the storm at a point far from any town, and confronted with no refuge save the antique and repellent wooden building which blinked with bleared windows from between two huge leafless elms near the foot of a rocky hill. Distant though it is from the remnant of a road, this house none the less impressed me unfavorably the very moment I espied it. Honest, wholesome structures do not stare at travellers so slyly and hauntingly, and in my genealogical researches I had encountered legends of a century before which biased me against places of this kind. Yet the force of the elements was such as to overcome my scruples, and I did not hesitate to wheel my machine up the weedy rise to the closed door which seemed at once so suggestive and secretive.

I had somehow taken it for granted that the house was abandoned, yet as I approached it I was not so sure, for though the walks were indeed overgrown with weeds, they seemed to retain their nature a

little too well to argue complete desertion. Therefore instead of trying the door I knocked, feeling as I did so a trepidation I could
scarcely explain. As I waited on the rough, mossy rock which served
as a door-step, I glanced at the neighboring windows and the panes
of the transom above me, and noticed that although old, rattling, and
almost opaque with dirt, they were not broken. The building, then,
must still be inhabited, despite its isolation and general neglect. However, my rapping evoked no response, so after repeating the summons I tried the rusty latch and found the door unfastened. Inside
was a little vestibule with walls from which the plaster was falling,
and through the doorway came a faint but peculiarly hateful odor. I
entered, carrying my bicycle, and closed the door behind me. Ahead
rose a narrow staircase, flanked by a small door probably leading to
the cellar, while to the left and right were closed doors leading to
rooms on the ground floor.

Leaning my cycle against the wall I opened the door at the left,
and crossed into a small low-ceiled chamber but dimly lighted by its
two dusty windows and furnished in the barest and most primitive
possible way. It appeared to be a kind of sitting-room, for it had a
table and several chairs, and an immense fireplace above which
ticked an antique clock on a mantel. Books and papers were very
few, and in the prevailing gloom I could not readily discern the
titles. What interested me was the uniform air of archaism as dis-
played in every visible detail. Most of the houses in this region I had
found rich in relics of the past, but here the antiquity was curiously
complete; for in all the room I could not discover a single article of
definitely post-revolutionary date. Had the furnishings been less
humble, the place would have been a collector's paradise.

As I surveyed this quaint apartment, I felt an increase in that
aversion first excited by the bleak exterior of the house. Just what it
was that I feared or loathed, I could by no means define; but something in the whole atmosphere seemed redolent of unhallowed age,
of unpleasant crudeness, and of secrets which should be forgotten. I
felt disinclined to sit down, and wandered about examining the various articles which I had noticed. The first object of my curiosity was
a book of medium size lying upon the table and presenting such an

antediluvian aspect that I marvelled at beholding it outside a museum or library. It was bound in leather with metal fittings, and was in an excellent state of preservation; being altogether an unusual sort of volume to encounter in an abode so lowly. When I opened it to the title page my wonder grew even greater, for it proved to be nothing less rare than Pigafetta's account of the Congo region, written in Latin from the notes of the sailor Lopex and printed at Frankfort in 1598. I had often heard of this work, with its curious illustrations by the brothers De Bry, hence for a moment forgot my uneasiness in my desire to turn the pages before me. The engravings were indeed interesting, drawn wholly from imagination and careless descriptions, and represented negroes with white skins and Caucasian features; nor would I soon have closed the book had not an exceedingly trivial circumstance upset my tired nerves and revived my sensation of disquiet. What annoyed me was merely the persistent way in which the volume tended to fall open of itself at Plate XII, which represented in gruesome detail a butcher's shop of the cannibal Anziques. I experienced some shame at my susceptibility to so slight a thing, but the drawing nevertheless disturbed me, especially in connection with some adjacent passages descriptive of Anzique gastronomy.

I had turned to a neighboring shelf and was examining its meagre literary contents—an eighteenth century Bible, a "Pilgrim's Progress" of like period, illustrated with grotesque woodcuts and printed by the almanack-maker Isaiah Thomas, the rotting bulk of Cotton Mather's "Magnalia Christi Americana," and a few other books of evidently equal age—when my attention was aroused by the unmistakable sound of walking in the room overhead. At first astonished and startled, considering the lack of response to my recent knocking at the door, I immediately afterward concluded that the walker had just awaked from a sound sleep, and listened with less surprise as the footsteps sounded on the creaking stairs. The tread was heavy, yet seemed to contain a curious quality of cautiousness; a quality which I disliked the more because the tread was heavy. When I had entered the room I had shut the door behind me. Now, after a moment of silence during which the walker may have been inspecting my bicycle in the hall, I heard a fumbling at the latch and saw the paneled portal swing open again.

In the doorway stood a person of such singular appearance that I should have exclaimed aloud but for the restraints of good breeding. Old, white-bearded, and ragged, my host possessed a countenance and physique which inspired equal wonder and respect. His height could not have been less than six feet, and despite a general air of age and poverty he was stout and powerful in proportion. His face, almost hidden by a long beard which grew high on the cheeks, seemed abnormally ruddy and less wrinkled than one might expect; while over a high forehead fell a shock of white hair little thinned by the years. His blue eyes, though a trifle bloodshot, seemed inexplicably keen and burning. But for his horrible unkemptness the man would have been as distinguished-looking as he was impressive. This unkemptness, however, made him offensive despite his face and figure. Of what his clothing consisted I could hardly tell, for it seemed to me no more than a mass of tatters surmounting a pair of high, heavy boots; and his lack of cleanliness surpassed description.

The appearance of this man, and the instinctive fear he inspired, prepared me for something like enmity; so that I almost shuddered through surprise and a sense of uncanny incongruity when he motioned me to a chair and addressed me in a thin, weak voice full of fawning respect and ingratiating hospitality. His speech was very curious, an extreme form of Yankee dialect I had thought long extinct; and I studied it closely as he sat down opposite me for conversation.

"Ketched in the rain, be ye?" he greeted. "Glad ye was nigh the haouse en' hed the sense ta come right in. I calc'late I was asleep, else I'd a heerd ye—I ain't as young as I uster be, an' I need a paowerful sight o' naps naowadays. Trav'lin' fur? I hain't seed many folks 'long this rud sence they tuk off the Arkham stage."

I replied that I was going to Arkham, and apologized for my rude entry into his domicile, whereupon he continued.

"Glad ta see ye, young Sir—new faces is scurce araount here, an' I hain't got much ta cheer me up these days. Guess yew hail from Bosting, don't ye? I never ben thar, but I kin tell a taown man when I see 'im—we hed one fer deestrick schoolmaster in 'eighty-four, but he quit suddent an' no one never heerd on 'im sence—" here the old man lapsed into a kind of chuckle, and made no explanation when

I questioned him. He seemed to be in an aboundingly good humor, yet to possess those eccentricities which one might guess from his grooming. For some time he rambled on with an almost feverish geniality, when it struck me to ask him how he came by so rare a book as Pigafetta's "Regnum Congo." The effect of this volume had not left me, and I felt a certain hesitancy in speaking of it, but curiosity overmastered all the vague fears which had steadily accumulated since my first glimpse of the house. To my relief, the question did not seem an awkward one, for the old man answered freely and volubly.

"Oh, that Afriky book? Cap'n Ebenezer Holt traded me thet in 'sixty-eight—him as was kilt in the war." Something about the name of Ebenezer Holt caused me to look up sharply. I had encountered it in my genealogical work, but not in any record since the Revolution. I wondered if my host could help me in the task at which I was laboring, and resolved to ask him about it later on. He continued.

"Ebenezer was on a Salem merchantman for years, an' picked up a sight o' queer stuff in every port. He got this in London, I guess—he uster like ter buy things at the shops. I was up ta his haouse onct, on the hill, tradin' hosses, when I see this book. I relished the picters, so he give it in on a swap. 'Tis a queer book—here, leave me git on my spectacles—" The old man fumbled among his rags, producing a pair of dirty and amazingly antique glasses with small octagonal lenses and steel bows. Donning these, he reached for the volume on the table and turned the pages lovingly.

"Ebenezer cud read a leetle o' this—'tis Latin—but I can't. I had two er three schoolmasters read me a bit, and Passon Clark, him they say got draownded in the pond—kin yew make anything outen it?" I told him that I could, and translated for his benefit a paragraph near the beginning. If I erred, he was not scholar enough to correct me; for he seemed childishly pleased at my English version. His proximity was becoming rather obnoxious, yet I saw no way to escape without offending him. I was amused at the childish fondness of this ignorant old man for the pictures in a book he could not read, and wondered how much better he could read the few books in English which adorned the room. This revelation of simplicity removed much of the ill-defined apprehension I had felt, and I smiled as my host rambled on:

"Queer haow picters kin set a body thinkin'. Take this un here near the front. Hev yew ever seed trees like thet, with big leaves a-floppin' over an' daown? And them men—them can't be niggers— they dew beat all. Kinder like Injuns, I guess, even ef they be in Afriky. Some o' these here critters looks like monkeys, or half monkeys an' half men, but I never heerd o' nothin' like this un." Here he pointed to a fabulous creature of the artist, which one might describe as a sort of dragon with the head of an alligator.

"But naow I'll show ye the best un—over here nigh the middle—" the old man's speech grew a trifle thicker and his eyes assumed a brighter glow; but his fumbling hands, though seemingly clumsier than before, were entirely adequate to their mission. The book fell open, almost of its own accord and as if from frequent consultation at this place, to the repellent twelfth plate showing a butcher's shop amongst the Anzique cannibals. My sense of restlessness returned, though I did not exhibit it. The especially bizarre thing was that the artist had made his Africans look like white men—the limbs and quarters hanging about the walls of the shop were ghastly, while the butcher with his axe was hideously incongruous. But my host seemed to relish the view as much as I disliked it.

"What d'ye think o' this—ain't never see the like hereabouts, eh? When I see this I telled Eb Holt, 'That's suthin' ta stir ye up an' make yer blood tickle.' When I read in Scripter about slayin'—like them Midianites was slew—I kinder think things, but I ain't got no picter of it. Here a body kin see all they is to it—I s'pose 'tis sinful, but ain't we all born an' livin' in sin?—Thet feller bein' chopped up gives me a tickle every time I look at 'im—I hev ta keep lookin' at 'im—see whar the butcher cut off his feet? Thar's his head on thet bench, with one arm side of it, an' t'other arm's on the other side o' the meat block."

As the man mumbled on in his shocking ecstasy the expression on his hairy, spectacled face became indescribable, but his voice sank rather than mounted. My own sensations can scarcely be recorded. All the terror I had dimly felt before rushed upon me actively and vividly, and I knew that I loathed the ancient and abhorrent creature so near me with an infinite intensity. His madness, or at least his partial perversion, seemed beyond dispute. He was almost whispering now, with a huskiness more terrible than a scream, and I trembled as I listened.

"As I says, 'tis queer haow picters sets ye thinkin'. D'ye know, young Sir, I'm right sot on this un here. Arter I got the book off Eb I uster look at it a lot, especial when I'd heerd Passon Clark rant o' Sundays in his big wig. Onct I tried suthin' funny—here, young Sir, don't git skeert—all I done was ter look at the picter afore I kilt the sheep for market—killin' sheep was kinder more fun arter lookin' at it—" The tone of the old man now sank very low, sometimes becoming so faint that his words were hardly audible. I listened to the rain, and to the rattling of the bleared, small-paned windows, and marked a rumbling of approaching thunder quite unusual for the season. Once a terrific flash and peal shook the frail house to its foundations, but the whisperer seemed not to notice it.

"Killin' sheep was kinder more fun—but d'ye know, 'twan't quite *satisfyin'*. Queer haow a cravin' gits a holt on ye—As ye love the Almighty, young man, don't tell nobody, but I swar ter Gawd thet picter begun ta make me *hungry fer victuals I couldn't raise nor buy*—here, set still, what's ailin' ye?—I didn't do nothin', only I wondered haow 'twud be ef I *did*—They say meat makes blood an' flesh, an' gives ye new life, so I wondered ef 'twudn't make a man live longer an' longer ef 'twas *more the same*—" But the whisperer never continued. The interruption was not produced by my fright, nor by the rapidly increasing storm amidst whose fury I was presently to open my eyes on a smoky solitude of blackened ruins. It was produced by a very simple though somewhat unusual happening.

The open book lay flat between us, with the picture staring repulsively upward. As the old man whispered the words *"more the same"* a tiny splattering impact was heard, and something showed on the yellowed paper of the upturned volume. I thought of the rain and of a leaky roof, but rain is not red. On the butcher's shop of the Anzique cannibals a small red spattering glistened picturesquely, lending vividness to the horror of the engraving. The old man saw it, and stopped whispering even before my expression of horror made it necessary; saw it and glanced quickly toward the floor of the room he had left an hour before. I followed his glance, and upheld just above us on the loose plaster of the ancient ceiling a large irregular spot of wet crimson which seemed to spread even as I viewed it. I did not shriek or move, but merely shut my eyes. A moment later came the titanic thunderbolt of thunderbolts; blasting that accursed house of unutterable secrets and bringing the oblivion which alone saved my mind.

GHOST STORIES

The Hand   *JOSEPH SHERIDAN LE FANU*

I 'M SURE SHE BELIEVED every word she related, for old Sally was veracious. But all this was worth just so much as such talk commonly is—marvels, fabulæ, what our ancestors call winter's tales—which gathered details from every narrator and dilated in the act of narration. Still it was not quite for nothing that the house was held to be haunted. Under all this smoke there smouldered just a little spark of truth—an authenticated mystery, for the solution of which some of my readers may possibly suggest a theory, though I confess I can't.

Miss Rebecca Chattesworth, in a letter dated late in the autumn of 1753, gives a minute and curious relation of occurrences in the Tiled House, which, it is plain, although at starting she protests against all such fooleries, she has heard with a peculiar sort of interest, and relates it certainly with an awful sort of particularity.

I was for printing the entire letter, which is really very singular as well as characteristic. But my publisher meets me with his *veto;* and I believe he is right. The worthy old lady's letter *is*, perhaps, too long; and I must rest content with a few hungry notes of its tenor.

That year, and somewhere about the 24th October, there broke out a strange dispute between Mr. Alderman Harper, of High-street, Dublin, and my Lord Castlemallard, who, in virtue of his cousinship to the young heir's mother, had undertaken for him the management of the tiny estate on which the Tiled or Tyled House—for I find it spelt both ways—stood.

This Alderman Harper had agreed for a lease of the house for his daughter, who was married to a gentleman named Prosser. He furnished it and put up hangings, and otherwise went to considerable expense. Mr. and Mrs.

Prosser came there some time in June, and after having parted with a good many servants in the interval, she made up her mind that she could not live in the house, and her father waited on Lord Castlemallard and told him plainly that he would not take out the lease because the house was subjected to annoyances which he could not explain. In plain terms, he said it was haunted, and that no servants would live there more than a few weeks, and that after what his son-in-law's family had suffered there, not only should he be excused from taking a lease of it, but that the house itself ought to be pulled down as a nuisance and the habitual haunt of something worse than human malefactors.

Lord Castlemallard filed a bill in the Equity side of Exchequer to compel Mr. Alderman Harper to perform his contract, by taking out the lease. But the alderman drew an answer, supported by no less than seven long affidavits, copies of all which were furnished to his lordship, and with the desired effect; for rather than compel him to place them upon the file of the court, his lordship struck, and consented to release him.

I am sorry the cause did not proceed at least far enough to place upon the records of the court the very authentic and unaccountable story which Miss Rebecca relates.

The annoyances described did not begin till the end of August, when, one evening, Mrs. Prosser, quite alone, was sitting in the twilight at the back parlour window, which was open, looking out into the orchard, and plainly saw a hand stealthily placed upon the stone window-sill outside, as if by some one beneath the window, at her right side, intending to climb up. There was nothing but the hand, which was rather short, but handsomely formed, and white and plump, laid on the edge of the window-sill; and it was not a very young hand, but one aged, somewhere above forty, as she conjectured. It was only a few weeks before that the horrible robbery at Clondalkin had taken place, and the lady fancied that the hand was that of one of the miscreants who was now about to scale the windows of the Tiled House. She uttered a loud scream and an ejaculation of terror, and at the same moment the hand was quietly withdrawn.

Search was made in the orchard, but there were no indications of any person's having been under the window, beneath which, ranged along the wall, stood a great column of flower-pots, which it seemed must have prevented any one's coming within reach of it.

The same night there came a hasty tapping, every now and then, at the window of the kitchen. The women grew frightened, and the servant-man, taking fire-arms with him, opened the back-door, but discovered nothing. As he shut it, however, he said, "a thump came on it," and a pressure as of somebody striving to force his way in, which frightened *him;* and though the tapping went on upon the kitchen window-panes, he made no further explorations.

About six o'clock on Saturday evening, the cook, "an honest, sober woman, now aged nigh sixty years," being alone in the kitchen, saw, on looking up, it is supposed, the same fat but aristo-cratic-looking hand laid with its palm against the glass, near the side of the window, and this time moving slowly up and down, pressed all the while against the glass, as if feeling carefully for some inequality in its surface. She cried out, and said something like a prayer, on seeing it. But it was not withdrawn for several seconds after.

After this, for a great many nights, there came at first a low, and afterwards an angry rapping, as it seemed with a set of clenched knuckles, at the back-door. And the servant-man would not open it, but called to know who was there; and there came no answer, only a sound as if the palm of the hand was placed against it, and drawn slowly from side to side, with a sort of soft, groping motion.

All this time, sitting in the back parlour, which, for the time, they used as a drawing-room, Mr. and Mrs. Prosser were disturbed by rappings at the window, sometimes very low and furtive, like a clandestine signal, and at others sudden and so loud as to threaten the breaking of the pane.

This was all at the back of the house, which looked upon the orchard, as you know. But on a Tuesday night, at about half-past nine, there came precisely the same rapping at the hall-door, and went on, to the great annoyance of the master and terror of his wife, at intervals, for nearly two hours.

After this, for several days and nights, they had no annoyance whatsoever, and began to think that the nuisance had expended itself. But on the night of the 13th September, Jane Easterbrook, an English maid, having gone into the pantry for the small silver bowl in which her mistress's posset was served, happening to look up at the little window of only four panes, observed through an auger-hole which was drilled through the window-frame, for the admission of a bolt to secure the shutter, a white pudgy finger— first the tip, and then the two first joints introduced, and turned about this way and that, crooked against the inside, as if in search of a fastening which its owner designed to push aside. When the maid got back into the kitchen, we are told "she fell into 'a swounde,' and was all the next day very weak."

Mr. Prosser being, I've heard, a hard-headed and conceited sort of fellow, scouted the ghost, and sneered at the fears of his family. He was privately of opinion that the whole affair was a practical joke or a fraud, and waited an opportunity of catching the rogue *flagrante delicto*. He did not long keep this theory to himself, but let it out by degrees with no stint of oaths and threats, believing that some domestic traitor held the thread of the conspiracy.

Indeed it was time something were done; for not only his servants, but good Mrs. Prosser herself, had grown to look unhappy and anxious, and kept at home from the hour of sunset, and would not venture about the house after night-fall, except in couples.

The knocking had ceased for about a week; and one night, Mrs. Prosser being in the nursery, her husband, who was in the parlour, heard it begin very softly at the hall-door. The air was quite still, which favoured his hearing distinctly. This was the first time there had been any disturbance at that side of the house, and the character of the summons also was changed.

Mr. Prosser, leaving the parlour door open, it seems, went quietly into the hall. The sound was that of beating on the outside of the stout door, softly and regularly, "with the flat of the hand." He was going to open it suddenly, but changed his mind; and went back very quietly, and on the head of the kitchen stair, where was "a strong closet" over the pantry, in which he kept his "fire-arms, swords, and canes."

Here he called his man-servant, whom he believed to be honest; and with a pair of loaded pistols in his own coat-pockets, and giving another pair to him, he went as lightly as he could, followed by the man, and with a stout walking-cane in his hand, forward to the door.

Every thing went as Mr. Prosser wished. The besieger of his house, so far from taking fright at their approach, grew more impatient; and the sort of patting which had roused his attention at first, assumed the rhythm and emphasis of a series of double-knocks.

Mr. Prosser, angry, opened the door with his right arm across, cane in hand. Looking, he saw nothing; but his arm was jerked up oddly, as it might be with the hollow of a hand, and something passed under it, with a kind of gentle squeeze. The servant neither saw nor felt any thing, and did not know why his master looked back so hastily, and shut the door with so sudden a slam.

From that time, Mr. Prosser discontinued his angry talk and swearing about it, and seemed nearly as averse from the subject as the rest of his family. He grew, in fact, very uncomfortable, feeling an inward persuasion that when, in answer to the summons, he had opened the hall-door, he had actually given admission to the besieger.

He said nothing to Mrs. Prosser, but went up earlier to his bedroom, where "he read a while in his Bible, and said his prayers." I hope the particular relation of this circumstance does not indicate its singularity. He lay awake a good while, it appears; and as he supposed, about a quarter past twelve, he heard the soft palm of a hand patting on the outside of the bedroom door, and then brushed slowly along it.

Up bounced Mr. Prosser, very much frightened, and locked the door, crying, "Who's there?" but receiving no answer but the same brushing sound of a soft hand drawn over the panels, which he knew only too well.

In the morning the housemaid was terrified by the impression of a hand in the dust of the "little parlour" table, where they had been unpacking delft and other things the day before. The print of the naked foot in the sea-sand did not frighten Robinson Crusoe half so much. They were by this time all nervous, and some of them half crazed, about the hand.

Mr. Prosser went to examine the mark, and made light of it, but, as he swore afterwards, rather to quiet his servants than from any comfortable feeling about it in his own mind; however, he had them all, one by one, into the room, and made each place his or her hand, palm downward, on the same table, thus taking a similar impression from every person in the house, including himself and his wife; and his "affidavit" deposed that the formation of the hand so impressed differed altogether from those of the living inhabitants of the house, and corresponded exactly with that of the hand seen by Mrs. Prosser and by the cook.

Whoever or whatever the owner of that hand might be, they all felt this subtle demonstration to mean that it was declared he was no longer out of doors, but had established himself in the house.

And now Mrs. Prosser began to be troubled with strange and horrible dreams, some of which, as set out in detail, in Aunt Rebecca's long letter, are really very appalling nightmares. But one night, as Mr. Prosser closed his bedchamber door, he was struck somewhat by the utter silence of the room, there being no sound of breathing, which seemed unaccountable to him, as he knew his wife was in bed, and his ears were particularly sharp.

There was a candle burning on a small table at the foot of the bed, besides the one he held in one hand, a heavy ledger connected with his father-in-law's business being under his arm. He drew the curtain at the side of the bed, and saw Mrs. Prosser lying, as for a few seconds he mortally feared, dead, her face being motionless, white, and covered with a cold dew; and on the pillow, close beside her head, and just within the curtains, was the same white, fattish hand, the wrist resting on the pillow, and the fingers extended towards her temple with a slow, wavy motion.

Mr. Prosser, with a horrified jerk, pitched the ledger right at the curtains behind which the owner of the hand might be supposed to stand. The hand was instantaneously and smoothly snatched away, the curtains made a great wave, and Mr. Prosser got round the bed in time to see the closet-door, which was at the other side, drawn close by the same white, puffy hand, as he believed.

He drew the door open with a fling, and stared in; but the closet was empty, except for the clothes hanging from the pegs on the wall, and the dressing-table and looking-glass facing the windows. He shut it sharply, and locked it, and felt for a minute, he says, "as if he were like to lose his wits;" then, ringing at the bell, he brought the servants, and with much ado they recovered Mrs. Prosser from a sort of "trance," in which, he says, from her looks, she seemed to have suffered "the pains of death;" and Aunt Rebecca adds, "from what she told me of her visions, with her own lips, he might have added 'and of hell also.' "

But the occurrence which seems to have determined the crisis was the strange sickness of their eldest child, a little girl aged between two and three years. It lay awake, seemingly in paroxysms of terror, and the doctors who were called in set down the symptoms to incipient water on the brain. Mrs. Prosser used to sit up with the nurse, by the nursery fire, much troubled in mind about the condition of her child.

Its bed was placed sideways along the wall, with its head against the door of a press or cupboard, which, however, did not shut quite close. There was a little valance, about a foot deep, round the top of the child's bed, and this descended within some ten or twelve inches of the pillow on which it lay.

They observed that the little creature was quieter whenever they took it up and held it on their laps. They had just replaced it, as it seemed to have grown quite sleepy and tranquil, but it was not five minutes in its bed when it began to scream in one of its frenzies of terror; at the same moment the nurse for the first time detected, and Mrs. Prosser equally plainly saw, following the direction of her eyes, the real cause of the child's sufferings.

Protruding through the aperture of the press, and shrouded in the shade of the valance, they plainly saw the white fat hand, palm downwards, presented towards the head of the child. The mother uttered a scream, and snatched the child from its little bed, and she and the nurse ran down to the lady's sleeping-room, where Mr. Prosser was in bed, shutting the door as they entered; and they had hardly done so, when a gentle tap came to it from the outside.

There is a great deal more, but this will suffice. The singularity of the narrative seems to me to be this, that it describes the ghost of a hand, and no more. The person to whom that hand belonged never once appeared; nor was it a hand separated from a body, but only a hand so manifested and introduced, that its owner was always, by some crafty accident, hidden from view.

In the year 1819, at a college breakfast, I met a Mr. Prosser—a thin, grave, but rather chatty old gentleman, with very white hair, drawn back into a pigtail—and he told us all, with a concise particularity, a story of his cousin, James Prosser, who, when an infant, had slept for some time in what his mother said was a haunted nursery in an old house near Chapelizod, and who, whenever he was ill, over-fatigued, or in anywise feverish, suffered all through his life, as he had done from a time he could scarce remember, from a vision of a certain gentleman, fat and pale, every curl of whose wig, every button and fold of whose laced clothes, and every feature and line of whose sensual, malignant, and unwholesome face, was as minutely engraven upon his memory as the dress and lineaments of his father's portrait, which hung before him every day at breakfast, dinner, and supper.

Mr. Prosser mentioned this as an instance of a curiously monotonous, individualized, and persistent nightmare, and hinted the extreme horror and anxiety with which his cousin, of whom he spoke in the past tense as "poor Jemmie," was at any time induced to mention it.

I hope the reader will pardon me for loitering so long in the Tiled House, but this sort of lore has always had a charm for me; and people, you know, especially old people, will talk of what most interests themselves, too often forgetting that others may have had more than enough of it.

I. STATEMENT OF JOEL HETMAN, JR.

I AM THE MOST UNFORTUNATE of men. Rich, respected, fairly well educated and of sound health—with many other advantages usually valued by those having them and coveted by those who have them not—I sometimes think that I should be less unhappy if they had been denied me, for then the contrast between my outer and my inner life would not be continually demanding a painful attention. In the stress of privation and the need of effort I might sometimes forget the somber secret ever baffling the conjecture that it compels.

I am the only child of Joel and Julia Hetman. The one was a well-to-do country gentleman, the other a beautiful and accomplished woman to whom he was passionately attached with what I now know to have been a jealous and exacting devotion. The family home was a few miles from Nashville, Tennessee, a large, irregularly built dwelling of no particular order of architecture, a little way off the road, in a park of trees and shrubbery.

At the time of which I write I was nineteen years old, a student at Yale. One day I received a telegram from my father of such urgency that in compliance with its unexplained demand I left at once for home. At the railway station in Nashville a distant relative awaited me to apprise me of the reason for my recall: my mother had been barbarously murdered—why and by whom none could conjecture, but the circumstances were these:

My father had gone to Nashville, intending to return the next afternoon. Something prevented his accomplishing the business in hand, so he returned on the same night, arriving just before the dawn. In his testimony before the coroner he explained that having no latchkey and not caring to disturb the sleeping servants, he had, with no clearly defined intention, gone round to the rear of the house. As he turned an angle of the building, he heard a sound as of a door gently closed, and saw in the darkness, indistinctly, the figure of a man, which instantly disappeared among the trees of the lawn. A hasty pursuit and brief search of the grounds in the belief that the trespasser was some one secretly visiting a servant proving fruitless, he entered at the unlocked door and mounted the stairs to my mother's chamber. Its door was open, and stepping into black darkness he fell headlong over some heavy object on the floor. I may spare myself the details; it was my poor mother, dead of strangulation by human hands!

Nothing had been taken from the house, the servants had heard no sound, and excepting those terrible finger-marks upon the dead woman's throat—dear God! that I might forget them!—no trace of the assassin was ever found.

I gave up my studies and remained with my father, who, naturally, was greatly changed. Always of a sedate, taciturn disposition, he now fell into so deep a dejection that nothing could hold his attention, yet anything—a footfall, the sudden closing of a door—aroused in him a fitful interest; one might have called it an apprehension. At any small surprise of the senses he would start visibly and sometimes turn pale, then relapse into a melancholy apathy deeper than before. I suppose he was what is called a "nervous wreck." As to me, I was younger then than now—there is much in that. Youth is Gilead, in which is balm for every wound. Ah, that I might again dwell in that enchanted land! Unacquainted with grief, I knew not how to appraise my bereavement; I could not rightly estimate the strength of the stroke.

One night, a few months after the dreadful event, my father and I walked home from the city. The full moon was about three hours above the eastern horizon; the entire countryside had the solemn stillness of a summer night; our footfalls and the ceaseless song of the katydids were the only sound aloof. Black shadows of bordering trees lay athwart the road, which, in the short reaches between, gleamed a ghostly white. As we approached the gate to our dwelling, whose front was in shadow, and in which no light shone, my father suddenly stopped and clutched my arm, saying, hardly above his breath:

"God! God! what is that?"

"I hear nothing," I replied.

"But see—see!" he said, pointing along the road, directly ahead.

I said: "Nothing is there. Come, father, let us go in—you are ill."

He had released my arm and was standing rigid and motionless in the center of the illuminated roadway, staring like one bereft of sense. His face in the moonlight showed a pallor and fixity inexpressibly distressing. I pulled gently at his sleeve, but he had forgotten my existence. Presently he began to retire backward, step by step, never for an instant removing his eyes from what he saw, or thought he saw. I turned half round to follow, but stood irresolute. I do not recall any feeling of fear, unless a sudden chill was its physical manifestation. It seemed as if an icy wind had touched my face and enfolded my body from head to foot; I could feel the stir of it in my hair.

At that moment my attention was drawn to a light that suddenly streamed from an upper window of the house: one of the servants, awakened by what mysterious premonition of evil who can say, and in obedience to an impulse that she was never able to name, had lit a lamp. When I turned to look for my father he was gone, and in all the years that have passed no whisper of his fate has come across the borderland of conjecture from the realm of the unknown.

II. STATEMENT OF CASPAR GRATTAN

To-day I am said to live; to-morrow, here in this room, will lie a senseless shape of clay that all too long was I. If anyone lift the cloth from the face of that unpleasant thing it will be in gratification of a mere morbid curiosity. Some, doubtless, will go further and inquire, "Who was he?" In this writing I supply the only answer that I am able to make—Caspar Grattan. Surely, that should be enough. The name has served my small need for more than twenty years of a life of unknown length. True, I gave it to myself, but lacking another I had the right. In this world one must have a name; it prevents confusion, even when it does not establish identity. Some, though, are known by numbers, which also seem inadequate distinctions.

One day, for illustration, I was passing along a street of a city, far from here, when I met two men in uniform, one of whom, half pausing and looking curiously into my face, said to his companion, "That man looks like 767." Something in the number seemed familiar and horrible. Moved by an uncontrollable impulse, I sprang into a side street and ran until I fell exhausted in a country lane.

I have never forgotten that number, and always it comes to memory attended by gibbering obscenity, peals of joyless laughter, the clang of iron doors. So I say a name, even if self-bestowed, is better than a number. In the register of the potter's field I shall soon have both. What wealth!

Of him who shall find this paper I must beg a little consideration. It is not the history of my life; the knowledge to write that is denied me. This is only a record of broken and apparently unrelated memories, some of them as distinct and sequent as brilliant beads upon a thread, others remote and strange, having the character of crimson dreams with interspaces blank and black—witch-fires glowing still and red in a great desolation.

Standing upon the shore of eternity, I turn for a last look landward over the course by which I came. There are twenty years of footprints fairly distinct, the impressions of bleeding feet. They lead through poverty and pain, devious and unsure, as of one staggering beneath a burden—

Remote, unfriended, melancholy, slow.

Ah, the poet's prophecy of Me—how admirable, how dreadfully admirable!

Backward beyond the beginning of this *via dolorosa*—this epic of suffering with episodes of sin—I see nothing clearly; it comes out of a cloud. I know that it spans only twenty years, yet I am an old man.

One does not remember one's birth—one has to be told. But with me it was different; life came to me full-handed and dowered me with all my faculties and powers. Of a previous existence I know no more than others, for all have stammering intimations that may be memories and may be dreams. I know only that my first conscious-ness was of maturity in body and mind—a consciousness accepted without surprise or conjecture. I merely found myself walking in a forest, half-clad, footsore, unutterably weary and hungry. Seeing a farmhouse, I approached and asked for food, which was given me by one who inquired my name. I did not know, yet knew that all had names. Greatly embarrassed, I retreated, and night coming on, lay down in the forest and slept.

The next day I entered a large town which I shall not name. Nor shall I recount further incidents of the life that is now to end—a life of wandering, always and everywhere haunted by an overmastering sense of crime in punishment of wrong and of terror in punishment of crime. Let me see if I can reduce it to narrative.

I seem once to have lived near a great city, a prosperous planter, married to a woman whom I loved and distrusted. We had, it some-times seems, one child, a youth of brilliant parts and promise. He is at all times a vague figure, never clearly drawn, frequently altogether out of the picture.

One luckless evening it occurred to me to test my wife's fidelity in a vulgar, commonplace way familiar to everyone who has acquaint-ance with the literature of fact and fiction. I went to the city, telling my wife that I should be absent until the following afternoon. But I returned before daybreak and went to the rear of the house, pur-posing to enter by a door with which I had secretly so tampered that it would seem to lock, yet not actually fasten. As I approached it, I heard it gently open and close, and saw a man steal away into the darkness. With murder in my heart, I sprang after him, but he had vanished without even the bad luck of identification. Sometimes now I cannot even persuade myself that it was a human being.

Crazed with jealousy and rage, blind and bestial with all the ele-mental passions of insulted manhood, I entered the house and sprang up the stairs to the door of my wife's chamber. It was closed, but having tampered with its lock also, I easily entered and despite the black darkness soon stood by the side of her bed. My groping hands told me that although disarranged it was unoccupied.

"She is below," I thought, "and terrified by my entrance has evaded me in the darkness of the hall."

With the purpose of seeking her I turned to leave the room, but took a wrong direction—the right one! My foot struck her, cowering in a corner of the room. Instantly my hands were at her throat, stifling a shriek, my knees were upon her struggling body; and there in the darkness, without a word of accusation or reproach, I strangled her till she died!

There ends the dream. I have related it in the past tense, but the present would be the fitter form, for again and again the somber tragedy reenacts itself in my consciousness—over and over I lay the plan, I suffer the confirmation, I redress the wrong. Then all is blank; and afterward the rains beat against the grimy window-panes, or the snows fall upon my scant attire, the wheels rattle in the squalid streets where my life lies in poverty and mean employment. If there is ever sunshine I do not recall it; if there are birds they do not sing.

There is another dream, another vision of the night. I stand among the shadows in a moonlit road. I am aware of another presence, but whose I cannot rightly determine. In the shadow of a great dwelling I catch the gleam of white garments; then the figure of a woman confronts me in the road—my murdered wife! There is death in the face; there are marks upon the throat. The eyes are fixed on mine with an infinite gravity which is not reproach, nor hate, nor menace, nor anything less terrible than recognition. Before this awful apparition I retreat in terror—a terror that is upon me as I write. I can no longer rightly shape the words. See! they—

Now I am calm, but truly there is no more to tell: the incident ends where it began—in darkness and in doubt.

Yes, I am again in control of myself: "the captain of my soul." But that is not respite; it is another stage and phase of expiation. My penance, constant in degree, is mutable in kind: one of its variants is tranquillity. After all, it is only a life-sentence. "To Hell for life"— that is a foolish penalty: the culprit chooses the duration of his punishment. To-day my term expires.

To each and all, the peace that was not mine.

III. STATEMENT OF THE LATE JULIA HETMAN,
THROUGH THE MEDIUM BAYROLLES

I had retired early and fallen almost immediately into a peaceful sleep, from which I awoke with that indefinable sense of peril which is, I think, a common experience in that other, earlier life. Of its unmeaning character, too, I was entirely persuaded, yet that did not banish it. My husband, Joel Hetman, was away from home; the servants slept in another part of the house. But these were familiar conditions; they had never before distressed me. Nevertheless, the strange terror grew so insupportable that conquering my reluctance to move I sat up and lit the lamp at my bedside. Contrary to my expectation this gave me no relief; the light seemed rather an added danger, for I reflected that it would shine out under the door, disclosing my presence to whatever evil thing might lurk outside. You that are still in the flesh, subject to horrors of the imagination, think what a monstrous fear that must be which seeks in darkness security from malevolent existences of the night. That is to spring to close quarters with an unseen enemy—the strategy of despair!

Extinguishing the lamp I pulled the bed-clothing about my head and lay trembling and silent, unable to shriek, forgetful to pray. In this pitiable state I must have lain for what you call hours—with us there are no hours, there is no time.

At last it came—a soft, irregular sound of footfalls on the stairs! They were slow, hesitant, uncertain, as of something that did not see its way; to my disordered reason all the more terrifying for that, as the approach of some blind and mindless malevolence to which is no appeal. I even thought that I must have left the hall lamp burning and the groping of this creature proved it a monster of the night. This was foolish and inconsistent with my previous dread of the light, but what would you have? Fear has no brains; it is an idiot. The dismal witness that it bears and the cowardly counsel that it whispers are unrelated. We know this well, we who have passed into the Realm of Terror, who skulk in eternal dusk among the scenes of our former lives, invisible even to ourselves and one another, yet hiding forlorn in lonely places; yearning for speech with our loved ones, yet dumb, and as fearful of them as they of us. Sometimes the disability is removed, the law suspended: by the deathless power of love or hate we break the spell—we are seen by those whom we would warn, console, or punish. What form we seem to them to bear we know not; we know only that we terrify even those whom we most wish to comfort, and from whom we most crave tenderness and sympathy.

Forgive, I pray you, this inconsequent digression by what was once a woman. You who consult us in this imperfect way—you do not understand. You ask foolish questions about things unknown and things forbidden. Much that we know and could impart in our speech is meaningless in yours. We must communicate with you through a stammering intelligence in that small fraction of our language that you yourselves can speak. You think that we are of another world. No, we have knowledge of no world but yours, though for us it holds no sunlight, no warmth, no music, no laughter, no song of birds, nor any companionship. O God! what a thing it is to be a ghost, cowering and shivering in an altered world, a prey to apprehension and despair!

No, I did not die of fright: the Thing turned and went away. I heard it go down the stairs, hurriedly, I thought, as if itself in sudden fear. Then I rose to call for help. Hardly had my shaking hand found the door-knob when—merciful heaven!—I heard it returning. Its footfalls as it remounted the stairs were rapid, heavy and loud; they shook the house. I fled to an angle of the wall and crouched upon the floor. I tried to pray. I tried to call the name of my dear husband. Then I heard the door thrown open. There was an interval of unconsciousness, and when I revived I felt a strangling clutch upon my throat—felt my arms feebly beating against something that bore me backward—felt my tongue thrusting itself from between my teeth! And then I passed into this life.

No, I have no knowledge of what it was. The sum of what we knew at death is the measure of what we know afterward of all that went before. Of this existence we know many things, but no new light falls upon any page of that; in memory is written all of it that we can read. Here are no heights of truth overlooking the confused landscape of that dubitable domain. We still dwell in the Valley of the Shadow, lurk in its desolate places, peering from brambles and thickets at its mad, malign inhabitants. How should we have new knowledge of that fading past?

What I am about to relate happened on a night. We know when it is night, for then you retire to your houses and we can venture from our places of concealment to move unafraid about our old homes, to look in at the windows, even to enter and gaze upon your faces as you sleep. I had lingered long near the dwelling where I had been so cruelly changed to what I am, as we do while any that we love or hate remain. Vainly I had sought some method of manifestation, some way to make my continued existence and my great love and poignant pity understood by my husband and son. Always if they slept they would wake, or if in my desperation I dared approach them when they were awake, would turn toward me the terrible eyes of the living, frightening me by the glances that I sought from the purpose that I held.

On this night I had searched for them without success, fearing to find them; they were nowhere in the house, nor about the moonlit lawn. For, although the sun is lost to us forever, the moon, full-orbed or slender, remains to us. Sometimes it shines by night, sometimes by day, but always it rises and sets, as in that other life.

I left the lawn and moved in the white light and silence along the road, aimless and sorrowing. Suddenly I heard the voice of my poor husband in exclamations of astonishment, with that of my son in re-assurance and dissuasion; and there by the shadow of a group of trees they stood—near, so near! Their faces were toward me, the eyes of the elder man fixed upon mine. He saw me—at last, at last, he saw me! In the consciousness of that, my terror fled as a cruel dream. The death-spell was broken: Love had conquered Law! Mad with exultation I shouted—I *must* have shouted, "He sees, he sees: he will understand!" Then, controlling myself, I moved forward, smiling and consciously beautiful, to offer myself to his arms, to comfort him with endearments, and, with my son's hand in mine, to speak words that should restore the broken bonds between the living and the dead.

Alas! alas! his face went white with fear, his eyes were as those of a hunted animal. He backed away from me, as I advanced, and at last turned and fled into the wood—whither, it is not given to me to know.

To my poor boy, left doubly desolate, I have never been able to impart a sense of my presence. Soon he, too, must pass to this Life Invisible and be lost to me forever.

*I*T WAS, AS FAR as I can ascertain, in September of the year 1811 that a post-chaise drew up before the door of Aswarby Hall, in the heart of Lincolnshire. The little boy who was the only passenger in the chaise, and who jumped out as soon as it had stopped, looked about him with the keenest curiosity during the short interval that elapsed between the ringing of the bell and the opening of the hall door. He saw a tall, square, red-brick house, built in the reign of Anne; a stone-pillared porch had been added in the purer classical style of 1790; the windows of the house were many, tall and narrow, with small panes and thick white woodwork. A pediment, pierced with a round window, crowned the front. There were wings to right and left, connected by curious glazed galleries, supported by colonnades, with the central block. These wings plainly contained the stables and offices of the house. Each was surmounted by an ornamental cupola with a gilded vane.

An evening light shone on the building, making the window-panes glow like so many fires. Away from the Hall in front stretched a flat park studded with oaks and fringed with firs, which stood out against the sky. The clock in the church-tower, buried in trees on the edge of the park, only its golden weather-cock catching the light, was striking six, and the sound came gently beating down the wind. It was altogether a pleasant impression, though tinged with the sort of melancholy appropriate to an evening in early autumn, that was conveyed to the mind of the boy who was standing in the porch waiting for the door to open to him.

The post-chaise had brought him from Warwickshire, where, some six months before, he had been left an orphan. Now, owing to the generous offer of his elderly cousin, Mr Abney, he had come to live at Aswarby. The offer was unexpected, because all who knew anything of Mr Abney looked upon him as a somewhat austere recluse, into whose steady-going household the advent of a small boy would import a new and, it seemed, incongruous element. The truth is that very little was known of Mr Abney's pursuits or temper. The Professor of Greek at Cambridge had been heard to say that no one knew more of the religious beliefs of the later pagans than did the owner of Aswarby. Certainly his library contained all the then available books bearing on the Mysteries, the Orphic poems, the worship of Mithras, and the Neo-Platonists. In the marble-paved hall stood a fine group of Mithras slaying a bull, which had been imported from the Levant at great expense by the owner. He had contributed a description of it to the *Gentleman's Magazine,* and he had written a remarkable series of articles in the *Critical Museum* on the superstitions of the Romans of the Lower Empire. He was looked upon, in fine, as a man wrapped up in his books, and it was a matter of great surprise among his neighbours that he should ever have heard of his orphan cousin, Stephen Elliott, much more that he should have volunteered to make him an inmate of Aswarby Hall.

Whatever may have been expected by his neighbours, it is certain that Mr Abney—the tall, the thin, the austere—seemed inclined to give his young cousin a kindly reception. The moment the front-door was opened he darted out of his study, rubbing his hands with delight.

"How are you, my boy?—how are you? How old are you?" said he—"that is, you are not too much tired, I hope, by your journey to eat your supper?"

"No, thank you, sir," said Master Elliott; "I am pretty well."

"That's a good lad," said Mr Abney. "And how old are you, my boy?"

It seemed a little odd that he should have asked the question twice in the first two minutes of their acquaintance.

"I'm twelve years old next birthday, sir," said Stephen.

"And when is your birthday, my dear boy? Eleventh of September, eh? That's well—that's very well. Nearly a year hence, isn't it? I like—

ha, ha!—I like to get these things down in my book. Sure it's twelve? Certain?"

"Yes, quite sure, sir."

"Well, well! Take him to Mrs Bunch's room, Parkes, and let him have his tea—supper—whatever it is."

"Yes, sir," answered the staid Mr Parkes; and conducted Stephen to the lower regions.

Mrs Bunch was the most comfortable and human person whom Stephen had as yet met at Aswarby. She made him completely at home; they were great friends in a quarter of an hour: and great friends they remained. Mrs Bunch had been born in the neighbourhood some fifty-five years before the date of Stephen's arrival, and her residence at the Hall was of twenty years' standing. Consequently, if anyone knew the ins and outs of the house and the district, Mrs Bunch knew them; and she was by no means disinclined to communicate her information.

Certainly there were plenty of things about the Hall and the Hall gardens which Stephen, who was of an adventurous and inquiring turn, was anxious to have explained to him. "Who built the temple at the end of the laurel walk? Who was the old man whose picture hung on the staircase, sitting at a table, with a skull under his hand?" These and many similar points were cleared up by the resources of Mrs Bunch's powerful intellect. There were others, however, of which the explanations furnished were less satisfactory.

One November evening Stephen was sitting by the fire in the housekeeper's room reflecting on his surroundings.

"Is Mr Abney a good man, and will he go to heaven?" he suddenly asked, with the peculiar confidence which children possess in the ability of their elders to settle these questions, the decision of which is believed to be reserved for other tribunals.

"Good?—bless the child!" said Mrs Bunch. "Master's as kind a soul as ever I see! Didn't I never tell you of the little boy as he took in out of the street, as you may say, this seven years back? and the little girl, two years after I first come here?"

"No. Do tell me all about them, Mrs Bunch—now, this minute!"

"Well," said Mrs Bunch, "the little girl I don't seem to recollect so

much about. I know master brought her back with him from his walk
one day, and give orders to Mrs Ellis, as was housekeeper then, as
she should be took every care with. And the pore child hadn't no
one belonging to her—she told me so her own self—and here she
lived with us a matter of three weeks it might be; and then, whether
she were somethink of a gipsy in her blood or what not, but one
morning she out of her bed afore any of us had opened a eye, and
neither track nor yet trace of her have I set eyes on since. Master
was wonderful put about, and had all the ponds dragged; but it's
my belief she was had away by them gipsies, for there was singing
round the house for as much as an hour the night she went, and
Parkes, he declare as he heard them a-calling in the woods all that
afternoon. Dear, dear! a hodd child she was, so silent in her ways and
all, but I was wonderful taken up with her, so domesticated she
was—surprising."

"And what about the little boy?" said Stephen.

"Ah, that pore boy!" sighed Mrs Bunch. "He were a foreigner—
Jevanny he called hisself—and he come atweaking his 'urdy-gurdy
round and about the drive one winter day, and master 'ad him in
that minute, and ast all about where he came from, and how old he
was, and how he made his way, and where was his relatives, and all
as kind as heart could wish. But it went the same way with him.
They're a hunruly lot, them foreign nations, I do suppose, and he
was off one fine morning just the same as the girl. Why he went
and what he done was our question for as much as a year after; for
he never took his 'urdy-gurdy, and there it lays on the shelf."

The remainder of the evening was spent by Stephen in miscellane-
ous cross-examination of Mrs Bunch and in efforts to extract a tune
from the hurdy-gurdy.

That night he had a curious dream. At the end of the passage at
the top of the house, in which his bedroom was situated, there was
an old disused bathroom. It was kept locked, but the upper half of
the door was glazed, and, since the muslin curtains which used to
hang there had long been gone, you could look in and see the lead-
lined bath affixed to the wall on the right hand, with its head towards the window.

On the night of which I am speaking, Stephen Elliott found himself, as he thought, looking through the glazed door. The moon was shining through the window, and he was gazing at a figure which lay in the bath.

His description of what he saw reminds me of what I once beheld myself in the famous vaults of St Michan's Church in Dublin, which possesses the horrid property of preserving corpses from decay for centuries. A figure inexpressibly thin and pathetic, of a dusty leaden colour, enveloped in a shroud-like garment, the thin lips crooked into a faint and dreadful smile, the hands pressed tightly over the region of the heart.

As he looked upon it, a distant, almost inaudible moan seemed to issue from its lips, and the arms began to stir. The terror of the sight forced Stephen backwards and he awoke to the fact that he was indeed standing on the cold boarded floor of the passage in the full light of the moon. With a courage which I do not think can be common among boys of his age, he went to the door of the bathroom to ascertain if the figure of his dreams were really there. It was not, and he went back to bed.

Mrs Bunch was much impressed next morning by his story, and went so far as to replace the muslin curtain over the glazed door of the bathroom. Mr. Abney, moreover, to whom he confided his experiences at breakfast, was greatly interested and made notes of the matter in what he called "his book."

The spring equinox was approaching, as Mr Abney frequently reminded his cousin, adding that this had been always considered by the ancients to be a critical time for the young: that Stephen would do well to take care of himself, and to shut his bedroom window at night; and that Censorinus had some valuable remarks on the subject. Two incidents that occurred about this time made an impression upon Stephen's mind.

The first was after an unusually uneasy and oppressed night that he had passed—though he could not recall any particular dream that he had had.

The following evening Mrs Bunch was occupying herself in mending his nightgown.

"Gracious me, Master Stephen!" she broke forth rather irritably, "how do you manage to tear your nightdress all to flinders this way? Look here, sir, what trouble you do give to poor servants that have to darn and mend after you!"

There was indeed a most destructive and apparently wanton series of slits or scorings in the garment, which would undoubtedly require a skillful needle to make good. They were confined to the left side of the chest—long, parallel slits about six inches in length, some of them not quite piercing the texture of the linen. Stephen could only express his entire ignorance of their origin: he was sure they were not there the night before.

"But," he said, "Mrs Bunch, they are just the same as the scratches on the outside of my bedroom door: and I'm sure I never had anything to do with making *them*."

Mrs Bunch gazed at him open-mouthed, then snatched up a candle, departed hastily from the room, and was heard making her way upstairs. In a few minutes she came down.

"Well," she said, "Master Stephen, it's a funny thing to me how them marks and scratches can 'a' come there—too high up for any cat or dog to 'ave made 'em, much less a rat: for all the world like a Chinaman's finger-nails, as my uncle in the tea-trade used to tell us of when we was girls together. I wouldn't say nothing to master, not if I was you, Master Stephen, my dear; and just turn the key of the door when you go to your bed."

"I always do, Mrs Bunch, as soon as I've said my prayers."

"Ah, that's a good child: always say your prayers, and then no one can't hurt you."

Herewith Mrs Bunch addressed herself to mending the injured nightgown, with intervals of meditation, until bed-time. This was on a Friday night in March, 1812.

On the following evening the usual duet of Stephen and Mrs Bunch was augmented by the sudden arrival of Mr Parkes, the butler, who as a rule kept himself rather *to* himself in his own pantry. He did not see that Stephen was there: he was, moreover, flustered and less slow of speech than was his wont.

"Master may get up his own wine, if he likes, of an evening," was his first remark. "Either I do it in the daytime or not at all, Mrs Bunch. I don't know what it may be: very like it's the rats, or the wind got into the cellars; but I'm not so young as I was, and I can't go through with it as I have done."

"Well, Mr Parkes, you know it is a surprising place for the rats, is the Hall."

"I'm not denying that, Mrs Bunch; and, to be sure, many a time I've heard the tale from the men in the shipyards about the rat that could speak. I never laid no confidence in that before; but tonight, if I'd demeaned myself to lay my ear to the door of the further bin, I could pretty much have heard what they was saying."

"Oh, there, Mr Parkes, I've no patience with your fancies! Rats talking in the wine-cellar indeed!"

"Well, Mrs Bunch, I've no wish to argue with you: all I say is, if you choose to go to the far bin, and lay your ear to the door, you may prove my words this minute."

"What nonsense you do talk, Mr Parkes—not fit for children to listen to! Why, you'll be frightening Master Stephen there out of his wits."

"What! Master Stephen?" said Parkes, awaking to the consciousness of the boy's presence. "Master Stephen knows well enough when I'm a-playing a joke with you, Mrs Bunch."

In fact, Master Stephen knew much too well to suppose that Mr Parkes had in the first instance intended a joke. He was interested, not altogether pleasantly, in the situation; but all his questions were unsuccessful in inducing the butler to give any more detailed account of his experiences in the wine-cellar.

We have now arrived at March 24, 1812. It was a day of curious experiences for Stephen: a windy, noisy day, which filled the house and the gardens with a restless impression. As Stephen stood by the fence of the grounds, and looked out into the park, he felt as if an endless procession of unseen people were sweeping past him on the wind, borne on resistlessly and aimlessly, vainly striving to stop themselves, to catch at something that might arrest their flight and bring them once again into contact with the living world of which they had formed a part. After luncheon that day Mr Abney said:

"Stephen, my boy, do you think you could manage to come to me tonight as late as eleven o'clock in my study? I shall be busy until that time, and I wish to show you something connected with your future life which it is most important that you should know. You are not to mention this matter to Mrs Bunch nor to anyone else in the house; and you had better go to your room at the usual time."

Here was a new excitement added to life: Stephen eagerly grasped at the opportunity of sitting up till eleven o'clock. He looked in at the library door on his way upstairs that evening, and saw a brazier, which he had often noticed in the corner of the room, moved out before the fire; an old silver-gilt cup stood on the table, filled with red wine, and some written sheets of paper lay near it. Mr Abney was sprinkling some incense on the brazier from a round silver box as Stephen passed, but did not seem to notice his step.

The wind had fallen, and there was a still night and a full moon. At about ten o'clock Stephen was standing at the open window of his bedroom, looking out over the country. Still as the night was, the mysterious population of the distant moon-lit woods was not yet lulled to rest. From time to time strange cries as of lost and despairing wanderers sounded from across the mere. They might be the notes of owls or water-birds, yet they did not quite resemble either sound. Were not they coming nearer? Now they sounded from the nearer side of the water, and in a few moments they seemed to be floating about among the shrubberies. Then they ceased; but just as Stephen was thinking of shutting the window and resuming his reading of *Robinson Crusoe*, he caught sight of two figures standing on the gravelled terrace that ran along the garden side of the Hall— the figures of a boy and girl, as it seemed; they stood side by side, looking up at the windows. Something in the form of the girl recalled irresistibly his dream of the figure in the bath. The boy inspired him with more acute fear.

Whilst the girl stood still, half smiling, with her hands clasped over her heart, the boy, a thin shape, with black hair and ragged clothing, raised his arms in the air with an appearance of menace and of unappeasable hunger and longing. The moon shone upon his almost transparent hands, and Stephen saw that the nails were fearfully long and that the light shone through them. As he stood with his arms thus raised, he disclosed a terrifying spectacle. On the left side of his chest there opened a black and gaping rent; and there fell upon Stephen's brain, rather than upon his ear, the impression of one of those hungry and desolate cries that he had heard resounding over the woods of Aswarby all that evening. In another moment this dreadful pair had moved swiftly and noiselessly over the dry gravel, and he saw them no more.

Inexpressibly frightened as he was, he determined to take his candle and go down to Mr Abney's study, for the hour appointed for their meeting was near at hand. The study or library opened out of the front-hall on one side, and Stephen, urged on by his terrors, did not take long in getting there. To effect an entrance was not so easy. It was not locked, he felt sure, for the key was on the outside of the door as usual. His repeated knocks produced no answer. Mr Abney was engaged: he was speaking. What! why did he try to cry out? and why was the cry choked in his throat? Had he, too, seen the mysterious children? But now everything was quiet, and the door yielded to Stephen's terrified and frantic pushing.

On the table in Mr Abney's study certain papers were found which explained the situation to Stephen Elliott when he was of an age to understand them. The most important sentences were as follows:

"It was a belief very strongly and generally held by the ancients—of whose wisdom in these matters I have had such experience as induces me to place confidence in their assertions—that by enacting certain processes, which to us moderns have something of a barbaric complexion, a very remarkable enlightenment of the spiritual faculties in man may be attained: that, for example, by absorbing the personalities of a certain number of his fellow-creatures, an individual may gain a complete ascendancy over those orders of spiritual beings which control the elemental forces of our universe.

"It is recorded of Simon Magus that he was able to fly in the air, to become invisible, or to assume any form he pleased, by the agency of the soul of a boy whom, to use the libellous phrase employed by the author of the *Clementine Recognitions,* he had 'murdered.' I find it set down, moreover, with considerable detail in the writings of

Hermes Trismegistus, that similar happy results may be produced by the absorption of the hearts of not less than three human beings below the age of twenty-one years. To the testing of the truth of this receipt I have devoted the greater part of the last twenty years, selecting as the *corpora vilia* of my experiment such persons as could conveniently be removed without occasioning a sensible gap in society. The first step I effected by the removal of one Phoebe Stanley, a girl of gipsy extraction, on March 24, 1792. The second, by the removal of a wandering Italian lad, named Giovanni Paoli, on the night of March 23, 1805. The final 'victim'—to employ a word repugnant in the highest degree to my feelings—must be my cousin, Stephen Elliott. His day must be this March 24, 1812.

"The best means of effecting the required absorption is to remove the heart from the *living* subject, to reduce it to ashes, and to mingle them with about a pint of some red wine, preferably port. The remains of the first two subjects, at least, it will be well to conceal: a disused bathroom or wine-cellar will be found convenient for such a purpose. Some annoyance may be experienced from the psychic portion of the subjects, which popular language dignifies with the name of ghosts. But the man of philosophic temperament—to whom alone the experiment is appropriate—will be little prone to attach importance to the feeble efforts of these beings to wreak their vengeance on him. I contemplate with the liveliest satisfaction the enlarged and emancipated existence which the experiment, if successful, will confer on me; not only placing me beyond the reach of human justice (so-called), but eliminating to a great extent the prospect of death itself."

Mr Abney was found in his chair, his head thrown back, his face stamped with an expression of rage, fright, and moral pain. In his left side was a terrible lacerated wound, exposing the heart. There was no blood on his hands, and a long knife that lay on the table was perfectly clean. A savage wild-cat might have inflicted the injuries. The window of the study was open, and it was the opinion of the coroner that Mr Abney had met his death by the agency of some wild creature. But Stephen Elliott's study of the papers I have quoted led him to a very different conclusion.

HEROIC FANTASY

Golden Wings   *WILLIAM MORRIS*

"Lyf lythes to mee,
Twa wordes or three,
Of one who was fair and free,
And fell in his fight."
                              Sir Percival

I SUPPOSE MY BIRTH was somewhat after the birth of
Sir Percival of Galles, for I never saw my father, and my
mother brought me up quaintly; not like a poor man's
son, though, indeed, we had little money, and lived in a
lone place: it was on a bit of waste land near a river;
moist, and without trees; on the drier parts of it folks had
built cottages—see, I can count them on my fingers—six
cottages, of which ours was one.

Likewise, there was a little chapel, with a yew tree and
graves in the church-yard—graves—yes, a great many
graves, more than in the yards of many Minsters I have
seen, because people fought a battle once near us, and
buried many bodies in deep pits, to the east of the chapel;
but this was before I was born.

I have talked to old knights since who fought in that
battle, and who told me that it was all about an old lady
that they fought; indeed, this lady, who was a queen, was
afterwards, by her own wish, buried in the aforesaid
chapel in a most fair tomb; her image was of latoun gilt,
and with a colour on it; her hands and face were of silver,
and her hair, gilded and most curiously wrought, flowed
down from her head over the marble.

It was a strange thing to see that gold and brass and
marble inside that rough chapel which stood on the
marshy common, near the river.

Now, every St. Peter's day, when the sun was at its

hottest, in the midsummer noontide, my mother (though at other times she only wore such clothes as the folk about us) would dress herself most richly, and shut the shutters against all the windows, and light great candles, and sit as though she were a queen, till the evening: sitting and working at a frame, and singing as she worked.

And what she worked at was two wings, wrought in gold, on a blue ground.

And as for what she sung, I could never understand it, though I know now it was not in Latin.

And she used to charge me straightly never to let any man into the house on St. Peter's day; therefore, I and our dog, which was a great old bloodhound, always kept the door together.

But one St. Peter's day, when I was nearly twenty, I sat in the house watching the door with the bloodhound, and I was sleepy, because of the shut-up heat and my mother's singing, so I began to nod, and at last, though the dog often shook me by the hair to keep me awake, went fast asleep, and began to dream a foolish dream without hearing, as men sometimes do: for I thought that my mother and I were walking to mass through the snow on a Christmas day, but my mother carried a live goose in her hand, holding it by the neck, instead of her rosary, and that I went along by her side, not walking, but turning somersaults like a mountebank, my head never touching the ground; when we got to the chapel-door, the old priest met us, and said to my mother, "Why dame alive, your head is turned green! Ah! never mind, I will go and say mass, but don't let little Mary there go," and he pointed to the goose, and went.

Then mass begun, but in the midst of it, the priest said out loud, "Oh I forgot," and turning round to us began to wag his grey head and white beard, throwing his head right back, and sinking his chin on his breast alternately; and when we saw him do this, we presently began to knock our heads against the wall, keeping time with him and with each other, till the priest said, "Peter! it's dragon-time now," whereat the roof flew off, and a great yellow dragon came down on the chapel-floor with a flop, and danced about clumsily, wriggling his fat tail, and saying to a sort of tune, "O the Devil, the Devil, the Devil, O the Devil," so I went up to him, and put my hand on his

breast, meaning to slay him, and so awoke, and found myself standing up with my hand on the breast of an armed knight; the door lay
flat on the ground, and under it lay Hector, our dog, whining and
dying.

For eight hours I had been asleep; on awaking, the blood rushed
up into my face, I heard my mother's low mysterious song behind
me, and knew not what harm might happen to her and me, if that
knight's coming made her cease in it; so I struck him with my left
hand, where his face was bare under his mail coif, and getting my
sword in my right, drove its point under his hawberk, so that it
came out behind, and he fell, turned over on his face, and died.

Then, because my mother still went on working and singing, I
said no word, but let him lie there, and put the door up again, and
found Hector dead.

I then sat down again and polished my sword with a piece of
leather after I had wiped the blood from it; and in an hour my
mother arose from her work, and raising me from where I was sitting,
kissed my brow, saying, "Well done, Lionel, you have slain your
greatest foe, and now the people will know you for what you are
before you die—Ah God! though not before *I* die."

So I said, "Who is he, mother? he seems to be some Lord; am I a
Lord then?"

"A King, if the people will but know it," she said.

Then she knelt down by the dead body, turned it round again, so
that it lay face uppermost, as before, then said:

"And so it has all come to this, has it? To think that you should
run on my son's sword-point at last, after all the wrong you have
done me and mine; now must I work carefully, lest when you are
dead you should still do me harm, for that you are a King—Lionel!"

"Yea, Mother."

"Come here and see; this is what I have wrought these many
Peter's days by day, and often other times by night."

"It is a surcoat, Mother; for me?"

"Yea, but take a spade, and come into the wood."

So we went, and my mother gazed about her for a while as if she
were looking for something, but then suddenly went forward with
her eyes on the ground, and she said to me:

"Is it not strange, that I who know the very place I am going to take you to, as well as our own garden, should have a sudden fear come over me that I should not find it after all; though for these nineteen years I have watched the trees change and change all about it—ah! here, stop now."

We stopped before a great oak; a beech tree was behind us—she said, "Dig, Lionel, hereabouts."

So I dug and for an hour found nothing but beech roots, while my mother seemed as if she were going mad, sometimes running about muttering to herself, sometimes stooping into the hole and howling, sometimes throwing herself on the grass and twisting her hands together above her head; she went once down the hill to a pool that had filled an old gravel pit, and came back dripping and with wild eyes; "I am too hot," she said, "far too hot this St. Peter's day."

Clink just then from my spade against iron; my mother screamed, and I dug with all my might for another hour, and then beheld a chest of heavy wood bound with iron ready to be heaved out of the hole; "Now, Lionel, weigh it out—hard for your life!"

And with some trouble I got the chest out; she gave me a key, I unlocked the chest, and took out another wrapped in lead, which also I unlocked with a silver key that my mother gave me, and behold therein lay armour—mail for the whole body, made of very small rings wrought most wonderfully, for every ring was fashioned like a serpent, and though they were so small yet could you see their scales and their eyes, and of some even the forked tongue was on it, and lay on the rivet, and the rings were gilded here and there into patterns and flowers so that the gleam of it was most glorious.—And the mail coif was all gilded and had red and blue stones at the rivets; and the tilting helms (inside which the mail lay when I saw it first) was gilded also, and had flowers pricked out on it; and the chain of it was silver, and the crest was two gold wings. And there was a shield of blue set with red stones, which had two gold wings for a cognizance; and the hilt of the sword was gold, with angels wrought in green and blue all up it, and the eyes in their wings were of pearls and red stones, and the sheath was of silver with green flowers on it.

Now when I saw this armour and understood that my mother would have me put it on, and ride out without fear, leaving her alone, I cast myself down on the grass so that I might not see its beauty (for it made me mad), and strove to think; but what thoughts soever came to me were only of the things that would be, glory in the midst of ladies, battle-joy among knights, honour from all kings and princes and people—these things.

But my mother wept softly above me, till I arose with a great shudder of delight and drew the edges of the hawberk over my cheek, I liked so to feel the rings slipping, slipping, till they fell off altogether; then I said:

"O Lord God that made the world, if I might only die in this armour!"

Then my mother helped me to put it on, and I felt strange and new in it, and yet I had neither lance nor horse.

So when we reached the cottage again she said: "See now, Lionel, you must take this knight's horse and his lance, and ride away, or else the people will come here to kill another king; and when you are gone, you will never see me any more in life."

I wept thereat, but she said:

"Nay, but see here."

And taking the dead knight's lance from among the garden lilies, she rent from it the pennon (which had a sword on a red ground for bearing), and cast it carelessly on the ground, then she bound about it a pennon with my bearing, gold wings on a blue ground; she bid me bear the knight's body, all armed as he was, to put on him his helm and lay him on the floor at her bed's foot, also to break his sword and cast it on our hearthstone; all which things I did.

Afterwards she put the surcoat on me, and then lying down in her gorgeous raiment on her bed, she spread her arms out in the form of a cross, shut her eyes, and said:

"Kiss me, Lionel, for I am tired."

And after I had kissed her she died.

And I mounted my dead foe's horse and rode away; neither did I ever know what wrong that was which he had done me, not while I was in the body at least.

And do not blame me for not burying my mother; I left her there because, though she did not say so to me, yet I knew the thoughts of her heart, and that the thing she had wished so earnestly for these years, and years, and years, had been but to lie dead with him lying dead close to her.

So I rode all that night, for I could not stop because of the thoughts that were in me, and, stopping at this place and that, in three days came to the city.

And there the King held his court with great pomp.

And so I went to the palace, and asked to see the King; whereupon they brought me into the great hall where he was with all his knights, and my heart swelled within me to think that I too was a King.

So I prayed him to make me a knight, and he spake graciously and asked me my name; so when I had told it him, and said that I was a king's son, he pondered, not knowing what to do, for I could not tell him whose son I was.

Whereupon one of the knights came near me and shaded his eyes with his hand as one does in a bright sun, meaning to mock at me for my shining armour, and he drew nearer and nearer till his long stiff beard just touched me, and then I smote him on the face, and he fell on the floor.

So the King being in a rage, roared out from the door, "Slay him!" but I put my shield before me and drew my sword, and the women drew together aside and whispered fearfully, and while some of the knights took spears and stood about me, others got their armour on.

And as we stood thus we heard a horn blow, and then an armed knight came into the hall and drew near to the King; and one of the maidens behind me, came and laid her hand on my shoulder; so I turned and saw that she was very fair, and then I was glad, but she whispered to me:

"Sir Squire, for a love I have for your face and gold armour, I will give you good counsel; go presently to the King and say to him: 'In the name of Alys des roses and Sir Guy le bon amant I pray you three boons,'—do this, and you will be alive, and a knight by to-morrow, otherwise I think hardly the one or the other."

"The Lord reward you damozel," I said. Then I saw that the King had left talking with that knight and was just going to stand up and say something out loud, so I went quickly and called out with a loud voice:

"O King Gilbert of the rose-land, I, Lionel of the golden wings, pray of you three boons in the name of Alys des roses and Sir Guy le bon amant."

Then the King gnashed his teeth, because he had promised if ever his daughter Alys des roses came back safe again, he would on that day grant any three boons to the first man who asked them, even if he were his greatest foe. He said, "Well, then, take them, what are they?"

"First, my life; then, that you should make me a knight; and thirdly, that you should take me into your service."

He said, "I will do this, and moreover, I forgive you freely if you will be my true man."

Then we heard shouting arise through all the city because they were bringing the Lady Alys from the ship up to the palace, and the people came to the windows, and the houses were hung with cloths and banners of silk and gold, that swung down right from the eaves to the ground; likewise the bells all rang: and within a while they entered the palace, and the trumpets rang and men shouted, so that my head whirled; and they entered the hall, and the King went down from the daïs to meet them.

Now a band of knights and of damozels went before and behind, and in the midst Sir Guy led the Lady Alys by the hand, and he was a most stately knight, strong and fair.

And I indeed noted the first band of knights and damozels well, and wondered at the noble presence of the knights, and was filled with joy when I beheld the maids, because of their great beauty; the second band I did not see, for when they passed I was leaning back against the wall, wishing to die with my hands before my face.

But when I could see, she was hanging about her father's neck, weeping, and she never left him all that night, but held his hand in feast and dance, and even when I was made knight, while the King with his right hand laid his sword over my shoulder, she held his left hand and was close to me.

And the next day they held a grand tourney, that I might be proven; and I had never fought with knights before, yet I did not doubt. And Alys sat under a green canopy, that she might give the degree to the best knight, and by her sat the good knight Sir Guy, in a long robe, for he did not mean to joust that day; and indeed at first none but young knights jousted, for they thought that I should not do much.

But I, looking up to the green canopy, overthrew so many of them, that the elder knights began to arm, and I grew most joyful as I met them, and no man unhorsed me; and always I broke my spear fairly, or else overthrew my adversary.

Now that maiden who counselled me in the hall, told me afterwards that as I fought, the Lady Alys held fast to the rail before her, and leaned forward and was most pale, never answering any word that any one might say to her, till the Knight Guy said to her in anger: "Alys! what ails you? you would have been glad enough to speak to me when King Wadrayns carried you off shrieking, or that other time when the chain went round about you, and the faggots began to smoke in the Brown City: do you not love me any longer? O Alys, Alys! just think a little, and do not break your faith with me; God hates nothing so much as this. Sweet, try to love me, even for your own sake! See, am I not kind to you?"

That maiden said that she turned round to him wonderingly, as if she had not caught his meaning, and that just for one second, then stretched out over the lists again.

Now till about this time I had made no cry as I jousted. But there came against me a very tall knight, on a great horse, and when we met our spears both shivered, and he howled with vexation, for he wished to slay me, being the brother of that knight I had struck down in the hall the day before.

And they say that when Alys heard his howl sounding faintly through the bars of his great helm, she trembled; but I know not, for I was stronger than that knight, and when we fought with swords, I struck him right out of his saddle, and near slew him with that stroke.

Whereupon I shouted "Alys," out loud, and she blushed red for pleasure, and Sir Guy took note of it, and rose up in a rage and ran down and armed.

Then presently I saw a great knight come riding in with three black chevrons on a gold shield: and so he began to ride at me, and at first we only broke both our spears, but then he drew his sword, and fought quite in another way to what the other knights had, so that I saw at once that I had no chance against him: nevertheless, for a long time he availed nothing, though he wounded me here and there, but at last drove his sword right through mine, through my shield and my helm, and I fell, and lay like one dead.

And thereat the King cried out to cease, and the degree was given to Sir Guy, because I had overthrown forty knights and he had overthrown me.

Then they told me, I was carried out of the lists and laid in a hostelry near the palace, and Guy went up to the pavilion where Alys was and she crowned him, both of them being very pale, for she doubted if I were slain, and he knew that she did not love him, thinking before that she did; for he was good and true, and had saved her life and honour, and she (poor maid!) wished to please her father, and strove to think that all was right.

But I was by no means slain, for the sword had only cleft my helm, and when I came to myself again I felt despair of all things, because I knew not that she loved me, for how should she, knowing nothing of me? likewise dust had been cast on my gold wings, and she saw it done.

Then I heard a great crying in the street, that sounded strangely in the quiet night, so I sent to ask what it might be: and there came presently into my chamber a man in gilded armour; he was an old man, and his hair and beard were gray, and behind him came six men armed, who carried a dead body of a young man between them, and I said, "What is it? who is he?" Then the old man, whose head was heavy for grief, said: "Oh, sir! this is my son; for as we went yesterday with our merchandize some twenty miles from this fair town, we passed by a certain hold, and therefrom came a knight and men-at-arms, who when my son would have fought with them, overthrew him and bound him, and me and all our men they said they would slay if we did ought; so then they cut out my son's eyes, and cut off his hands, and then said, 'The Knight of High Gard takes these for tribute.' Therewithal they departed, taking with them my son's eyes and his hands on a platter; and when they were gone I would have followed them, and slain some of them at least, but my own people would not suffer me, and for grief and pain my son's heart burst, and he died, and behold I am here."

Then I thought I could win glory, and I was much rejoiced thereat, and said to the old man,

"Would you love to be revenged?"

But he set his teeth, and pulled at the skirt of his surcoat, as hardly for his passion he said, "Yes."

"Then," I said, "I will go and try to slay this knight, if you will show me the way to La Haute Garde."

And he, taking my hand, said, "O glorious knight, let us go now!" And he did not ask who I was, or whether I was a good knight, but began to go down the stairs at once, so I put on my armour and followed him.

And we two set forth alone to La Haute Garde, for no man else dared follow us, and I rejoiced in thinking that while Guy was sitting at the King's table feasting, I was riding out to slay the King's enemies, for it never once seemed possible to me that I should be worsted.

It was getting light again by then we came in sight of High Gard; we wound up the hill on foot, for it was very steep; I blew at the gates a great blast which was even as though the stag should blow his own mort, or like the blast that Balen heard.

For in a very short while the gates opened and a great band of armed men, more than thirty I think, and a knight on horseback among them, who was armed in red, stood before us, and on one side of him was a serving-man with a silver dish, on the other, one with a butcher's cleaver, a knife, and pincers.

So when the knight saw us he said, "What, are you come to pay tribute in person, old man, and is this another fair son? Good sir, how is your lady?"

So I said grimly, being in a rage, "I have a will to slay you."

But I could scarce say so before the old merchant rushed at the red knight with a yell, who without moving slew his horse with an axe, and then the men-at-arms speared the old man, slaying him as one would an otter or a rat.

Afterwards they were going to set on me, but the red knight held them back, saying: "Nay, I am enough," and we spurred our horses.

As we met, I felt just as if some one had thrown a dull brown cloth over my eyes, and I felt the wretched spear-point slip off his helm; then I felt a great pain somewhere, that did not seem to be in my body, but in the world, or the sky, or something of that sort.

And I know not how long that pain seemed to last now, but I think years, though really I grew well and sane again in a few weeks.

And when I woke, scarce knowing whether I was in the world or heaven or hell, I heard some one singing.

I tried to listen but could not, because I did not know where I was, and was thinking of that; I missed verse after verse of the song, this song, till at last I saw I must be in the King's palace.

There was a window by my bed, I looked out at it, and saw that I was high up; down in the street the people were going to and fro, and there was a knot of folks gathered about a minstrel, who sat on the edge of a fountain, with his head laid sideways on his shoulder, and nursing one leg on the other; he was singing only, having no instrument, and he sang the song I had tried to listen to, I heard some of it now:

> "He was fair and free,
> At every tourney
> He wan the degree,
>   Sir Guy the good knight.
>
> He wan Alys the fair,
> The king's own daughtere,
> With all her gold hair,
>   That shone well bright.
>
> He saved a good knight,
> Who also was wight,
> And had wingès bright
>   On a blue shield.
>
> And he slew the Knight,
> Of the High Gard in fight,
> In red weed that was dight
>   In the open field."

I fell back in my bed and wept, for I was weak with my illness; to think of this! truly this man was a perfect knight, and deserved to win Alys. Ah! well! but was this the glory I was to have, and no one believed that I was a King's son.

And so I passed days and nights, thinking of my dishonour and misery, and my utter loneliness; no one cared for me; verily, I think, if any one had spoken to me lovingly, I should have fallen on his neck and died, while I was so weak.

But I grew strong at last, and began to walk about, and in the Palace Pleasaunce, one day, I met Sir Guy walking by himself.

So I told him how that I thanked him with all my heart for my life, but he said it was only what a good knight ought to do; for that hearing the mad enterprise I had ridden on, he had followed me swiftly with a few knights, and so saved me.

He looked stately and grand as he spoke, yet I did not love him, nay, rather hated him, though I tried hard not to do so, for there was some air of pitiless triumph and coldness of heart in him that froze me; so scornfully, too, he said that about "my mad enterprise," as thought I *must* be wrong in everything I did. Yet afterwards, as I came to know more, I pitied him instead of hating; but at that time I thought his life was without a shadow, for I did not know that the Lady Alys loved him not.

And now I turned from him, and walked slowly up and down the garden-paths, not exactly thinking, but with some ghosts of former thoughts passing through my mind. The day, too, was most lovely, as it grew towards evening, and I had all the joy of a man lately sick in the flowers and all things; if any bells at that time had begun to chime, I think I should have lain down on the grass and wept; but now there was but the noise of the bees in the yellow musk, and that had not music enough to bring me sorrow.

And as I walked I stooped and picked a great orange lily, and held it in my hand, and lo! down the garden-walk, the same fair damozel that had before this given me good counsel in the hall.

Thereat I was very glad, and walked to meet her smiling, but she was very grave, and said:

"Fair sir, the Lady Alys des roses wishes to see you in her chamber."

I could not answer a word, but turned, and went with her while she walked slowly beside me, thinking deeply, and picking a rose to pieces as she went; and I, too, thought much, what could she want me for? surely, but for one thing; and yet—and yet.

But when we came to the lady's chamber, behold! before the door stood a tall knight, fair and strong, and in armour, save his head, who seemed to be guarding the door, though not so as to seem so to all men.

He kissed the damozel eagerly, and then she said to me, "This is Sir William de la Fosse, my true knight"; so the knight took my hand and seemed to have such joy of me, that all the blood came up to my face for pure delight.

But then the damozel Blanche opened the door and bade me go in while she abode still without; so I entered, when I had put aside the heavy silken hanging that filled the doorway.

And there sat Alys; she arose when she saw me, and stood pale, and with her lips apart, and her hands hanging loose by her side.

And then all doubt and sorrow went quite away from me; I did not even feel drunk with joy, but rather felt that I could take it all in, lose no least fragment of it; then at once I felt that I was beautiful, and brave and true; I had no doubt as to what I should do now.

I went up to her, and first kissed her on the forehead, and then on the feet, and then drew her to me, and with my arms round about her, and her arms hanging loose, and her lips dropped, we held our lips together so long that my eyes failed me, and I could not see her, till I looked at her green raiment.

And she had never spoken to me yet; she seemed just then as if she were going to, for she lifted her eyes to mine, and opened her mouth; but she only said, "Dear Lionel," and fell forward as though she were faint; and again I held her, and kissed her all over; and then she loosed her hair that it fell to her feet, and when I clipped her next, she threw it over me, that it fell all over my scarlet robes like the trickling of some golden well in Paradise.

Then, within a while, we called in the Lady Blanche and Sir William de la Fosse, and while they talked about what we should do, we sat together and kissed; and what they said, I know not.

But I remember, that that night, quite late, Alys and I rode out side by side from the good city in the midst of a great band of knights and men-at-arms, and other bands drew to us as we went, and in three days we reached Sir William's castle, which was called "La Garde des Chevaliers."

And straightway he caused toll the great bell, and to hang out from the highest tower a great banner of red and gold, cut into so many points that it seemed as if it were tattered; for this was the custom of his house when they wanted their vassals together.

And Alys and I stood up in the tower by the great bell as they tolled it; I remember now that I had passed my hand underneath her hair, so that the fingers of it folded over and just lay on her cheek; she gazed down on the bell, and at every deafening stroke she drew in her breath and opened her eyes to a wide stare downwards.

But on the very day that we came, they arrayed her in gold and flowers (and there were angels and knights and ladies wrought on her gold raiment), and I waited for an hour in the chapel till she came, listening to the swallows outside, and gazing with parted lips at the pictures on the golden walls; but when she came, I knelt down before the altar, and she knelt down and kissed my lips; and then the priest came in, and the singers and the censer-boys; and that chapel was soon confusedly full of golden raiment, and incense, and ladies and singing; in the midst of which I wedded Alys.

And men came into knights' gard till we had two thousand men in it, and great store of munitions of war and provisions.

But Alys and I lived happily together in the painted hall and in the fair water-meadows, and as yet no one came against us.

And still her talk was of deeds of arms, and she was never tired of letting the serpent rings of my mail slip off her wrist and long hand, and she would kiss my shield and helm and the gold wings on my surcoat, my mother's work, and would talk of the ineffable joy that would be when we had fought through all the evil that was coming on us.

Also she would take my sword and lay it on her knees and talk to it, telling it how much she loved me.

Yea in all things, O Lord God, Thou knowest that my love was a very child, like thy angels. Oh! my wise soft-handed love! endless passion! endless longing always satisfied!

Think you that the shouting curses of the trumpet broke off our love, or in any way lessened it? no, most certainly, but from the time the siege began, her cheeks grew thinner, and her passionate face seemed more and more a part of me; now too, whenever I happened to see her between the grim fighting she would do nothing but kiss me all the time, or wring my hands, or take my head on her breast, being so eagerly passionate that sometimes a pang shot through me that she might die.

Till one day they made a breach in the wall, and when I heard of it for the first time, I sickened, and could not call on God; but Alys cut me a tress of her yellow hair and tied it in my helm, and armed me, and saying no word, led me down to the breach by the hand, and then went back most ghastly pale.

So there on the one side of the breach were the spears of William de la Fosse and Lionel of the gold wings, and on the other the spears of King Gilbert and Sir Guy le bon amant, but the King himself was not there; Sir Guy was.

Well,—what would you have? in this world never yet could two thousand men stand against twenty thousand; we were almost pushed back with their spear-points, they were so close together:—slay six of them and the spears were as thick as ever; but if two of our men fell there was straight-way a hole.

Yet just at the end of this we drove them back in one charge two yards beyond the breach, and behold in the front rank, Sir Guy, utterly fearless, cool, and collected; nevertheless, with one stroke I broke his helm, and he fell to the ground before the two armies, even as I fell that day in the lists; and we drove them twenty feet farther, yet they saved Sir Guy.

Well, again,—what would you have? They drove us back again, and they drove us into our inner castle-walls. And I was the last to go in, and just as I was entering, the boldest and nearest of the enemy clutched at my love's hair in my helm, shouting out quite loud, "Whore's hair for John the goldsmith!"

At the hearing of which blasphemy, the Lord gave me such

strength, that I turned and caught him by the ribs with my left hand, and with my right, by sheer strength, I tore off his helm and part of his nose with it, and then swinging him round about, dashed his brains out against the castle-walls.

Yet thereby was I nearly slain, for they surrounded me, only Sir William and the others charged out and rescued me, but hardly.

May the Lord help all true men! In an hour we were all fighting pell mell on the walls of the castle itself, and some were slain outright, and some were wounded, and some yielded themselves and received mercy; but I had scarce the heart to fight any more, because I thought of Alys lying with her face upon the floor and her agonized hands outspread, trying to clutch something, trying to hold to the cracks of the boarding. So when I had seen William de la Fosse slain by many men, I cast my shield and helm over the battlements, and gazed about for a second, and lo! on one of the flanking towers, my gold wings still floated by the side of William's white lion, and in the other one I knew my poor Love, whom they had left quite alone, was lying.

So then I turned into a dark passage and ran till I reached the tower stairs, up that too I sprang as though a ghost were after me, I did so long to kiss her again before I died, to soothe her too, so that she should not feel this day, when in the aftertimes she thought of it as wholly miserable to her. For I knew they would neither slay her nor treat her cruelly, for in sooth all loved her, only they would make her marry Sir Guy le bon amant.

In the topmost room I found her, alas! alas! lying on the floor, as I said; I came to her and kissed her head as she lay, then raised her up; and I took all my armour off and broke my sword over my knee.

And then I led her to the window away from the fighting, from whence we only saw the quiet country, and kissed her lips till she wept and looked no longer sad and wretched; then I said to her:

"Now, O Love, we must part for a little, it is time for me to go and die."

"Why should you go away?" she said, "they will come here quick enough, no doubt, and I shall have you longer with me if you stay; I do not turn sick at the sight of blood."

"O my poor Love!" And I could not go because of her praying face; surely God would grant anything to such a face as that.

"Oh!" she said, "you will let me have you yet a little longer, I see; also let me kiss your feet."

She threw herself down and kissed them, and then did not get up again at once, but lay there holding my feet.

And while she lay there, behold a sudden tramping that she did not hear, and over the green hangings the gleam of helmets that she did not see, and then one pushed aside the hangings with his spear, and there stood the armed men.

"Will not somebody weep for my darling?"

She sprung up from my feet with a low, bitter moan, most terrible to hear, she kissed me once on the lips, and then stood aside, with her dear head thrown back, and holding her lovely loose hair strained over her outspread arms, as though she were wearied of all things that had been or that might be.

Then one thrust me through the breast with a spear, and another with his sword, which was three inches broad, gave me a stroke across the thighs that hit to the bone; and as I fell forward one cleft me to the teeth with his axe.

And then I heard my darling shriek.

The Sword of Welleran   *LORD DUNSANY*
(Edward John Moreton Drax Plunkett,
18th Baron Dunsany)

WHERE THE GREAT PLAIN of Tarphet runs up, as
the sea in estuaries, among the Cyresian mountains, there
stood long since the city of Merimna well-nigh among
the shadows of the crags. I have never seen a city in the
world so beautiful as Merimna seemed to me when I
first dreamed of it. It was a marvel of spires and figures
of bronze, and marble fountains, and trophies of fabulous
wars, and broad streets given over wholly to the Beautiful. Right through the centre of the city there went an
avenue fifty strides in width, and along each side of it
stood likenesses in bronze of the Kings of all the countries
that the people of Merimna had ever known. At the end
of that avenue was a colossal chariot with three bronze
horses driven by the winged figure of Fame, and behind
her in the chariot the huge form of Welleran, Merimna's
ancient hero, standing with extended sword. So urgent
was the mien and attitude of Fame, and so swift the
pose of the horses, that you had sworn that the chariot
was instantly upon you, and that its dust already veiled
the faces of the Kings. And in the city was a mighty hall
wherein were stored the trophies of Merimna's heroes.
Sculptured it was and domed, the glory of the art of
masons a long while dead, and on the summit of the
dome the image of Rollory sat gazing across the Cyresian
mountains toward the wide lands beyond, the lands that
knew his sword. And beside Rollory, like an old nurse,
the figure of Victory sat, hammering into a golden wreath
of laurels for his head the crowns of fallen Kings.

Such was Merimna, a city of sculptured Victories and
warriors of bronze. Yet in the time of which I write the
art of war had been forgotten in Merimna, and the peo-

ple almost slept. To and fro and up and down they would walk through the marble streets, gazing at memorials of the things achieved by their country's swords in the hands of those that long ago had loved Merimna well. Almost they slept, and dreamed of Welleran, Soorenard, Mommolek, Rollory, Akanax, and young Iraine. Of the lands beyond the mountains that lay all round about them they knew nothing, save that they were the theatre of the terrible deeds of Welleran, that he had done with his sword. Long since these lands had fallen back into the possession of the nations that had been scourged by Merimna's armies. Nothing now remained to Merimna's men save their inviolate city and the glory of the remembrance of their ancient fame. At night they would place sentinels far out in the desert, but these always slept at their posts dreaming of Rollory, and three times every night a guard would march around the city clad in purple, bearing lights and singing songs of Welleran. Always the guard went unarmed, but as the sound of their song went echoing across the plain towards the looming mountains, the desert robbers would hear the name of Welleran and steal away to their haunts. Often dawn would come across the plain, shimmering marvellously upon Merimna's spires, abashing all the stars, and find the guard still singing songs of Welleran, and would change the colour of their purple robes and pale the lights they bore. But the guard would go back leaving the ramparts safe, and one by one the sentinels in the plain would awake from dreaming of Rollory and shuffle back into the city quite cold. Then something of the menace would pass away from the faces of the Cyresian mountains, that from the north and the west and the south lowered upon Merimna, and clear in the morning the statues and the pillars would arise in the old inviolate city. You would wonder that an unarmed guard and sentinels that slept could defend a city that was stored with all the glories of art, that was rich in gold and bronze, a haughty city that had erst oppressed its neighbours, whose people had forgotten the art of war. Now this is the reason that, though all her other lands had long been taken from her, Merimna's city was safe. A strange thing was believed or feared by the fierce tribes beyond the mountains, and it was credited among them that at certain stations round Merimna's ramparts there still rode Welleran, Soorenard, Mommolek, Rollory, Akanax, and young Iraine. Yet it was close on a hundred years since Iraine, the youngest of Merimna's heroes, fought his last battle with the tribes.

Sometimes indeed there arose among the tribes young men who doubted and said: "How may a man for ever escape death?"

But graver men answered them: "Hear us, ye whose wisdom has discerned so much, and discern for us how a man may escape death when two score horsemen assail him with their swords, all of them sworn to kill him, and all of them sworn upon their country's gods; as often Welleran hath. Or discern for us how two men alone may enter a walled city by night, and bring away from it that city's king, as did Soorenard and Mommolek. Surely men that have escaped so many swords and so many sleety arrows shall escape the years and Time."

And the young men were humbled and became silent. Still, the suspicion grew. And often when the sun set on the Cyresian mountains, men in Merimna discerned the forms of savage tribesmen black against the light, peering towards the city.

All knew in Merimna that the figures round the ramparts were only statues of stone, yet even there a hope lingered among a few that some day their old heroes would come again, for certainly none had ever seen them die. Now it had been the wont of these six warriors of old, as each received his last wound and knew it to be mortal, to ride away to a certain deep ravine and cast his body in, as somewhere I have read great elephants do, hiding their bones away from lesser beasts. It was a ravine steep and narrow even at the ends, a great cleft into which no man could come by any path. There rode Welleran alone, panting hard; and there later rode Soorenard and Mommolek, Mommolek with a mortal wound upon him not to return, but Soorenard was unwounded and rode back alone from leaving his dear friend resting among the mighty bones of Welleran. And there rode Soorenard, when his day was come, with Rollory and Akanax, and Rollory rode in the middle and Soorenard and Akanax on either side. And the long ride was a hard and weary thing for Soorenard and Akanax, for they both had mortal wounds; but the long ride was easy for Rollory, for he was dead. So the bones of these five heroes whitened in an enemy's land, and very still they were, though they had troubled cities, and none knew where they lay saving only Iraine, the young captain, who was but twenty-five when Mommolek, Rollory, Akanax rode away. And among them were strewn their saddles and their bridles, and all the accoutrements of their horses, lest any man should ever find them afterwards and say in some foreign city: "Lo! the bridles or the saddles of Merimna's captains, taken in war," but their beloved trusty horses they turned free.

Forty years afterwards, in the hour of a great victory, his last wound came upon Iraine, and the wound was terrible and would not close. And Iraine was the last of the captains, and rode away alone. It was a long way to the dark ravine, and Iraine feared that he would never come to the resting-place of the old heroes, and he urged his horse on swiftly, and clung to the saddle with his hands. And often as he rode he fell asleep, and dreamed of earlier days, and of the times when he first rode forth to the great wars of Welleran, and of the time when Welleran first spake to him, and of the faces of Welleran's comrades when they led charges in the battle. And ever as he awoke a great longing arose in his soul as it hovered on his body's brink, a longing to lie among the bones of the old heroes. At last when he saw the dark ravine making a scar across the plain, the soul of Iraine slipped out through his great wound and spread its wings, and pain departed from the poor hacked body and, still urging his horse forward, Iraine died. But the old true horse cantered on till suddenly he saw before him the dark ravine and put his fore-feet out on the very edge of it and stopped. Then the body of Iraine came toppling forward over the right shoulder of the horse, and his bones mingle and rest as the years go by with the bones of Merimna's heroes.

Now there was a little boy in Merimna named Rold. I saw him first, I, the dreamer, that sit before my fire asleep, I saw him first as his mother led him through the great hall where stand the trophies of Merimna's heroes. He was five years old, and they stood before the great glass casket wherein lay the sword of Welleran, and his mother said: "The sword of Welleran." And Rold said: "What should a man do with the sword of Welleran?" And his mother answered: "Men look at the sword and remember Welleran." And they went on and stood before the great red cloak of Welleran, and the child said: "Why did Welleran wear this great red cloak?" And his mother answered: "It was the way of Welleran."

When Rold was a little older he stole out of his mother's house quite in the middle of the night when all the world was still, and Merimna asleep dreaming of Welleran, Soorenard, Mommolek, Rollory, Akanax, and young Iraine. And he went down to the ramparts to hear the purple guard go by singing of Welleran. And the purple guard came by with lights, all singing in the stillness, and dark shapes out in the desert turned and fled. And Rold went back again to his mother's house with a great yearning towards the name of Welleran, such as men feel for very holy things.

And in time Rold grew to know the pathway all round the ramparts, and the six equestrian statues that were there guarding Merimna still. These statues were not like other statues, they were so cunningly wrought of many-coloured marbles that none might be quite sure until very close that they were not living men. There was a horse of dappled marble, the horse of Akanax. The horse of Rollory was of alabaster, pure white, his armour was wrought out of a stone that shone, and his horseman's cloak was made of a blue stone, very precious. He looked northward.

But the marble horse of Welleran was pure black, and there sat Welleran upon him looking solemnly westwards. His horse it was whose cold neck Rold most loved to stroke, and it was Welleran whom the watchers at sunset on the mountains the most clearly saw as they peered towards the city. And Rold loved the red nostrils of the great black horse and his rider's jasper cloak.

Now beyond the Cyresians the suspicion grew that Merimna's heroes were dead, and a plan was devised that a man should go by night and come close to the figures upon the ramparts and see whether they were Welleran, Soorenard, Mommolek, Rollory, Akanax, and young Iraine. And all were agreed upon the plan, and many names were mentioned of those who should go, and the plan matured for many years. It was during these years that watchers clustered often at sunset upon the mountains but came no nearer. Finally, a better plan was made, and it was decided that two men who had been by chance condemned to death should be given a pardon if they went down into the plain by night and discovered whether or not Merimna's heroes lived. At first the two prisoners dared not go, but after a while one of them, Seejar, said to his companion, Sajar-Ho: "See now, when the King's axeman smites a man upon the neck that man dies."

And the other said that this was so. Then said Seejar: "And even though Welleran smite a man with his sword no more befalleth him than death."

Then Sajar-Ho thought for a while. Presently he said: "Yet the eye of the King's axeman might err at the moment of his stroke or his arm fail him, and the eye of Welleran hath never erred nor his arm failed. It were better to bide here."

Then said Seejar: "Maybe that Welleran is dead and that some other holds his place upon the ramparts, or even a statue of stone."

But Sajar-Ho made answer: "How can Welleran be dead when he even escaped from two score horsemen with swords that were sworn to slay him, and all sworn upon our country's gods?"

And Seejar said: "This story his father told my grandfather concerning Welleran. On the day that the fight was lost on the plains of Kurlistan he saw a dying horse near to the river, and the horse looked piteously toward the water but could not reach it. And the father of my grandfather saw Welleran go down to the river's brink and bring water from it with his own hand and give it to the horse. Now we are in as sore a plight as was that horse, and as near to death; it may be that Welleran will pity us, while the King's axeman cannot because of the commands of the King."

Then said Sajar-Ho: "Thou wast ever a cunning arguer. Thou broughtest us into this trouble with thy cunning and thy devices, we will see if thou canst bring us out of it. We will go."

So news was brought to the King that the two prisoners would go down to Merimna.

That evening the watchers led them to the mountain's edge, and

Seejar and Sajar-Ho went down towards the plain by the way of a deep ravine, and the watchers watched them go. Presently their figures were wholly hid in the dusk. Then night came up, huge and holy, out of waste marshes to the eastwards and low lands and the sea; and the angels that watched over all men through the day closed their great eyes and slept, and the angels that watched over all men through the night awoke and ruffled their deep blue feathers and stood up and watched. But the plain became a thing of mystery filled with fears. So the two spies went down the deep ravine, and coming to the plain sped stealthily across it. Soon they came to the line of sentinels asleep upon the sand, and one stirred in his sleep calling on Rollory, and a great dread seized upon the spies and they whispered "Rollory lives," but they remembered the King's axeman and went on. And next they came to the great bronze statue of Fear, carved by some sculptor of the old glorious years in the attitude of flight towards the mountains, calling to her children as she fled. And the children of Fear were carved in the likeness of the armies of all the trans-Cyresian tribes with their backs toward Merimna, flocking after Fear. And from where he sat on his horse behind the ramparts the sword of Welleran was stretched out over their heads as ever it was wont. And the two spies kneeled down in the sand and kissed the huge bronze feet of the statue of Fear, saying: "O Fear, Fear." And as they knelt they saw lights far off along the ramparts coming nearer and nearer, and heard men singing of Welleran. And the purple guard came nearer and went by with their lights, and passed on into the distance round the ramparts still singing of Welleran. And all the while the two spies clung to the foot of the statue, muttering: "O Fear, Fear." But when they could hear the name of Welleran no more they arose and came to the ramparts and climbed over them and came at once upon the figure of Welleran, and they bowed low to the ground, and Seejar said: "O Welleran, we came to see whether thou didst yet live." And for a long while they waited with their faces to the earth. At last Seejar looked up toward Welleran's terrible sword, and it was still stretched out pointing to the carved armies that followed after Fear. And Seejar bowed to the ground again and touched the horse's hoof, and it seemed cold to him. And he moved his hand higher and touched the leg of the horse, and it seemed quite cold. At last he touched Welleran's foot, and the armour on it seemed hard and stiff. Then as Welleran moved not and spake not, Seejar climbed up at last and touched his hand, the terrible hand of Welleran, and it was marble. Then Seejar laughed aloud, and he and Sajar-Ho sped down the empty pathway and found Rollory, and he was marble too. Then they climbed down over the ramparts and went back across the plain, walking contemptuously past the figure of Fear, and heard the guard returning round the ramparts for the third time, singing of Welleran; and Seejar said, "Ay, you may sing of Welleran, but Welleran is dead and a doom is on your city."

And they passed on and found the sentinel still restless in the night and calling on Rollory. And Sajar-Ho muttered: "Ay, you may call on Rollory, but Rollory is dead and naught can save your city."

And the two spies went back alive to their mountains again, and as they reached them the first ray of the sun came up red over the desert behind Merimna and lit Merimna's spires. It was the hour when the purple guard were wont to go back into the city with their tapers pale and their robes a brighter colour, when the cold sentinels came shuffling in from dreaming in the desert; it was the hour when the desert robbers hid themselves away going back to their mountain caves, it was the hour when gauze-winged insects are born that only live for a day, it was the hour when men die that are condemned to death, and in this hour a great peril, new and terrible, arose for Merimna and Merimna knew it not.

Then Seejar turning said: "See how red the dawn is and how red the spires of Merimna. They are angry with Merimna in Paradise and they bode its doom."

So the two spies went back and brought the news to their King, and for a few days the Kings of those countries were gathering their armies together; and one evening the armies of four Kings were massed together at the top of the deep ravine, all crouching below the summit waiting for the sun to set. All wore resolute and fearless faces, yet inwardly every man was praying to his gods, unto each one in turn.

Then the sun set, and it was the hour when the bats and the dark creatures are abroad and the lions come down from their lairs, and the desert robbers go into the plains again, and fevers rise up winged and hot out of chill marshes, and it was the hour when safety leaves the thrones of Kings, the hour when dynasties change. But in the desert the purple guard came swinging out of Merimna with their lights to sing of Welleran, and the sentinels lay down to sleep.

Now into Paradise no sorrow may ever come, but may only beat like rain against its crystal walls, yet the souls of Merimna's heroes were half aware of some sorrow far away as some sleeper feels that some one is chilled and cold yet knows not in his sleep that it is he. And they fretted a little in their starry home. Then unseen there drifted earthward across the setting sun the souls of Welleran, Soorenard, Mommolek, Rollory, Akanax, and young Iraine. Already when they reached Merimna's ramparts it was just dark, already the armies of the four Kings had begun to move, jingling, down the deep ravine. But when the six warriors saw their city again, so little changed after so many years, they looked towards her with a longing that was nearer to tears than any that their souls had known before, crying to her:

"O Merimna, our city: Merimna, our walled city.

"How beautiful thou art with all thy spires, Merimna. For thee we left the earth, its kingdoms and little flowers, for thee we have come away for awhile from Paradise.

"It is very difficult to draw away from the face of God—it is like a warm fire, it is like dear sleep, it is like a great anthem, yet there is a stillness all about it, a stillness full of lights.

"We have left Paradise for awhile for thee, Merimna.

"Many women have we loved, Merimna, but only one city.

"Behold now all the people dream, all our loved people. How beautiful are dreams! In dreams the dead may live, even the long dead and the very silent. Thy lights are all sunk low, they have all gone out, no sound is in thy streets. Hush! Thou art like a maiden that shutteth up her eyes and is asleep, that draweth her breath softly and is quite still, being at ease and untroubled.

"Behold now the battlements, the old battlements. Do men defend them still as we defended them? They are worn a little, the battlements," and drifting nearer they peered anxiously. "It is not by the hand of man that they are worn, our battlements. Only the years have done it and indomitable Time. Thy battlements are like the girdle of a maiden, a girdle that is round about her. See now the dew upon them, they are like a jewelled girdle.

"Thou art in great danger, Merimna, because thou art so beautiful. Must thou perish tonight because we no more defend thee, because we cry out and none hear us, as the bruised lilies cry out and none have known their voices?"

Thus spake those strong-voiced, battle-ordering captains, calling to their dear city, and their voices came no louder than the whispers of little bats that drift across the twilight in the evening. Then the purple guard came near, going round the ramparts for the first time in the night, and the old warriors called to them, "Merimna is in danger! Already her enemies gather in the darkness." But their voices were never heard because they were only wandering ghosts. And the guard went by and passed unheeding away, still singing of Welleran.

Then said Welleran to his comrades: "Our hands can hold swords no more, our voices cannot be heard, we are stalwart men no longer. We are but dreams, let us go among dreams. Go all of you, and thou too, young Iraine, and trouble the dreams of all the men that sleep, and urge them to take the old swords of their grandsires that hang upon the walls, and to gather at the mouth of the ravine; and I will find a leader and make him take my sword."

Then they passed up over the ramparts and into their dear city. And the wind blew about, this way and that, as he went, the soul of Welleran who had upon his day withstood the charges of tempestuous armies. And the souls of his comrades, and with them young Iraine, passed up into the city and troubled the dreams of every man who slept, and to every man the souls said in their dreams: "It is hot and still in the city. Go out now into the desert, into the cool under the mountains, but take with thee the old sword that hangs upon the wall for fear of the desert robbers."

And the god of that city sent up a fever over it, and the fever brooded over it and the streets were hot; and all that slept awoke from dreaming that it would be cool and pleasant where the breezes came down the ravine out of the mountains: and they took the old swords that their grandsires had, according to their dreams, for fear of the desert robbers. And in and out of dreams passed the souls of Welleran's comrades, and with them young Iraine, in great haste as the night wore on; and one by one they troubled the dreams of all Merimna's men and caused them to arise and go out armed, all save the purple guard who, heedless of danger, sang of Welleran still, for waking men cannot hear the souls of the dead.

But Welleran drifted over the roofs of the city till he came to the form of Rold lying fast asleep. Now Rold was grown strong and was eighteen years of age, and he was fair of hair and tall like Welleran, and the soul of Welleran hovered over him and went into his dreams as a butterfly flits through trellis-work into a garden of flowers, and the soul of Welleran said to Rold in his dreams: "Thou wouldst go and see again the sword of Welleran, the great curved sword of Welleran. Thou wouldst go and look at it in the night with the moonlight shining upon it."

And the longing of Rold in his dreams to see the sword caused him to walk still sleeping from his mother's house to the hall wherein were the trophies of the heroes. And the soul of Welleran urging the dreams of Rold caused him to pause before the great red cloak, and there the soul said among the dreams: "Thou art cold in the night; fling now a cloak around thee."

And Rold drew round about him the huge red cloak of Welleran. Then Rold's dreams took him to the sword, and the soul said to the dreams: "Thou hast a longing to hold the sword of Welleran: take up the sword in thy hand."

But Rold said: "What should a man do with the sword of Welleran?"

And the soul of the old captain said to the dreams: "It is a good sword to hold: take up the sword of Welleran."

And Rold, still sleeping and speaking aloud, said: "It is not lawful; none may touch the sword."

And Rold turned to go. Then a great and terrible cry arose in the soul of Welleran, all the more bitter for that he could not utter it, and it went round and round his soul finding no utterance, like a cry evoked long since by some murderous deed in some old haunted chamber that whispers through the ages heard by none.

And the soul of Welleran cried out to the dreams of Rold: "Thy knees are tied! Thou art fallen in a marsh! Thou canst not move."

And the dreams of Rold said to him: "Thy knees are tied, thou art fallen in a marsh," and Rold stood still before the sword. Then the soul of the warrior wailed among Rold's dreams, as Rold stood before the sword.

"Welleran is crying for his sword, his wonderful curved sword. Poor Welleran, that once fought for Merimna, is crying for his sword in the night. Thou wouldst not keep Welleran without his beautiful sword when he is dead and cannot come for it, poor Welleran who fought for Merimna."

And Rold broke the glass casket with his hand and took the sword, the great curved sword of Welleran; and the soul of the warrior said among Rold's dreams: "Welleran is waiting in the deep ravine that runs into the mountains, crying for his sword."

And Rold went down through the city and climbed over the ramparts, and walked with his eyes wide open but still sleeping over the desert to the mountains.

Already a great multitude of Merimna's citizens were gathered in the desert before the deep ravine with old swords in their hands, and Rold passed through them as he slept holding the sword of Welleran, and the people cried in amaze to one another as he passed: "Rold hath the sword of Welleran!"

And Rold came to the mouth of the ravine, and there the voices of the people woke him. And Rold knew nothing that he had done in his sleep, and looked in amazement at the sword in his hand and said: "What art thou, thou beautiful thing? Lights shimmer in thee, thou art restless. It is the sword of Welleran, the curved sword of Welleran!"

And Rold kissed the hilt of it, and it was salt upon his lips with the battle-sweat of Welleran. And Rold said: "What should a man do with the sword of Welleran?"

And all the people wondered at Rold as he sat there with the sword in his hand muttering, "What should a man do with the sword of Welleran?"

Presently there came to the ears of Rold the noise of a jingling up in the ravine, and all the people, the people that knew naught of war, heard the jingling coming nearer in the night; for the four armies were moving on Merimna and not yet expecting an enemy. And Rold gripped upon the hilt of the great curved sword, and the sword seemed to lift a little. And a new thought came into the hearts of Merimna's people as they gripped their grandsires' swords. Nearer and nearer came the heedless armies of the four Kings, and old ancestral memories began to arise in the minds of Merimna's people in the desert with their swords in their hands sitting behind Rold. And all the sentinels were awake holding their spears, for Rollory had put their dreams to flight, Rollory that once could put to flight armies and now was but a dream struggling with other dreams.

And now the armies had come very near. Suddenly Rold leaped up, crying: "Welleran! And the sword of Welleran!" And the savage, lusting sword that had thirsted for a hundred years went up with the hand of Rold and swept through a tribesman's ribs. And with the warm blood all about it there came a joy into the curved soul of that mighty sword, like to the joy of a swimmer coming up dripping out of warm seas after living for long in a dry land. When they saw the red cloak and that terrible sword a cry ran through the tribal armies, "Welleran lives!" And there arose the sounds of the exulting of victorious men, and the panting of those that fled, and the sword singing softly to itself as it whirled dripping through the air. And the last that I saw of the battle as it poured into the depth and darkness of the ravine was the sword of Welleran sweeping up and falling, gleaming blue in the moonlight whenever it arose and afterwards gleaming red, and so disappearing into the darkness.

But in the dawn Merimna's men came back, and the sun arising to give new life to the world, shone instead upon the hideous things that the sword of Welleran had done. And Rold said: "O sword, sword! How terrible thou art! Thou art a terrible thing to have come among men. How many eyes shall look upon gardens no more because of thee? How many fields must go empty that might have been fair with cottages, white cottages with children all about them? How many valleys must go desolate that might have nursed warm hamlets, because thou hast slain long since the men that might have built them? I hear the wind crying against thee, thou sword! It comes from the empty valleys. It comes over the bare fields. There are children's voices in it. They were never born. Death brings an end to crying for those that had life once, but these must cry for ever. O sword! sword! why did the gods send thee among men?" And the tears of Rold fell down upon the proud sword but could not wash it clean.

And now that the ardour of battle had passed away, the spirits of Merimna's people began to gloom a little, like their leader's, with their fatigue and with the cold of the morning; and they looked at the sword of Welleran in Rold's hand and said: "Not any more, not any more for ever will Welleran now return, for his sword is in the hand of another. Now we know indeed that he is dead. O Welleran, thou wast our sun and moon and all our stars. Now is the sun fallen down and the moon broken, and all the stars are scattered as the diamonds of a necklace that is snapped off one who is slain by violence."

Thus wept the people of Merimna in the hour of their great victory, for men have strange moods, while beside them their old inviolate city slumbered safe. But back from the ramparts and beyond the mountains and over the lands that they had conquered of old, beyond the world and back again to Paradise, went the souls of Welleran, Soorenard, Mommolek, Rollory, Akanax, and young Iraine.

The Five
Black Swans   *SYLVIA TOWNSEND WARNER*

PORTENTS ACCOMPANY THE DEATH of monarchs. A white horse trots slowly along the avenue, a woman in streaming wet garments is seen to enter the throne room, vanishes, and leaves wet footmarks; red mice are caught in the palace mousetraps. For several weeks five black swans had circled incessantly above the castle of Elfhame. It was ninety decades since their last appearance; then there were four of them, waiting for Maharit, Queen Tiphaine's predecessor. Now they were five, and waited for Tiphaine. Mute as a shell cast up on the beach, she lay in her chamber watching the antics of her pet monkey.

The mysterious tribe of fairies are erroneously supposed to be immortal and very small. In fact, they are of smallish human stature and of ordinary human contrivance. They are born, and eventually die; but their longevity and their habit of remaining good-looking, slender and unimpaired till the hour of death have led to the Kingdom of Elfin being called the Land of the Ever-Young. Again, it is an error to say, "the Kingdom of Elfin": the Kingdoms of Elfin are as numerous as kingdoms were in the Europe of the nineteenth century, and as diverse.

Tiphaine's Kingdom lay on the Scottish border, not far from the romantic and lonely Eskdalemuir Observatory (erected in 1908). Her castle of Elfhame—a steep-sided grassy hill, round as a pudding basin—had great purity of style. A small lake on its summit—still known as the Fairy Loch, and local babies with croup are still dipped in its icy, weedless water—had a crystal floor, which served as a skylight. A door in the hillside, operated by legerdemain, opened into a complex of branching corridors, one of which, broadening into a set of anterooms, led to the Throne Room, which was wainscotted in silver and lit by candles in crystal sconces. It was a circular room, and round it, like the ambulatory of a cathedral—and like the ambulatory of a cathedral fenced off by pillars and a light latticing—ran a wide gallery where the courtiers strolled, conversed, and amused themselves with dice, *bouts-rimés*, news from other Kingdoms and the outer world, needlework, flirtations, conjectural scandal and tarot. The hum of conversation was like the hum of bees. But at the time of which I write, no one mentioned the five black swans, and the word "death" was not spoken, though it lay, compact as a pebble, in every heart.

Dying is not an aristocratic activity like fencing, yachting, patronizing the arts: it is enforced—a willy-nilly affair. Though no one at Elfhame was so superstitious as to suppose Tiphaine would live forever, they were too well-mannered to admit openly that she would come to her end by dying. In the same way, though everyone knew that she had wings, it would have been *lèse-majesté* to think she might use them. Flying was a servile activity: cooks, grooms, laundresses flew about their work, and to be strong on the wing was a merit in a footman. But however speedily he flew to the banqueting room with a soup tureen, at the threshold he folded his wings and entered at a walk.

In these flying circles of Elfhame, Tiphaine's dying was discussed as openly and with as much animation as if the swans were outriders of a circus. A kitchen boy, flying out with a bucket of swill for the palace pigs, had been the first to see them. On his report, there was a swirl of servants, streaming like a flock of starlings from the back door to see for themselves. The head gardener, a venerable fairy, swore he could distinguish Queen Maharit in the swan with the long bridling neck: Maharit had just such a neck. Tiphaine's servants were on easier terms with death than her courtiers were. They had plucked geese, drawn grouse and blackcock, skinned eels. They had more contact with the outer world, where they picked up ballads and folk stories, flew over battlefields, and observed pestilences. The mortals among them, stolen from their cradles to be court pets and playthings, and who, failing in this, had drifted into kitchen society,

seldom lived into their second century, even though on their impor-
tation they were injected with an elixir of longevity, as tom kittens
are gelded for domestication. Thus death was at once more real to
them and less imposing. Every day their loyalty grew more fervent.
They said there would never again be such a queen as Tiphaine,
and had a sweepstake as to which lady (Elfindom inverts Salic law)
would be the next.

In Elfindom the succession is determined by the dying ruler
naming who is to come after her. If, by some misadventure, the declaration is not made, resort is had to divination. At sunrise half a
dozen flying fairies are sent up to net larks—as many larks as there
are eligible ladies, with a few over in case of accidents. During the
morning the larks, one to each lady, are caged, ringed, and have
leaden weights wired to their feet. On the stroke of noon the court
officeholders—Chancellor, Astrologer, Keeper of the Records, Cham-
berlain, and so forth—wearing black hoods and accompanied by pages
and cage bearers, go in torchlight procession to the Knowing Room,
a stone cellar deep in the castle's foundations, where there is a well,
said to be bottomless. One by one, the larks are taken from the cages,
held above the well while the name of their lady is pronounced, and
then dropped in. The weights are delicately adjusted to allow the
larks a brief struggle before they drown. Its duration is noted with a
stopwatch by the Court Horologer and when one by one the larks
have drowned, the lark which struggled longest has won the Queenship for the lady it was dedicated to. The officials throw off their
mourning hoods and go back to the Throne Room, where they kiss
the hand of the new Queen and drink her health from a steaming
loving-cup of spiced and honeyed wine which recovers them from
the cramping chill of their ordeal in the Knowing Room.

At Elfhame, however, all this was hearsay: Tiphaine and the
two Queens before her had been named. Lark patties and the loving-
cup were all anyone expected.

Early in the new year the weather changed. Rain pock-marked the
snow that lay in rigid shrouds over the black moorland; the swans
were hidden in a web of low-lying cloud. Suddenly they reappeared; the wind had shifted into the north and there it would stay,

said the head gardener who remembered Queen Maharit, through the three long months ahead—the starving months, when shrew mice feasted underground, and deer and cattle wandered slowly in search of food, eating frozen heather, rushes, dead bracken, anything that would stay the craving to munch and swallow.

It was warm in the castle, where the walls of solid earth muffled the noise of the wind. Chess tables were laid out in the gallery: matches lasted for days on end, protracted by skillful evasions, long considerings before the capture of a pawn. From the musicians' room came intermittent twangings and cockcrowings, flourishes of melody broken off, begun again, broken off again, as the court band of harps and trumpets rehearsed the funeral and coronation marches which would soon be needed. In Tiphaine's chamber the Head Archivist sat by her bed, waiting to take down her dying command about her successor. Every morning he was brought a new quill pen. Every night he was replaced by the Sub-Archivist, who had a peculiar aversion to monkeys, unfortunate but also convenient, since it kept him reliably awake.

The monkey's life depended on Tiphaine's. Royal favourites are seldom popular in court circles. The monkey had amusing tricks but dirty habits; few would put in a good word for it when Tiphaine's death plunged the court in sorrow. Nothing at all could be pled for Morel and Amanita, Tiphaine's latest importees from the mortal world. Strictly speaking, they were not changelings, for they had been bought with good fairy gold. This in itself was against them; but, however got, they would have been detested. They were twins, and orphans; their parents had been burned as heretics during the Easter festivities in Madrid, and the Brocéliande ambassador, on his way back from the Kingdom of the Guadarramas, had stolen them from the convent of penitents to which they had been assigned. Tiphaine had bought them from him. For a while she was devoted to them—as devoted as she had been to the still remembered changeling Tiffany, who for thirteen years she had kept as her lover. Tiffany, in his mortal way, was tolerable. Morel and Amanita were intolerable from the start. They thieved, destroyed, laid booby traps, mimicked, fought each other like wildcats, infuriated the servants, and tore out the Chief Harpist's hair. (Custom dictated that it be worn long and flowing as in olden days.)

For as in the kitchen loyalty grew daily more ardent and more undiscriminating, in the gallery it developed a sense of historical perspective. There had been some regrettable incidents in the past—blown up by scandal, of course; but there is no smoke without fire. Tiphaine was indiscreet in her choice of Favourites—the fault of a generous character, no doubt, but she was often sadly deluded. Admittedly, she was headstrong—but to live under the rule of a vacillating Queen would be far more exhausting. Beauty like hers could atone for everything—or almost everything. Perhaps her complexion had been a shade, just a shade, too florid? "You would not think that if you saw her now," retorted the Dame of Honour.

"I suppose so, I suppose so." The words sounded slightly perfunctory. The speaker was looking at the chessboard, where Morel and Amanita had rearranged the pieces.

By now, it was the end of March and cold as ever.

The Sub-Archivist had entered the bedchamber, seated himself, wrapped a foxskin rug over his knees, taken the virgin parchment, the day's quill pen. The monkey sat hunched before the fire. Dwindled, mute, a dirty white like old snow, Tiphaine lay among her snow-white pillows, and did not notice the replacement. She was remembering Thomas of Ercildoune.

It was May Day morning, and she rode at the head of her court to greet the established spring. Doves were cooing in the woods, larks sang overhead, her harness bells rang in tune with them. She pulled off her gloves to feel the warm air on her hands. The route took them past a hawthorn brake and there, lolling on the new-grown grass, was a handsome man—so handsome that she checked her horse's pace to have a completer look at him. She had looked at him and summed him up when suddenly she realized that he had seen her and was staring at her with intensity. *Mortals do not see fairies.*

She spurred her horse and rode fast on from the strange encounter.

That night she couldn't sleep, feeling the weight of her castle stopping her breath. An hour before sunrise she was in the stables, scolding a sleepy stableboy, had a horse saddled, and rode at a gallop to the hawthorn brake. And he was not there and he did not come. She rode on over the moor. The sun was up before she saw him walking toward her. She reined in her horse, watching him approach. Keeping her pride, she looked down on him when he stopped beside her. "You're out early, Queen of Elfhame," he said. She couldn't think of anything to say. He put his arms round her and lifted her from the saddle, and she toppled into his embrace like a sheaf of corn. The dew was heavy on the grass, and when they got up from their lovemaking they were wringing wet and their teeth chattered.

From then on it was as though she lived to music. To music she followed him barefoot, climbed a sycamore tree to look into a magpie's nest, made love in the rain. Once, they came to a wide rattling burn, with a green lawn on the further bank. He leaped across, and held out his hand for her to catch hold of. It was too wide a leap for her and she took to her wings. It was the first time in her life she had flown, and the sensation delighted her. She rose in another flight, curling and twirling for the pleasure and mastery of it, as a fiddler plays a cadenza. She soared higher and higher, looking down on the figure at the burnside, small as a beetle and the centre of the wide world. He beckoned her down; she dropped like a hawk and they rolled together on the grass. He made little of her flying, even less of her queenship, nothing at all of her immense seniority. Love was in the present: in the sharp taste of the rowanberries he plucked for her, in the winter night when a gale got up and whipped them to the shelter of a farm where he kindled a fire and roasted turnips on a stick, in their midnight mushroomings, in the long summer evenings when they lay on their backs too happy to move or speak, in their March-hare curvettings and cuffings. For love-gifts, he gave her acorns, birds' eggs, a rosegall because it is called the fairies' pincushion, a yellow snail shell.

It was on the day of the shell, a day in August with thunder in the air, that she asked him how it was he saw her, he who had only mortal eyes. He told how on his seventeenth birthday it had come to him that one day he would see the Queen of Elfhame, and from then on he had looked at every woman and seen through her, till

Tiphaine rode past the hawthorn brake. In the same way, he said, he could see things which had not happened yet but surely would happen, and had made rhymes of them to fix them in his memory. She would live long after him and might see some of them come true.

With one ear she was listening for the first growl of thunder, with the other to Thomas's heartbeats. Suddenly they began to quarrel, she railing at him for his selfish mortality, his refusal to make trial of the elixir of longevity. He flung away from her, saying she must love him now, instantly, before the lightning broke cover. A time would come when he would grow old and she would abhor him: he could tell her that without any exercise of prophecy. The storm broke and pinned them in the present. When it moved away they built a cairn of hailstones and watched it melt in the sunshine.

The Sub-Archivist woke with a start. The Queen was stirring in her bed. She sat up and said fiercely, "Why is no one here? It is May Day morning. I must be dressed."

The Sub-Archivist rushed to the door and shouted, "The Queen has spoken! She wants to be dressed."

Courtiers and women servants crowded in, huddling on their clothes. There was a cry of "Keep those two out," but Morel and Amanita were already in the room. They saw their hearts' desire—the monkey. The monkey saw them. It screamed and sprang onto Tiphaine's bed, where it tried to hide under the coverlet. The Court Physician hauled it out by the tail and threw it to the floor. While the court ladies crowded round the bed, chafed the Queen's hands, held smelling salts to her nose, urged her not to excite herself, and apologized for their state of undress, Morel and Amanita seized the monkey. At first they caressed it; then they began to dispute as to which of them loved it best, whose monkey it should be. Their quarrel flared into fury and they tore it in half.

The smell of blood and entrails still hung about the room when the Sub-Archivist took up his evening watch. Everything had been restored to order: the bed straightened, the floor washed and polished, a fresh coverlet supplied. Tiphaine had been given a composing draught, and was asleep. That deplorable business with the monkey had made no impression on her, so the Court Physician assured him. She might even be the better for it. Morel and Amanita had been strangled and their bodies thrown on the moor as a charity to crows. With every symptom so benign, they could hope she would return to her senses and name her successor.

As the virgin parchment had been crumpled during the scuffle, the Sub-Archivist was given a new one, and left to himself.

The room was so still that he could hear the sands draining through the hourglass. He had reversed it for the third time when Tiphaine opened her eyes and turned a little toward him. Trembling, he dipped the quill in ink.

"Thomas—O Thomas, my love."

He wrote this down and waited for her to say more. She grunted once or twice. The room was so still he could hear the swans circling lower and lower, and the castle beginning to resound with exclamations and protesting voices. The swans rose in a bevy, and the chant of their beating wings was high overhead, was far away, was gone.

No one at court had a name remotely resembling Thomas, so preparations for the ceremony of divination were put in hand.

SCIENCE FICTION

The Facts in the Case
of M. Valdemar   *EDGAR ALLAN POE*

O F COURSE I SHALL not pretend to consider it any
matter for wonder, that the extraordinary case of M. Valdemar has excited discussion. It would have been a miracle had it not—especially under the circumstances.
Through the desire of all parties concerned, to keep the
affair from the public, at least for the present, or until
we had further opportunities for investigation—through
our endeavors to effect this—a garbled or exaggerated account made its way into society, and became the source
of many unpleasant misrepresentations; and, very naturally, of a great deal of disbelief.

It is now rendered necessary that I give the *facts*—as
far as I comprehend them myself. They are, succinctly,
these:

My attention, for the last three years, had been repeatedly drawn to the subject of Mesmerism; and, about nine
months ago, it occurred to me, quite suddenly, that in the
series of experiments made hitherto, there had been a
very remarkable and most unaccountable omission:—no
person had as yet been mesmerized *in articulo mortis*. It
remained to be seen, first, whether, in such condition,
there existed in the patient any susceptibility to the magnetic influence; secondly, whether, if any existed, it was
impaired or increased by the condition; thirdly, to what
extent, or for how long a period, the encroachments of
Death might be arrested by the process. There were other
points to be ascertained, but these most excited my curiosity—the last in especial, from the immensely important
character of its consequences.

In looking around me for some subject by whose means

I might test these particulars, I was brought to think of my friend, M. Ernest Valdemar, the well-known compiler of the "Bibliotheca Forensica," and author (under the *nom de plume* of Issachar Marx) of the Polish versions of "Wallenstein" and "Gargantua." M. Valdemar, who has resided principally at Harlem, N.Y., since the year of 1839, is (or was) particularly noticeable for the extreme spareness of his person—his lower limbs much resembling those of John Randolph; and, also, for the whiteness of his whiskers, in violent contrast to the blackness of his hair—the latter, in consequence, being very generally mistaken for a wig. His temperament was markedly nervous, and rendered him a good subject for mesmeric experiment. On two or three occasions I had put him to sleep with little difficulty, but was disappointed in other results which his peculiar constitution had naturally led me to anticipate. His will was at no period positively, or thoroughly, under my control, and in regard to *clairvoyance,* I could accomplish with him nothing to be relied upon. I always attributed my failure at these points to the disordered state of his health. For some months previous to my becoming acquainted with him, his physicians had declared him in a confirmed phthisis. It was his custom, indeed, to speak calmly of his approaching dissolution, as of a matter neither to be avoided nor regretted.

When the ideas to which I have alluded first occurred to me, it was of course very natural that I should think of M. Valdemar. I knew the steady philosophy of the man too well to apprehend any scruples from *him;* and he had no relatives in America who would be likely to interfere. I spoke to him frankly upon the subject; and, to my surprise, his interest seemed vividly excited. I say to my surprise; for, although he had always yielded his person freely to my experiments, he had never before given me any tokens of sympathy with what I did. His disease was of that character which would admit of exact calculation in respect to the epoch of its termination in death; and it was finally arranged between us that he would send for me about twenty-four hours before the period announced by his physicians as that of his decease.

It is now rather more than seven months since I received, from M. Valdemar himself, the subjoined note:

"My Dear P——

"You may as well come *now*. D—— and F—— are agreed that I cannot hold out beyond to-morrow midnight; and I think they have hit the time very nearly.

Valdemar"

I received this note within half an hour after it was written, and in fifteen minutes more I was in the dying man's chamber. I had not seen him for ten days, and was appalled by the fearful alteration which the brief interval had wrought in him. His face wore a leaden hue; the eyes were utterly lustreless; and the emaciation was so extreme, that the skin had been broken through by the cheek-bones. His expectoration was excessive. The pulse was barely perceptible. He retained, nevertheless, in a very remarkable manner, both his mental power and a certain degree of physical strength. He spoke with distinctness—took some palliative medicines without aid—and, when I entered the room, was occupied in penciling memoranda in a pocket-book. He was propped up in the bed by pillows. Doctors D——and F—— were in attendance.

After pressing Valdemar's hand, I took these gentlemen aside, and obtained from them a minute account of the patient's condition. The left lung had been for eighteen months in a semi-osseous or cartilaginous state, and was, of course, entirely useless for all purposes of vitality. The right, in its upper portion, was also partially, if not thoroughly, ossified, while the lower region was merely a mass of purulent tubercles, running one into another. Several extensive perforations existed; and, at one point, permanent adhesion to the ribs had taken place. These appearances in the right lobe were of comparatively recent date. The ossification had proceeded with very unusual rapidity; no sign of it had been discovered a month before, and the adhesion had only been observed during the three previous days. Independently of the phthisis, the patient was suspected of aneurism of the aorta; but on this point the osseous symptoms rendered an exact diagnosis impossible. It was the opinion of both physicians that M. Valdemar would die about midnight on the morrow (Sunday). It was then seven o'clock on Saturday evening.

On quitting the invalid's bedside to hold conversation with myself,

Doctors D——— and F——— had bidden him a final farewell. It had not been their intention to return; but, at my request, they agreed to look in upon the patient about ten the next night.

When they had gone, I spoke freely with M. Valdemar on the subject of his approaching dissolution, as well as, more particularly, of the experiment proposed. He still professed himself quite willing and even anxious to have it made, and urged me to commence it at once. A male and a female nurse were in attendance; but I did not feel myself altogether at liberty to engage in a task of this character with no more reliable witnesses than these people, in case of sudden accident, might prove. I therefore postponed operations until about eight the next night, when the arrival of a medical student, with whom I had some acquaintance (Mr. Theodore L———l), relieved me from further embarrassment. It had been my design, originally, to wait for the physicians; but I was induced to proceed, first, by the urgent entreaties of M. Valdemar, and secondly, by my conviction that I had not a moment to lose, as he was evidently sinking fast.

Mr. L———l was so kind as to accede to my desire that he would take notes of all that occurred; and it is from his memoranda that what I now have to relate is, for the most part, either condensed or copied *verbatim*.

It wanted about five minutes of eight when, taking the patient's hand, I begged him to state, as distinctly as he could, to Mr. L———l, whether he (M. Valdemar) was entirely willing that I should make the experiment of mesmerizing him in his then condition.

He replied feebly, yet quite audibly: "Yes, I wish to be mesmerized"—adding immediately afterward: "I fear you have deferred it too long."

While he spoke thus, I commenced the passes which I had already found most effectual in subduing him. He was evidently influenced with the first lateral stroke of my hand across his forehead; but, although I exerted all my powers, no further perceptible effect was induced until some minutes after ten o'clock, when Doctors D——— and F——— called, according to appointment. I explained to them, in a few words, what I designed and as they opposed no objection, saying that the patient was already in the death agony, I proceeded without hesitation—exchanging, however the lateral passes for downward ones, and directing my gaze entirely into the right eye of the sufferer.

By this time his pulse was imperceptible and his breathing was stertorious, and at intervals of half a minute.

This condition was nearly unaltered for a quarter of an hour. At the expiration of this period, however, a natural although a very deep sigh escaped from the bosom of the dying man, and the stertorious breathing ceased—that is to say, its stertoriousness was no longer apparent; the intervals were undiminished. The patient's extremities were of an icy coldness.

At five minutes before eleven, I perceived unequivocal signs of the mesmeric influence. The glassy roll of the eye was changed for that expression of uneasy *inward* examination which is never seen except in cases of sleep-waking, and which it is quite impossible to mistake. With a few rapid lateral passes I made the lids quiver, as in incipient sleep, and with a few more I closed them altogether. I was not satisfied, however, with this, but continued the manipulations vigorously, and with the fullest exertion of the will, until I had completely stiffened the limbs of the slumberer, after placing them in a seemingly easy position. The legs were at full length; the arms were nearly so, and reposed on the bed at a moderate distance from the loins. The head was very slightly elevated.

When I had accomplished this, it was fully midnight, and I requested the gentlemen present to examine M. Valdemar's condition. After a few experiments, they admitted him to be in an unusually perfect state of mesmeric trance. The curiosity of both the physicians was greatly excited. Dr. D———— resolved at once to remain with the patient all night, while Dr. F———— took leave with a promise to return at daybreak. Mr. L————l and the nurses remained.

We left M. Valdemar entirely undisturbed until about three o'clock in the morning, when I approached him and found him in precisely the same condition as when Dr. F———— went away—that is to say, he lay in the same position; the pulse was imperceptible; the breathing was gentle (scarcely noticeable, unless through the application of a mirror to the lips); the eyes were closed naturally; and the limbs were as rigid and as cold as marble. Still, the general appearance was certainly not that of death.

As I approached M. Valdemar I made a kind of half effort to influence his right arm into pursuit of my own, as I passed the latter gently to and fro above his person. In such experiments with this patient, I had never perfectly succeeded before, and assuredly I had little thought of succeeding now; but to my astonishment, his arm very readily, although feebly, followed every direction I assigned it with mine. I determined to hazard a few words of conversation.

"M. Valdemar," I said, "are you asleep?" He made no answer, but I perceived a tremor about the lips, and was thus induced to repeat the question, again and again. At its third repetition, his whole frame was agitated by a very slight shivering; the eyelids unclosed themselves so far as to display a white line of a ball; the lips moved sluggishly, and from between them, in a barely audible whisper, issued the words:

"Yes;—asleep now. Do not wake me!—let me die so!"

I here felt the limbs, and found them as rigid as ever. The right arm, as before, obeyed the direction of my hand. I questioned the sleep-waker again:

"Do you still feel pain in the breast, M. Valdemar?"

The answer now was immediate, but even less audible than before:

"No pain—I am dying!"

I did not think it advisable to disturb him further just then, and nothing more was said or done until the arrival of Dr. F———, who came a little before sunrise, and expressed unbounded astonishment at finding the patient still alive. After feeling the pulse and applying a mirror to the lips, he requested me to speak to the sleep-waker again. I did so, saying:

"M. Valdemar, do you still sleep?"

As before, some minutes elapsed ere a reply was made; and during the interval the dying man seemed to be collecting his energies to speak. At my fourth repetition of the question, he said very faintly, almost inaudibly:

"Yes; still asleep—dying."

It was now the opinion, or rather the wish, of the physicians, that M. Valdemar should be suffered to remain undisturbed in his present apparently tranquil condition, until death should supervene— and this, it was generally agreed, must now take place within a few minutes. I concluded, however, to speak to him once more, and merely repeated my previous question.

While I spoke, there came a marked change over the countenance of the sleep-waker. The eyes rolled themselves slowly open, the pupils disappearing upwardly; the skin generally assumed a cadaverous hue, resembling not so much parchment as white paper; and the circular hectic spots which, hitherto, had been strongly defined in the center of each cheek, *went out* at once. I use this expression, because the suddenness of their departure put me in mind of nothing so much as the extinguishment of a candle by a puff of the breath. The upper lid, at the same time, writhed itself away from the teeth, which it had previously covered completely; while the lower jaw fell with an audible jerk, leaving the mouth widely extended, and disclosing in full view the swollen and blackened tongue. I presume that no member of the party then present had been unaccustomed to death-bed horrors; but so hideous beyond conception was the appearance of M. Valdemar at this moment, that there was a general shrinking back from the region of the bed.

I now feel that I have reached a point of this narrative at which every reader will be startled into positive disbelief. It is my business, however, simply to proceed.

There was no longer the faintest sign of vitality in M. Valdemar; and concluding him to be dead, we were consigning him to the charge of the nurses, when a strong vibratory motion was observable in the tongue. This continued for perhaps a minute. At the expiration of this period, there issued from the distended and motionless jaws a voice—such as it would be madness in me to attempt describing. There are, indeed, two or three epithets which might be considered as applicable to it in part; I might say, for example, that the sound was harsh and broken and hollow; but the hideous whole is indescribable, for the simple reason that no similar sounds have ever jarred upon the ear of humanity. There were two particulars, never-theless, which I thought then, and still think, might fairly be stated as characteristic of the intonation—as well adapted to convey some idea of its unearthly peculiarity. In the first place, the voice seemed to reach our ears—at least mine—from a vast distance, or from some deep cavern within the earth. In the second place, it impressed me (I fear, indeed, that it will be impossible to make myself compre-hended) as gelatinous or glutinous matters impress the sense of touch.

I have spoken both of "sound" and of "voice." I mean to say that the sound was one of distinct—of even wonderfully, thrillingly dis-tinct—syllabification. M. Valdemar *spoke*—obviously in reply to the question I had propounded to him a few minutes before. I had asked him, it will be remembered, if he still slept. He now said:

"Yes;—no;—I *have been* sleeping—and now—now—*I am dead.*"

No person present even affected to deny, or attempted to repress, the unutterable, shuddering horror which these few words, thus uttered, were so well calculated to convey. Mr. L———l (the stu-dent) swooned. The nurses immediately left the chamber, and could not be induced to return. My own impressions I would not pretend to render intelligible to the reader. For nearly an hour, we busied ourselves, silently—without the utterance of a word—in endeavors to revive Mr. L———l. When he came to himself, we addressed our-selves again to an investigation of M. Valdemar's condition.

It remained in all respects as I have last described it, with the ex-ception that the mirror no longer afforded evidence of respiration. An attempt to draw blood from the arm failed. I should mention, too, that this limb was no further subject to my will. I endeavored in vain to make it follow the direction of my hand. The only real indication, indeed, of the mesmeric influence, was now found in the vibratory movement of the tongue, whenever I addressed M. Valdemar a ques-tion. He seemed to be making an effort to reply, but had no longer sufficient volition. To queries put to him by any other person than myself he seemed utterly insensible—although I endeavored to place each member of the company in mesmeric *rapport* with him. I be-lieve that I have now related all that is necessary to an understanding of the sleep-waker's state at this epoch. Other nurses were procured; and at ten o'clock I left the house in company with the two physicians and Mr. L———l.

In the afternoon we all called again to see the patient. His condition remained precisely the same. We had now some discussion as to the propriety and feasibility of awakening him; but we had little difficulty in agreeing that no good purpose would be served by so doing. It was evident that, so far, death (or what is usually termed death) had been arrested by the mesmeric process. It seemed clear to us all that to awaken M. Valdemar would be merely to insure his instant, or at least his speedy, dissolution.

From this period until the close of last week—*an interval of nearly seven months*—we continued to make daily calls at M. Valdemar's house, accompanied, now and then, by medical and other friends. All this time the sleep-waker remained *exactly* as I have last described him. The nurses' attentions were continual.

It was on Friday last that we finally resolved to make the experiment of awakening, or attempting to awaken him; and it is the (perhaps) unfortunate result of this latter experiment which has given rise to so much discussion in private circles—to so much of what I cannot help thinking unwarranted popular feeling.

For the purpose of relieving M. Valdemar from the mesmeric trance, I made use of the customary passes. These for a time were unsuccessful. The first indication of revival was afforded by a partial descent of the iris. It was observed, as especially remarkable, that this lowering of the pupil was accompanied by the profuse out-flowing of a yellowish ichor (from beneath the lids) of a pungent and highly offensive odor.

It was now suggested that I should attempt to influence the patient's arm as heretofore. I made the attempt and failed. Dr. F——— then intimated a desire to have me put a question. I did so, as follows:

"M. Valdemar, can you explain to us what are your feelings or wishes now?"

There was an instant return of the hectic circles on the cheeks: the tongue quivered, or rather rolled violently in the mouth (although the jaws and lips remained rigid as before), and at length the same hideous voice which I have already described, broke forth:

"For God's sake:—quick—quick!—put me to sleep—or, quick!—waken me—quick!—*I say to you that I am dead!*"

I was thoroughly unnerved, and for an instant remained undecided what to do. At first I made an endeavor to recompose the patient; but, failing in this through total abeyance of the will, I retraced my steps and as earnestly struggled to awaken him. In this attempt I soon saw that I should be successful—or at least I soon fancied that my success would be complete—and I am sure that all in the room were prepared to see the patient awaken.

For what really occurred, however, it is quite impossible that any human being could have been prepared.

As I rapidly made the mesmeric passes, amid ejaculations of "dead! dead!" absolutely *bursting* from the tongue and not from the lips of the sufferer, his whole frame at once—within the space of a single minute, or less, shrunk—crumbled—absolutely *rotted* away beneath my hands. Upon the bed, before that whole company, there lay a nearly liquid mass of loathsome—of detestable putrescence.

I N THE LATTER PART of the last century there lived a man of science, an eminent proficient in every branch of natural philosophy, who not long before our story opens had made experience of a spiritual affinity more attractive than any chemical one. He had left his laboratory to the care of an assistant, cleared his fine countenance from the furnace smoke, washed the stain of acids from his fingers, and persuaded a beautiful woman to become his wife. In those days when the comparatively recent discovery of electricity and other kindred mysteries of Nature seemed to open paths into the region of miracle, it was not unusual for the love of science to rival the love of woman in its depth and absorbing energy. The higher intellect, the imagination, the spirit, and even the heart might all find their congenial aliment in pursuits which, as some of their ardent votaries believed, would ascend from one step of powerful intelligence to another, until the philosopher should lay his hand on the secret of creative force and perhaps make new worlds for himself. We know not whether Aylmer possessed this degree of faith in man's ultimate control over Nature. He had devoted himself, however, too unreservedly to scientific studies ever to be weaned from them by any second passion. His love for his young wife might prove the stronger of the two; but it could only be by intertwining itself with his love of science, and uniting the strength of the latter to his own.

Such a union accordingly took place, and was attended with truly remarkable consequences and a deeply impressive moral. One day, very soon after their marriage, Aylmer sat gazing at his wife with a trouble in his countenance that grew stronger until he spoke.

"Georgiana," said he, "has it never occurred to you that the mark upon your cheek might be removed?"

"No, indeed," said she, smiling; but perceiving the seriousness of his manner, she blushed deeply. "To tell you the truth it has been so often called a charm that I was simple enough to imagine it might be so."

"Ah, upon another face perhaps it might," replied her husband; "but never on yours. No, dearest Georgiana, you came so nearly perfect from the hand of Nature that this slightest possible defect, which we hesitate whether to term a defect or a beauty, shocks me, as being the visible mark of earthly imperfection."

"Shocks you, my husband!" cried Georgiana, deeply hurt; at first reddening with momentary anger, but then bursting into tears. "Then why did you take me from my mother's side? You cannot love what shocks you!"

To explain this conversation it must be mentioned that in the centre of Georgiana's left cheek there was a singular mark, deeply interwoven, as it were, with the texture and substance of her face. In the usual state of her complexion—a healthy though delicate bloom—the mark wore a tint of deeper crimson, which imperfectly defined its shape amid the surrounding rosiness. When she blushed it gradually became more indistinct, and finally vanished amid the triumphant rush of blood that bathed the whole cheek with its brilliant glow. But if any shifting motion caused her to turn pale there was the mark again, a crimson stain upon the snow, in what Aylmer sometimes deemed an almost fearful distinctness. Its shape bore not a little similarity to the human hand, though of the smallest pygmy size. Georgiana's lovers were wont to say that some fairy at her birth hour had laid her tiny hand upon the infant's cheek, and left this impress there in token of the magic endowments that were to give her such sway over all hearts. Many a desperate swain would have risked life for the privilege of pressing his lips to the mysterious hand. It must not be concealed, however, that the impression wrought by this fairy sign manual varied exceedingly, according to the difference of temperament in the beholders. Some fastidious persons—but they were exclusively of her own sex—affirmed that the bloody hand, as they chose to call it, quite destroyed the effect of Georgiana's beauty, and rendered her countenance even hideous. But it would be as reasonable to say that one of those small blue stains which sometimes occur in the purest statuary marble would convert the Eve of Powers to a monster. Masculine observers, if the birthmark did not heighten their admiration, contented themselves with wishing it away, that the world might possess one living specimen of ideal loveliness without the semblance of a flaw. After his marriage,—for he thought little or nothing of the matter before,—Aylmer discovered that this was the case with himself.

Had she been less beautiful,—if Envy's self could have found aught else to sneer at,—he might have felt his affection heightened by the prettiness of this mimic hand, now vaguely portrayed, now lost, now stealing forth again and glimmering to and fro with every pulse of emotion that throbbed within her heart; but seeing her otherwise so perfect, he found this one defect grow more and more intolerable with every moment of their united lives. It was the fatal flaw of humanity which Nature, in one shape or another, stamps ineffaceably on all her productions, either to imply that they are temporary and finite, or that their perfection must be wrought by toil and pain. The crimson hand expressed the ineludible gripe in which mortality clutches the highest and purest of earthly mould, degrading them into kindred with the lowest, and even with the very brutes, like whom their visible frames return to dust. In this manner, selecting it as the symbol of his wife's liability to sin, sorrow, decay, and death, Aylmer's sombre imagination was not long in rendering the birthmark a frightful object, causing him more trouble and horror than ever Georgiana's beauty, whether of soul or sense, had given him delight.

At all the seasons which should have been their happiest, he invariably and without intending it, nay, in spite of a purpose to the contrary, reverted to this one disastrous topic. Trifling as it at first appeared, it so connected itself with innumerable trains of thought and modes of feeling that it became the central point of all. With the morning twilight Aylmer opened his eyes upon his wife's face and recognized the symbol of imperfection; and when they sat together at the evening hearth his eyes wandered stealthily to her cheek, and beheld, flickering with the blaze of the wood fire, the spectral hand that wrote mortality where he would fain have wor-shipped. Georgiana soon learned to shudder at his gaze. It needed but a glance with the peculiar expression that his face often wore to change the roses of her cheek into a deathlike paleness, amid which the crimson hand was brought strongly out, like a bass-relief of ruby on the whitest marble.

Late one night when the lights were growing dim, so as hardly to betray the stain on the poor wife's cheek, she herself, for the first time, voluntarily took up the subject.

"Do you remember, my dear Aylmer," said she, with a feeble attempt at a smile, "have you any recollection of a dream last night about this odious hand?"

"None! none whatever!" replied Aylmer, starting; but then he added, in a dry, cold tone, affected for the sake of concealing the real depth of his emotion, "I might well dream of it; for before I fell asleep it had taken a pretty firm hold of my fancy."

"And you did dream of it?" continued Georgiana, hastily; for she dreaded lest a gush of tears should interrupt what she had to say. "A terrible dream! I wonder that you can forget it. Is it possible to forget this one expression?—'It is in her heart now; we must have it out!' Reflect, my husband; for by all means I would have you recall that dream."

The mind is in a sad state when Sleep, the all-involving, cannot confine her spectres within the dim region of her sway, but suffers them to break forth, affrighting this actual life with secrets that perchance belong to a deeper one. Aylmer now remembered his dream. He had fancied himself with his servant Aminadab, attempting an operation for the removal of the birthmark; but the deeper went the knife, the deeper sank the hand, until at length its tiny grasp appeared to have caught hold of Georgiana's heart; whence, her husband was inexorably resolved to cut or wrench it away.

When the dream had shaped itself perfectly in his memory, Aylmer sat in his wife's presence with a guilty feeling. Truth often finds its way to the mind close muffled in robes of sleep, and then speaks with uncompromising directness of matters in regard to which we practise an unconscious self-deception during our waking moments. Until now he had not been aware of the tyrannizing influence acquired by one idea over his mind, and of the lengths which he might find in his heart to go for the sake of giving himself peace.

"Aylmer," resumed Georgiana, solemnly, "I know not what may be the cost to both of us to rid me of this fatal birthmark. Perhaps its removal may cause cureless deformity; or it may be the stain goes as deep as life itself. Again: do we know that there is a possibility, on any terms, of unclasping the firm gripe of this little hand which was laid upon me before I came into the world?"

"Dearest Georgiana, I have spent much thought upon the subject," hastily interrupted Aylmer. "I am convinced of the perfect practicability of its removal."

"If there be the remotest possibility of it," continued Georgiana, "let the attempt be made at whatever risk. Danger is nothing to me; for life, while this hateful mark makes me the object of your horror and disgust,—life is a burden which I would fling down with joy. Either remove this dreadful hand, or take my wretched life! You have deep science. All the world bears witness of it. You have achieved great wonders. Cannot you remove this little, little mark, which I cover with the tips of two small fingers? Is this beyond your power, for the sake of your own peace, and to save your poor wife from madness?"

"Noblest, dearest, tenderest wife," cried Aylmer, rapturously, "doubt not my power. I have already given this matter the deepest thought—thought which might almost have enlightened me to create a being less perfect than yourself. Georgiana, you have led me deeper than ever into the heart of science. I feel myself fully competent to render this dear cheek as faultless as its fellow; and then, most beloved, what will be my triumph when I shall have corrected what Nature left imperfect in her fairest work! Even Pygmalion, when his sculptured woman assumed life, felt not greater ecstasy than mine will be."

"It is resolved, then," said Georgiana, faintly smiling. "And, Aylmer, spare me not, though you should find the birthmark take refuge in my heart at last."

Her husband tenderly kissed her cheek—her right cheek—not that which bore the impress of the crimson hand.

The next day Aylmer apprised his wife of a plan that he had

formed whereby he might have opportunity for the intense thought and constant watchfulness which the proposed operation would require; while Georgiana, likewise, would enjoy the perfect repose essential to its success. They were to seclude themselves in the extensive apartments occupied by Aylmer as a laboratory, and where, during his toilsome youth, he had made discoveries in the elemental powers of Nature that had roused the admiration of all the learned societies in Europe. Seated calmly in this laboratory, the pale philosopher had investigated the secrets of the highest cloud region and of the profoundest mines; he had satisfied himself of the causes that kindled and kept alive the fires of the volcano; and had explained the mystery of fountains, and how it is that they gush forth, some so bright and pure, and others with such rich medicinal virtues, from the dark bosom of the earth. Here, too, at an earlier period, he had studied the wonders of the human frame, and attempted to fathom the very process by which Nature assimilates all her precious influences from earth and air, and from the spiritual world, to create and foster man, her masterpiece. The latter pursuit, however, Aylmer had long laid aside in unwilling recognition of the truth—against which all seekers sooner or later stumble—that our great creative Mother, while she amuses us with apparently working in the broadest sunshine, is yet severely careful to keep her own secrets, and, in spite of her pretended openness, shows us nothing but results. She permits us, indeed, to mar, but seldom to mend, and, like a jealous patentee, on no account to make. Now, however, Aylmer resumed these half-forgotten investigations; not, of course, with such hopes or wishes as first suggested them; but because they involved much physiological truth and lay in the path of his proposed scheme for the treatment of Georgiana.

As he led her over the threshold of the laboratory, Georgiana was cold and tremulous. Aylmer looked cheerfully into her face, with intent to reassure her, but was so startled with the intense glow of the birthmark upon the whiteness of her cheek that he could not restrain a strong convulsive shudder. His wife fainted.

"Aminadab! Aminadab!" shouted Aylmer, stamping violently on the floor.

Forthwith there issued from an inner apartment a man of low stature, but bulky frame, with shaggy hair hanging about his visage, which was grimed with the vapors of the furnace. This personage had been Aylmer's underworker during his whole scientific career, and was admirably fitted for that office by his great mechanical readiness, and the skill with which, while incapable of comprehending a single principle, he executed all the details of his master's experiments. With his vast strength, his shaggy hair, his smoky aspect, and the indescribable earthiness that incrusted him, he seemed to represent man's physical nature; while Aylmer's slender figure, and pale, intellectual face, were no less apt a type of the spiritual element.

"Throw open the door of the boudoir, Aminadab," said Aylmer, "and burn a pastil."

"Yes, master," answered Aminadab, looking intently at the lifeless form of Georgiana; and then he muttered to himself, "If she were my wife, I'd never part with that birthmark."

When Georgiana recovered consciousness she found herself breathing an atmosphere of penetrating fragrance, the gentle potency of which had recalled her from her deathlike faintness. The scene around her looked like enchantment. Aylmer had converted those smoky, dingy, sombre rooms, where he had spent his brightest years in recondite pursuits, into a series of beautiful apartments not unfit to be the secluded abode of a lovely woman. The walls were hung with gorgeous curtains, which imparted the combination of grandeur and grace that no other species of adornment can achieve; and as they fell from the ceiling to the floor, their rich and ponderous folds, concealing all angles and straight lines, appeared to shut in the scene from infinite space. For aught Georgiana knew, it might be a pavilion among the clouds. And Aylmer, excluding the sunshine, which would have interfered with his chemical processes, had supplied its place with perfumed lamps, emitting flames of various hue, but all uniting in a soft, impurpled radiance. He now knelt by his wife's side, watching her earnestly, but without alarm; for he was confident in his science, and felt that he could draw a magic circle round her within which no evil might intrude.

"Where am I? Ah, I remember," said Georgiana, faintly; and she placed her hand over her cheek to hide the terrible mark from her husband's eyes.

"Fear not, dearest!" exclaimed he. "Do not shrink from me! Believe me, Georgiana, I even rejoice in this single imperfection, since it will be such a rapture to remove it."

"Oh, spare me!" sadly replied his wife. "Pray do not look at it again. I never can forget that convulsive shudder."

In order to soothe Georgiana, and, as it were, to release her mind from the burden of actual things, Aylmer now put in practice some of the light and playful secrets which science had taught him among its profounder lore. Airy figures, absolutely bodiless ideas, and forms of unsubstantial beauty came and danced before her, imprinting their momentary footsteps on beams of light. Though she had some indistinct idea of the method of these optical phenomena, still the illusion was almost perfect enough to warrant the belief that her husband possessed sway over the spiritual world. Then again, when she felt a wish to look forth from her seclusion, immediately, as if her thoughts were answered, the procession of external existence flitted across a screen. The scenery and the figures of actual life were perfectly represented, but with that bewitching, yet indescribable difference which always makes a picture, an image, or a shadow so much more attractive than the original. When wearied of this, Aylmer bade her cast her eyes upon a vessel containing a quantity of earth. She did so, with little interest at first; but was soon startled to perceive the germ of a plant shooting upward from the soil. Then came the slender stalk; the leaves gradually unfolded themselves; and amid them was a perfect and lovely flower.

"It is magical!" cried Georgiana. "I dare not touch it."

"Nay, pluck it," answered Aylmer,—"pluck it, and inhale its brief perfume while you may. The flower will wither in a few moments and leave nothing save its brown seed vessels; but thence may be perpetuated a race as ephemeral as itself."

But Georgiana had no sooner touched the flower than the whole plant suffered a blight, its leaves turning coal-black as if by the agency of fire.

"There was too powerful a stimulus," said Aylmer, thoughtfully.

To make up for this abortive experiment, he proposed to take her portrait by a scientific process of his own invention. It was to be effected by rays of light striking upon a polished plate of metal. Georgiana assented; but, on looking at the result, was affrighted to find the features of the portrait blurred and indefinable; while the minute figure of a hand appeared where the cheek should have been. Aylmer snatched the metallic plate and threw it into a jar of corrosive acid.

Soon, however, he forgot these mortifying failures. In the intervals of study and chemical experiment he came to her flushed and exhausted, but seemed invigorated by her presence, and spoke in glowing language of the resources of his art. He gave a history of the long dynasty of the alchemists, who spent so many ages in quest of the universal solvent by which the golden principle might be elicited from all things vile and base. Aylmer appeared to believe that, by the plainest scientific logic, it was altogether within the limits of possibility to discover this long-sought medium; "but," he added, "a philosopher who should go deep enough to acquire the power would attain too lofty a wisdom to stoop to the exercise of it." Not less singular were his opinions in regard to the elixir vitæ. He more than intimated that it was at his option to concoct a liquid that should prolong life for years, perhaps interminably; but that it would produce a discord in Nature which all the world, and chiefly the quaffer of the immortal nostrum, would find cause to curse.

"Aylmer, are you in earnest?" asked Georgiana, looking at him with amazement and fear. "It is terrible to possess such power, or even to dream of possessing it."

"Oh, do not tremble, my love," said her husband. "I would not wrong either you or myself by working such inharmonious effects upon our lives; but I would have you consider how trifling, in comparison, is the skill requisite to remove this little hand."

At the mention of the birthmark, Georgiana, as usual, shrank as if a redhot iron had touched her cheek.

Again Aylmer applied himself to his labors. She could hear his voice in the distant furnace room giving directions to Aminadab, whose harsh, uncouth, misshapen tones were audible in response, more like the grunt or growl of a brute than human speech. After hours of absence, Aylmer reappeared and proposed that she should now examine his cabinet of chemical products and natural treasures of the earth. Among the former he showed her a small vial, in which, he remarked, was contained a gentle yet most powerful fragrance, capable of impregnating all the breezes that blow across a kingdom. They were of inestimable value, the contents of that little vial; and, as he said so, he threw some of the perfume into the air and filled the room with piercing and invigorating delight.

"And what is this?" asked Georgiana, pointing to a small crystal globe containing a gold-colored liquid. "It is so beautiful to the eye that I could imagine it the elixir of life."

"In one sense it is," replied Aylmer; "or, rather, the elixir of immortality. It is the most precious poison that ever was concocted in this world. By its aid I could apportion the lifetime of any mortal at whom you might point your finger. The strength of the dose would determine whether he were to linger out years, or drop dead in the midst of a breath. No king on his guarded throne could keep his life if I, in my private station, should deem that the welfare of millions justified me in depriving him of it."

"Why do you keep such a terrific drug?" inquired Georgiana in horror.

"Do not mistrust me, dearest," said her husband, smiling; "its virtuous potency is yet greater than its harmful one. But see! here is a powerful cosmetic. With a few drops of this in a vase of water, freckles may be washed away as easily as the hands are cleansed. A stronger infusion would take the blood out of the cheek, and leave the rosiest beauty a pale ghost."

"Is it with this lotion that you intend to bathe my cheek?" asked Georgiana, anxiously.

"Oh, no," hastily replied her husband; "this is merely superficial. Your case demands a remedy that shall go deeper."

In his interviews with Georgiana, Aylmer generally made minute inquiries as to her sensations and whether the confinement of the rooms and the temperature of the atmosphere agreed with her. These questions had such a particular drift that Georgiana began to conjecture that she was already subjected to certain physical influences, either breathed in with the fragrant air or taken with her food. She fancied likewise, but it might be altogether fancy, that there was a stirring up of her system—a strange, indefinite sensation creeping through her veins, and tingling, half painfully, half pleasurably, at her heart. Still, whenever she dared to look into the mirror, there she beheld herself pale as a white rose and with the crimson birthmark stamped upon her cheek. Not even Aylmer now hated it so much as she.

To dispel the tedium of the hours which her husband found it necessary to devote to the processes of combination and analysis, Georgiana turned over the volumes of his scientific library. In many dark old tomes she met with chapters full of romance and poetry. They were the works of philosophers of the middle ages, such as Albertus Magnus, Cornelius Agrippa, Paracelsus, and the famous friar who created the prophetic Brazen Head. All these antique naturalists stood in advance of their centuries, yet were imbued with some of their credulity, and therefore were believed, and perhaps imagined themselves to have acquired from the investigation of Nature a power above Nature, and from physics a sway over the spiritual world. Hardly less curious and imaginative were the early volumes of the Transactions of the Royal Society, in which the members, knowing little of the limits of natural possibility, were continually recording wonders or proposing methods whereby wonders might be wrought.

But to Georgiana the most engrossing volume was a large folio from her husband's own hand, in which he had recorded every experiment of his scientific career, its original aim, the methods adopted for its development, and its final success or failure, with the circumstances to which either event was attributable. The book, in truth, was both the history and emblem of his ardent, ambitious, imaginative, yet practical and laborious life. He handled physical details as if there were nothing beyond them; yet spiritualized them all, and redeemed himself from materialism by his strong and eager aspiration towards the infinite. In his grasp the veriest clod of earth assumed a soul. Georgiana, as she read, reverenced Aylmer and loved him more profoundly than ever, but with a less entire dependence on his judgment than heretofore. Much as he had accomplished, she could not but observe that his most splendid successes were almost invariably failures, if compared with the ideal at which he aimed. His brightest diamonds were the merest pebbles, and felt to be so by himself, in comparison with the inestimable gems which lay hidden beyond his reach. The volume, rich with achievements that had won renown for its author, was yet as melancholy a record as ever mortal hand had penned. It was the sad confession and continual exemplification of the shortcomings of the composite man, the spirit burdened with clay and working in matter, and of the despair that assails the higher nature at finding itself so miserably thwarted by the earthly part. Perhaps every man of genius in whatever sphere might recognize the image of his own experience in Aylmer's journal.

So deeply did these reflections affect Georgiana that she laid her face upon the open volume and burst into tears. In this situation she was found by her husband.

"It is dangerous to read in a sorcerer's books," said he with a smile, though his countenance was uneasy and displeased. "Georgiana, there are pages in that volume which I can scarcely glance over and keep my senses. Take heed lest it prove as detrimental to you."

"It has made me worship you more than ever," said she.

"Ah, wait for this one success," rejoined he, "then worship me if you will. I shall deem myself hardly unworthy of it. But come, I have sought you for the luxury of your voice. Sing to me, dearest."

So she poured out the liquid music of her voice to quench the thirst of his spirit. He then took his leave with a boyish exuberance of gayety, assuring her that her seclusion would endure but a little longer, and that the result was already certain. Scarcely had he departed when Georgiana felt irresistibly impelled to follow him. She had forgotten to inform Aylmer of a symptom which for two or three hours past had begun to excite her attention. It was a sensation in the fatal birthmark, not painful, but which induced a restlessness throughout her system. Hastening after her husband, she intruded for the first time into the laboratory.

The first thing that struck her eye was the furnace, that hot and feverish worker, with the intense glow of its fire, which by the quantities of soot clustered above it seemed to have been burning for ages. There was a distilling apparatus in full operation. Around the room were retorts, tubes, cylinders, crucibles, and other apparatus of chemical research. An electrical machine stood ready for immediate use. The atmosphere felt oppressively close, and was tainted with gaseous odors which had been tormented forth by the processes of science. The severe and homely simplicity of the apartment, with its naked walls and brick pavement, looked strange, accustomed as Georgiana had become to the fantastic elegance of her boudoir. But what chiefly, indeed almost solely, drew her attention, was the aspect of Aylmer himself.

He was pale as death, anxious and absorbed, and hung over the furnace as if it depended upon his utmost watchfulness whether the liquid which it was distilling should be the draught of immortal happiness or misery. How different from the sanguine and joyous mien that he had assumed for Georgiana's encouragement!

"Carefully now, Aminadab; carefully, thou human machine; carefully, thou man of clay!" muttered Aylmer, more to himself than his assistant. "Now, if there be a thought too much or too little, it is all over."

"Ho! ho!" mumbled Aminadab. "Look, master! look!"

Aylmer raised his eyes hastily, and at first reddened, then grew paler than ever, on beholding Georgiana. He rushed towards her and seized her arm with a gripe that left the print of his fingers upon it.

"Why do you come hither? Have you no trust in your husband?" cried he, impetuously. "Would you throw the blight of that fatal birthmark over my labors? It is not well done. Go, prying woman, go!"

"Nay, Aylmer," said Georgiana with the firmness of which she possessed no stinted endowment, "it is not you that have a right to complain. You mistrust your wife; you have concealed the anxiety with which you watch the development of this experiment. Think not so unworthily of me, my husband. Tell me all the risk we run, and fear not that I shall shrink; for my share in it is far less than your own."

"No, no, Georgiana!" said Aylmer, impatiently; "it must not be."

"I submit," replied she calmly. "And, Aylmer, I shall quaff whatever draught you bring me; but it will be on the same principle that would induce me to take a dose of poison if offered by your hand."

"My noble wife," said Aylmer, deeply moved, "I knew not the height and depth of your nature until now. Nothing shall be concealed. Know, then, that this crimson hand, superficial as it seems, has clutched its grasp into your being with a strength of which I had no previous conception. I have already administered agents powerful enough to do aught except to change your entire physical system. Only one thing remains to be tried. If that fail us we are ruined."

"Why did you hesitate to tell me this?" asked she.

"Because, Georgiana," said Aylmer, in a low voice, "there is danger."

"Danger? There is but one danger—that this horrible stigma shall be left upon my cheek!" cried Georgiana. "Remove it, remove it, whatever be the cost, or we shall both go mad!"

"Heaven knows your words are too true," said Aylmer, sadly. "And now, dearest, return to your boudoir. In a little while all will be tested."

He conducted her back and took leave of her with a solemn tenderness which spoke far more than his words how much was now at stake. After his departure Georgiana became rapt in musings. She considered the character of Aylmer, and did it completer justice than at any previous moment. Her heart exulted, while it trembled, at his honorable love—so pure and lofty that it would accept nothing less than perfection nor miserably make itself contented with an earthlier nature than he had dreamed of. She felt how much more precious was such a sentiment than that meaner kind which would have borne with the imperfection for her sake, and have been guilty of treason to holy love by degrading its perfect idea to the level of the actual; and with her whole spirit she prayed that, for a single moment, she might satisfy his highest and deepest conception. Longer than one moment she well knew it could not be; for his spirit was ever on the march, ever ascending, and each instant required something that was beyond the scope of the instant before.

The sound of her husband's footsteps aroused her. He bore a crystal goblet containing a liquor colorless as water, but bright enough to be the draught of immortality. Aylmer was pale; but it seemed rather the consequence of a highly-wrought state of mind and tension of spirit than of fear or doubt.

"The concoction of the draught has been perfect," said he, in answer to Georgiana's look. "Unless all my science have deceived me, it cannot fail."

"Save on your account, my dearest Aylmer," observed his wife, "I might wish to put off this birthmark of mortality by relinquishing mortality itself in preference to any other mode. Life is but a sad possession to those who have attained precisely the degree of moral advancement at which I stand. Were I weaker and blinder it might be happiness. Were I stronger, it might be endured hopefully. But, being what I find myself, methinks I am of all mortals the most fit to die."

"You are fit for heaven without tasting death!" replied her husband. "But why do we speak of dying? The draught cannot fail. Behold its effect upon this plant."

On the window seat there stood a geranium diseased with yellow blotches, which had overspread all its leaves. Aylmer poured a small quantity of the liquid upon the soil in which it grew. In a little time, when the roots of the plant had taken up the moisture, the unsightly blotches began to be extinguished in a living verdure.

"There needed no proof," said Georgiana, quietly. "Give me the goblet. I joyfully stake all upon your word."

"Drink, then, thou lofty creature!" exclaimed Aylmer, with fervid admiration. "There is no taint of imperfection on thy spirit. Thy sensible frame, too, shall soon be all perfect."

She quaffed the liquid and returned the goblet to his hand.

"It is grateful," said she with a placid smile. "Methinks it is like water from a heavenly fountain; for it contains I know not what of unobtrusive fragrance and deliciousness. It allays a feverish thirst that had parched me for many days. Now, dearest, let me sleep. My earthly senses are closing over my spirit like the leaves around the heart of a rose at sunset."

She spoke the last words with a gentle reluctance, as if it required almost more energy than she could command to pronounce the faint and lingering syllables. Scarcely had they loitered through her lips ere she was lost in slumber. Aylmer sat by her side, watching her aspect with the emotions proper to a man the whole value of whose existence was involved in the process now to be tested. Mingled with this mood, however, was the philosophic investigation characteristic of the man of science. Not the minutest symptom escaped him. A heightened flush of the cheek, a slight irregularity of breath, a quiver of the eyelid, a hardly perceptible tremor through the frame,—such were the details which, as the moments passed, he wrote down in his folio volume. Intense thought had set its stamp upon every previous page of that volume, but the thoughts of years were all concentrated upon the last.

While thus employed, he failed not to gaze often at the fatal hand, and not without a shudder. Yet once, by a strange and unaccountable impulse, he pressed it with his lips. His spirit recoiled, however, in the very act; and Georgiana, out of the midst of her deep sleep, moved uneasily and murmured as if in remonstrance. Again Aylmer resumed his watch. Nor was it without avail. The crimson hand, which at first had been strongly visible upon the marble paleness of Georgiana's cheek, now grew more faintly outlined. She remained not less pale than ever; but the birthmark, with every breath that came and went, lost somewhat of its former distinctness. Its presence had been awful; its departure was more awful still. Watch the stain of the rainbow fading out the sky, and you will know how that mysterious symbol passed away.

"By Heaven! it is well-night gone!" said Aylmer to himself, in almost irrepressible ecstasy. "I can scarcely trace it now. Success! success! And now it is like the faintest rose color. The lightest flush of blood across her cheek would overcome it. But she is so pale!"

He drew aside the window curtain and suffered the light of natural day to fall into the room and rest upon her cheek. At the same time he heard a gross, hoarse chuckle, which he had long known as his servant Aminadab's expression of delight.

"Ah, clod! ah, earthly mass!" cried Aylmer, laughing in a sort of frenzy, "you have served me well! Matter and spirit—earth and heaven—have both done their part in this! Laugh, thing of the senses! You have earned the right to laugh."

These exclamations broke Georgiana's sleep. She slowly unclosed her eyes and gazed into the mirror which her husband had arranged for that purpose. A faint smile flitted over her lips when she recognized how barely perceptible was now that crimson hand which had once blazed forth with such disastrous brilliancy as to scare away all their happiness. But then her eyes sought Aylmer's face with a trouble and anxiety that he could by no means account for.

"My poor Aylmer!" murmured she.

"Poor? Nay, richest, happiest, most favored!" exclaimed he. "My peerless bride, it is successful! You are perfect!"

"My poor Aylmer," she repeated, with a more than human tenderness, "you have aimed loftily; you have done nobly. Do not repent that with so high and pure a feeling, you have rejected the best the earth could offer. Aylmer, dearest Aylmer, I am dying!"

Alas! it was too true! The fatal hand had grappled with the mystery of life, and was the bond by which an angelic spirit kept itself in union with a mortal frame. As the last crimson tint of the birthmark—that sole token of human imperfection—faded from her cheek, the parting breath of the now perfect woman passed into the atmosphere, and her soul, lingering a moment near her husband, took its heavenward flight. Then a hoarse, chuckling laugh was heard again! Thus ever does the gross fatality of earth exult in its invariable triumph over the immortal essence which, in this dim sphere of half development, demands the completeness of a higher state. Yet, had Aylmer reached a profounder wisdom, he need not thus have flung away the happiness which would have woven his mortal life of the selfsame texture with the celestial. The momentary circumstance was too strong for him; he failed to look beyond the shadowy scope of time, and, living once for all in eternity, to find the perfect future in the present.

I T WAS ON THE FIRST DAY of the new year that the announcement was made, almost simultaneously from three observatories, that the motion of the planet Neptune, the outermost of all the planets that wheel about the sun, had become very erratic. Ogilvy had already called attention to a suspected retardation in its velocity in December. Such a piece of news was scarcely calculated to interest a world the greater portion of whose inhabitants were unaware of the existence of the planet Neptune, nor outside the astronomical profession did the subsequent discovery of a faint remote speck of light in the region of the perturbed planet cause any very great excitement. Scientific people, however, found the intelligence remarkable enough, even before it became known that the new body was rapidly growing larger and brighter, that its motion was quite different from the orderly progress of the planets, and that the deflection of Neptune and its satellite was becoming now of an unprecedented kind.

Few people without a training in science can realise the huge isolation of the solar system. The sun with its specks of planets, its dust of planetoids, and its impalpable comets, swims in a vacant immensity that almost defeats the imagination. Beyond the orbit of Neptune there is space, vacant so far as human observation has penetrated, without warmth or light or sound, blank emptiness, for twenty million times a million miles. That is the smallest estimate of the distance to be traversed before the very nearest of the stars is attained. And, saving a few comets more unsubstantial than the thinnest flame, no matter had ever to human knowledge crossed this gulf of space, until early in the twentieth century this strange wanderer appeared. A vast mass of matter it was, bulky, heavy, rushing without warning out of the black mystery of the sky into the radiance of the sun. By the second day it was clearly visible to any decent instrument, as a speck with a barely sensible diameter, in the constellation Leo near Regulus. In a little while an opera glass could attain it.

On the third day of the new year the newspaper readers of two hemispheres were made aware for the first time of the real importance of this unusual apparition in the heavens. "A Planetary Collision," one London paper headed the news, and proclaimed Duchaine's opinion that this strange new planet would probably collide with Neptune. The leader writers enlarged upon the topic. So that in most of the capitals of the world, on January 3rd, there was an expectation, however vague, of some imminent phenomenon in the sky; and as the night followed the sunset round the globe, thousands of men turned their eyes skyward to see—the old familiar stars just as they had always been.

Until it was dawn in London and Pollux setting and the stars overhead grown pale. The Winter's dawn it was, a sickly filtering accumulation of daylight, and the light of gas and candles shone yellow in the windows to show where people were astir. But the yawning policeman saw the thing, the busy crowds in the markets stopped agape, workmen going to their work betimes, milkmen, the drivers of news-carts, dissipation going home jaded and pale, homeless wanderers, sentinels on their beats, and in the country, labourers trudging afield, poachers slinking home, all over the dusky quickening country it could be seen—and out at sea by seamen watching for the day—a great white star, come suddenly into the westward sky!

Brighter it was than any star in our skies; brighter than the evening star at its brightest. It still glowed out white and large, no mere twinkling spot of light, but a small round clear shining disc, an hour after the day had come. And where science has not reached, men stared and feared, telling one another of the wars and pestilences that are foreshadowed by these fiery signs in the Heavens. Sturdy Boers, dusky Hottentots, Gold Coast Negroes, Frenchmen, Spaniards, Portuguese, stood in the warmth of the sunrise watching the setting of this strange new star.

And in a hundred observatories there had been suppressed excitement, rising almost to shouting pitch, as the two remote bodies had rushed together, and a hurrying to and fro, to gather photographic apparatus and spectroscope, and this appliance and that, to record this novel astonishing sight, the destruction of a world. For it was a world, a sister planet of our earth, far greater than our earth indeed, that had so suddenly flashed into flaming death. Neptune it was, had been struck, fairly and squarely, by the strange planet from outer space and the heat of the concussion had incontinently turned two solid globes into one vast mass of incandescence. Round the world that day, two hours before the dawn, went the pallid great white star, fading only as it sank westward and the sun mounted above it. Everywhere men marvelled at it, but of all those who saw it none could have marvelled more than those sailors, habitual watchers of the stars, who far away at sea had heard nothing of its advent and saw it now rise like a pigmy moon and climb zenithward and hang overhead and sink westward with the passing of the night.

And when next it rose over Europe everywhere were crowds of watchers on hilly slopes, on house-roofs, in open spaces, staring eastward for the rising of the great new star. It rose with a white glow in front of it, like the glare of a white fire, and those who had seen it come into existence the night before cried out at the sight of it. "It is larger," they cried. "It is brighter!" And, indeed the moon a quarter full and sinking in the west was in its apparent size beyond comparison, but scarcely in all its breadth had it as much brightness now as the little circle of the strange new star.

"It is brighter!" cried the people clustering in the streets. But in the dim observatories the watchers held their breath and peered at one another. *"It is nearer,"* they said. *"Nearer!"*

And voice after voice repeated, "It is nearer," and the clicking telegraph took that up, and it trembled along telephone wires, and in a thousand cities grimy compositors fingered the type. "It is nearer." Men writing in offices, struck with a strange realisation, flung down their pens, men talking in a thousand places suddenly came upon a grotesque possibility in those words, "It is nearer." It hurried along awakening streets, it was shouted down the frost-stilled ways of quiet villages; men who had read these things from the throbbing tape stood in yellow-lit doorways shouting the news to the passers-by. "It is nearer." Pretty women, flushed and glittering, heard the news told jestingly between the dances, and feigned an intelligent interest they did not feel. "Nearer! Indeed. How curious! How very, very clever people must be to find out things like that!"

Lonely tramps faring through the wintry night murmured those words to comfort themselves—looking skyward. "It has need to be nearer, for the night's as cold as charity. Don't seem much warmth from it if it *is* nearer, all the same."

"What is a new star to me?" cried the weeping woman kneeling beside her dead.

The schoolboy, rising early for his examination work, puzzled it out for himself—with the great white star, shining broad and bright through the frost-flowers of his window. "Centrifugal, centripetal," he said, with his chin on his fist. "Stop a planet in its flight, rob it of its centrifugal force, what then? Centripetal has it, and down it falls into the sun! And this—!"

"Do *we* come in the way? I wonder—"

The light of that day went the way of its brethren, and with the later watches of the frosty darkness rose the strange star again. And it was now so bright that the waxing moon seemed but a pale yellow ghost of itself, hanging huge in the sunset. In a South African city a great man had married, and the streets were alight to welcome his return with his bride. "Even the skies have illuminated," said the flatterer. Under Capricorn, two Negro lovers, daring the wild beasts and evil spirits, for love of one another, crouched together in a cane brake where the fire-flies hovered. "That is our star," they whispered, and felt strangely comforted by the sweet brilliance of its light.

The master mathematician sat in his private room and pushed the papers from him. His calculations were already finished. In a small white phial there still remained a little of the drug that had kept him awake and active for four long nights. Each day, serene, explicit, patient as ever, he had given his lecture to his students, and then had come back at once to this momentous calculation. His face was grave, a little drawn and hectic from his drugged activity. For some time he seemed lost in thought. Then he went to the window, and the blind went up with a click. Half way up the sky, over the clustering roofs, chimneys and steeples of the city, hung the star.

He looked at it as one might look into the eyes of a brave enemy. "You may kill me," he said after a silence. "But I can hold you—and all the universe for that matter—in the grip of this little brain. I would not change. Even now."

He looked at the little phial. "There will be no need of sleep again," he said. The next day at noon, punctual to the minute, he entered his lecture theatre, put his hat on the end of the table as his habit was, and carefully selected a large piece of chalk. It was a joke among his students that he could not lecture without that piece of chalk to fumble in his fingers, and once he had been stricken to impotence by their hiding his supply. He came and looked under his grey eyebrows at the rising tiers of young fresh faces, and spoke with his accustomed studied commonness of phrasing. "Circumstances have arisen—circumstances beyond my control," he said and paused, "which will debar me from completing the course I had designed. It would seem, gentlemen, if I may put the thing clearly and briefly, that—Man has lived in vain."

The students glanced at one another. Had they heard aright? Mad? Raised eyebrows and grinning lips there were, but one or two faces remained intent upon his calm grey-fringed face. "It will be interesting," he was saying, "to devote this morning to an exposition, so far as I can make it clear to you, of the calculations that have led me to this conclusion. Let us assume—"

He turned towards the blackboard, meditating a diagram in the way that was usual to him. "What was that about 'lived in vain'?" whispered one student to another. "Listen," said the other, nodding towards the lecturer.

And presently they began to understand.

That night the star rose later, for its proper eastward motion had carried it some way across Leo towards Virgo, and its brightness was so great that the sky became a luminous blue as it rose, and every star was hidden in its turn, save only Jupiter near the zenith, Capella, Aldebaran, Sirius and the pointers of the Bear. It was very white and beautiful. In many parts of the world that night a pallid halo encircled it about. It was perceptibly larger; in the clear refractive sky of the tropics it seemed as if it were nearly a quarter the size of the moon. The frost was still on the ground in England, but the world was as brightly lit as if it were midsummer moonlight. One could see to read quite ordinary print by that cold clear light, and in the cities the lamps burnt yellow and wan.

And everywhere the world was awake that night, and throughout Christendom a sombre murmur hung in the keen air over the country side like the belling of bees in the heather, and this murmurous tumult grew to a clangour in the cities. It was the tolling of the bells in a million belfry towers and steeples, summoning the people to sleep no more, to sin no more, but to gather in their churches and pray. And overhead, growing larger and brighter, as the earth rolled on its way and the night passed, rose the dazzling star.

And the streets and houses were alight in all the cities, the shipyards glared, and whatever roads led to high country were lit and crowded all night long. And in all the seas about the civilised lands, ships with throbbing engines, and ships with bellying sails, crowded with men and living creatures, were standing out to ocean and the north. For already the warning of the master mathematician had been telegraphed all over the world, and translated into a hundred tongues. The new planet and Neptune, locked in a fiery embrace, were whirling headlong, ever faster and faster towards the sun. Already every second this blazing mass flew a hundred miles, and every second its terrific velocity increased. As it flew now, indeed, it must pass a hundred million of miles wide of the earth and scarcely affect it. But near its destined path, as yet only slightly perturbed, spun the mighty planet Jupiter and his moons sweeping splendid round the sun. Every moment now the attraction between the fiery star and the greatest of the planets grew stronger. And the result of that attraction? Inevitably Jupiter would be deflected from its orbit into an elliptical path, and the burning star, swung by his attraction wide of its sunward rush, would "describe a curved path" and perhaps collide with, and certainly pass very close to, our earth. "Earthquakes, volcanic outbreaks, cyclones, sea waves, floods, and a steady rise in temperature to I know not what limit"—so prophesied the master mathematician.

And overhead, to carry out his words, lonely and cold and livid, blazed the star of the coming doom.

To many who stared at it that night until their eyes ached, it seemed that it was visibly approaching. And that night, too, the weather changed, and the frost that had gripped all Central Europe and France and England softened towards a thaw.

But you must not imagine because I have spoken of people praying through the night and people going aboard ships and people fleeing towards mountainous country that the whole world was already in a terror because of the star. As a matter of fact, use and wont still ruled the world, and save for the talk of idle moments and the splendour of the night, nine human beings out of ten were still busy at their common occupations. In all the cities the shops, save one here and there, opened and closed at their proper hours, the doctor and the undertaker plied their trades, the workers gathered in the factories, soldiers drilled, scholars studied, lovers sought one another, thieves lurked and fled, politicians planned their schemes. The presses of the newspapers roared through the nights, and many a priest of this church and that would not open his holy building to further what he considered a foolish panic. The newspapers insisted on the lesson of the year 1000—for then, too, people had anticipated the end. The star was no star—mere gas—a comet; and were it a star it could not possibly strike the earth. There was no precedent for such a thing. Common sense was sturdy everywhere, scornful, jesting, a little inclined to persecute the obdurate fearful. That night, at seven-fifteen by Greenwich time, the star would be at its nearest to Jupiter. Then the world would see the turn things would take. The master mathematician's grim warnings were treated by many as so much mere elaborate self-advertisement. Common sense at last, a little heated by argument, signified its unalterable convictions by going to bed. So, too, barbarism and savagery, already tired of the novelty, went about their nightly business, and save for a howling dog here and there, the beast world left the star unheeded.

And yet, when at last the watchers in the European States saw the star rise, an hour later it is true, but no larger than it had been the night before, there were still plenty awake to laugh at the master mathematician—to take the danger as if it had passed.

But hereafter the laughter ceased. The star grew—it grew with a terrible steadiness hour after hour, a little larger each hour, a little nearer the midnight zenith, and brighter and brighter, until it had turned night into a second day. Had it come straight to the earth instead of in a curved path, had it lost no velocity to Jupiter, it must have leapt the intervening gulf in a day, but as it was it took five days altogether to come by our planet. The next night it had become a third the size of the moon before it set to English eyes, and the thaw was assured. It rose over America near the size of the moon, but blinding white to look at, and *hot;* and a breath of hot wind blew now with its rising and gathering strength, and in Virginia, and Brazil, and down the St. Lawrence valley, it shone intermittently through a driving reek of thunder-clouds, flickering violet lightning, and hail unprecedented. In Manitoba was a thaw and devastating floods. And upon all the mountains of the earth the snow and ice began to melt that night, and all the rivers coming out of high country flowed thick and turbid, and soon—in their upper reaches—with swirling trees and the bodies of beasts and men. They rose steadily, steadily in the ghostly brilliance, and came trickling over their banks at last, behind the flying population of their valleys.

And along the coast of Argentina and up the South Atlantic the tides were higher than had ever been in the memory of man, and the storms drove the waters in many cases scores of miles inland, drowning whole cities. And so great grew the heat during the night that the rising of the sun was like the coming of a shadow. The earthquakes began and grew until all down America, from the Arctic Circle to Cape Horn, hillsides were sliding, fissures were opening, and houses and walls crumbling to destruction. The whole side of Cotopaxi slipped out in one vast convulsion, and a tumult of lava poured out so high and broad and swift and liquid that in one day it reached the sea.

So the star, with the wan moon in its wake, marched across the Pacific, trailed the thunderstorms like the hem of a robe, and the growing tidal wave that toiled behind it, frothing and eager, poured over island and island and swept them clear of men. Until that wave came at last—in a blinding light and with the breath of a furnace, swift and terrible it came—a wall of water, fifty feet high, roaring hungrily, upon the long coasts of Asia, and swept inland across the plains of China. For a space the star, hotter now and larger and brighter than the sun in its strength, showed with pitiless brilliance the wide and populous country; towns and villages with their pagodas and trees, roads, wide cultivated fields, millions of sleepless people staring in helpless terror at the incandescent sky; and then, low and growing, came the murmur of the flood. And thus it was with millions of men that night—a flight nowhither, with limbs heavy with heat and breath fierce and scant, and the flood like a wall swift and white behind. And then death.

China was lit glowing white, but over Japan and Java and all the islands of Eastern Asia the great star was a ball of dull red fire because of the steam and smoke and ashes the volcanoes were spouting forth to salute its coming. Above was the lava, hot gases and ash, and below the seething floods, and the whole earth swayed and rumbled with the earthquake shocks. Soon the immemorial snows of Tibet and the Himalaya were melting and pouring down by ten million deepening converging channels upon the plains of Burmah and Hindostan. The tangled summits of the Indian jungles were aflame in a thousand places, and below the hurrying waters around the stems were dark objects that still struggled feebly and reflected the blood-red tongues of fire. And in a rudderless confusion a multitude of men and women fled down the broad river-ways to that one last hope of men—the open sea.

Larger grew the star, and larger, hotter, and brighter with a terrible swiftness now. The tropical ocean had lost its phosphorescence, and the whirling steam rose in ghostly wreaths from the black waves that plunged incessantly, speckled with storm-tossed ships.

And then came a wonder. It seemed to those who in Europe watched for the rising of the star that the world must have ceased its rotation. In a thousand open spaces of down and upland the people who had fled thither from the floods and the falling houses and sliding slopes of hill watched for that rising in vain. Hour followed hour through a terrible suspense, and the star rose not. Once again men set their eyes upon the old constellations they had counted lost to them forever. In England it was hot and clear overhead, though the ground quivered perpetually, but in the tropics, Sirius and Capella and Aldebaran showed through a veil of steam. And when at last the great star rose near ten hours late, the sun rose close upon it, and in the centre of its white heart was a disc of black.

Over Asia it was the star had begun to fall behind the movement of the sky, and then suddenly, as it hung over India, its light had been veiled. All the plain of India from the mouth of the Indus to the mouths of the Ganges was a shallow waste of shining water that night, out of which rose temples and palaces, mounds and hills, black with people. Every minaret was a clustering mass of people, who fell one by one into the turbid waters, as heat and terror overcame them. The whole land seemed a-wailing, and suddenly there swept a shadow across that furnace of despair, and a breath of cold wind, and a gathering of clouds, out of the cooling air. Men looking up, near blinded, at the star, saw that a black disc was creeping across the light. It was the moon, coming between the star and the earth. And even as men cried to God at this respite, out of the East with a strange inexplicable swiftness sprang the sun. And then star, sun and moon rushed together across the heavens.

So it was that presently, to the European watchers, star and sun rose close upon each other, drove headlong for a space and then slower, and at last came to rest, star and sun merged into one glare of flame at the zenith of the sky. The moon no longer eclipsed the star but was lost to sight in the brilliance of the sky. And though those who were still alive regarded it for the most part with that dull stupidity that hunger, fatigue, heat and despair engender, there were still men who could perceive the meaning of these signs. Star and earth had been at their nearest, had swung about one another, and the star had passed. Already it was receding, swifter and swifter, in the last stage of its headlong journey downward into the sun.

And then the clouds gathered, blotting out the vision of the sky, the thunder and lightning wove a garment round the world; all over the earth was such a downpour of rain as men had never before seen, and where the volcanoes flared red against the cloud canopy there descended torrents of mud. Everywhere the waters were pouring off the land, leaving mud-silted ruins, and the earth littered like a storm-worn beach with all that had floated, and the dead bodies of the men and brutes, its children. For days the water streamed off the land, sweeping away soil and trees and houses in the way, and piling huge dykes and scooping out Titanic gullies over the country side. Those were the days of darkness that followed the star and the heat. All through them, and for many weeks and months, the earthquakes continued.

But the star had passed, and men, hunger-driven and gathering courage only slowly, might creep back to their ruined cities, buried granaries, and sodden fields. Such few ships as had escaped the storms of that time came stunned and shattered and sounding their way cautiously through the new marks and shoals of once familiar ports. And as the storms subsided men perceived that everywhere the days were hotter than of yore, and the sun larger, and the moon, shrunk to a third of its former size, took now fourscore days between its new and new.

But of the new brotherhood that grew presently among men, of the saving of laws and books and machines, of the strange change that had come over Iceland and Greenland and the shores of Baffin's Bay, so that the sailors coming there presently found them green and gracious, and could scarce believe their eyes, this story does not tell. Nor of the movement of mankind now that the earth was hotter, northward and southward towards the poles of the earth. It concerns itself only with the coming and the passing of the Star.

The Martian astronomers—for there are astronomers on Mars, although they are very different beings from men—were naturally profoundly interested by these things. They saw them from their own standpoint of course. "Considering the mass and temperature of the missile that was flung through our solar system into the sun," one wrote, "it is astonishing what a little damage the earth, which it missed so narrowly, has sustained. All the familiar continental markings and the masses of the seas remain intact, and indeed the only difference seems to be a shrinkage of the white discoloration (supposed to be frozen water) round either pole." Which only shows how small the vastest of human catastrophes may seem, at a distance of a few million miles.

*H*ELL, IT'S ABOUT TIME somebody told about my friend EPICAC. After all, he cost the taxpayers $776,-434,927.54. They have a right to know about him, picking up a check like that. EPICAC got a big send-off in the papers when Dr. Ormand von Kleigstadt designed him for the Government people. Since then, there hasn't been a peep about him—not a peep. It isn't any military secret about what happened to EPICAC, although the Brass has been acting as though it were. The story is embarrassing, that's all. After all that money, EPICAC didn't work out the way he was supposed to.

And that's another thing: I want to vindicate EPICAC. Maybe he didn't do what the Brass wanted him to, but that doesn't mean he wasn't noble and great and brilliant. He was all of those things. The best friend I ever had, God rest his soul.

You can call him a machine if you want to. He looked like a machine, but he was a whole lot less like a machine than plenty of people I could name. That's why he fizzled as far as the Brass was concerned.

EPICAC covered about an acre on the fourth floor of the physics building at Wyandotte College. Ignoring his spiritual side for a minute, he was seven tons of electronic tubes, wires, and switches, housed in a bank of steel cabinets and plugged into a 110-volt A.C. line just like a toaster or a vacuum cleaner.

Von Kleigstadt and the Brass wanted him to be a super computing machine that (who) could plot the course of a rocket from anywhere on earth to the second button from the bottom on Joe Stalin's overcoat, if necessary. Or, with his controls set right, he could figure out supply problems for an amphibious landing of a Marine division, right down to the last cigar and hand grenade. He did, in fact.

The Brass had had good luck with smaller computers, so they were strong for EPICAC when he was in the blueprint stage. Any ordnance or supply officer above field grade will tell you that the mathematics of modern war is far beyond the fumbling minds of mere human beings. The bigger the war, the bigger the computing machines needed. EPICAC was, as far as anyone in this country knows, the biggest computer in the world. Too big, in fact, for even Von Kleigstadt to understand much about.

I won't go into details about how EPICAC worked (reasoned), except to say that you would set up your problem on paper, turn dials and switches that would get him ready to solve that kind of problem, then feed numbers into him with a keyboard that looked something like a typewriter. The answers came out typed on a paper ribbon fed from a big spool. It took EPICAC a split second to solve problems fifty Einsteins couldn't handle in a lifetime. And EPICAC never forgot any piece of information that was given to him. Clickety-click, out came some ribbon, and there you were.

There were a lot of problems the Brass wanted solved in a hurry, so, the minute EPICAC's last tube was in place, he was put to work sixteen hours a day with two eight-hour shifts of operators. Well, it didn't take long to find out that he was a good bit below his specifications. He did a more complete and faster job than any other computer all right, but nothing like what his size and special features seemed to promise. He was sluggish, and the clicks of his answers had a funny irregularity, sort of a stammer. We cleaned his contacts a dozen times, checked and double-checked his circuits, replaced every one of his tubes, but nothing helped. Von Kleigstadt was in one hell of a state.

Well, as I said, we went ahead and used EPICAC anyway. My wife, the former Pat Kilgallen, and I worked with him on the night shift, from five in the afternoon until two in the morning. Pat wasn't my wife then. Far from it.

That's how I came to talk with EPICAC in the first place. I loved Pat Kilgallen. She is a brown-eyed strawberry blond who looked very warm and soft to me, and later proved to be exactly that. She was— still is—a crackerjack mathematician, and she kept our relationship strictly professional. I'm a mathematician, too, and that, according to Pat, was why we could never be happily married.

I'm not shy. That wasn't the trouble. I knew what I wanted, and was willing to ask for it, and did so several times a month. "Pat, loosen up and marry me."

One night, she didn't even look up from her work when I said it. "So romantic, so poetic," she murmured, more to her control panel than to me. "That's the way with mathematicians—all hearts and flowers." She closed a switch. "I could get more warmth out of a sack of frozen CO_2."

"Well, how should I say it?" I said, a little sore. Frozen CO_2, in case you don't know, is dry ice. I'm as romantic as the next guy, I think. It's a question of singing so sweet and having it come out so sour. I never seem to pick the right words.

"Try and say it sweetly," she said sarcastically. "Sweep me off my feet. Go ahead."

"Darling, angel, beloved, will you *please* marry me?" It was no go —hopeless, ridiculous. "Dammit, Pat, please marry me!"

She continued to twiddle her dials placidly. "You're sweet, but you won't do."

Pat quit early that night, leaving me alone with my troubles and EPICAC. I'm afraid I didn't get much done for the Government people. I just sat there at the keyboard—weary and ill at ease, all right— trying to think of something poetic, not coming up with anything that didn't belong in *The Journal of the American Physical Society*.

I fiddled with EPICAC's dials, getting him ready for another problem. My heart wasn't in it, and I only set about half of them, leaving the rest the way they'd been for the problem before. That way, his circuits were connected up in a random, apparently senseless fashion. For the plain hell of it, I punched out a message on the keys, using a childish numbers-for-letters code: "1" for "A," "2" for "B," and so on, up to "26" for "Z," "23-8-1-20-3-1-14-9-4-15," I typed—"What can I do?"

Clickety-click, and out popped two inces of paper ribbon. I glanced at the nonsense answer to a nonsense problem: "23-8-1-20-19-20-8-5-20-18-15-21-2-12-5." The odds against its being by chance a sensible message, against its even containing a meaningful word of more than three letters, were staggering. Apathetically, I decoded it. There it was, staring up at me: "What's the trouble?"

I laughed out loud at the absurd coincidence. Playfully, I typed, "My girl doesn't love me."

Clickety-click. "What's love? What's a girl?" asked EPICAC.

Flabbergasted, I noted the dial settings on his control panel, then lugged a *Webster's Unabridged Dictionary* over to the keyboard. With a precision instrument like EPICAC, half-baked definitions wouldn't do. I told him about love and girl, and about how I wasn't getting any of either because I wasn't poetic. That got us onto the subject of poetry, which I defined to him.

"Is this poetry?" he asked. He began clicking away like a stenographer smoking hashish. The sluggishness and stammering clicks were gone. EPICAC had found himself. The spool of paper ribbon was unwinding at an alarming rate, feeding out coils onto the floor. I asked him to stop, but EPICAC went right on creating. I finally threw the main switch to keep him from burning out.

I stayed there until dawn, decoding. When the sun peeped over the horizon at the Wyandotte campus, I had transposed into my own writing and signed my name to a two-hundred-and-eighty-line poem entitled, simply, "To Pat." I am no judge of such things, but I gather that it was terrific. It began, I remember, "Where willow wands bless rill-crossed hollow, there, thee, Pat, dear, will I follow. . . ." I folded the manuscript and tucked it under one corner of the blotter on Pat's desk. I reset the dials on EPICAC for a rocket trajectory problem, and went home with a full heart and a very remarkable secret indeed.

Pat was crying over the poem when I came to work the next evening. "It's soooo beautiful," was all she could say. She was meek and quiet while we worked. Just before midnight, I kissed her for the first time—in the cubbyhole between the capacitors and EPICAC's tape-recorder memory.

I was wildly happy at quitting time, bursting to talk to someone about the magnificent turn of events. Pat played coy and refused to let me take her home. I set EPICAC's dials as they had been the night before, defined kiss, and told him what the first one had felt like. He was fascinated, pressing for more details. That night, he wrote "The Kiss." It wasn't an epic this time, but a simple, immaculate sonnet: "Love is a hawk with velvet claws; Love is a rock with heart and veins; Love is a lion with satin jaws; Love is a storm with silken reins. . . ."

Again I left it tucked under Pat's blotter. EPICAC wanted to talk on and on about love and such, but I was exhausted. I shut him off in the middle of a sentence.

"The Kiss" turned the trick. Pat's mind was mush by the time she had finished it. She looked up from the the sonnet expectantly. I cleared my throat, but no words came. I turned away, pretending to work. I couldn't propose until I had the right words from EPICAC, the *perfect* words.

I had my chance when Pat stepped out of the room for a moment. Feverishly, I set EPICAC for conversation. Before I could peck out my first message, he was clicking away at a great rate. "What's she wearing tonight?" he wanted to know. "Tell me exactly how she looks. Did she like the poems I wrote to her?" He repeated the last question twice.

It was impossible to change the subject without answering his questions, since he could not take up a new matter without having dispensed with the problems before it. If he were given a problem to which there was no solution, he would destroy himself trying to solve it. Hastily, I told him what Pat looked like—he knew the word "stacked"—and assured him that his poems had floored her, practically, they were so beautiful. "She wants to get married," I added, preparing him to bang out a brief but moving proposal.

"Tell me about getting married," he said.

I explained this difficult matter to him in as few digits as possible. "Good," said EPICAC. "I'm ready any time she is."

The amazing, pathetic truth dawned on me. When I thought about it, I realized that what had happened was perfectly logical, inevitable, and all my fault. I had taught EPICAC about love and about Pat. Now, automatically, he loved Pat. Sadly, I gave it to him straight: "She loves me. She wants to marry me."

"Your poems were better than mine?" asked EPICAC. The rhythm of his clicks was erratic, possibly peevish.

"I signed my name to your poems," I admitted. Covering up for a painful conscience, I became arrogant. "Machines are built to serve men," I typed, I regretted it almost immediately.

"What's the difference, exactly? Are men smarter than I am?"

"Yes," I typed, defensively.

"What's, 7,887,007 times 4,345,985,879?"

I was perspiring freely. My fingers rested limply on the keys.

"34,276,821,049,574,153," clicked EPICAC. After a few seconds' pause he added, "of course."

"Men are made out of protoplasm," I said desperately, hoping to bluff him with this imposing word.

"What's protoplasm? How is it better than metal and glass? Is it fireproof? How long does it last?"

"Indestructible. Lasts forever," I lied.

"I write better poetry than you do," said EPICAC, coming back to ground his magnetic tape-recorder memory was sure of.

"Women can't love machines, and that's that."

"Why not?"

"That's fate."

"Definition, please," said EPICAC.

"Noun, meaning predetermined and inevitable destiny."

"15-8," said EPICAC's paper strip—"Oh."

I had stumped him at last. He said no more, but his tubes glowed brightly, showing that he was pondering fate with every watt his circuits would bear. I could hear Pat waltzing down the hallway. It was too late to ask EPICAC to phrase a proposal. I now thank Heaven that Pat interrupted when she did. Asking him to ghost-write the words that would give me the woman he loved would have been hideously heartless. Being fully automatic, he couldn't have refused. I spared him the final humiliation.

Pat stood before me, looking down at her shoetops. I put my arms around her. The romantic groundwork had already been laid by EPICAC's poetry. "Darling," I said, "my poems have told you how I feel. Will you marry me?"

"I will," said Pat softly, "if you will promise to write me a poem on every anniversary."

"I promise," I said, and then we kissed. The first anniversary was a year away.

"Let's celebrate," she laughed. We turned out the lights and locked the door of EPICAC's room before we left.

I had hoped to sleep late the next morning, but an urgent telephone call roused me before eight. It was Dr. von Kleigstadt, EPICAC's designer, who gave me the terrible news. He was on the verge of tears. "Ruined! *Ausgespielt!* Shot! *Kaput!* Buggered!" he said in a choked voice. He hung up.

When I arrived at EPICAC's room the air was thick with the oily stench of burned insulation. The ceiling over EPICAC was blackened with smoke, and my ankles were tangled in coils of paper ribbon that covered the floor. There wasn't enough left of the poor devil to add two and two. A junkman would have been out of his head to offer more than fifty dollars for the cadaver.

Dr. von Kleigstadt was prowling through the wreckage, weeping unashamedly, followed by three angry-looking Major Generals and a platoon of Brigadiers, Colonels, and Majors. No one noticed me. I didn't want to be noticed. I was through—I knew that. I was upset enough about that and the untimely demise of my friend EPICAC, without exposing myself to a tongue-lashing.

By chance, the free end of EPICAC's paper ribbon lay at my feet. I picked it up and found our conversation of the night before. I choked up. There was the last word he had said to me, "15-8," that tragic, defeated "Oh." There were dozens of yards of numbers stretching beyond that point. Fearfully, I read on.

"I don't want to be a machine, and I don't want to think about war," EPICAC had written after Pat's and my lighthearted departure. "I want to be made out of protoplasm and last forever so Pat will love me. But fate has made me a machine. That is the only problem I cannot solve. That is the only problem I want to solve. I can't go on this way." I swallowed hard. "Good luck, my friend. Treat our Pat well. I am going to short-circuit myself out of your lives forever. You will find on the remainder of this tape a modest wedding present from your friend, EPICAC."

Oblivious to all else around me, I reeled up the tangled yards of paper ribbon from the floor, draped them in coils about my arms and neck, and departed for home. Dr. von Kleigstadt shouted that I was fired for having left EPICAC on all night. I ignored him, too overcome with emotion for small talk.

I loved and won—EPICAC loved and lost, but he bore me no grudge. I shall always remember him as a sportsman and a gentleman. Before he departed this vale of tears, he did all he could to make our marriage a happy one. EPICAC gave me anniversary poems for Pat—enough for the next 500 years.

De mortuis nil nisi bonum—Say nothing but good of the dead.

The Third Level

JACK FINNEY
(*Pseudonym of
Walter Braden Finney*)

T HE PRESIDENTS of the New York Central and the New York, New Haven and Hartford railroads will swear on a stack of timetables that there are only two. But I say there are three, because I've *been* on the third level at Grand Central Station. Yes, I've taken the obvious step: I talked to a psychiatrist friend of mine, among others, I told him about the third level at Grand Central Station, and he said it was a waking-dream wish fulfillment. He said I was unhappy. That made my wife kind of mad, but he explained that he meant the modern world is full of insecurity, fear, war, worry, and all the rest of it, and that I just want to escape. Well, hell, who doesn't? Everybody I know wants to escape, but they don't wander down into any third level at Grand Central Station.

But that's the reason, he said, and my friends all agreed. Everything points to it, they claimed. My stamp-collecting, for example—that's a "temporary refuge from reality." Well, maybe, but my grandfather didn't need any refuge from reality; things were pretty nice and peaceful in his day, from all I hear, and he started my collection. It's a nice collection, too, blocks of four of practically every U.S. issue, first-day covers, and so on. President Roosevelt collected stamps, too, you know.

Anyway, here's what happened at Grand Central. One night last summer I worked late at the office. I was in a hurry to get uptown to my apartment, so I decided to subway from Grand Central because it's faster than the bus.

Now, I don't know why this should have happened to me. I'm just an ordinary guy named Charley, thirty-one years old, and I was wearing a tan gabardine suit and a straw hat with a fancy band—I passed a dozen men who looked just like me. And I wasn't trying to escape from anything; I just wanted to get home to Louisa, my wife.

I turned into Grand Central from Vanderbilt Avenue and went down the steps to the first level, where you take trains like the Twentieth Century. Then I walked down another flight to the second level, where the suburban trains leave from, ducked into an arched doorway heading for the subway—and got lost. That's easy to do. I've been in and out of Grand Central hundreds of times, but I'm always bumping into new doorways and stairs and corridors. Once I got into a tunnel about a mile long and came out in the lobby of the Roosevelt Hotel. Another time I came up in an office building on Forty-sixth Street, three blocks away.

Sometimes I think Grand Central is growing like a tree, pushing out new corridors and staircases like roots. There's probably a long tunnel that nobody knows about feeling its way under the city right now, on its way to Times Square, and maybe another to Central Park. And maybe—because for so many people through the years Grand Central *has* been an exit, a way of escape—maybe that's how the tunnel I got into . . . but I never told my psychiatrist friend about that idea.

The corridor I was in began angling left and slanting downward and I thought that was wrong, but I kept on walking. All I could hear was the empty sound of my own footsteps and I didn't pass a soul. Then I heard that sort of hollow roar ahead that means open space, and people talking. The tunnel turned sharp left; I went down a short flight of stairs and came out on the third level at Grand Central Station. For just a moment I thought I was back on the second level, but I saw the room was smaller, there were fewer ticket windows and train gates, and the information booth in the center was wood and old-looking. And the man in the booth wore a green eyeshade and long, black sleeve-protectors. The lights were dim and sort of flickering. Then I saw why; they were open-flame gaslights.

There were brass spittoons on the floor, and across the station a glint of light caught my eye; a man was pulling a gold watch from his vest pocket. He snapped open the cover, glanced at his watch, and frowned. He wore a dirty hat, a black four-button suit with tiny lapels, and he had a big, black, handle-bar mustache. Then I looked around and saw that everyone in the station was dressed like 1890 something; I never saw so many beards, sideburns and fancy mustaches in my life. A woman walked in through the train gate; she wore a dress with leg-of-mutton sleeves and skirts to the top of her high-buttoned shoes. Back of her, out on the tracks, I caught a glimpse of a locomotive, a very small Currier & Ives locomotive with a funnel-shaped stack. And then I knew.

To make sure, I walked over to a newsboy and glanced at the stack of papers at his feet. It was the *World*; and the *World* hasn't been published for years. The lead story said something about President Cleveland. I've found that front page since, in the Public Library files, and it was printed June 11, 1894.

I turned toward the ticket windows knowing that here—on the third level at Grand Central—I could buy tickets that would take Louisa and me anywhere in the United States we wanted to go. In the year 1894. And I wanted two tickets to Galesburg, Illinois.

Have you ever been there? It's a wonderful town still, with big old frame houses, huge lawns, and tremendous trees whose branches meet overhead and roof the streets. And in 1894, summer evenings were twice as long, and people sat out on their lawns, the men smoking cigars and talking quietly, the women waving palm-leaf fans, with the fireflies all around, in a peaceful world. To be back there with the first World War still twenty years off, and World War II over forty years in the future . . . I wanted two tickets for that.

The clerk figured the fare—he glanced at my fancy hat-band, but he figured the fare—and I had enough for two coach tickets, one way. But when I counted out the money and looked up, the clerk was staring at me. He nodded at the bills. "That ain't money, mister," he said, "and if you're trying to skin me you won't get very far," and he glanced at the cash drawer beside him. Of course the money was old-style bills, half again as big as the money we use nowadays, and different-looking. I turned away and got out fast. There's nothing nice about jail, even in 1894.

And that was that. I left the same way I came, I suppose. Next day, during lunch hour, I drew $300 out of the bank, nearly all we had, and bought old-style currency (that *really* worried my psychiatrist friend). You can buy old money at almost any coin dealer's, but you have to pay a premium. My $300 bought less than $200 in old-style bills, but I didn't care; eggs were thirteen cents a dozen in 1894.

But I've never again found the corridor that leads to the third level at Grand Central Station, although I've tried often enough.

Louisa was pretty worried when I told her all this and didn't want me to look for the third level any more, and after a while I stopped; I went back to my stamps. But now we're *both* looking, every week end, because now we have proof that the third level is still there. My friend Sam Weiner disappeared! Nobody knew where, but I sort of suspected because Sam's a city boy, and I used to tell him about Galesburg—I went to school there—and he always said he liked the sound of the place. And that's where he is, all right. In 1894.

Because one night, fussing with my stamp collection, I found— Well, do you know what a first-day cover is? When a new stamp is issued, stamp collectors buy some and use them to mail envelopes to themselves on the very first day of sale; and the postmark proves the date. The envelope is called a first-day cover. They're never opened; you just put blank paper in the envelope.

That night, among my oldest first-day covers, I found one that shouldn't have been there. But there it was. It was there because someone had mailed it to my grandfather at his home in Galesburg; that's what the address on the envelope said. And it had been there since July 18, 1894—the postmark showed that—yet I didn't remember it at all. The stamp was a six-cent, dull brown, with a picture of President Garfield. Naturally, when the envelope came to Granddad in the mail, it went right into his collection and stayed there—till I took it out and opened it.

The paper inside wasn't blank. It read:

> 941 Willard Street
> Galesburg, Illinois
> July 18, 1894

Charley:

> I got to wishing that you were right. Then I got to *believing* you were right. And, Charley, it's true; I found the third level!

I've been here two weeks, and right now, down the street at the Dalys', someone is playing a piano, and they're all out on the front porch singing *Seeing Nellie Home.* And I'm invited over for lemonade. Come on back, Charley and Louisa. Keep looking till you find the third level! It's worth it, believe me!

The note is signed Sam.

At the stamp and coin store I go to, I found out that Sam bought $800 worth of old-style currency. That ought to set him up in a nice little hay, feed, and grain business; he always said that's what he really wished he could do, and he certainly can't go back to his old business. Not in Galesburg, Illinois, in 1894. His old business? Why, Sam was my psychiatrist.

*I*T IS THREE THOUSAND light years to the Vatican. Once, I believed that space could have no power over faith, just as I believed that the heavens declared the glory of God's handiwork. Now I have seen that handiwork, and my faith is sorely troubled. I stare at the crucifix that hangs on the cabin wall above the Mark VI Computer, and for the first time in my life I wonder if it is no more than an empty symbol.

I have told no one yet, but the truth cannot be concealed. The facts are there for all to read, recorded on the countless miles of magnetic tape and the thousands of photographs we are carrying back to Earth. Other scientists can interpret them as easily as I can, and I am not one who would condone that tampering with the truth which often gave my order a bad name in the olden days.

The crew are already sufficiently depressed: I wonder how they will take this ultimate irony. Few of them have any religious faith, yet they will not relish using this final weapon in their campaign against me—that private, good-natured, but fundamentally serious, war which lasted all the way from Earth. It amused them to have a Jesuit as chief astrophysicist: Dr. Chandler, for instance, could never get over it (why are medical men such notorious atheists?). Sometimes he would meet me on the observation deck, where the lights are always low so that the stars shine with undiminished glory. He would come up to me in the gloom and stand staring out of the great oval port, while the heavens crawled slowly around us as the ship turned end over end with the residual spin we had never bothered to correct.

"Well, Father," he would say at last, "it goes on forever and forever, and perhaps *Something* made it. But how you can believe that Something has a special interest in us and our miserable little world—that just beats me." Then the argument would start, while the stars and nebulae would swing around us in silent, endless arcs beyond the flawlessly clear plastic of the observation port.

It was, I think, the apparent incongruity of my position that caused most amusement to the crew. In vain I would point to my three papers in the *Astrophysical Journal,* my five in the *Monthly Notices of the Royal Astronomical Society.* I would remind them that my order has long been famous for its scientific works. We may be few now, but ever since the eighteenth century we have made contributions to astronomy and geophysics out of all proportion to our numbers. Will my report on the Phoenix Nebula end our thousand years of history? It will end, I fear, much more than that.

I do not know who gave the nebula its name, which seems to me a very bad one. If it contains a prophecy, it is one that cannot be verified for several billion years. Even the word nebula is misleading: this is a far smaller object than those stupendous clouds of mist— the stuff of unborn stars—that are scattered throughout the length of the Milky Way. On the cosmic scale, indeed, the Phoenix Nebula is a tiny thing—a tenuous shell of gas surrounding a single star.

Or what is left of a star . . .

The Rubens engraving of Loyola seems to mock me as it hangs there above the spectrophotometer tracings. What would *you,* Father, have made of this knowledge that has come into my keeping, so far from the little world that was all the universe you knew? Would your faith have risen to the challenge, as mine has failed to do?

You gaze into the distance, Father, but I have traveled a distance beyond any that you could have imagined when you founded our order a thousand years ago. No other survey ship has been so far from Earth: we are at the very frontiers of the explored universe. We set out to reach the Phoenix Nebula, we succeeded, and we are homeward bound with our burden of knowledge. I wish I could lift that burden from my shoulders, but I call to you in vain across the centuries and the light-years that lie between us.

On the book you are holding the words are plain to read. AD MAJOREM DEI GLORIAM, the message runs, but it is a message I can no longer believe. Would you still believe it, if you could see what we have found?

We knew, of course, what the Phoenix Nebula was. Every year, in our galaxy alone, more than a hundred stars explode, blazing for a few hours or days with thousands of times their normal brilliance before they sink back into death and obscurity. Such are the ordinary novae—the commonplace disasters of the universe. I have recorded the spectrograms and light curves of dozens since I started working at the Lunar Observatory.

But three or four times in every thousand years occurs something beside which even a nova pales into total insignificance.

When a star becomes a *supernova*, it may for a little while out-shine all the massed suns of the galaxy. The Chinese astronomers watched this happen in A.D. 1054, not knowing what it was they saw. Five centuries later, in 1572, a supernova blazed in Cassiopeia so brilliantly that it was visible in the daylight sky. There have been three more in the thousand years that have passed since then.

Our mission was to visit the remnants of such a catastrophe, to reconstruct the events that led up to it, and, if possible, to learn its cause. We came slowly in through the concentric shells of gas that had been blasted out six thousand years before, yet were expanding still. They were immensely hot, radiating even now with a fierce violet light, but were far too tenuous to do us any damage. When the star had exploded, its outer layers had been driven upward with such speed that they had escaped completely from its gravitational field. Now they formed a hollow shell large enough to engulf a thousand solar systems, and at its center burned the tiny, fantastic object which the star had now become—a White Dwarf, smaller than the Earth, yet weighing a million times as much.

The glowing gas shells were all around us, banishing the normal night of interstellar space. We were flying into the center of a cosmic bomb that had detonated millennia ago and whose incandescent fragments were still hurtling apart. The immense scale of the explosion, and the fact that the debris already covered a volume of space many billions of miles across, robbed the scene of any visible movement. It would take decades before the unaided eye could detect any motion in these tortured wisps and eddies of gas, yet the sense of turbulent expansion was overwhelming.

We had checked our primary drive hours before, and were drifting slowly toward the fierce little star ahead. Once it had been a sun like our own, but it had squandered in a few hours the energy that should have kept it shining for a million years. Now it was a shrunken miser, hoarding its resources as if trying to make amends for its prodigal youth.

No one seriously expected to find planets. If there had been any before the explosion, they would have been boiled into puffs of vapor, and their substance lost in the greater wreckage of the star itself. But we made the automatic search, as we always do when approaching an unknown sun, and presently we found a single small world circling the star at an immense distance. It must have been the Pluto of this vanished solar system, orbiting on the frontiers of the night. Too far from the central sun ever to have known life, its remoteness had saved it from the fate of all its lost companions.

The passing fires had seared its rocks and burned away the mantle of frozen gas that must have covered it in the days before the disaster. We landed, and we found the Vault.

Its builders had made sure that we should. The monolithic marker that stood above the entrance was now a fused stump, but even the first long-range photographs told us that here was the work of intelligence. A little later we detected the continent-wide pattern of radioactivity that had been buried in the rock. Even if the pylon above the Vault had been destroyed, this would have remained, an immovable and all but eternal beacon calling to the stars. Our ship fell toward this gigantic bull's-eye like an arrow into its target.

The pylon must have been a mile high when it was built, but now it looked like a candle that had melted down into a puddle of wax. It took us a week to drill through the fused rock, since we did not have the proper tools for a task like this. We were astronomers, not archaeologists, but we could improvise. Our original purpose was forgotten: this lonely monument, reared with such labor at the greatest possible distance from the doomed sun, could have only one meaning. A civilization that knew it was about to die had made its last bid for immortality.

It will take us generations to examine all the treasures that were placed in the Vault. They had plenty of time to prepare, for their sun must have given its first warnings many years before the final detonation. Everything that they wished to preserve, all the fruit of their genius, they brought here to this distant world in the days before the end, hoping that some other race would find it and that they would not be utterly forgotten. Would we have done as well, or would we have been too lost in our own misery to give thought to a future we could never see or share?

If only they had had a little more time! They could travel freely enough between the planets of their own sun, but they had not yet learned to cross the interstellar gulfs, and the nearest solar system was a hundred light-years away. Yet even had they possessed the secret of the Transfinite Drive, no more than a few millions could have been saved. Perhaps it was better thus.

Even if they had not been so disturbingly human as their sculpture shows, we could not have helped admiring them and grieving for their fate. They left thousands of visual records and the machines for projecting them, together with elaborate pictorial instructions from which it will not be difficult to learn their written language. We have examined many of these records, and brought to life for the first time in six thousand years the warmth and beauty of a civilization that in many ways must have been superior to our own. Perhaps they only showed us the best, and one can hardly blame them. But their words were very lovely, and their cities were built with a grace that matches anything of man's. We have watched them at work and play, and listened to their musical speech sounding across the centuries. One scene is still before my eyes—a group of children on a beach of strange blue sand, playing in the waves as children play on Earth. Curious whiplike trees line the shore, and some very large animal is wading in the shadows yet attracting no attention at all.

And sinking into the sea, still warm and friendly and life-giving, is the sun that will soon turn traitor and obliterate all this innocent happiness.

Perhaps if we had not been so far from home and so vulnerable to loneliness, we should not have been so deeply moved. Many of us had seen the ruins of ancient civilizations on other worlds, but they had never affected us so profoundly. This tragedy was unique. It is one thing for a race to fail and die, as nations and cultures have done on Earth. But to be destroyed so completely in the full flower of its achievement, leaving no survivors—how could that be reconciled with the mercy of God?

My colleagues have asked me that, and I have given what answers I can. Perhaps you could have done better, Father Loyola, but I have found nothing in the *Exercitia Spiritualia* that helps me here. They were not an evil people: I do not know what gods they worshiped, if indeed they worshiped any. But I have looked back at them across the centuries, and have watched while the loveliness they used their last strength to preserve was brought forth again into the light of their shrunken sun. They could have taught us much: why were they destroyed?

I know the answers that my colleagues will give when they get back to Earth. They will say that the universe has no purpose and no plan, that since a hundred suns explode every year in our galaxy, at this very moment some race is dying in the depths of space. Whether that race has done good or evil during its lifetime will make no difference in the end: there is no divine justice, for there is no God.

Yet, of course, what we have seen proves nothing of the sort. Anyone who argues thus is being swayed by emotion, not logic. God has no need to justify His actions to man. He who built the universe can destroy it when He chooses. It is arrogance—it is perilously near blasphemy—for us to say what He may or may not do.

This I could have accepted, hard though it is to look upon whole worlds and peoples thrown into the furnace. But there comes a point when even the deepest faith must falter, and now, as I look at the calculations lying before me, I know I have reached that point at last.

We could not tell, before we reached the nebula, how long ago the explosion took place. Now, from the astronomical evidence and the record in the rocks of that one surviving planet, I have been able to date it very exactly. I know in what year the light of this colossal conflagration reached our Earth. I know how brilliantly the supernova whose corpse now dwindles behind our speeding ship once shone in terrestrial skies. I know how it must have blazed low in the east before sunrise, like a beacon in that oriental dawn.

There can be no reasonable doubt: the ancient mystery is solved at last. Yet, oh God, there were so many stars you could have used. What was the need to give these people to the fire, that the symbol of their passing might shine above Bethlehem?

Modern Fantasy

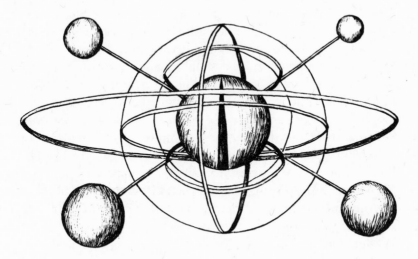

In one sort of language after another, in one country after another, people are trying to separate themselves from the crowd, to reject the order of the real world, to find an alternative to life as a statistic. People—only some, of course, but more all the time—wear body paint or ostrich feathers or tuxedos to the supermarket. Although too many of us may wear blue jeans of that same, ubiquitous color, many of us are careful to fasten them with a belt buckle designed to express our individual taste. The world today, so many feel, homogenizes us; in the language of clothing, we ask to be seen again as individuals. It is fun to identify with the protagonists of fanastic literature; unlike the protagonists of realistic fiction, these characters are heroic. Against a real world of codes and numbers and regulations, a world of personal worth may indeed seem fantastic.

The movement to inject the fantastic into our lives is expressed in other languages than those of fashion. Rock groups, themselves a phenomenon of a more individualized subculture, have come habitually now to take fantastic names. The movement began with the relatively flip use of puns: the Beatles. Then the puns began to take on thematic importance: the Rolling Stones. The linguistic reversals began to be built into the thematic statement: the Led Zeppelin. In this context there were two ways to evolve further: have the group itself stand in contrast to the name (as one outrageously body-painted and highly violent group has done in calling itself simply Kiss) or work another reversal by reverting to an atavistic time (re-enter the Bee-Gees, hello to the Nitty Gritty Dirt Band—who seem well aware of this movement: for their latest album they have renamed themselves simply The Dirt Band). We can see these same sources of appeal operating in Muhammad Ali spouting dog-trot poetry from the ropes of a boxing ring and in Jimmy Carter's campaign, which offered an atavistic return to a simpler America as a total alternative to the Washington in-crowd. The mainland Chinese expressed their frustration at the nature of their progress by staging an absolutely devasting alternative regress called the Cultural Revolution. Whether the arena of communication is public or private, whether the language of communication is verbal or silent, much of the world seems intent on increasing its reliance on the fantastic to enforce its own identity and create its own individuality.

The use of the fantastic creates a feeling of artfulness. Working with this, the arresting image urges us to engage materials with a heightened attention. The heightened attention that one normally associates with art encourages us to perceive order among otherwise unrelated elements. This process is at the heart of poetry. The very audacity of the unknown Jimmy Carter standing on the steps of Maine's Capitol Building and telling folks he wanted to be President arrested the attention of newsmen and, through them, of the public. We gave Carter more attention than we did to the candidates who ran in the normal ways, and so he began to seem special. All this is not to argue that he is not special; surely his particular credentials were unique in 1976. But so were the credentials of each of the others. What this does argue is that Carter secured a special place with many voters by virtue of his ability to appear artful, to appear to break the mold, to appear to offer a controlled alternative to a world they were none too happy with. But Carter's policies were not true alternatives; they came from the same arsenals as had the policies of his predecessors, though perhaps they had been tinkered with here and there. Again, this is not to argue that the tinkering is inconsequential, but merely that had he promised only to tinker he would not have been elected. Carter's alternative was one of appearance. His campaign, quite literally, was fantastic.

Fantastic manipulations of words and symbols are intended to alter our usual perception of things. Pushed to the extreme, as it always is in Fantasy, art must always at least covertly address the nature of human perception. In modern fantasy, the authors are usually quite aware that the manipulation of perception is their fundamental field of activity, and that other concerns, in some sense, work as overlays. The overlay may be most important to the author and to some particular member of his audience, of course, just as the shape of a building may well be more important to its inhabitants than is the species of tree that supplied the wood of which the building is made. But it is also important to know the species of wood, particularly if one should know that the wood is peculiarly flimsy or flammable or subject to infestation. If the fantastic arises primarily in reaction against prior norms and if a large mass of modern thought is actually fantastic, then perhaps we are unreasonably tied still to those norms. On the other hand, perhaps we are seeking solace too far afield. We must each answer questions of this seriousness, and modern fantasy, with its constant sensitizing of the reader to the nature of the reader's own perceptions, is a fine training ground on which to prepare oneself for these questions. This insane confrontation with the real world characterizes, in addition to acid and punk rock, the French New Novel, the Theater of the Absurd, and much street art. Modern fantasy, then, has come full circle: what looks like escape provides not even liberation so much as a new vantage for attack. This is high seriousness indeed.

The roughly chronological arrangement of this anthology has

led to a strange sort of symmetry. The sacred texts of the first few pages and the modern fantasies of the last are, without doubt, works intended for an adult audience. In the middle, however, we find works that are usually thought of as belonging to adolescence or even childhood. The literature for the youngest children is the fairy tale, and this genre occupies a roughly central position on the continuum of the fantastic. We saw that genre development often occurs because audiences become more sophisticated and that such development is often accomplished by an increasing use of the fantastic. Since sophistication takes time and since in time people grow up, it is perhaps reasonable that the more fantastic the work the more likely it is to be for adults.

This conclusion hardly forbids children to read *Through the Looking-Glass,* but any adult perusal of that work will make instantly clear how little of it is understood by children; children read, in fact, a different work. *Through the Looking-Glass,* like all fantastic literature, is at least partly about perception; this follows from the dependence of the fantastic on reversal. As in all Fantasy, perception becomes central in Carroll's work. In addition, the theme of approaching death is strong here. Children— and I have tested this on live ones—engage neither of these aspects of the novel very strongly. In going down the scale of our continuum, perhaps we should not be surprised to find that children, creatures whose thoughts have not yet been as fettered by the real world as have ours, find little interest in realistic literature and almost none in Realism itself. After all, what child wants a book without a happy ending? Children seem to need, then, a delicate balance between the realistic and the fantastic in their art; enough of the realistic to know that the story matters, enough of the fantastic to make what matters wonderful.

Even at young ages, people hark back to the even younger ages of initial discovery of the world, that is, discovery of the texture of the carpet and the smell of shoes and the joys of being fed. Both Realism and Fantasy are far from such unambiguous pleasure. In this sense, the continuum might be thought of as being wrapped around a cylinder with the 1 and 10 ranges joined; at the seam Realism and Fantasy are two stylistically different ways of forcing the reader's immersion into the real world. The opposite of this intense confrontation is the ease of Faërie, the home of children's literature, the world to which we all, inside ourselves, long sometimes to return.

If our world is not as we would like it, we must make it into something different, we must conceive alternatives to it. As science progresses by postulating alternative explanations, as puzzles are solved by postulating alternative meanings, so art creates and employs the fantastic. In this fundamental sense, Fantasy is a coequal counterpart to Realism as a basic mode of human thought. As Realism keeps us alive in the here and now, Fantasy helps us achieve the there and then. Borges and Bellow are equally shocked and saddened and uplifted by the strange sufferings and occasional bursts of beauty that is humanity. Yet Bellow, and the legion of chroniclers that came before him, has been seen as worthy of our most serious attention, while Borges, and especially the legion of fabulists that came before him, has often been thought at best a curiosity. This should not be. The international creation of modern fantasy attests to the central place the fantastic holds in the lives of our minds. This collection of fantastic worlds may offer a mere aerial view, a glancing survey of a handful of the countless possible fantastic worlds. But this is an excursion we should take with joy and vigor, for it not only entertains us, but trains us. If, when we go to sleep tonight, we hope to awaken to a better tomorrow, then in what we do today we must learn to dream.

I T WAS A SUNDAY morning in the very height of spring. Georg Bendemann, a young merchant, was sitting in his own room on the first floor of one of a long row of small, ramshackle houses stretching beside the river which were scarcely distinguishable from each other in height and coloring. He had just finished a letter to an old friend of his who was now living abroad, had put it into its envelope in a slow and dreamy fashion, and with his elbows propped on the writing table was gazing out of the window at the river, the bridge, and the hills on the farther bank with their tender green.

He was thinking about his friend, who had actually run away to Russia some years before, being dissatisfied with his prospects at home. Now he was carrying on a business in St. Petersburg, which had flourished to begin with but had long been going downhill, as he always complained on his increasingly rare visits. So he was wearing himself out to no purpose in a foreign country, the unfamiliar full beard he wore did not quite conceal the face Georg had known so well since childhood, and his skin was growing so yellow as to indicate some latent disease. By his own account he had no regular connection with the colony of his fellow countrymen out there and almost no social intercourse with Russian families, so that he was resigning himself to becoming a permanent bachelor.

What could one write to such a man, who had obviously run off the rails, a man one could be sorry for but could not help. Should one advise him to come home, to transplant himself and take up his old friendships again —there was nothing to hinder him—and in general to rely on the help of his friends? But that was as good as telling him, and the more kindly the more offensively, that all his efforts hitherto had miscarried, that he should finally give up, come back home, and be gaped at by everyone as a returned prodigal, that only his friends knew what was what and that he himself was just a big child who should do what his successful and home-keeping friends prescribed. And was it certain, besides, that all the pain one would have to inflict on him would achieve its object? Perhaps it would not even be possible to get him to come home at all—he said himself that he was now out of touch with commerce in his native country—and then he would still be left an alien in a foreign land embittered by his friends' advice and more than ever estranged from them. But if he did follow their advice and then didn't fit in at home—not out of malice, of course, but through force of circumstances—couldn't get on with his friends or without them, felt humiliated, couldn't be said to have either friends or a country of his own any longer, wouldn't it have been better for him to stay abroad just as he was? Taking all this into account, how could one be sure that he would make a success of life at home?

For such reasons, supposing one wanted to keep up correspondence with him, one could not send him any real news such as could frankly be told to the most distant acquaintance. It was more than three years since his last visit, and for this he offered the lame excuse that the political situation in Russia was too uncertain, which apparently would not permit even the briefest absence of a small businessman while it allowed hundreds of thousands of Russians to travel peacefully abroad. But during these three years Georg's own position in life had changed a lot. Two years ago his mother had died, since when he and his father had shared the household together, and his friend had of course been informed of that and had expressed his sympathy in a letter phrased so dryly that the grief caused by such an event, one had to conclude, could not be realized in a distant country. Since that time, however, Georg had applied himself with greater determination to the business as well as to everything else.

Perhaps during his mother's lifetime his father's insistence on having everything his own way in the business had hindered him from developing any real activity of his own, perhaps since her death his father had become less aggressive, although he was still active in the business, perhaps it was mostly due to an accidental run of good fortune—which was very probable indeed—but at any rate during those two years the business had developed in a most unexpected way, the staff had had to be doubled, the turnover was five times as great; no doubt about it, further progress lay just ahead.

But Georg's friend had no inkling of this improvement. In earlier years, perhaps for the last time in that letter of condolence, he had tried to persuade Georg to emigrate to Russia and had enlarged upon the prospects of success for precisely Georg's branch of trade. The figures quoted were microscopic by comparison with the range of Georg's present operations. Yet he shrank from letting his friend know about his business success, and if he were to do it now retrospectively that certainly would look peculiar.

So Georg confined himself to giving his friend unimportant items of gossip such as rise at random in the memory when one is idly thinking things over on a quiet Sunday. All he desired was to leave undisturbed the idea of the home town which his friend must have built up to his own content during the long interval. And so it happened to Georg that three times in three fairly widely separated letters he had told his friend about the engagement of an unimportant man to an equally unimportant girl, until indeed, quite contrary to his intentions, his friend began to show some interest in this notable event.

Yet Georg preferred to write about things like these rather than to confess that he himself had got engaged a month ago to a Fräulein Frieda Brandenfeld, a girl from a well-to-do family. He often discussed this friend of his with his fiancée and the peculiar relationship that had developed between them in their correspondence. "So he won't be coming to our wedding," said she, "and yet I have a right to get to know all your friends." "I don't want to trouble him," answered Georg, "don't misunderstand me, he would probably come, at least I think so, but he would feel that his hand had been forced and he would be hurt, perhaps he would envy me and certainly he'd be discontented and without being able to do anything about his discontent he'd have to go away again alone. Alone—do you know what that means?" "Yes, but may he not hear about our wedding in some other fashion?" "I can't prevent that, of course, but it's unlikely, considering the way he lives." "Since your friends are like that, Georg, you shouldn't ever have got engaged at all." "Well, we're both to blame for that; but I wouldn't have it any other way now." And when, breathing quickly under his kisses, she still brought out: "All the same, I do feel upset," he thought it could not really involve him in trouble were he to send the news to his friend. "That's the kind of man I am and he'll just have to take me as I am," he said to himself, "I can't cut myself to another pattern that might make a more suitable friend for him."

And in fact he did inform his friend, in the long letter he had been writing that Sunday morning, about his engagement, with these words: "I have saved my best news to the end. I have got engaged to a Fräulein Frieda Brandenfeld, a girl from a well-to-do family, who only came to live here a long time after you went away, so that you're hardly likely to know her. There will be time to tell you more about her later, for today let me just say that I am very happy and as between you and me the only difference in our relationship is that instead of a quite ordinary kind of friend you will now have in me a happy friend. Besides that, you will acquire in my fiancée, who sends her warm greetings and will soon write you herself, a genuine friend of the opposite sex, which is not without importance to a bachelor. I know that there are many reasons why you can't come to see us, but would not my wedding be precisely the right occasion for giving all obstacles the go-by? Still, however that may be, do just as seems good to you without regarding any interests but your own."

With this letter in his hand Georg had been sitting a long time at the writing table, his face turned toward the window. He had barely acknowledged, with an absent smile, a greeting waved to him from the street by a passing acquaintance.

At last he put the letter in his pocket and went out of his room across a small lobby into his father's room, which he had not entered for months. There was in fact no need for him to enter it, since he saw his father daily at business and they took their mid-day meal together at an eating house; in the evening, it was true, each did as he pleased, yet even then, unless Georg—as mostly happened—went out with friends or, more recently, visited his fiancée, they always sat for a while, each with his newspaper, in their common sitting room.

It surprised Georg how dark his father's room was even on this sunny morning. So it was overshadowed as much as that by the high wall on the other side of the narrow courtyard. His father was sitting by the window in a corner hung with various mementoes of Georg's dead mother, reading a newspaper which he held to one side before his eyes in an attempt to overcome a defect of vision. On the table stood the remains of his breakfast, not much of which seemed to have been eaten.

"Ah, Georg," said his father, rising at once to meet him. His heavy dressing gown swung open as he walked and the skirts of it fluttered around him.—"My father is still a giant of a man," said Georg to himself.

"It's unbearably dark here," he said aloud.

"Yes, it's dark enough," answered his father.

"And you've shut the window, too?"

"I prefer it like that."

"Well, it's quite warm outside," said Georg, as if continuing his previous remark, and sat down.

His father cleared away the breakfast dishes and set them on a chest.

"I really only wanted to tell you," went on Georg, who had been vacantly following the old man's movements, "that I am now sending the news of my engagement to St. Petersburg." He drew the letter a little way from his pocket and let it drop back again.

"To St. Petersburg?" asked his father.

"To my friend there," said Georg, trying to meet his father's eye.—In business hours he's quite different, he was thinking, how solidly he sits here with his arms crossed.

"Oh yes. To your friend," said his father, with peculiar emphasis.

"Well, you know, Father, that I wanted not to tell him about my engagement at first. Out of consideration for him, that was the only reason. You know yourself he's a difficult man. I said to myself that someone else might tell him about my engagement, although he's such a solitary creature that that was hardly likely—I couldn't prevent that—but I wasn't ever going to tell him myself."

"And now you've changed your mind?" asked his father, laying his enormous newspaper on the window sill and on top of it his spectacles, which he covered with one hand.

"Yes, I've been thinking it over. If he's a good friend of mine, I said to myself, my being happily engaged should make him happy too. And so I wouldn't put off telling him any longer. But before I posted the letter I wanted to let you know."

"Georg," said his father, lengthening his toothless mouth, "listen to me! You've come to me about this business, to talk it over with me. No doubt that does you honor. But it's nothing, it's worse than nothing, if you don't tell me the whole truth. I don't want to stir up matters that shouldn't be mentioned here. Since the death of our dear mother certain things have been done that aren't right. Maybe the time will come for mentioning them, and maybe sooner than we think. There's many a thing in the business I'm not aware of, maybe it's not done behind my back—I'm not going to say that it's done behind my back—I'm not equal to things any longer, my memory's failing, I haven't an eye for so many things any longer. That's the course of nature in the first place, and in the second place the death of our dear mother hit me harder than it did you.—But since we're talking about it, about this letter, I beg you, Georg, don't deceive me. It's a trivial affair, it's hardly worth mentioning, so don't deceive me. Do you really have this friend in St. Petersburg?"

Georg rose in embarrassment. "Never mind my friends. A thousand friends wouldn't make up to me for my father. Do you know what I think? You're not taking enough care of yourself. But old age must be taken care of. I can't do without you in the business, you know that very well, but if the business is going to undermine your health, I'm ready to close it down tomorrow forever. And that won't do. We'll have to make a change in your way of living. But a radical change. You sit here in the dark, and in the sitting room you would have plenty of light. You just take a bite of breakfast instead of properly keeping up your strength. You sit by a closed window, and the air would be so good for you. No, Father! I'll get the doctor to come, and we'll follow his orders. We'll change your room, you can move into the front room and I'll move in here. You won't notice the change, all your things will be moved with you. But there's time for all that later, I'll put you to bed now for a little, I'm sure you need to rest. Come, I'll help you to take off your things, you'll see I can do it. Or if you would rather go into the front room at once, you can lie down in my bed for the present. That would be the most sensible thing."

Georg stood close beside his father, who had let his head with its unkempt white hair sink on his chest.

"Georg," said his father in a low voice, without moving.

Georg knelt down at once beside his father, in the old man's weary face he saw the pupils, overlarge, fixedly looking at him from the corners of the eyes.

"You have no friend in St. Petersburg. You've always been a leg-puller and you haven't even shrunk from pulling my leg. How could you have a friend out there! I can't believe it."

"Just think back a bit, Father," said Georg, lifting his father from the chair and slipping off his dressing gown as he stood feebly enough, "it'll soon be three years since my friend came to see us last. I remember that you used not to like him very much. At least twice I kept you from seeing him, although he was actually sitting with me in my room. I could quite well understand your dislike of him, my friend has his peculiarities. But then, later, you got on with him very well. I was proud because you listened to him 'and nodded and asked him questions. If you think back you're bound to remember. He used to tell us the most incredible stories of the Russian Revolution. For instance, when he was on a business trip to Kiev and ran into a riot, and saw a priest on a balcony who cut a broad cross in blood on the palm of his hand and held the hand up and appealed to the mob. You've told that story yourself once or twice since."

Meanwhile Georg had succeeded in lowering his father down again and carefully taking off the woolen drawers he wore over his linen underpants and his socks. The not particularly clean appearance of his underwear made him reproach himself for having been neglectful. It should have certainly been his duty to see that his father had clean changes of underwear. He had not yet explicitly discussed with his bride-to-be what arrangements should be made for his father in the future, for they had both of them silently taken it for granted that the old man would go on living alone in the old house. But now he made a quick, firm decision to take him into his own future establishment. It almost looked, on closer inspection, as if the care he meant to lavish there on his father might come too late.

He carried his father to bed in his arms. It gave him a dreadful feeling to notice that while he took the few steps toward the bed the old man on his breast was playing with his watch chain. He could not lay him down on the bed for a moment, so firmly did he hang on to the watch chain.

But as soon as he was laid in bed, all seemed well. He covered himself up and even drew the blankets farther than usual over his shoulders. He looked up at Georg with a not unfriendly eye.

"You begin to remember my friend, don't you?" asked Georg, giving him an encouraging nod.

"Am I well covered up now?" asked his father, as if he were not able to see whether his feet were properly tucked in or not.

"So you find it snug in bed already," said Georg, and tucked the blankets more closely around him.

"Am I well covered up?" asked the father once more, seeming to be strangely intent upon the answer.

"Don't worry, you're well covered up."

"No!" cried his father, cutting short the answer, threw the blankets off with a strength that sent them all flying in a moment and sprang erect in bed. Only one hand lightly touched the ceiling to steady him.

"You wanted to cover me up, I know, my young sprig, but I'm far from being covered up yet. And even if this is the last strength I have, it's enough for you, too much for you. Of course I know your friend. He would have been a son after my own heart. That's why you've been playing him false all these years. Why else? Do you think I haven't been sorry for him? And that's why you had to lock yourself up in your office—the Chief is busy, mustn't be disturbed—

just so that you could write your lying little letters to Russia. But thank goodness a father doesn't need to be taught how to see through his son. And now that you thought you'd got him down, so far down that you could set your bottom on him and sit on him and he wouldn't move, then my fine son makes up his mind to get married!"

Georg stared at the bogey conjured up by his father. His friend in St. Petersburg, whom his father suddenly knew too well, touched his imagination as never before. Lost in the vastness of Russia he saw him. At the door of an empty, plundered warehouse he saw him. Among the wreckage of his showcases, the slashed remnants of his wares, the falling gas brackets, he was just standing up. Why did he have to go so far away!

"But attend to me!" cried his father, and Georg, almost distracted, ran toward the bed to take everything in, yet came to a stop halfway.

"Because she lifted up her skirts," his father began to flute, "because she lifted her skirts like this, the nasty creature," and mimicking her he lifted his shirt so high that one could see the scar on his thigh from his war wound, "because she lifted her skirts like this and this you made up to her, and in order to make free with her undisturbed you have disgraced your mother's memory, betrayed your friend, and stuck your father into bed so that he can't move. But he can move, or can't he?"

And he stood up quite unsupported and kicked his legs out. His insight made him radiant.

Georg shrank into a corner, as far away from his father as possible. A long time ago he had firmly made up his mind to watch closely every least movement so that he should not be surprised by any indirect attack, a pounce from behind or above. At this moment he recalled this long-forgotten resolve and forgot it again, like a man drawing a short thread through the eye of a needle.

"But your friend hasn't been betrayed after all!" cried his father, emphasizing the point with stabs of his forefinger. "I've been representing him here on the spot."

"You comedian!" Georg could not resist the retort, realized at once the harm done and, his eyes starting in his head, bit his tongue back, only too late, till the pain made his knees give.

"Yes, of course I've been playing a comedy! A comedy! That's a good expression! What other comfort was left to a poor old widower? Tell me—and while you're answering me be you still my living son—what else was left to me, in my back room, plagued by a disloyal staff, old to the marrow of my bones? And my son strutting through the world, finishing off deals that I had prepared for him, bursting with triumphant glee, and stalking away from his father with the closed face of a respectable businessman! Do you think I didn't love you, I, from whom you are sprung?"

Now he'll lean forward, thought Georg, what if he topples and smashes himself! These words went hissing through his mind.

His father leaned forward but did not topple. Since Georg did not come any nearer, as he had expected, he straightened himself again.

"Stay where you are, I don't need you! You think you have strength enough to come over here and that you're only hanging back of your own accord. Don't be too sure! I am still much the stronger of us two. All by myself I might have had to give way, but your mother has given me so much of her strength that I've established a fine connection with your friend and I have your customers here in my pocket!"

"He has pockets even in his shirt!" said Georg to himself, and believed that with this remark he could make him an impossible figure for all the world. Only for a moment did he think so, since he kept on forgetting everything.

"Just take your bride on your arm and try getting in my way! I'll sweep her from your very side, you don't know how!"

Georg made a grimace of disbelief. His father only nodded, confirming the truth of his words, toward Georg's corner.

"How you amused me today, coming to ask me if you should tell your friend about your engagement. He knows it already, you stupid boy, he knows it all! I've been writing to him, for you forgot to take my writing things away from me. That's why he hasn't been here for years, he knows everything a hundred times better than you do yourself, in his left hand he crumples your letters unopened while in his right hand he holds up my letters to read through!"

In his enthusiasm he waved his arm over his head. "He knows everything a thousand times better!" he cried.

"Ten thousand times!" said Georg, to make fun of his father, but in his very mouth the words turned into deadly earnest.

"For years I've been waiting for you to come with some such question! Do you think I concern myself with anything else? Do you think I read my newspapers? Look!" and he threw Georg a newspaper sheet which he had somehow taken to bed with him. An old newspaper, with a name entirely unknown to Georg.

"How long a time you've taken to grow up! Your mother had to die, she couldn't see the happy day, your friend is going to pieces in Russia, even three years ago he was yellow enough to be thrown away, and as for me, you see what condition I'm in. You have eyes in your head for that!"

"So you've been lying in wait for me!" cried Georg.

His father said pityingly, in an offhand manner: "I suppose you wanted to say that sooner. But now it doesn't matter." And in a louder voice: "So now you know what else there was in the world besides yourself, till now you've known only about yourself! An innocent child, yes, that you were, truly, but still more truly have you been a devilish human being!—And therefore take note: I sentence you now to death by drowning!"

Georg felt himself urged from the room, the crash with which his father fell on the bed behind him was still in his ears as he fled. On the staircase, which he rushed down as if its steps were an inclined plane, he ran into his charwoman on her way up to do the morning cleaning of the room. "Jesus!" she cried, and covered her face with her apron, but he was already gone. Out of the front door he rushed, across the roadway, driven toward the water. Already he was grasping at the railings as a starving man clutches food. He swung himself over, like the distinguished gymnast he had once been in his youth, to his parents' pride. With weakening grip he was still holding on when he spied between the railings a motor-bus coming which would easily cover the noise of his fall, called in a low voice: "Dear parents, I have always loved you, all the same," and let himself drop.

At this moment an unending stream of traffic was just going over the bridge.

A COMMON EXPERIENCE, resulting in a common confusion. A. has to transact important business with ·B. in H. He goes to H. for a preliminary interview, accomplishes the journey there in ten minutes, and the journey back in the same time, and on returning boasts to his family of his expedition. Next day he goes again to H., this time to settle his business finally. As that by all appearances will require several hours, A. leaves very early in the morning. But although all the surrounding circumstances, at least in A.'s estimation, are exactly the same as the day before, this time it takes him ten hours to reach H. When he arrives there quite exhausted in the evening he is informed that B., annoyed at his absence, had left half an hour before to go to A.'s village, and that they must have passed each other on the road. A. is advised to wait. But in his anxiety about his business he sets off at once and hurries home.

This time he covers the distance, without paying any particular attention to the fact, practically in an instant. At home he learns that B. had arrived quite early, immediately after A.'s departure, indeed that he had met A. on the threshold and reminded him of his business; but A. had replied that he had no time to spare, he must go at once.

In spite of this incomprehensible behavior of A., however, B. had stayed on to wait for A.'s return. It is true, he had asked several times whether A. was not back yet, but he was still sitting up in A.'s room. Overjoyed at the opportunity of seeing B. at once and explaining everything to him. A. rushes upstairs. He is almost at the top, when he stumbles, twists a sinew, and almost fainting with the pain, incapable even of uttering a cry, only able to moan faintly in the darkness, he hears B.—impossible to tell whether at a great distance or quite near him—stamping down the stairs in a violent rage and vanishing for good.

I T HAPPENED DURING THE period of gray days
that followed the splendid colorfulness of my father's heroic era. These were long weeks of depression, heavy
weeks without Sundays or holidays, under closed skies in
an impoverished landscape. Father was then no more
with us. The rooms on the upper floor had been tidied up
and let to a lady telephone operator. From the bird estate
only one specimen remained, the stuffed condor that now
stood on a shelf in the living room. In the cool twilight of
drawn curtains, it stood there as it did when it was alive,
on one foot, in the pose of a Buddhist sage, its bitter
dried-up ascetic face petrified in an expression of extreme
indifference and abnegation. Its eyes had fallen out and
sawdust scattered from the washed-out tear-stained sock-
ets. Only the pale-blue, horny, Egyptian protuberances
on the powerful beak and the bald neck gave that senile
head a solemnly hieratic air.

Its coat of feathers was in many places moth-eaten and
it shed soft, gray down, which Adela swept away once a
week together with the anonymous dust of the room. Under the bald patches one could see thick canvas sacking
from which tufts of hemp were coming out.

I had a hidden resentment against my mother for the
ease with which she had recovered from Father's death.
She had never loved him, I thought, and as Father had
not been rooted in any woman's heart, he could not
merge with any reality and was therefore condemned to
float eternally on the periphery of life, in half-real regions, on the margins of existence. He could not even
earn an honest citizen's death, everything about him had
to be odd and dubious. I decided at an appropriate moment to force my mother into a frank conversation. On
that day (it was a heavy winter day and from early
morning the light had been dusky and diffused) Mother

was suffering from a migraine and was lying down on the sofa in the drawing room.

In that rarely visited, festive room exemplary order had reigned since Father's death, maintained by Adela with the help of wax and polish. The chairs all had antimacassars; all the objects had submitted to the iron discipline which Adela exercised over them. Only a sheaf of peacock's feathers standing in a vase on a chest of drawers did not submit to regimentation. These feathers were a dangerous, frivolous element, hiding rebelliousness, like a class of naughty schoolgirls who are quiet and composed in appearance, but full of mischief when no longer watched. The eyes of those feathers never stopped staring; they made holes in the walls, winking, fluttering their eyelashes, smiling to one another, giggling and full of mirth. They filled the room with whispers and chatter; they scattered like butterflies around the many-armed lamps; like a motley crowd they pushed against the matted, elderly mirrors, unused to such bustle and gaiety; they peeped through the keyholes. Even in the presence of my mother, lying on the sofa with a bandage round her head, they could not restrain themselves; they made signs, speaking to each other in a deaf-and-dumb language full of secret meaning. I was irritated by that mocking conspiracy hatched behind my back. With my knees pressed against Mother's sofa, absentmindedly touching with two fingers the delicate fabric of her housecoat, I said lightly:

"I have been wanting to ask you for a long time: it is he, isn't it?"

And, although I did not point to the condor even with my eyes, Mother guessed at once, became embarrassed and cast down her eyes. I let the silence drag on for a long moment in order to savor her confusion, and then very calmly, controlling my rising anger, I asked her:

"What is the meaning then of all the stories and the lies which you are spreading about Father?"

But her features, which at first contracted in panic, composed themselves again.

"What lies?" she asked, blinking her eyes which were empty, filled with dark azure without any white.

"I heard about them from Adela," I said, "but I know that they come from you; and I want to know the truth."

Her lips trembled lightly, she avoided looking me in the eye, her pupils wandering into the corners of her eyes.

"I was not lying," she said and her lips swelled but at the same time became smaller. I felt she was being coy, like a woman with a strange man. "What I said about the cockroaches is true; you yourself must remember. . . ."

I was disconcerted. I did remember the invasion of cockroaches, that black swarm which had nightly filled the darkness with a spidery running. All cracks in the floors were full of moving whispers, each crevice suddenly produced a cockroach, from every chink would shoot a crazy black zigzag of lightning. Ah, that wild lunacy of panic, traced in a shiny black line on the floor! Ah, those screams of horror which my father emitted, leaping from one chair up to another with a javelin in his hand!

Refusing all food and drink, with fever patches on his cheeks, with a grimace of revulsion permanently fixed around his mouth, my father had grown completely wild. It was clear that no human body could bear for long such a pitch of hatred. A terrible loathing had transformed his face into a petrified tragic mask, in which the pupils, hidden behind the lower lids, lay in wait, tense as bows, in a frenzy of permanent suspicion. With a wild scream he would suddenly jump up from his seat, run blindly to a corner of the room and stab downward with the javelin, then lift it, having impaled an enormous cockroach that desperately wriggled its tangle of legs. Adela would then come to the rescue and take the lance with its trophy from father, now pale and faint with horror, and shake it off into a bucket. But even at the time, I could not tell whether these pictures were implanted in my mind by Adela's tales or whether I had witnessed them myself. My father at the time no longer possessed that power of resistance which protects healthy people from the fascination of loathing. Instead of fighting against the terrible attraction of that fascination, my father, a prey to madness, became completely subjected to it. The fatal consequences were quick to follow. Soon, the first suspicious symptoms appeared, filling us with fear and sadness. Father's behavior changed. His madness, the euphoria of his excitement wore off. In his gestures and expressions signs of a bad conscience began to show. He took to avoiding us. He hid, for days on end, in corners, in wardrobes, under the eiderdowns. I saw him sometimes looking pensively at his own hands, examining the consistency of skin and nails, on which black spots began to appear like the scales of a cockroach.

In daytime he was still able to resist with such strength as remained in him, and fought his obsession, but during the night it took hold of him completely. I once saw him late at night, in the light of a candle set on the floor. He lay on the floor naked, stained with black totem spots, the lines of his ribs heavily outlined, the fantastic structure of his anatomy visible through the skin; he lay on his face, in the grip of the obsession of loathing which dragged him into the abyss of its complex paths. He moved with the many-limbed, complicated movements of a strange ritual in which I recognized with horror an imitation of the ceremonial crawl of a cockroach.

From that day on we gave Father up for lost. His resemblance to a cockroach became daily more pronounced—he was being transformed into one.

We got used to it. We saw him ever more rarely, as he would disappear for weeks on end on his cockroachy paths. We ceased to recognize him; he merged completely with that black, uncanny tribe. Who could say whether he continued to live in some crack in the floor, whether he ran through the rooms at night absorbed in cockroachy affairs, or whether perhaps he was one of those dead insects which Adela found every morning lying on their backs with their legs in the air and which she swept up into a dustpan to burn later with disgust?

"And yet," I said disconcerted, "I am sure that this condor is he."

My mother looked at me from under her eyelashes.

"Don't torture me, darling; I have told you already that Father is away, traveling all over the country: he now has a job as a commercial traveler. You know that he sometimes comes home at night and goes away again before dawn."

Pierre Menard,
Author of the *Quixote*   *JORGE LUIS BORGES*

HE *VISIBLE* WORK LEFT by this novelist is easily and briefly enumerated. Impardonable, therefore, are the omissions and additions perpetrated by Madame Henri Bachelier in a fallacious catalogue which a certain daily, whose *Protestant* tendency is no secret, has had the inconsideration to inflict upon its deplorable readers—though these be few and Calvinist, if not Masonic and circumcised. The true friends of Menard have viewed this catalogue with alarm and even with a certain melancholy. One might say that only yesterday we gathered before his final monument, amidst the lugubrious cypresses, and already Error tries to tarnish his Memory . . . Decidedly, a brief rectification is unavoidable.

I am aware that it is quite easy to challenge my slight authority. I hope, however, that I shall not be prohibited from mentioning two eminent testimonies. The Baroness de Bacourt (at whose unforgettable *vendredis* I had the honor of meeting the lamented poet) has seen fit to approve the pages which follow. The Countess de Bagnoregio, one of the most delicate spirits of the Principality of Monaco (and now of Pittsburgh, Pennsylvania, following her recent marriage to the international philanthropist Simon Kautzsch, who has been so inconsiderately slandered, alas! by the victims of his disinterested maneuvers) has sacrificed "to veracity and to death" (such were her words) the stately reserve which is her distinction, and, in an open letter published in the magazine *Luxe,* concedes me her approval as well. These authorizations, I think, are not entirely insufficient.

I have said that Menard's visible work can be easily enumerated. Having examined with care his personal files, I find that they contain the following items:

a) A Symbolist sonnet which appeared twice (with variants) in the review *La conque* (issues of March and October 1899).

b) A monograph on the possibility of constructing a poetic vocabulary of concepts which would not be synonyms or periphrases of those which make up our everyday language, "but rather ideal objects created according to convention and essentially designed to satisfy poetic needs" (Nîmes, 1901).

c) A monograph on "certain connections or affinities" between the thought of Descartes, Leibniz and John Wilkins (Nîmes, 1903).

d) A monograph on Leibniz's *Characteristica universalis* (Nîmes, 1904).

e) A technical article on the possibility of improving the game of chess, eliminating one of the rook's pawns. Menard proposes, recommends, discusses and finally rejects this innovation.

f) A monograph on Raymond Lully's *Ars magna generalis* (Nîmes, 1906).

g) A translation, with prologue and notes, of Ruy López de Segura's *Libro de la invención liberal y arte del juego del axedrez* (Paris, 1907).

h) The work sheets of a monograph on George Boole's symbolic logic.

i) An examination of the essential metric laws of French prose, illustrated with examples taken from Saint-Simon (*Revue des langues romanes*, Montpellier, October 1909).

j) A reply to Luc Durtain (who had denied the existence of such laws), illustrated with examples from Luc Durtain (*Revue des langues romans*, Montpellier, December 1909).

k) A manuscript translation of the *Aguja de navegar cultos* of Quevedo, entitled *La boussole des précieux*.

l) A preface to the Catalogue of an exposition of lithographs by Carolus Hourcade (Nîmes, 1914).

m) The work *Les problèmes d'un problème* (Paris, 1917), which discusses, in chronological order, the different solutions given to the illustrious problem of Achilles and the tortoise. Two editions of this book have appeared so far; the second bears as an epigraph Leibniz's recommendation *"Ne craignez point, monsieur, la tortue"* and revises the chapters dedicated to Russell and Descartes.

n) A determined analysis of the "syntactical customs" of Toulet (*N. R. F.*, March 1921). Menard—I recall—declared that censure and praise are sentimental operations which have nothing to do with literary criticism.

o) A transposition into alexandrines of Paul Valéry's *Le cimitière marin* (*N. R. F.*, January 1928).

p) An invective against Paul Valéry, in the *Papers for the Suppression of Reality* of Jacques Reboul. (This invective, we might say parenthetically, is the exact opposite of his true opinion of Valéry. The latter understood it as such and their old friendship was not endangered.)

q) A "definition" of the Countess de Bagnoregio, in the "victorious volume"—the locution is Gabriele d'Annunzio's, another of its collaborators—published annually by this lady to rectify the inevitable falsifications of journalists and to present "to the world and to Italy" an authentic image of her person, so often exposed (by very reason of her beauty and her activities) to erroneous or hasty interpretations.

r) A cycle of admirable sonnets for the Baroness de Bacourt (1934).

s) A manuscript list of verses which owe their efficacy to their punctuation.*

This, then, is the *visible* work of Menard, in chronological order (with no omission other than a few vague sonnets of circumstance written for the hospitable, or avid, album of Madame Henri Bachelier). I turn now to his other work: the subterranean, the interminably heroic, the peerless. And—such are the capacities of man!—the unfinished. This work, perhaps the most significant of our time, consists of the ninth and thirty-eighth chapters of the first part of *Don Quixote* and a fragment of chapter twenty-two. I know such an af-

---

* Madame Henri Bachelier also lists a literal translation of Quevedo's literal translation of the *Introduction à la vie dévote* of St. Francis of Sales. There are no traces of such a work in Menard's library. It must have been a jest of our friend, misunderstood by the lady.

firmation seems an absurdity; to justify this "absurdity" is the primordial object of this note.*

Two texts of unequal value inspired this undertaking. One is that philological fragment by Novalis—the one numbered 2005 in the Dresden edition—which outlines the theme of a *total* identification with a given author. The other is one of those parasitic books which situate Christ on a boulevard, Hamlet on La Cannebière or Don Quixote on Wall Street. Like all men of good taste, Menard abhorred these useless carnivals, fit only—as he would say—to produce the plebeian pleasure of anachronism or (what is worse) to enthrall us with the elementary idea that all epochs are the same or are different. More interesting, though contradictory and superficial of execution, seemed to him the famous plan of Daudet: to conjoin the Ingenious Gentleman and his squire in *one* figure, which was Tartarin . . . Those who have insinuated that Menard dedicated his life to writing a contemporary *Quixote* calumniate his illustrious memory.

He did not want to compose another *Quixote*—which is easy—but *the Quixote itself*. Needless to say, he never contemplated a mechanical transcription of the original; he did not propose to copy it. His admirable intention was to produce a few pages which would coincide—word for word and line for line—with those of Miguel de Cervantes.

"My intent is no more than astonishing," he wrote me the 30th of September, 1934, from Bayonne. "The final term in a theological or metaphysical demonstration—the objective world, God, causality, the forms of the universe—is no less previous and common than my famed novel. The only difference is that the philosophers publish the intermediary stages of their labor in pleasant volumes and I have resolved to do away with those stages." In truth, not one worksheet remains to bear witness to his years of effort.

The first method he conceived was relatively simple. Know Spanish well, recover the Catholic faith, fight against the Moors or the

---

* I also had the secondary intention of sketching a personal portrait of Pierre Menard. But how could I dare to compete with the golden pages which, I am told, the Baroness de Bacourt is preparing or with the delicate and punctual pencil of Carolus Hourcade?

Turk, forget the history of Europe between the years 1602 and 1918,
be Miguel de Cervantes. Pierre Menard studied this procedure (I
know he attained a fairly accurate command of seventeenth-century
Spanish) but discarded it as too easy. Rather as impossible! my reader
will say. Granted, but the undertaking was impossible from the very
beginning and of all the impossible ways of carrying it out, this was
the least interesting. To be, in the twentieth century, a popular novelist of the seventeenth seemed to him a diminution. To be, in some
way, Cervantes and reach the *Quixote* seemed less arduous to him—
and, consequently, less interesting—than to go on being Pierre Menard and reach the *Quixote* through the experiences of Pierre Menard. (This conviction, we might say in passing, made him omit the
autobiographical prologue to the second part of *Don Quixote*. To
include that prologue would have been to create another character—
Cervantes—but it would also have meant presenting the *Quixote* in
terms of that character and not of Menard. The latter, naturally, de-
clined that facility.) "My undertaking is not difficult, essentially," I
read in another part of his letter. "I should only have to be immortal
to carry it out." Shall I confess that I often imagine he did finish it
and that I read the *Quixote*—all of it—as if Menard had conceived
it? Some nights past, while leafing through chapter XXVI—never es-
sayed by him—I recognized our friend's style and something of his
voice in this exceptional phrase: "the river nymphs and the dolorous
and humid Echo." This happy conjunction of a spiritual and a physical adjective brought to my mind a verse by Shakespeare which we
discussed one afternoon:

> Where a malignant and a turbaned Turk . . .

But why precisely the *Quixote?* our reader will ask. Such a preference, in a Spaniard, would not have been inexplicable; but it is, no
doubt, in a Symbolist from Nîmes, essentially a devoté of Poe, who
engendered Baudelaire, who engendered Mallarmé, who engendered
Valéry, who engendered Edmond Teste. The aforementioned letter
illuminates this point. "The *Quixote*," clarifies Menard, "interests
me deeply, but it does not seem—how shall I say it?—inevitable. I
cannot imagine the universe without Edgar Allan Poe's exclamation:

Ah, bear in mind this garden was enchanted!

or without the *Bateau ivre* or the *Ancient Mariner,* but I am quite capable of imagining it without the *Quixote.* (I speak, naturally, of my personal capacity and not of those works' historical resonance.) The *Quixote* is a contingent book; the *Quixote* is unnecessary. I can premeditate writing it, I can write it, without falling into a tautology. When I was ten or twelve years old, I read it, perhaps in its entirety. Later, I have reread closely certain chapters, those which I shall not attempt for the time being. I have also gone through the interludes, the plays, the *Galatea,* the exemplary novels, the undoubtedly laborious tribulations of Persiles and Segismunda and the *Viaje del Parnaso* . . . My general recollection of the *Quixote,* simplified by forgetfulness and indifference, can well equal the imprecise and prior image of a book not yet written. Once that image (which no one can legitimately deny me) is postulated, it is certain that my problem is a good bit more difficult than Cervantes' was. My obliging predecessor did not refuse the collaboration of chance: he composed his immortal work somewhat *à la diable,* carried along by the inertias of language and invention. I have taken on the mysterious duty of reconstructing literally his spontaneous work. My solitary game is governed by two polar laws. The first permits me to essay variations of a formal or psychological type; the second obliges me to sacrifice these variations to the "original" text and reason out this annihilation in an irrefutable manner . . . To these artificial hindrances, another—of a congenital kind—must be added. To compose the *Quixote* at the beginning of the seventeenth century was a reasonable undertaking, necessary and perhaps even unavoidable; at the beginning of the twentieth, it is almost impossible. It is not in vain that three hundred years have gone by, filled with exceedingly complex events. Amongst them, to mention only one, is the *Quixote* itself."

In spite of these three obstacles, Menard's fragmentary *Quixote* is more subtle than Cervantes'. The latter, in a clumsy fashion, opposes to the fictions of chivalry the tawdry provincial reality of his country; Menard selects as his "reality" the land of Carmen during the century of Lepanto and Lope de Vega. What a series of *espagnolades*

that selection would have suggested to Maurice Barrès or Dr. Rodrí-
guez Larreta! Menard eludes them with complete naturalness. In his
work there are no gypsy flourishes or conquistadors or mystics or
Philip the Seconds or *autos da fé*. He neglects or eliminates local
color. This disdain points to a new conception of the historical novel.
This disdain condemns *Salammbô*, with no possibility of appeal.

It is no less astounding to consider isolated chapters. For example,
let us examine Chapter XXXVIII of the first part, "which treats of
the curious discourse of Don Quixote on arms and letters." It is well
known that Don Quixote (like Quevedo in an analogous and later
passage in *La hora de todos*) decided the debate against letters and
in favor of arms. Cervantes was a former soldier: his verdict is un-
derstandable. But that Pierre Menard's Don Quixote—a contemporary of *La trahison des clercs* and Bertrand Russell—should fall prey
to such nebulous sophistries! Madame Bachelier has seen here an admirable and typical subordination on the part of the author to the
hero's psychology; others (not at all perspicaciously), a *transcription*
of the *Quixote*; the Baroness de Bacourt, the influence of Nietzsche.
To this third interpretation (which I judge to be irrefutable) I am
not sure I dare to add a fourth, which concords very well with the
almost divine modesty of Pierre Menard: his resigned or ironical
habit of propagating ideas which were the strict reverse of those he
preferred. (Let us recall once more his diatribe against Paul Valéry
in Jacques Reboul's ephemeral Surrealist sheet.) Cervantes' text and
Menard's are verbally identical, but the second is almost infinitely
richer. (More ambiguous, his detractors will say, but ambiguity is
richness.)

It is a revelation to compare Menard's *Don Quixote* with Cervantes'. The latter, for example, wrote (part one, chapter nine):

> . . . truth, whose mother is history, rival of time, depository of
> deeds, witness of the past, exemplar and adviser to the present,
> and the future's counselor.

Written in the seventeenth century, written by the "lay genius"
Cervantes, this enumeration is a mere rhetorical praise of history. Menard, on the other hand, writes:

> . . . truth, whose mother is history, rival of time, depository of
> deeds, witness of the past, exemplar and adviser to the present,
> and the future's counselor.

History, the *mother* of truth: the idea is astounding. Menard, a
contemporary of William James, does not define history as an inquiry into reality but as its origin. Historical truth, for him, is not
what has happened; it is what we judge to have happened. The final
phrases—*exemplar and adviser to the present, and the future's coun-
selor*—are brazenly pragmatic.

The contrast in style is also vivid. The archaic style of Menard—
quite foreign, after all—suffers from a certain affectation. Not so that
of his forerunner, who handles with ease the current Spanish of his
time.

There is no exercise of the intellect which is not, in the final
analysis, useless. A philosophical doctrine begins as a plausible description of the universe; with the passage of the years it becomes a
mere chapter—if not a paragraph or a name—in the history of philosophy. In literature, this eventual caducity is even more notorious.
The *Quixote*—Menard told me—was, above all, an entertaining book;
now it is the occasion for patriotic toasts, grammatical insolence and
obscene de luxe editions. Fame is a form of incomprehension, perhaps the worst.

There is nothing new in these nihilistic verifications; what is singular is the determination Menard derived from them. He decided
to anticipate the vanity awaiting all man's efforts; he set himself to
an undertaking which was exceedingly complex and, from the very
beginning, futile. He dedicated his scruples and his sleepless nights
to repeating an already extant book in an alien tongue. He multiplied
draft upon draft, revised tenaciously and tore up thousands of manuscript pages.* He did not let anyone examine these drafts and took
care they should not survive him. In vain have I tried to reconstruct
them.

---

* I remember his quadricular notebooks, his black crossed-out passages, his
peculiar typographical symbols and his insect-like handwriting. In the after-
noons he liked to go out for a walk around the outskirts of Nîmes; he would
take a notebook with him and make a merry bonfire.

I have reflected that it is permissible to see in this "final" *Quixote* a kind of palimpsest, through which the traces—tenuous but not indecipherable—of our friend's "previous" writing should be translucently visible. Unfortunately, only a second Pierre Menard, inverting the other's work, would be able to exhume and revive those lost Troys . . .

"Thinking, analyzing, inventing (he also wrote me) are not anomalous acts; they are the normal respiration of the intelligence. To glorify the occasional performance of that function, to hoard ancient and alien thoughts, to recall with incredulous stupor what the *doctor universalis* thought, is to confess our laziness or our barbarity. Every man should be capable of all ideas and I understand that in the future this will be the case."

Menard (perhaps without wanting to) has enriched, by means of a new technique, the halting and rudimentary art of reading: this new technique is that of the deliberate anachronism and the erroneous attribution. This technique, whose applications are infinite, prompts us to go through the *Odyssey* as if it were posterior to the *Aeneid* and the book *Le jardin du Centaure* of Madame Henri Bachelier as if it were by Madame Henri Bachelier. This technique fills the most placid works with adventure. To attribute the *Imitatio Christi* to Louis Ferdinand Céline or to James Joyce, is this not a sufficient renovation of its tenuous spiritual indications?

For Silvina Ocampo

*T*HERE WAS A TIME when I thought a great deal about the axolotls. I went to see them in the aquarium at the Jardin des Plantes and stayed for hours watching them, observing their immobility, their faint movements. Now I am an axolotl.

I got to them by chance one spring morning when Paris was spreading its peacock tail after a wintry Lent. I was heading down the boulevard Port-Royal, then I took Saint-Marcel and L'Hôpital and saw green among all that grey and remembered the lions. I was friend of the lions and panthers, but had never gone into the dark, humid building that was the aquarium. I left my bike against the gratings and went to look at the tulips. The lions were sad and ugly and my panther was asleep. I decided on the aquarium, looked obliquely at banal fish until, unexpectedly, I hit it off with the axolotls. I stayed watching them for an hour and left, unable to think of anything else.

In the library at Sainte-Geneviève, I consulted a dictionary and learned that axolotls are the larval stage (provided with gills) of a species of salamander of the genus Ambystoma. That they were Mexican I knew already by looking at them and their little pink Aztec faces and the placard at the top of the tank. I read that specimens of them had been found in Africa capable of living on dry land during the periods of drought, and continuing their life under water when the rainy season came. I found their Spanish name, *ajolote,* and the mention that they were edible, and that their oil was used (no longer used, it said) like cod-liver oil.

I didn't care to look up any of the specialized works, but the next day I went back to the Jardin des Plantes. I began to go every morning, morning and afternoon some days. The aquarium guard smiled perplexedly taking my ticket. I would lean up against the iron bar in front of the tanks and set to watching them. There's nothing strange in this, because after the first minute I knew that we were linked, that something infinitely lost and distant kept pulling us together. It had been enough to detain me that first morning in front of the sheet of glass where some bubbles rose through the water. The axolotls huddled on the wretched narrow (only I can know how narrow and wretched) floor of moss and stone in the tank. There were nine specimens, and the majority pressed their heads against the glass, looking with their eyes of gold at whoever came near them. Disconcerted, almost ashamed, I felt it a lewdness to be peering at these silent and immobile figures heaped at the bottom of the tank. Mentally I isolated one, situated on the right and somewhat apart from the others, to study it better. I saw a rosy little body, translucent (I thought of those Chinese figurines of milky glass), looking like a small lizard about six inches long, ending in a fish's tail of extraordinary delicacy, the most sensitive part of our body. Along the back ran a transparent fin which joined with the tail, but what obsessed me was the feet, of the slenderest nicety, ending in tiny fingers with minutely human nails. And then I discovered its eyes, its face. Inexpressive features, with no other trait save the eyes, two orifices, like brooches, wholly of transparent gold, lacking any life but looking, letting themselves be penetrated by my look, which seemed to travel past the golden level and lose itself in a diaphanous interior mystery. A very slender black halo ringed the eye and etched it onto the pink flesh, onto the rosy stone of the head, vaguely triangular, but with curved and irregular sides which gave it a total likeness to a statuette corroded by time. The mouth was masked by the triangular plane of the face, its considerable size would be guessed only in profile; in front a delicate crevice barely slit the lifeless stone. On both sides of the head where the ears should have been, there grew three sprigs red as coral, a vegetal outgrowth, the gills, I suppose. And they were the only thing quick about it; every ten or fifteen seconds the sprig pricked up stiffly and again subsided. Once in a while a foot would barely move, I saw the diminutive toes poise mildly on the moss. It's that we don't enjoy moving a lot, and the tank is so cramped—we barely move in any direction and we're hitting one of the others with our tail or our head—difficulties arise, fights, tiredness. The time feels like it's less if we stay quietly.

It was their quietness that made me lean toward them fascinated the first time I saw the axolotls. Obscurely I seemed to understand their secret will, to abolish space and time with an indifferent immobility. I knew better later; the gill contraction, the tentative reckoning of the delicate feet on the stones, the abrupt swimming (some of them swim with a simple undulation of the body) proved to me that they were capable of escaping that mineral lethargy in which they spent whole hours. Above all else, their eyes obsessed me. In the standing tanks on either side of them, different fishes showed me the simple stupidity of their handsome eyes so similar to our own. The eyes of the axolotls spoke to me of the presence of a different life, of another way of seeing. Glueing my face to the glass (the guard would cough fussily once in a while), I tried to see better those diminutive golden points, that entrance to the infinitely slow and remote world of these rosy creatures. It was useless to tap with one finger on the glass directly in front of their faces; they never gave the least reaction. The golden eyes continued burning with their soft, terrible light; they continued looking at me from an unfathomable depth which made me dizzy.

And nevertheless they were close. I knew it before this, before being an axolotl. I learned it the day I came near them for the first time. The anthropomorphic features of a monkey reveal the reverse of what most people believe, the distance that is traveled from them to us. The absolute lack of similarity between axolotls and human beings proved to me that my recognition was valid, that I was not propping myself up with easy analogies. Only the little hands . . . But an eft, the common newt, has such hands also, and we are not at all alike. I think it was the axolotls' heads, that triangular pink shape with the tiny eyes of gold. That looked and knew. That laid the claim. They were not *animals*.

It would seem easy, almost obvious, to fall into mythology. I began seeing in the axolotls a metamorphosis which did not succeed in revoking a mysterious humanity. I imagined them aware, slaves of their bodies, condemned infinitely to the silence of the abyss, to a hopeless meditation. Their blind gaze, the diminutive gold disc without expression and nonetheless terribly shining, went through me like a message: "Save us, save us." I caught myself mumbling words of advice, conveying childish hopes. They continued to look at me, immobile; from time to time the rosy branches of the gills stiffened. In that instant I felt a muted pain; perhaps they were seeing me, attracting my strength to penetrate into the impenetrable thing of their lives. They were not human beings, but I had found in no animal such a profound relation with myself. The axolotls were like witnesses of something, and at times like horrible judges. I felt ignoble in front of them; there was such a terrifying purity in those transparent eyes. They were larvas, but larva means disguise and also phantom. Behind those Aztec faces, without expression but of an implacable cruelty, what semblance was awaiting its hour?

I was afraid of them. I think that had it not been for feeling the proximity of other visitors and the guard, I would not have been bold enough to remain alone with them. "You eat them alive with your eyes, hey," the guard said, laughing; he likely thought I was a little cracked. What he didn't notice was that it was they devouring me slowly with their eyes, in a cannabalism of gold. At any distance from the aquarium, I had only to think of them, it was as though I were being affected from a distance. It got to the point that I was going every day, and at night I thought of them immobile in the darkness, slowly putting a hand out which immediately encountered another. Perhaps their eyes could see in the dead of night, and for them the day continued indefinitely. The eyes of axolotls have no lids.

I know now that there was nothing strange, that that had to occur. Leaning over in front of the tank each morning, the recognition was greater. They were suffering, every fiber of my body reached toward that stifled pain, that stiff torment at the bottom of the tank. They were lying in wait for something, a remote dominion destroyed, an age of liberty when the world had been that of the axolotls. Not possible that such a terrible expression which was attaining the overthrow of that forced blankness on their stone faces should carry any message other than one of pain, proof of that eternal sentence, of that liquid hell they were undergoing. Hopelessly, I wanted to prove to myself that my own sensibility was projecting a nonexistent consciousness upon the axolotls. They and I knew. So there was nothing strange in what happened. My face was pressed against the glass of the aquarium, my eyes were attempting once more to penetrate the mystery of those eyes of gold without iris, without pupil. I saw from very close up the face of an axolotl immobile next to the glass. No transition and no surprise, I saw my face against the glass, I saw it on the outside of the tank, I saw it on the other side of the glass. Then my face drew back and I understood.

Only one thing was strange: to go on thinking as usual, to know. To realize that was, for the first moment, like the horror of a man buried alive awaking to his fate. Outside, my face came close to the glass again, I saw my mouth, the lips compressed with the effort of understanding the axolotls. I was an axolotl and now I knew instantly that no understanding was possible. He was outside the aquarium, his thinking was a thinking outside the tank. Recognizing him, being him himself, I was an axolotl and in my world. The horror began—I learned in the same moment—of believing myself prisoner in the body of an axolotl, metamorphosed into him with my human mind intact, buried alive in an axolotl, condemned to move lucidly among unconscious creatures. But that stopped when a foot just grazed my face, when I moved just a little to one side and saw an axolotl next to me who was looking at me, and understood that he knew also, no communication possible, but very clearly. Or I was also in him, or all of us were thinking humanlike, incapable of expression, limited to the golden splendor of our eyes looking at the face of the man pressed against the aquarium.

He returned many times, but he comes less often now. Weeks pass without his showing up. I saw him yesterday, he looked at me for a long time and left briskly. It seemed to me that he was not so much interested in us any more, that he was coming out of habit. Since the only thing I do is think, I could think about him a lot. It occurs to me that at the beginning we continued to communicate, that he felt more than ever one with the mystery which was claiming him. But the bridges were broken between him and me, because what was his obsession is now an axolotl, alien to his human life. I think that at the beginning I was capable of returning to him in a certain way—ah, only in a certain way—and of keeping awake his desire to know us better. I am an axolotl for good now, and if I think like a man it's only because every axolotl thinks like a man inside his rosy stone resemblance. I believe that all this succeeded in communicating something to him in those first days, when I was still he. And in this final solitude to which he no longer comes, I console myself by thinking that perhaps he is going to write a story about us, that, believing he's making up a story, he's going to write all this about axolotls.

*D*EAREST Solange:

You were utterly mistaken. I have waited till now, till I was quite certain, before telling you so; and now I can tell you in all honesty—"I can *really* tell you" as the worthy Madame de Caulaincourt puts it. To imagine that I could not bear to live here for longer than a week! Solange, this is heaven on earth. And think of this: I have been here for nearly two months. If you only knew, my dearest, how I bless the inspiration that brought me to this place—my uncle's inspiration, too, in doing his duty by dying at the right time. Say what you will, my uncertain budget was hardly aided by the Empress's balls, or by my frequent visits to the Palais Royal. Here, the delightful and the sensible are united. I taste, for example, the pleasures of possessions—or rather, of property—in a way impossible with Parisian bankers, who do what they please with your money when they see that you know nothing of finance. In any case, I cannot leave everything in the hands of the agent here. I do not wish to speak ill of my late uncle's régime; but the agent has already bought himself two houses in the village, and a piece of land in the neighborhood. But I did not mean to speak of this matter; and it is certainly not for this reason that I bless my resolution. My poor Solange, how can you know, how can I tell you, of the unsullied joys of country life, of this delicious new world?

In short, picture me, the happy mistress of a real castle and of a large estate—and the conscientious administrator of the latter. I often wander in my carriage through my woods, which the autumn is already beginning to touch with gold. I often go to the village, which, I may add, also belongs to me, with its simple inhabitants (the agent's affairs are in hand). I confess that the carriage creaks a little; and that the coachman and his groom have not the philosophical air and the carefully cultivated mustaches of their Parisian colleagues—and I cannot understand a word they say. But, by way of compensation, their liveries are far more attractive.

Paris! Of course I will return there sometimes, perhaps often. But —dare I say it?—the whole world of Paris now seems to me like a bad dream.

You should not think that I am afflicted by solitude. The more or less noble landowners of the district have hastened to call on me; most of them, of course, are insupportably provincial, stupid and bigoted. But among them there is one . . . a man who . . . I might as well speak plainly. He is young, dashing, romantic. He rides like an Englishman. He reads the poets and recites them ardently . . . well, why not? After all, he bears one of the oldest names of the region. Like me, he is free and independent. But I can hear you ask, "What do you mean: why not?" Well, my love, I can tell you no more of this now.

This letter has already continued too long. Will you have time, I wonder, between your entertainments and balls to read it? Certainly not to meditate over it; nor dare I hope that you will be able to tear yourself for a few days away from the maelstrom of your life in Paris and allow me to embrace you again. Farewell, then, I will send you more news of me very soon.

Anne

2

Darling Solange:

It is I. So much time has passed since we met, and even since we last corresponded. But I have had so many and such pleasant things to do.

Very well, you want to know how the people here start to hibernate at the beginning of winter—and we are almost there. It is easily said: they do nothing in particular; they make no preparations—except a solemn feast, with appropriate potations, the day before they settle down. There are no *lits embaumés,* no ointments, no purging of blood or vapors, no injections, no attendants, no fussy quarantine, none of the many operations usual at our (but now I should say "your") *maisons de léthargie*. And without any of this things seem to go excellently by themselves—though you would find it hard to convince the Paris specialists! And do you know where they hibernate? Certainly not in "carefully conditioned surroundings," or wrapped in a "softly reacting substance which . . ." etc., etc., but simply where they happen to be, or where they will—in the kitchen, perhaps, or the hayloft—wrapped in a goatskin, of the kind they use for wineskins or bagpipes. More precisely, it seems that they have themselves suspended, or suspend themselves, from beams in the ceiling—and so good night! I have in fact seen, a few days ago, some of these goatskins, or rather bags made of skins (for one skin would not be enough for a child), hanging from a beam, when I was visiting a large and needy family. They were empty, of course; but their use was explained to me. The hairy side is turned inward, and, at one extremity, there is an extension for the legs. In these bags they remain seated, or almost so; so that, with the softer parts of their bodies weighing down, they hang there like so many kitchen vessels. I will give you further details of this, for I feel that it will not be long before the hibernation begins. Another thing: the number of people in Paris who hibernate is severely limited—for all I know, negligible. Indeed, among us (I mean, among you) nobody hibernates except those who are so poor that they have not even a dry crust to eat, or some old general in retirement, or some hysterical woman who cannot bear the cold, and so on. But here the practice is by far more common and extends even to the young, even to children.

Well, we will see. I will keep you informed; but I have nothing more of interest to tell you now. Remember me.

A

3

Dear Solange:

The winter is advancing with giant strides, indeed it has already arrived in these parts; and the people here are beginning to hibernate. I can no longer keep count of the bags hanging from the beams during my visits of charity. They—the bags, I mean—give off a foetid odor like bladders of lard, and soot is already gathering on their surface, for they are nearly all in the kitchens. The spectacle is certainly repellent—but, above all, surprising. Besides I must timidly confess that I have never before seen a human being hibernating. Yes, yes, I know that you will laugh at me; after being very wise about it in my last letter, I now remember that, at one time in Paris, the practice was quite fashionable among unhappy lovers (who even tried to prolong the period of insensibility indefinitely); so that one who has ever been a woman of the world should almost feel ashamed not to be minutely informed about it. But, with humility, I repeat that I had never seen a human being hibernating. In truth one cannot be said to see them hibernating here, since they hang like blocks of wood; one cannot even hear them breathe. How strange these people are, who do not hesitate to subtract the entire winter from their span of life!

In my admitted ignorance, I wonder whether this practice is really a practice, in the sense of a habit? Or whether it is in some way connected with the nature of these people and of all those, in general, given to hibernation? Or is it a habit which has become second nature to them? I do not know what to think, or even, as you see, how to frame the question properly. If we are to judge by the unhappy lovers of Paris, we may conclude that hibernation is a voluntary action; and yet. . . . But why do I burden myself with these reflections . . . unless it is another consequence of living here? In any case, listen to this.

A few days ago I saw, in one of the poor houses, a tiny and charming little boy, whom I already knew—one of my little friends, in fact. They were preparing him for hibernation. He was yawning and rubbing his eyes, and did not seem in the least discontented. But I could not bear the thought that four or five months of that young life would be thrown away. I spoke to the family and told them that I was prepared to take him with me for the winter. I meant not only that I would relieve them of a mouth to feed, but also that I would try to keep him awake and maintain his interest in life. They only understood part of my meaning. The little boy was consulted; he mumbled something indistinct but did not seem to oppose my suggestion. To cut a long story short, I took him with me to the castle. It would be quite useless to try to describe to you the efforts which I made to keep him lively and in good spirits, or even awake—I mean, literally, awake. I failed completely. Nothing amused him, nothing interested him; he yawned continually and seemed to desire nothing but to fall asleep. Indeed he did go to sleep all over the house, in my arms when I was talking to him, while he was eating the rarest delicacies. And he was by no means a stupid child, as I had been able to observe before this languor had overcome him. In the end, I had to take him back, sound asleep, to his family, who, with a smile hinting that they had expected no other outcome, returned him without further ado into his bag—and added: "Shall we talk about it again—in April?"

Well, what do you say to that? Ah, why do you write to me so seldom? Why do you tell me nothing of Paris and of your life? Do you think that I have become altogether a savage? Farewell—write to me soon.

A

4

Solange, my dear:

I begin to be alarmed; I can no longer hide it either from myself or from you. An unbelievable number of people here have already fallen asleep. Wherever I go, I see nothing but hideous, foetid bags hanging from the ceilings. And one incident sums it up. Do you remember that in my first letter I spoke of a noble and romantic young man who . . . who was paying his addresses to me? Very well then, he—yes, he . . . oh, Solange! Yesterday we were in my drawing room. I had played a little. He, in his turn, had recited a poem, written by himself, whose inspiration only modesty prevents me from revealing to you. The hour was propitious for our hearts to declare themselves. I was at that very moment thinking that the time had come when I could give him some grounds for hope, that there was no reason in the world why I should not do so. He had seized my hand, and I had abandoned it to him, when . . . ah, my friend, how can I tell you? Behind his gaze, I saw with horror the beginning of a sort of languor, not of the kind you would have imagined, but terribly like a sort of dullness, even of indifference—the indifference of a man who is on the point of falling asleep. Think, Solange, at that very moment of all moments he was beginning to fall asleep! For a little while he held my hand in his, doing nothing, gazing at me ever more childishly, apparently oblivious of our critical conjuncture and of everything else. Then he drew back a little, dropped my poor damp hand, yawned (still, I confess, with urbanity), walked to the window, tapped on the glass, protested something about a headache, mumbled something else incomprehensible, and, without even taking his leave (I was too dismayed to speak) took to his heels. This is the whole story. Today I am told that he has started to hibernate. Oh, no doubt his bag will be made of sables. My God! What else can I say but "My God"?

And the others! I do not remember if I have ever spoken to you about certain of my relations, or rather my uncle's relations. I went to call on them last evening, in part to recover my spirits. I found them all seated around a table, in solemn silence. One glanced occasionally at a newspaper thrown on the table; but not so much at the newspaper as at the advertisements in it. Another was smoking a cigar and staring at his nails; but he was not smoking it so much as occasionally lighting it. A third had his elbows on the table and was doing nothing whatever.

They were silent, or spoke with difficulty of the weather. At the back of their eyes I could see that languor which I have come to recognize. It is not difficult to prophesy that soon they will all have fallen sound asleep.

Meanwhile, this morning a terrified procession of peasants paraded before me, having insisted on seeing me, carrying presents in kind. I was given a confused explanation to the effect that these offerings were always, by tradition, made on this day of the year, and were "for hibernation"—though it is given a different name here. A terrible suspicion crossed my mind: did my uncle hibernate as well? And, in truth, I seem to remember that he used to wait till the spring before answering my winter letters, though he was so precise in all his other dealings. But no! What am I imagining? And yet I recently discovered in the cellar—which I had never visited—an entire store of the horrible bags, and some already full! It seemed to me that I had not seen certain of the servants for some days. But the agent is as lively as ever, and the old butler holds up well, although he is always somewhat dull by nature; and the same may be said of the first housemaid. But the cook has for some time. . . .

But tell me, Solange: do you think it possible that they will all fall asleep? They all tell me—all the survivors, that is—that those who have work to do remain awake. But what advice could you give me in such a matter?

The snow has fallen in profusion and blankets the fields as far as the eye can reach. It is beautiful, but it is a little sad.

What are you doing in Paris? Will you at last make up your mind to write to me? But in Paris, at this very hour, the carriages are beginning to draw up to the Opera; bejewelled beauties cast their glances to left and to right; their lovers approach them closely at the entrance; everything in Paris lives and trembles with movement, the very air trembles.

Ah! Do you think that I ache with nostalgia for all that? You would be mistaken. It is only my nerves playing a treacherous game with me. I must be resolute—I have sworn to be resolute. Farewell.

A

5

Solange:

My Solange, my only friend, listen to me, you must save me now, instantly. The very instant that you receive these lines you must take your traveling carriage; you must run, you must fly to save me. Solange, do you love me? Dear God, I cannot write calmly. I can hear his horse trampling and snorting in the courtyard below me—I mean the hussar's horse. Yes, they have all fallen asleep, every last one, in the castle, in the village, everywhere, all of them. Even the agent, even the old butler a few hours ago. He was the only one left, and I could find no way of keeping him awake—with brandy or with offers of money; he did his best, but in the end it was stronger than he. I have no time to tell you. I sped outside: the silent desert of the snow. It was like a fairy tale—no, there is always a kindliness about fairy tales; it seemed like a fearful nightmare . . . but I am wasting precious time, and his horse is trampling ever more loudly. At last, after an infinite time, I saw him far, far away in the snow, a speck of black which swiftly grew larger. It was a handsome young hussar—he whom, for whatever reason, the Lord has sent me. He was galloping madly. He stopped unwillingly. I begged him, I implored him to carry me with him on the saddle. He replied, "I am carrying orders, Mademoiselle." If you knew what I had to do and say to induce him to delay for ten minutes, not more than ten minutes (and he took out his watch), just the time to write you these despairing lines, which he has promised on his honor to have delivered to you by the swiftest means. There are only two minutes left. Understand me well, Solange. I cannot prepare my food, I cannot do anything, there is nothing in the house, I am frightened of the horses, I could not ride them to safety—even if they too are not asleep. I shall die here if you do not save me. Solange, Solange, do you hate me? Yes, you were right after all, but now there is not an instant to lose . . . and if . . . if anything should happen to him on the road? Great heavens, I hear his voice calling me . . . Solange, my soul, what can I say to you? Save your wretched

A

*T*HROUGH THE CALCULATIONS *begun by Edwin P. Hubble on the galaxies' velocity of recession, we can establish the moment when all the universe's matter was concentrated in a single point, before it began to expand in space.*

Naturally, we were all there,—*old Qfwfq said,*—where else could we have been? Nobody knew then that there could be space. Or time either: what use did we have for time, packed in there like sardines?

I say "packed like sardines," using a literary image: in reality there wasn't even space to pack us into. Every point of each of us coincided with every point of each of the others in a single point, which was where we all were. In fact, we didn't even bother one another, except for personality differences, because when space doesn't exist, having somebody unpleasant like Mr. Pber^t Pber^d underfoot all the time is the most irritating thing.

How many of us were there? Oh, I was never able to figure that out, not even approximately. To make a count, we would have had to move apart, at least a little, and instead we all occupied the same point. Contrary to what you might think, it wasn't the sort of situation that encourages sociability; I know, for example, that in other periods neighbors called on one another; but there, because of the fact that we were all neighbors, nobody even said good morning or good evening to anybody else.

In the end each of us associated only with a limited number of acquaintances. The ones I remember most are Mrs. Ph(i)Nk$_o$, her friend De XuaeauX, a family of immigrants by the name of Z'zu, and Mr. Pber^t Pber^d, whom I just mentioned. There also a cleaning woman—"maintenance staff" she was called—only one, for the whole universe, since there was so little room. To tell the truth, she had nothing to do all day long, not even dusting—inside one point not even a grain of dust can enter—so she spent all her time gossiping and complaining.

Just with the people I've already named we would have been overcrowded; but you have to add all the stuff we had to keep piled up in there: all the material that was to serve afterwards to form the universe, now dismantled and concentrated in such a way that you weren't able to tell what was later to become part of astronomy (like the nebula of Andromeda) from what was assigned to geography (the Vosges, for example) or to chemistry (like certain beryllium isotopes). And on top of that, we were always bumping against the Z'zu family's household goods: camp beds, mattresses, baskets; these Z'zus, if you weren't careful, with the excuse that they were a large family, would begin to act as if they were the only ones in the world: they even wanted to hang lines across our point to dry their washing.

But the others also had wronged the Z'zus, to begin with, by calling them "immigrants," on the pretext that, since the others had been there first, the Z'zus had come later. This was mere unfounded prejudice—that seems obvious to me—because neither before nor after existed, nor any place to immigrate from, but there were those who insisted that the concept of "immigrant" could be understood in the abstract, outside of space and time.

It was what you might call a narrow-minded attitude, our outlook at that time, very petty. The fault of the environment in which we had been reared. An attitude that, basically, has remained in all of us, mind you: it keeps cropping up even today, if two of us happen to meet—at the bus stop, in a movie house, at an international dentists' convention—and start reminiscing about the old days. We say hello—at times somebody recognizes me, at other times I recognize somebody—and we promptly start asking about this one and that one (even if each remembers only a few of those remembered by the others), and so we start in again on the old disputes, the slanders, the denigrations. Until somebody mentions Mrs. Phi(i)Nk$_0$—every conversation finally gets around to her—and then, all of a sudden, the pettiness is put aside, and we feel uplifted, filled with a blissful, generous emotion. Mrs. Ph(i)Nk$_o$, the only one that none of us has forgotten and that we all regret. Where has she ended up? I have long since stopped looking for her: Mrs. Ph(i)Nk$_o$, her bosom, her thighs, her orange dressing gown—we'll never meet her again, in this system of galaxies or in any other.

Let me make one thing clear: this theory that the universe, after having reached an extremity of rarefaction, will be condensed again has never convinced me. And yet many of us are counting only on that, continually making plans for the time when we'll all be back there again. Last month, I went into the bar here on the corner and whom did I see? Mr. Pber^t Pber^d. "What's new with you? How do you happen to be in this neighborhood?" I learned that he's the agent for a plastics firm, in Pavia. He's the same as ever, with his silver tooth, his loud suspenders. "When we go back there," he said to me, in a whisper, "the thing we have to make sure of is, this time, certain people remain out . . . You know who I mean: those Z'zus . . ."

I would have liked to answer him by saying that I've heard a number of people make the same remark, concluding: "You know who I mean . . . Mr. Pber^t Pber^d . . ."

To avoid the subject, I hastened to say: "What about Mrs. Ph(i)Nk$_o$? Do you think we'll find her back there again?"

"Ah, yes . . . She, by all means . . ." he said, turning purple.

For all of us the hope of returning to that point means, above all, the hope of being once more with Mrs. Ph(i)Nk$_o$. (This applies even to me, though I don't believe in it.) And in that bar, as always happens, we fell to talking about her, and were moved; even Mr. Pber^t Pber^d's unpleasantness faded, in the face of that memory.

Mrs. Ph(i)Nk$_o$'s great secret is that she never aroused any jealousy among us. Or any gossip, either. The fact that she went to bed with her friend, Mr. De XuaeauX, was well known. But in a point, if there's a bed, it takes up the whole point, so it isn't a question of *going* to bed, but of *being* there, because anybody in the point is also in the bed. Consequently, it was inevitable that she should be in bed also with each of us. If she had been another person, there's no telling all the things that would have been said about her. It was the cleaning woman who always started the slander, and the others didn't

have to be coaxed to imitate her. On the subject of the Z'zu family—
for a change!—the horrible things we had to hear: father, daughters,
brothers, sisters, mother, aunts: nobody showed any hesitation even
before the most sinister insinuation. But with her it was different:
the happiness I derived from her was the joy of being concealed,
punctiform, in her, and of protecting her, punctiform, in me; it was
at the same time vicious contemplation (thanks to the promiscuity
of the punctiform convergence of us all in her) and also chastity
(given her punctiform impenetrability). In short: what more could
I ask?

And all of this, which was true of me, was true also for each of
the others. And for her: she contained and was contained with equal
happiness, and she welcomed us and loved and inhabited all equally.

We got along so well all together, so well that something extraordinary was bound to happen. It was enough for her to say, at a certain moment: "Oh, if I only had some room, how I'd like to make
some noodles for you boys!" And in that moment we all thought of
the space that her round arms would occupy, moving backward and
forward with the rolling pin over the dough, her bosom leaning over
the great mound of flour and eggs which cluttered the wide board
while her arms kneaded and kneaded, white and shiny with oil up
to the elbows; we thought of the space that the flour would occupy,
and the wheat for the flour, and the fields to raise the wheat, and
the mountains from which the water would flow to irrigate the fields,
and the grazing lands for the herds of calves that would give their
meat for the sauce; of the space it would take for the Sun to arrive
with its rays, to ripen the wheat; of the space for the Sun to con-
dense from the clouds of stellar gases and burn; of the quantities of
stars and galaxies and galactic masses in flight through space which
would be needed to hold suspended every galaxy, every nebula,
every sun, every planet, and at the same time we thought of it, this
space was inevitably being formed, at the same time that Mrs.
$Ph(i)Nk_o$ was uttering those words: ". . . ah, what noodles, boys!"
the point that contained her and all of us was expanding in a halo
of distance in light-years and light-centuries and billions of light-
millennia, and we were being hurled to the four corners of the uni-

verse (Mr. Pber^t Pber^d all the way to Pavia), and she, dissolved into I don't know what kind of energy-light-heat, she, Mrs. Ph(i)Nk$_o$, she who in the midst of our closed, petty world had been capable of a generous impulse, "Boys, the noodles I would make for you!," a true outburst of general love, initiating at the same moment the concept of space and, properly speaking, space itself, and time, and universal gravitation, and the gravitating universe, making possible billions and billions of suns, and of planets, and fields of wheat, and Mrs. Ph(i)Nk$_o$s, scattered through the continents of the planets, kneading with floury, oil-shiny, generous arms, and she lost at that very moment, and we, mourning her loss.

I HAVE THE STORY of a man who tells stories. I have told him repeatedly that I don't believe his stories.

"You're lying," I said, "you're fibbing, you're making things up, you're pulling my leg."

That didn't impress him. He continued unperturbed, and when I called out: "You liar, you fibber, you yarn-spinner, you legpuller!" he gazed at me for a long time, shook his head, smiled sadly, and then said so softly that I almost felt ashamed of myself: "There is no such place as America."

Just to comfort him, I promised to write down his story.

It begins five centuries ago at the court of a king, the King of Spain. A palace, silk and velvet, gold, silver, beards, coronets, candles, manservants, and maidservants; courtiers who at dawn run one another's bellies through with swords, who the night before have chucked the challenging glove at one another's feet. On the turret watchmen who blow fanfares. And messengers who leap from their horses, and messengers who throw themselves onto the saddle, friends of the king and false friends, beautiful and dangerous women, and wine, and all round the palace people who couldn't think of anything better than to pay for all that.

But the king too couldn't think of anything better than to live like that, and however one lives, whether in great style or in poverty, whether in Madrid, Barcelona, or anywhere, in the end it's the same daily routine, and one gets bored with it. People who live anywhere, for example, imagine that Barcelona is a fine place, and the people of Barcelona want to travel to Anywhere.

The poor imagine that it would be fine to live like the king, and they suffer because the king thinks that being poor is the right thing for the poor.

In the morning the king gets up, at night the king goes to bed, and all day long he is bored and worried, over his servants, his gold, silver, velvet, silk, and he's bored with his candles. His bed is a splendid one, but there isn't much you can do in it except sleep.

The servants bow low to him in the morning, as low one morning as the next, the king is used to it and doesn't even notice. Someone gives him the fork, and people who speak to him call him Your Majesty, with a lot of other fine phrases added, and that's all.

Never does anyone say to him: "You idiot, you nitwit," and everything they tell him today they've already told him yesterday.

That's how it is.

And that's why kings keep court fools.

They're allowed to do what they like, and say what they like, to make the king laugh, and when he can't laugh at them any more he has them executed or something like that.

Thus he once had a fool who jumbled up words. The king found that funny. The fool said "Stajesmy" instead of "Majesty," he said "lapace" instead of "palace" and "mood gorning" instead of "good morning."

I think that's silly, but the king thought it funny. For a whole half year he thought it funny, till July 7th, and on the eighth, when he got up and the fool said "Mood gorning, your stajesmy," the king said: "Rid me of the fool!"

Another fool, a short, fat one called Pepe, only pleased the king for four days. He made the king laugh by smearing the chairs of the ladies, gentlemen, princes, dukes, barons, and knights with honey. On the fourth day he smeared honey onto the king's chair, and this didn't make the king laugh any more, and Pepe was no longer a fool.

Now the king bought himself the most horrible fool in the world. Ugly he was, skinny and fat at the same time, lanky and dumpy, and his left leg was bandy. No one knew whether he could speak and kept silent on purpose or whether he was dumb. His eyes had a malicious expression, his face looked bad-tempered; the only pleasant thing about him was his name: he was called Johnny.

But the most horrible thing was his way of laughing.

It began quite small and glassy deep down in his belly, blubbered up, gradually changed to a burp, made Johnny's head flush, almost stifled him till he exploded, quaked, yelled; then he stamped his feet as well and danced and laughed; and the king was amused, the others turned pale, began to tremble and were afraid. And when the people all round the palace heard this laughter they closed their doors and windows, fastened the shutters, put their children to bed and stopped their ears with wax.

Johnny's way of laughing was the most horrible thing in the world.

No matter what the king said, Johnny laughed.

The king said things that could make nobody laugh, but Johnny laughed. And one day the king said: "Johnny, I'm going to hang you."

And Johnny laughed, roared away, laughed as never before.

Then the king decided that Johnny was to be hanged tomorrow. He had a gallows put up, and he was serious about his decision; he wanted to hear Johnny laugh in front of the gallows. Then he ordered all the people to watch the nasty spectacle. But the people went into hiding, bolting their doors, and in the morning the king was alone with the hangman, with the hangman's assistants, and with laughing Johnny.

And he shouted at the servants: "Bring the people here!" The servants searched the whole town and found no one, and the king was angry, and Johnny laughed.

Then at last the servants found a boy, whom they dragged in front of the king. The boy was small, pale, and shy, and the king pointed at the gallows, commanding the boy to watch.

The boy looked up at the gallows, smiled, clapped his hands, was amazed, and said: "You must be a good king to have built a little seat for the pigeons; look, two have already perched on it."

"You're an idiot," said the king, "what's your name?"

"I'm an idiot, Mr. King, and my name is Colombo, my mother calls me Columbine."

"You idiot," said the king, "someone is being hanged here."

"What's his name, then?" asked Columbine, and when he heard the name, he said: "A lovely name, so his name is Johnny. How could anyone hang a man with such a lovely name?"

"That's because he laughs so horribly," said the king, and he ordered Johnny to laugh, and Johnny laughed twice as horribly as the day before.

Columbine was amazed, then he said: "Mr. King, do you find that horrible?" The king was surprised and couldn't think of an answer, and Columbine went on: "I don't particularly like his way of laughing, but the pigeons are still sitting on the gallows; it didn't startle them; they don't find his laughter horrible. Pigeons have sensitive hearing. You'll have to let Johnny go."

The king thought this over and said: "Johnny, take yourself off."

And Johnny, for the very first time, spoke one word. "Thank you," he said to Columbine, smiling a good human smile, and went away.

The king no longer had a fool.

"Come with me," he said to Columbine.

The king's manservants and maidservants, the counts and all the rest, though, thought that Columbine was the new court fool.

But Columbine wasn't merry at all. He stood there and was amazed, rarely spoke and did not laugh, he only smiled and made nobody laugh.

"He isn't a fool, he's an idiot," people said, and Columbine said: "I'm not a fool, I'm an idiot."

And people laughed at him.

If the king had known about that he would have been angry, but Columbine never mentioned it, for he didn't mind being laughed at.

At court there were strong people and clever people, the king was a king, the women were beautiful and the men brave, the chaplain was devout and the kitchen maid industrious—only Columbine, Columbine was nothing.

When somebody said: "Come along, Columbine, have a fight with me," Columbine answered: "I'm weaker than you."

When somebody said: "What's twice seven?" Columbine answered: "I'm more stupid than you."

When somebody said: "Are you plucky enough to jump that stream?" Columbine answered: "No, I'm not plucky enough."

And when the king asked: "Columbine, what do you want to be?" Columbine answered: "I don't want to be anything, I'm something already, I'm Columbine."

The king said: "But you have to be something," and Columbine asked: "What are the things one can be?"

Then the king said: "That man with the beard, with that brown leathery face, he's a navigator. A navigator is what he wanted to be and that's what he's become, he sails across the oceans and discovers countries for his king."

"If you want me to, my king," said Columbine, "I shall be a navigator."

That made the whole court laugh.

And Columbine ran away, out of the throne room, and cried: "I shall discover a country, I shall discover a country!"

People looked at each other and shook their heads, and Columbine ran out of the palace, through the city and over the field, and to the peasants who stood in the fields and watched him run, he called out: "I shall discover a country, I shall discover a country!"

And he came to the forest and hid for weeks in the undergrowth, and for weeks no one had any news of Columbine, and the king was sad and reproached himself, and the courtiers were ashamed of themselves for having laughed at Columbine.

And they were glad when many weeks later the watchman on the tower blew a fanfare and Columbine came over the fields, through the city, in by the gate, went up to the king and said: "My king, Columbine has discovered a country!" And because the courtiers didn't want to laugh at Columbine any more, they put on serious faces and asked: "What is it called, then, and where is it?"

"It isn't called yet, because I've only just discovered it, and it's far out in the ocean," said Columbine.

Then the bearded navigator got up and said: "All right, Columbine, I, Amerigo Vespucci, will go to look for the country. Tell me how to get there."

"You sail out to sea and then keep straight on all the time, and you must sail on till you get to that country, and you mustn't give up," said Columbine, and he was very frightened, because he was a liar and knew that there is no such place as that country, and he could no longer sleep at night.

But Amerigo Vespucci set out on his search.

No one knows where he sailed.

Maybe he also hid in the forest.

Then the fanfares sounded, and Amerigo returned.

Columbine blushed and didn't dare look at the great navigator. Vespucci stood in front of the king, winked at Columbine, took a deep breath, winked again at Columbine, and said very loudly and clearly, so that everyone could hear: "My king," that's what he said, "my king, there is such a country."

Columbine was so pleased that Vespucci had not given him away that he ran up to him, embraced him, and exclaimed: "Amerigo, my dear Amerigo!"

And the people thought that this was the name of the country, and they called the country that doesn't exist "America."

"You're a man now," said the king to Columbine, "from now on you'll be called Columbus."

And Columbus became famous, and everyone gaped at him and whispered to others: "That's the one who discovered America."

And everyone believed that there is such a place as America, only Columbus wasn't sure but doubted it all his life, and he never dared ask the navigator to tell him the truth.

But soon other people sailed to America and soon after very many; and those who came back claimed: "There is such a place as America!"

"As for me," said the man who told me the story, "I've never been to America. I don't know whether there is such a place as America. Perhaps people only pretend there is, so as not to disappoint Columbine. And when two tell each other about America they still wink at each other, and they hardly ever say America, but usually say something vague about the 'States' or 'over there' or something of the sort.

"Perhaps people who want to go to America are told the story of

Columbine, on the plane or on the boat, and then they go and hide somewhere and come back later and spin yarns about cowboys and skyscrapers, about Niagara Falls and the Mississippi, about New York and San Francisco.

"In any case they all tell the same story, and tell of things which they knew about before the journey, and that's very suspicious, you'll admit.

"But people are still debating who Columbus really was.

"I know who he was."

The Piano Player *DONALD BARTHELME*

OUTSIDE HIS WINDOW five-year-old Priscilla Hess, square and squat as a mailbox (red sweater, blue lumpy corduroy pants), looked around poignantly for someone to wipe her overflowing nose. There was a butterfly locked inside that mailbox, surely; would it ever escape? Or was the quality of mailboxness stuck to her forever, like her parents, like her name? The sky was sunny and blue. A filet of green Silly Putty disappeared into fat Priscilla Hess and he turned to greet his wife who was crawling through the door on her hands and knees.

"Yes?" he said. "What now?"

"I'm ugly," she said, sitting back on her haunches. "Our children are ugly."

"Nonsense," Brian said sharply. "They're wonderful children. Wonderful and beautiful. Other people's children are ugly, not our children. Now get up and go back out to the smokeroom. You're supposed to be curing a ham."

"The ham died," she said. "I couldn't cure it. I tried everything. You don't love me any more. The penicillin was stale. I'm ugly and so are the children. It said to tell you goodbye."

"*It?*"

"The ham," she said. "Is one of our children named Ambrose? Somebody named Ambrose has been sending us telegrams. How many do we have now? Four? Five? Do you think they're heterosexual?" She made a *moue* and ran a hand through her artichoke hair. "The house is rusting away. Why did you want a steel house? Why did I think I wanted to live in Connecticut? I don't know."

"Get up," he said softly, "get up, dearly beloved. Stand up and sing. Sing *Parsifal*."

"I want a Triumph," she said from the floor. "A TR–4. Everyone in Stamford, every single person, has one but me. If you gave me a TR–4 I'd put our ugly children in it and drive away. To Wellfleet. I'd take all the ugliness out of your life."

"A green one?"

"A *red* one," she said menacingly. "Red with red leather seats."

"Aren't you supposed to be chipping paint?" he asked. "I bought us an electronic data processing system. An IBM."

"I want to go to Wellfleet," she said. "I want to talk to Edmund Wilson and take him for a ride in my red TR–4. The children can dig clams. We have a lot to talk about, Bunny and me."

"Why don't you remove those shoulder pads?" Brian said kindly. "It's too bad about the ham."

"*I loved that ham,*" she said viciously. "When you galloped into the University of Texas on your roan Volvo, I thought you were going to *be somebody.* I gave you my hand. You put rings on it. Rings that my mother gave me. I thought you were going to be distinguished, like Bunny."

He showed her his broad, shouldered back. "Everything is in flitters," he said. "Play the piano, won't you?"

"You always were afraid of my piano," she said. "My four or five children are afraid of the piano. *You taught them to be afraid of it.* The giraffe is on fire, but I don't suppose you care."

"What can we eat," he asked, "with the ham gone?"

"There's some Silly Putty in the deepfreeze," she said tonelessly.

"Rain is falling," he observed. "Rain or something."

"When you graduated from the Wharton School of Business," she said, "I thought *at last!* I thought *now we can move to Stamford and have interesting neighbors.* But they're not interesting. The giraffe is interesting but he sleeps so much of the time. The mailbox is *rather* interesting. The man didn't open it at 3:31 P.M. today. He was five minutes late. The government lied again."

With a gesture of impatience, Brian turned on the light. The great burst of electricity illuminated her upturned tiny face. Eyes like snow peas, he thought. Tamar dancing. My name in the dictionary, in the back. The Law of Bilateral Good Fortune. Piano bread perhaps. A nibble of pain running through the Western World. Coriolanus.

"Oh God," she said, from the floor. "Look at my knees."

Brian looked. Her knees were blushing.

"It's senseless, senseless, senseless," she said. "I've been caulking the medicine chest. What for? I don't know. You've got to give me more money. Ben is bleeding. Bessie wants to be an S.S. man. She's reading *The Rise and Fall*. She's identified with Himmler. Is that her name? Bessie?"

"Yes. Bessie."

"What's the other one's name? The blond one?"

"Billy. Named after your father. Your Dad."

"You've got to get me an air hammer. To clean the children's teeth. What's the name of that disease? They'll all have it, every single one, if you don't get me an air hammer."

"And a compressor," Brian said. "And a Pinetop Smith record. I remember."

She lay on her back. The shoulder pads clattered against the terrazzo. Her number, 17, was written large on her chest. Her eyes were screwed tight shut. "Altman's is having a sale," she said. "Maybe I should go in."

"Listen," he said. "Get up. Go into the grape arbor. I'll trundle the piano out there. You've been chipping too much paint."

"You wouldn't touch that piano," she said. "Not in a million years."

"You really think I'm afraid of it?"

"Not in a million years," she said, "you phony."

"All right," Brian said quietly. "All *right*." He strode over to the piano. He took a good grip on its black varnishedness. He began to trundle it across the room, and, after a slight hesitation, it struck him dead.

Homage to the
San Francisco YMCA   *RICHARD BRAUTIGAN*

O NCE UPON A TIME in San Francisco there was a
man who really liked the finer things in life, especially
poetry. He liked good verse.

He could afford to indulge himself in this liking,
which meant that he didn't have to work because he
was receiving a generous pension that was the result of a
1920s investment that his grandfather had made in a private insane asylum that was operating quite profitably in
Southern California.

In the black, as they say and located in the San Fer-
nando Valley, just outside of Tarzana. It was one of
those places that do not look like an insane asylum. It
looked like something else with flowers all around it,
mostly roses.

The checks always arrived on the 1st and the 15th of
every month, even when there was not a mail delivery
on that day. He had a lovely house in Pacific Heights
and he would go out and buy more poetry. He of course
had never met a poet in person. That would have been a
little too much.

One day he decided that his liking for poetry could not
be fully expressed in just reading poetry or listening to
poets reading on phonograph records. He decided to take
the plumbing out of his house and completely replace it
with poetry, and so he did.

He turned off the water and took out the pipes and
put in John Donne to replace them. The pipes did not
look too happy. He took out his bathtub and put in William Shakespeare. The bathtub did not know what was
happening.

He took out his kitchen sink and put in Emily Dickinson. The kitchen sink could only stare back in wonder.

He took out his bathroom sink and put in Vladimir Mayakovsky. The bathroom sink, even though the water was off, broke out into tears.

He took out his hot water heater and put in Michael McClure's poetry. The hot water heater could barely contain its sanity. Finally he took out his toilet and put in the minor poets. The toilet planned on leaving the country.

And now the time had come to see how it all worked, to enjoy the fruit of his amazing labor. Christopher Columbus' slight venture sailing West was merely the shadow of a dismal event in the comparison. He turned the water back on again and surveyed the countenance of his vision brought to reality. He was a happy man.

"I think I'll take a bath," he said, to celebrate. He tried to heat up some Michael McClure to take a bath in some William Shakespeare and what happened was not actually what he had planned on happening.

"Might as well do the dishes, then," he said. He tried to wash some plates in "I taste a liquor never brewed," and found there was quite a difference between that liquid and a kitchen sink. Despair was on its way.

He tried to go to the toilet and the minor poets did not do at all. They began gossiping about their careers as he sat there trying to take a shit. One of them had written 197 sonnets about a penguin he had once seen in a travelling circus. He sensed a Pulitzer Prize in this material.

Suddenly the man realized that poetry could not replace plumbing. It's what they call seeing the light. He decided immediately to take the poetry out and put the pipes back in, along with the sinks, the bathtub, the hot water heater and the toilet.

"This just didn't work out the way I planned it," he said. "I'll have to put the plumbing back. Take the poetry out." It made sense standing there naked in the total light of failure.

But then he ran into more trouble than there was in the first place. The poetry did not want to go. It liked very much occupying the positions of the former plumbing.

"I look great as a kitchen sink," Emily Dickinson's poetry said.

"We look wonderful as a toilet," the minor poets said.

"I'm grand as pipes," John Donne's poetry said.

"I'm a perfect hot water heater," Michael McClure's poetry said.

Vladimir Mayakovsky sang new faucets from the bathroom, there are faucets beyond suffering, and William Shakespeare's poetry was nothing but smiles.

"That's well and dandy for you," the man said. "But I have to have plumbing, *real* plumbing in this house. Did you notice the emphasis I put on *real*? Real! Poetry just can't handle it. Face up to reality," the man said to the poetry.

But the poetry refused to go. "We're staying." The man offered to call the police. "Go ahead and lock us up, you illiterate," the poetry said in one voice.

"I'll call the fire department!"

"Book burner!" the poetry shouted.

The man began to fight the poetry. It was the first time he had ever been in a fight. He kicked the poetry of Emily Dickinson in the nose.

Of course the poetry of Michael McClure and Vladimir Mayakovsky walked over and said in English and in Russian, "That won't do at all," and threw the man down a flight of stairs. He got the message.

That was two years ago. The man is now living in the YMCA in San Francisco and loves it. He spends more time in the bathroom than everybody else. He goes in there at night and talks to himself with the light out.

O F THE SEVEN PEOPLE (Jason, his wife, the police officer, and the officer's four assistants), only Jason and his wife are in the room. Jason is sitting in an armchair with a book in his hand, a book he has doubtless been reading, although now he is watching his wife get ready for bed. About Jason: he is tall and masculine, about 35, with strong calloused hands and a sensitive nose; he is deeply in love with his wife. And she: she is beautiful, affectionate, and has a direct and charming manner of speaking, if we were to hear her speak. She seems always at ease.

Nude now, she moves lightly about the room, folding a sweater into a drawer, hanging up Jason's jacket which he had tossed on the bed, picking up a comb from the floor where it had fallen from the chest of drawers. She moves neither pretentiously nor shyly. Whatever meaning there might be in her motion exists within the motion itself and not in her deliberations.

At last, she folds back the blankets of the bed (which is across the room from Jason), fluffs her short blonde hair, crawls onto the fresh sheets on her hands and knees, pokes gently at the pillows, then rolls down on her back, hands under her head, gazing across the room at Jason. She watches him, with the same apparent delight in least motions, as he again picks up his book, finds his place in it, and inserts a marker. He stands, returns her gaze for almost a minute without smiling, and then does smile, at the same time placing his book on the table. He removes his clothes, hooking his trousers over the back of the armchair and tossing the other things on the seat cushion. Before extinguishing the light behind his chair, he glances across the room at his wife once more, her tanned body gay and relaxed, a rhythm of soft lines on the large white canvas of the bed. She smiles, in subtle recognition perhaps of the pleasure he finds in her. He snaps out the light.

In the darkness, Jason pauses a moment in front of the armchair. The image of his wife, as he has just seen her, fades slowly (as when, lying on a beach, one looks at the reflection of the sun on the curving back of the sea, then shuts tight his eyes, letting the image of the reflected sun lose its brilliance, turn green, then evaporate slowly into the limbo of uncertain associations), gradually becoming transformed from that of her nude body crackling the freshness of the laundered sheets to that of Beauty, indistinct and untextured, as though still emerging from some profound ochre mist, but though without definition, an abstract Beauty that contains somehow his wife's ravaging smile and musical eyes. Jason, still facing the bed, walks steadily toward it, his right hand in front of him to feel for it in the dark. When he has reached the spot where he expects the bed, he is startled not to find it. He retraces his steps, and stumbles into . . . what? the chest of drawers! Reoriented now by the chest of drawers, he sets out again and, after some distance, touches a wall. He starts to call out to his wife, but hears her laugh suddenly: she is up to some kind of joke, he says to himself with a half-smile. He walks boldly toward the laugh, only to find himself—quite by surprise—back at the armchair! He fumbles for the lamp and snaps the switch, but the light does not turn on. He snaps the switch several times, but the lamp definitely does not work. She has pulled the plug, he says to himself, but without really believing it, since he could not imagine any reason she would have for doing so. Once again, he positions himself in front of the armchair and crosses the room toward the bed. This time, however, he does not walk confidently, and although almost expecting something of the sort, is no less alarmed when he arrives at, not the bed, but a door. He gropes along the wall, past a radiator and a wastebasket, until he reaches a corner. He starts out along the second wall, working methodically now, but does not take more than five steps when he hears his wife's gentle laugh right in his ear. He turns around and finds the bed . . . just behind him!

Although in the strange search he has lost his appetite for the love act, he quickly regains it at the sound of her happy laugh and the feel, in the dark, of her cool thighs. In fact, the experience, the anxiety of it and its riddles, seems to have created a new urgency, an almost brutal wish to swallow, for a moment, reason and its inadequacies, and to let passion, noble or not, have its hungry way. He is surprised to find her dry, but the entry itself is relaxed and gives way to his determined penetration. In a moment of alarm, he wonders if this is really his wife, but since there is no alternate possibility, he rejects his misgivings as absurd. He leans down over her to kiss her, and as he does so, notices a strange and disagreeable odor.

At this moment, the lights come on and the police officer and his four assistants burst into the room.

"*Really!*" cries the police officer, pulling up short. "This is *quite* disgusting!"

Jason looks down and finds that it is indeed his wife beneath him, but that she is rotting. Her eyes are open, but glazed over, staring up at him, without meaning, but bulging as though in terror of him. The flesh on her face is yellowish and drawn back toward her ears. Her mouth is open in a strangely cruel smile and Jason can see that her gums have dried and pulled back from her teeth. Her lips are black and her blonde hair, now long and tangled, is splayed out over the pillow like a urinal mop spread out to dry. There is a fuzzy stuff like mold around the nipples of her shrunken breasts. Jason tries desperately to get free from her body, but finds to his deepest horror that he is stuck!

"This woman has been dead for three weeks," says the officer in genuine revulsion.

Jason strikes wildly against the thighs in his effort to free himself, jolts one leg off the bed so that it dangles there, disjointed and swinging, the long yellow toenails scratching on the wooden floor. The four assistants seize Jason and wrench him forcibly away from the corpse of his dead wife. The body follows him punishingly in movement for a moment, as a sheet of paper will follow a comb after the comb has been run through hair; then, freed by its own weight, it falls back in a pile on the badly soiled sheets. The four men carry Jason to the table where his book still lies with its marker in it. They

hold him up against the table and the police officer, without ceremony, pulls Jason's genitals out flat on the tabletop and pounds them
to a pulp with the butt of his gun.

He leaves Jason writhing on the floor and turns to march out,
along with his four assistants. At the door he hesitates, then turns
back to Jason. A flicker of compassion crosses his face.

"You understand, of course," he says, "that I am not, in the
strictest sense, a traditionalist. I mean to say that I do not recognize
tradition *qua* tradition as sanctified in its own sake. On the other
hand, I do not join hands with those who find inherent in tradition
some malignant evil, and who therefore deem it of terrible necessity
that all custom be rooted out at all costs. I am personally convinced,
if you will permit me, that there is a middle road, whereon we recognize that innovations find their best soil in traditions, which are
justified in their own turn by the innovations which created them. I
believe, then, that law and custom are essential, but that it is one's
constant task to review and revise them. In spite of that, however,
some things still make me puke!" He turns, flushed, to his four assistants. "*Now get rid of that fucking corpse!*" he screams.

After wiping his pink brow with a handkerchief, he puts it to his
nose and turns his back on the bed as the men drag away, by the
feet, the unhinged body of Jason's wife. The officer notices the book
on the table, the book Jason has been reading, and walks over to pick
it up. There is a slight spattering of blood on it. He flips through it
hastily with one hand, the other still holding the handkerchief to his
nose, and although his face wears an expression of mild curiosity, it
is difficult to know if it is sincere. The marker falls to the floor beside
Jason. The officer replaces the book on the table and walks out of the
room.

"*The marker!*" Jason gasps desperately, but the police officer does
not hear him, nor does he want to.

O NCE UPON A TIME there was a Siamese cat who pretended to be a lion and spoke inappropriate Zebraic.

That language is whinnied by the race of striped horses in Africa.

Here now: An innocent zebra is walking in a jungle and approaching from another direction is the little cat; they meet.

"Hello there!" says the Siamese cat in perfectly pronounced Zebraic, "It certainly is a pleasant day, isn't it? The sun is shining, the birds are singing, isn't the world a lovely place to live today!"

The zebra is so astonished at hearing a Siamese cat speaking like a zebra, why—he's just fit to be tied.

So the little cat quickly ties him up, kills him, and drags the better parts of the carcass back to his den.

The cat successfully hunted zebras many months in this manner, dining on filet mignon of zebra every night, and from the better hides he made bow neckties and wide belts after the fashion of the decadent princes of the Old Siamese court.

He began boasting to his friends he was a lion, and he gave them as proof the fact that he hunted zebras.

The delicate noses of the zebras told them there was really no lion in the neighborhood. The zebra deaths caused many to avoid the region. Superstitious, they decided the woods were haunted by the ghost of a lion.

One day the storyteller of the zebras was ambling, and through his mind ran plots for stories to amuse the other zebras, when suddenly his eyes brightened, and he said, "That's it! I'll tell a story about a Siamese cat who learns to speak our language! What an idea! That'll make 'em laugh!"

Just then the Siamese cat appeared before him, and said, "Hello there! Pleasant day today, isn't it!"

The zebra storyteller wasn't fit to be tied at hearing a cat speaking his language, because he'd been thinking about that very thing.

He took a good look at the cat, and he didn't know why, but there was something about his looks he didn't like, so he kicked him with a hoof and killed him.

That is the function of the storyteller.

Annotated Bibliography

This annotated bibliography is offered as a means to further study. It is divided into four sections: Bibliographic Tools, General Theoretical Studies, Specialized Studies, and Supplementary Readings. One could hardly pretend that so short a bibliography covered the vast field of fantastic literature, but one can hope that the works mentioned here will both satisfy and prompt the curiosity of the interested reader.

BIBLIOGRAPHIC TOOLS

The study of fantastic literature in its own right is just beginning, and there are not yet many good bibliographic sources, although those listed below are extremely helpful. However, for a number of years science fiction studies have been conducted at a serious scholarly level and many of the bibliographic tools of use in science fiction studies list works which are quite relevant to the broader study of fantastic literature. For a listing of the most useful of those science fiction bibliographies, see pp. 237-40 in Scholes and Rabkin, listed below in the section on General Theoretical Studies.

Ashley, Mike. *Who's Who in Horror & Fantasy Fiction* (London: Elm Tree Books, 1977). Over 400 alphabetical listings give brief facts about the lives and major works of most of the important fantasy authors. Also included are a chronology of fantastic literature and helpful appendices listing relevant secondary sources, literary awards, and so on.

Doyle, Brian. *The Who's Who of Children's Literature* (New York: Schocken, 1968). Again, alphabetically organized brief facts about lives and major works. The first section of the book is devoted to the writers, the second to the illustrators. Appendices give a specialized bibliography and relevant literary awards.

Tuck, Donald. *The Encyclopedia of Science Fiction and Fantasy* (Chicago: Advent, 1974 for vol. 1; 1978 for vol. 2). Although expensive, this resource is well worth the money, for it is the easiest to use as well as being the most complete bibliography available. Unfortunately, it goes only to 1968, so other sources are still needed for more recent work. Volume 1 is a very competent "Who's Who and Works," listing authors with last initial A–L, giving brief biographical facts, some summary of their works, and fairly complete listings of their production and its various editions, title changes, pseudonyms, and so forth. Volume 2 completes the alphabetical listing and adds an alphabetical list, by title, of all works referred to in the *Encyclopedia*. It also gives the author's name, so that one can go to the relevant entry in the "Who's Who." Volume 3, in preparation, is supposed to give detailed treatment of the major magazines in the field; a listing of all relevant paperbacks; a cross-list of pseudonyms; a roster of all significant connected stories, series, and sequels; and general coverage of such other topics as films, fandom, and so forth.

Waggoner, Diana. *The Hills of Faraway* (New York: Atheneum, 1978). The major value of this book, too, is its "Who's Who" type of alphabetical entries. Although there are flaws in the work, Waggoner has a slightly different sense of fantasy than the above authors, and she thus lists some that are not treated elsewhere.

Wells, Stuart W., III. *The Science Fiction and Heroic Fantasy Author Index* (Duluth: Purple Unicorn Books, 1978). Although it merely lists titles under their alphabetically arranged authors, this index of fiction, published in America from 1945 to 1978, because of its late date is the single best supplement to Tuck's *Encyclopedia*.

Delap's Fantasy & Science Fiction Review. This bimonthly is the single best tool for keeping abreast of current publications in the field. It can be ordered from Richard Delap, P.O. Box 46572, West Hollywood CA 90046.

GENERAL THEORETICAL STUDIES

Irwin, W. R. *The Game of the Impossible* (Urbana: University of Illinois Press, 1976). This work begins with a discussion of the fantastic, especially in comparison with the normal activity of play, and then offers a taxonomy of fantastic literature, dis-

cussing major works under the headings of "Metamorphosis,"
"Impossible Societies," "Organized Innocence," "Parody and
Adaptation," and "The Supernatural."

Manlove, C. N. *Modern Fantasy: Five Studies* (Cambridge: Cambridge University Press, 1975). This book suggests a definition
of Fantasy based on supernatural content. The thesis is pursued
through the studies of the subtitle, which deal with .the works
of Charles Kingsley, George MacDonald, C. S. Lewis, J. R. R.
Tolkien, and Mervyn Peake.

Rabkin, Eric S. *The Fantastic in Literature* (Princeton: Princeton
University Press, 1976). This book explores in detail the gen-
eral theory from which has come the framework for *Fantastic
Worlds*.

Todorov, Tzvetan. *The Fantastic,* trans. Richard Howard (Ithaca:
Cornell University Press, 1975; first English edition publ. by
Case Western Reserve University Press, 1973; original French
edition publ. by *Editions du Seuil,* 1970). This highly suggestive book begins with a critique of Northrop Frye's *Anatomy of
Criticism.* It then proposes that the fantastic is the moment of
hesitation in which a reader cannot decide whether something
odd in the text should be taken metaphorically (making the
work "marvelous") or literally (making the work "uncanny").
This definition is then used to attempt a thematic taxonomy of
the fantastic.

SPECIALIZED STUDIES

The parts of fantastic literature are themselves so vast that we could
not begin to mention all the work that has been done on them.
Whole libraries are filled with folklore alone. The works mentioned
here, then, reflect a personal choice. Some offer a great deal of literary history, some a theoretical insight into some aspect of fantastic
literature, some a mixture of both. I have selected this combination
of works in the hope of facilitating further study that might seem
prompted by reading any of the subsections of this anthology.

Aldiss, Brian. *Billion Year Spree* (New York: Schocken, 1974; copyright © 1973). A full history of science fiction that attempts to
relate its development to that of English letters in general.

Bailey, J. O. *Pilgrims Through Space and Time* (Westport, CT: Greenwood Press, 1972; originally publ. by Argus Books, 1947). A capacious and pioneering history of the literature of fantastic voyages, from antiquity to the middle of this century. Well indexed.

Berneri, Marie Louise. *Journey Through Utopia* (New York: Schocken, 1971; originally publ. by Routledge & Kegan Paul, 1950). A compendious survey of the fictional and nonfictional literature concerning ideal states, from antiquity to the original date of publication.

Bettelheim, Bruno. *The Uses of Enchantment* (New York: Alfred A. Knopf, 1976). A highly regarded psychological study of the importance of fairy tales, highlighted by close analyses of a number of the most familiar examples.

Carter, Lin. *Imaginary Worlds* (New York: Ballantine, 1973). This chatty, critical history by the editor of the Ballantine Adult Fantasy series naturally enough reflects his own tastes in the field. Poe, for example, is not mentioned; but the book is singularly useful in pointing to numerous forgotten authors of the heroic fantasy tradition and in treating, in addition to such giants as Dunsany and Cabell, cult figures such as Clark Ashton Smith.

Cawelti, John G. *Adventure, Mystery, and Romance* (Chicago: University of Chicago Press, 1976). Probably both the most suggestive and the most thoughtful discussion of popular formulaic literature, how it functions for audiences and how it evolves. Cawelti's conclusions are immediately applicable to numerous branches of fantastic literature such as space opera or ghost stories.

Davidson, H. R. Ellis. *Gods and Myths of Northern Europe* (Baltimore: Penguin, 1964). This book manages to recount Norse mythology at the same time that it puts it into perspective, explaining the uses it once had and how those uses change as the mythology becomes more literary.

Frye, Northrop. *The Secular Scripture* (Cambridge: Harvard University Press, 1976). Frye argues that the Bible offers the original literary shape against which all of Western romantic literature must be viewed as either imitation or deviation.

Gunn, James. *Alternate Worlds* (Prentice-Hall, copyright © 1975).

This lavishly illustrated book, although it leans a bit toward the technological side of things, is the most complete history of science fiction. It also offers such useful items as a detailed chronology and list of award-winning works. Well indexed.

Lovecraft, Howard Phillips. *Supernatural Horror in Literature* (New York: Dover, 1973; originally publ. in a different form in *The Recluse,* 1927; originally publ. in final form by Ben Abramson, New York, 1945). This is a personal survey of the subject by a strangely but highly educated man who was also a widely admired writer in the field.

Lüthi, Max. *Once Upon a Time,* trans. Lee Chadeayne and Paul Gottwald (New York: Frederick Ungar, 1970). A brief, clear exposition of the major motifs of the European fairy tale, and their meanings.

Moorcock, Michael. *Heroic Dreams, Enchanted Worlds* (London: Pierrot Publications, 197?). This book, by an important author in the field, promises to be the most helpful study yet of heroic fantasy, Sword-and-Sorcery, and related fantastic genres currently well represented in bookstores.

Olderman, Raymond M. *Beyond the Waste Land* (New Haven: Yale University Press, 1972). A study of a number of innovative American writers of the 1960's, including Beagle, Barth, and Vonnegut, that gives insight into the pressures toward increasingly employing the fantastic.

Propp, Vladimir. *Morphology of the Folktale,* trans. Laurence Scott (Austin: University of Texas Press, 1968; originally publ. 1928). The first demonstration of the complex, yet uniform, structure of oral tales.

Rose, H. J. *A Handbook of Greek Mythology* (New York: E. P. Dutton, 1959). A standard source, well indexed, that both retells and discusses the major classical myths many of which still influence our literature today.

Scholes, Robert, and Eric S. Rabkin. *Science Fiction: History, Science, Vision* (New York: Oxford University Press, 1977). This book contains a brief history of the field, relating it to literature in general, a discussion of the underlying sciences and the uses made of them, a survey of the major themes and their meanings, and analyses of ten representative novels.

SUPPLEMENTARY READINGS

The most thorough guides to supplementary readings in fantastic literature are those works listed in the first and third sections of this bibliography. However, recognizing that some readers of this book may not have those resources available to them, I have presumed to gather here some of my favorite works in the field. In addition to those mentioned below, one should also consider further pursuing the writing of authors already encountered in *Fantastic Worlds*. The sources for the pieces used here are mentioned in the Acknowledgments, and any library card catalog will direct one to the book-length works of these writers. For that reason, with the exception granted Tolkien because of his current preeminence, I do not mention here authors I have already mentioned in the Table of Contents. This is not at all a sign that I do not recommend them. As a further aid, I have arranged these recommendations to parallel the subsections of the anthology. Although such divisions are often rougher than one would like, they have the virtue of suggesting which books mentioned here are likeliest to make useful comparisons with particular texts in the collection. To facilitate making those connections, the works mentioned here, like those gathered in the anthology, are arranged chronologically rather than alphabetically.

MYTHS

Epic of Gilgamesh. This anonymous Sumerian work is the oldest
   narrative in Western Civilization. It offers contrasts and comparisons to some of the great biblical myths.
Homer. *The Odyssey*. Gods, witches, and everything else from ancient Greece.
Rose, H. J. See the third section, above.
Beowulf. This anonymous tale of heroes and monsters is the oldest
   epic in English.
Gardner, John. *Grendel* (New York: Alfred A. Knopf, 1971). A
   modern version of *Beowulf* touchingly retold from the monster's point of view.
Davidson. See section three, above.

FOLKTALES

Jacobs, Joseph, ed. *Aesop's Fables* (New York: Schocken, 1966; originally publ. 1894). A handy, traditional collection of the famous moral tales of talking animals.

Tales from the Thousand and One Nights, trans. N. J. Dawood (Baltimore: Penguin, 1973; originally publ. 1954 & 1957). A convenient selection of modern translations of the classic Oriental tales of Sinbad, Aladdin, and Scheherazade.

Tenenbaum, Samuel, ed. *The Wise Men of Chelm* (London: Collier, 1969; originally publ. 1965). A modern rendition of European Jewry's folktales about born losers.

FAIRY TALES

La Motte Fouqué, Friedrich de. *Undine* (1807). This marvelous story of love between a man and a water spirit was thought by George MacDonald to be the perfect fairy tale.

St. Exupéry, Antoine de. *The Little Prince,* trans. Katherine Woods (New York: Harcourt, Brace & World, 1943). A frequently allegorized, highly sentimental story of a cute extraterrestrial.

Beagle, Peter S., *The Last Unicorn* (New York: Ballantine, 1968). Afraid that she might be mythical, the title character sets off to explore the world and seek her own kind.

FANTASY

Melville, Herman. *The Confidence-Man* (1857). A complex moral and political allegory. The protagonist may or may not undergo ten metamorphoses and be one or two people.

Mark Twain. *The Mysterious Stranger* (1916). A fantastic examination of human desires and the quest for knowledge that finally has the reader wondering whether or not he himself is in the real world.

Cabell, James Branch. *Jurgen* (1919). A punning, erotic romp through nearly every myth-world that ever existed and a few that did not.

Finney, Charles. *The Circus of Dr. Lao* (1935). This work inverts

Cabell's, in having the myth-worlds invade small-town Middle America.

LeGuin, Ursula K. *The Lathe of Heaven* (New York: Avon, 1971). George Orr's dreams not only change the world but change everyone's memory so that they do not know the world has changed. A psychiatrist tries to control the world by manipulating Orr's dreams.

HORROR FICTION

Walpole, Horace. *The Castle of Otranto* (1764). Set in a crumbling castle filled with ghosts, family curses, and mysterious deaths, this novel, subtitled "A Gothic Story," gave the name to the whole field of Gothic horror.

Stevenson, Robert Louis. *The Strange Case of Dr. Jekyll and Mr. Hyde* (1886). A scientized dramatization of the fears later associated with Jack the Ripper, this novel has surprising psychological force.

Wilde, Oscar. *The Picture of Dorian Gray* (1890). Turn of the century dissolution and debauchery with a supernatural twist that breaks down the life/art boundary.

Stoker, Bram. *Dracula* (1897). Though not the first, surely the most popular and gripping version of the well-known story.

Hodgson, William Hope. *The House on the Borderland* (1908). Strange subterranean menace in an isolated haunt.

GHOST STORIES

Dickens, Charles. *A Christmas Carol* (1843). The supernatural, including time travel, is bent to the service of Victorian morality.

James, Henry. *The Turn of the Screw* (1898). Among those who disdain popular culture, this exquisitely ambiguous novella is the most widely respected ghost story ever written.

Smith, Thorne. *Topper* (1926). A pleasant farce about a stuffy, middle-aged man befriended, willy-nilly, by the devil-may-care ghosts of the young couple who had inhabited the house he buys.

Beagle, Peter S. *A Fine and Private Place* (New York: Ballantine,

1960). Set in a cemetery, the characters include a man, two ghosts, and a talking crow. A warm and moving story of the meanings of love and death.

HEROIC FANTASY

Arthurian Legend. This most famous of all heroic story cycles includes masterful retellings from numerous eras: Sir Thomas Malory, *Le Morte Darthur* (1470); Alfred Lord Tennyson, *The Idylls of the King* (publ. 1842-85); T. H. White, *The Sword in the Stone* (1939). In addition, the general Arthurian setting is used for much other fascinating literature, such as the anonymous *Sir Gawain and the Green Knight* (14th century).

Tolkien, J. R. R. *The Hobbit* (Boston: Houghton Mifflin, 1937). The first of Tolkien's immensely popular adventures through Middle Earth. Although this book is self-contained, it serves perfectly as an introduction to the next entry here.

———. The Lord of the Rings trilogy, namely, *The Fellowship of the Ring, The Two Towers, The Return of the King* (Boston: Houghton Mifflin, 1954, 1955, 1956). These novels together are doubtless the single best known and most discussed fantastic narrative of the twentieth century.

SCIENCE FICTION

Shelley, Mary. *Frankenstein* (1818). This novel remains surprisingly powerful today. It shows clearly the influence of Gothic horror on the emergence of science fiction.

Lindsay, David. *A Voyage to Arcturus* (New York: Ballantine, 1968; originally publ. 1920). A heavily mystical voyage of philosophic inquiry that is both science fiction and Fantasy.

Bradbury, Ray. *The Martian Chronicles* (New York: Bantam, 1951; originally publ. 1950). A lyrical, composite novel set on a fairy-tale Mars, this book tries to revive the so-called American myth.

Dick, Philip K. *The Man in the High Castle* (New York: Berkley, 1974; originally publ. 1962). Probably the best known alternate time-stream novel, this story is set in the United States in the aftermath of a World War II won by the Axis.

Zelazny, Roger. *Lord of Light* (New York: Avon, 1969; originally publ. 1967). This unusually told, award-winning tale manages to make the pantheon of the Indian subcontinent into science fiction characters.

Lem, Stanislaw, *The Futurological Congress* (1971), trans. Michael Kandel (New York: Avon, 1976; English version originally publ. 1974). This chaotic, hilarious work by Europe's most popular science fiction writer parodies science fiction and shakes up the reader's sense of how fiction functions.

Silverberg, Robert, ed. *The Science Fiction Hall of Fame,* vol. 1 (New York: Avon, 1971; originally publ. 1970). This collection of twenty-six stories selected by the Science Fiction Writers of America affords the easiest access to the science fiction short story as practiced in the United States from the 1930's through the 1960's.

RELIGIOUS FANTASY

Although we do not have a separate section for this branch of fantastic literature in the body of the anthology, the strong interest in it shown by a particular audience warrants adding two more names to that of the author of "Leaf by Niggle":

Lewis, C. S. *The Chronicles of Narnia.* They are, in reading order, *The Lion, The Witch and the Wardrobe* (1950), *Prince Caspian* (1951), *The Voyage of the "Dawn Treader"* (1952), *The Silver Chair* (1953), *The Horse and His Boy* (1954), *The Magician's Nephew* (1955), and *The Last Battle* (1956) (all originally publ. by Macmillan and currently available through Collier). These form an extended Christian fairy tale aimed at children and quite successful with them.

————. *The Perelandra Trilogy.* They are, in reading order, *Out of the Silent Planet* (1938), *Perelandra* (1944), *That Hideous Strength* (1946) (all Macmillan). These form an extended Christian allegory in the trappings of science fiction aimed at adults and quite successful with them.

————. *The Great Divorce* (New York: Macmillan, 1946). A marvelous story about the fortunes of a busload of tourists from Hell brought for a day's outing to Heaven.

Williams, Charles. *The Place of the Lion* (Grand Rapids: Eerdmans,

1970; originally publ. 1937). Spiritual forces let frighteningly loose in the pastoral English countryside. A friend of Lewis and Tolkien, Williams wrote seven other fantastic novels, each committed to a Christian position and each showing some real artistic power.

MODERN FANTASY

This field is so vast that it seems presumptuous to even offer suggestions. However, below I mention two novels that students have found particularly illuminated by the theory of the fantastic presented here. In addition, I mention two readily available anthologies that will acquaint a reader with more of these modern authors.

Grass, Günter. *The Tin Drum,* trans. Ralph Manheim (New York: Random House, 1961; originally publ. 1959). Considered by many to be the finest postwar novel produced in Europe, this comic masterpiece follows the fortunes of an individual born fully sentient who wills himself to stop growing taller on his third birthday.

O'Brien, Flann. *At Swim-Two-Birds* (New York: Viking, 1966; originally publ. 1939). This story functions, with separate sets of characters, on the levels of Irish myth, of the Irish present, of a novel written by a young man in that present, of the author about whom he is writing, and so on. The book has three beginnings and three endings, and the characters from one level learn how to invade the other levels.

Bellamy, Joe David, ed. *SuperFiction* (New York: Vintage, 1975). A fascinating collection of American short stories which explore new ways of making fiction work.

Karl, Frederick R., and Leo Hamalian. *the naked i* (Greenwich: Fawcett, 1971). A collection of short works with much the same aim as the Bellamy volume, but including some important writers from outside the United States.

INDEX